ALIAS

THe UNDeRNeaTH

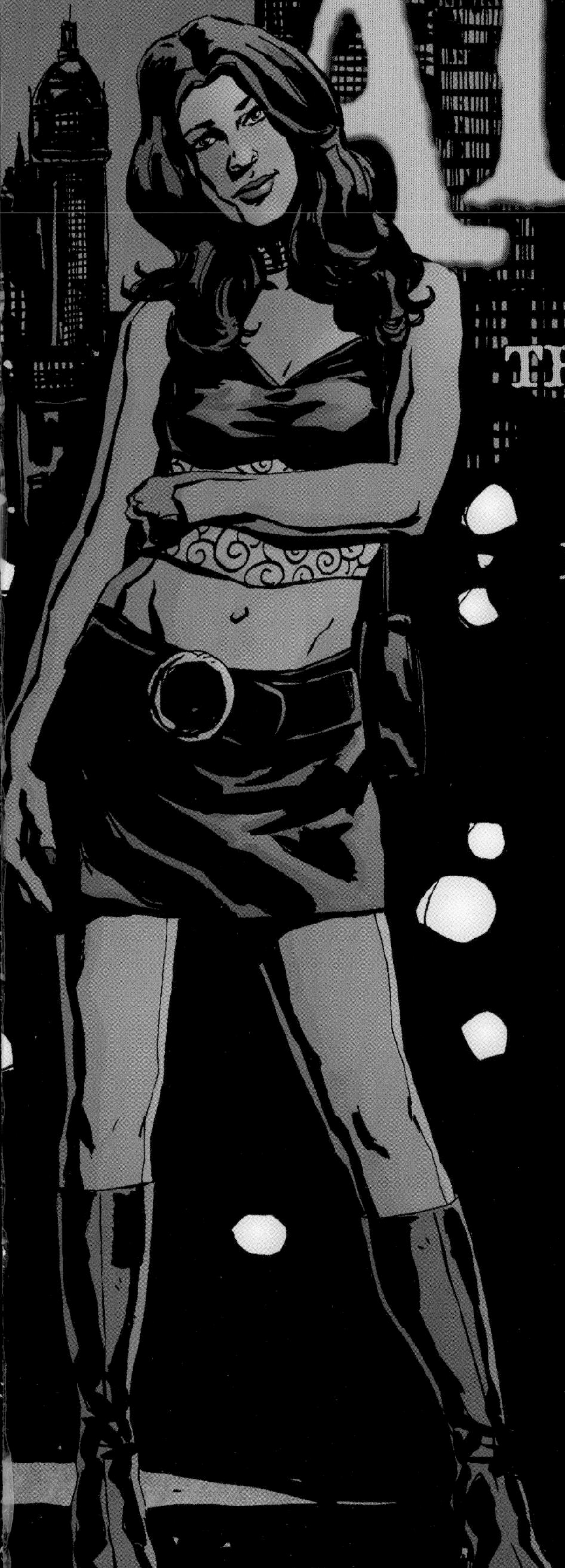

writer
Brian Michael Bendis

artist
Michael Gaydos

letters
Cory Petit
with Richard Starkings
and Comicraft's Wes Abbott
and Jason Levine

colors
Matt Hollingsworth

dream sequence art
Mark Bagely, Al Vey
and Dean White

cover art
David Mack

assistant editor
Nick Lowe

editors
Stuart Moore, C.B. Cebulski
& Joe Quesada

managing editor
Nanci Dakesian

associate managing editor
Kelly Lamy

editor in chief
Joe Quesada

president
Bill Jemas

Alias created by
Brian Michael Bendis

PREVIOUSLY IN ALIAS ...

Jessica Jones, a former costumed super hero, is now the owner and sole employee of Alias Investigations, a small private-investigative firm.

After a string of bad relationships, Jessica is fixed up with Scott Lang, a.k.a. Ant-Man. They are early in a potential relationship.

NEED A LAWYER?

...ve you been the victim of ...ofessional sabotage?

CALL
...MURDO...

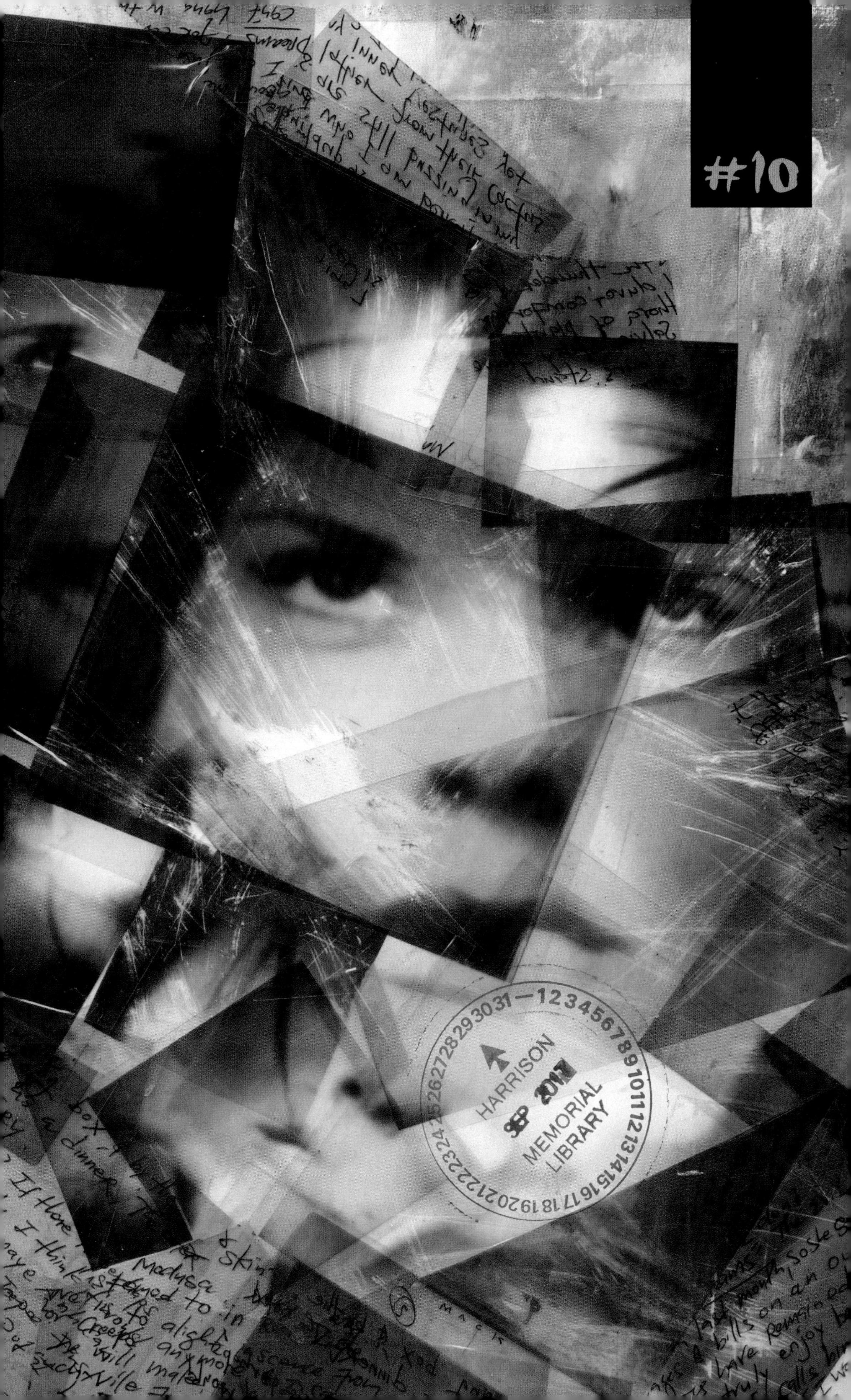
#10

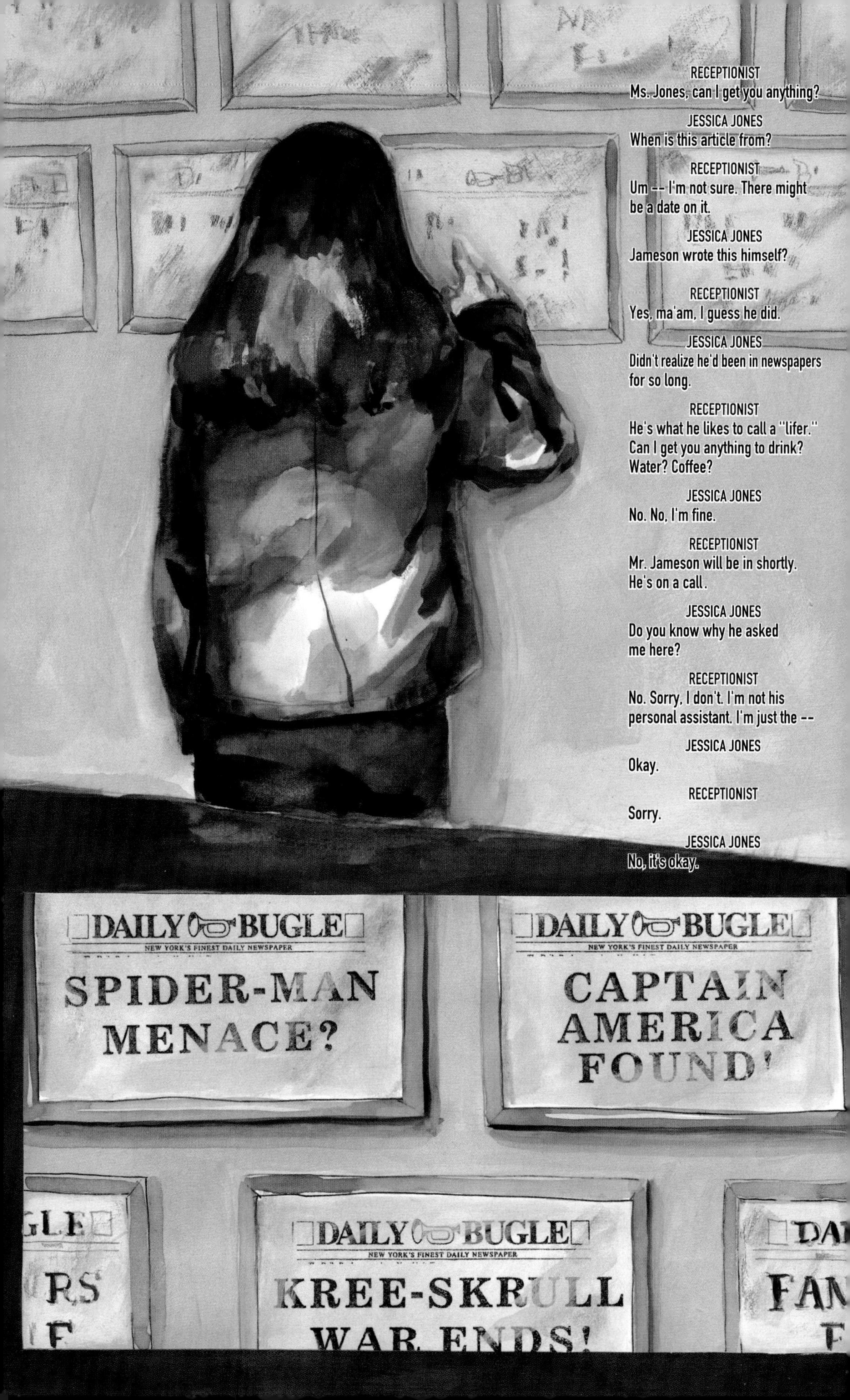
RECEPTIONIST
Ms. Jones, can I get you anything?
JESSICA JONES
When is this article from?
RECEPTIONIST
Um -- I'm not sure. There might be a date on it.
JESSICA JONES
Jameson wrote this himself?
RECEPTIONIST
Yes, ma'am, I guess he did.
JESSICA JONES
Didn't realize he'd been in newspapers for so long.
RECEPTIONIST
He's what he likes to call a "lifer." Can I get you anything to drink? Water? Coffee?
JESSICA JONES
No. No, I'm fine.
RECEPTIONIST
Mr. Jameson will be in shortly. He's on a call.
JESSICA JONES
Do you know why he asked me here?
RECEPTIONIST
No. Sorry, I don't. I'm not his personal assistant. I'm just the --
JESSICA JONES
Okay.
RECEPTIONIST
Sorry.
JESSICA JONES
No, it's okay.
DAILY BUGLE
NEW YORK'S FINEST DAILY NEWSPAPER
SPIDER-MAN MENACE?
DAILY BUGLE
NEW YORK'S FINEST DAILY NEWSPAPER
CAPTAIN AMERICA FOUND!
DAILY BUGLE
NEW YORK'S FINEST DAILY NEWSPAPER
KREE-SKRULL WAR ENDS!

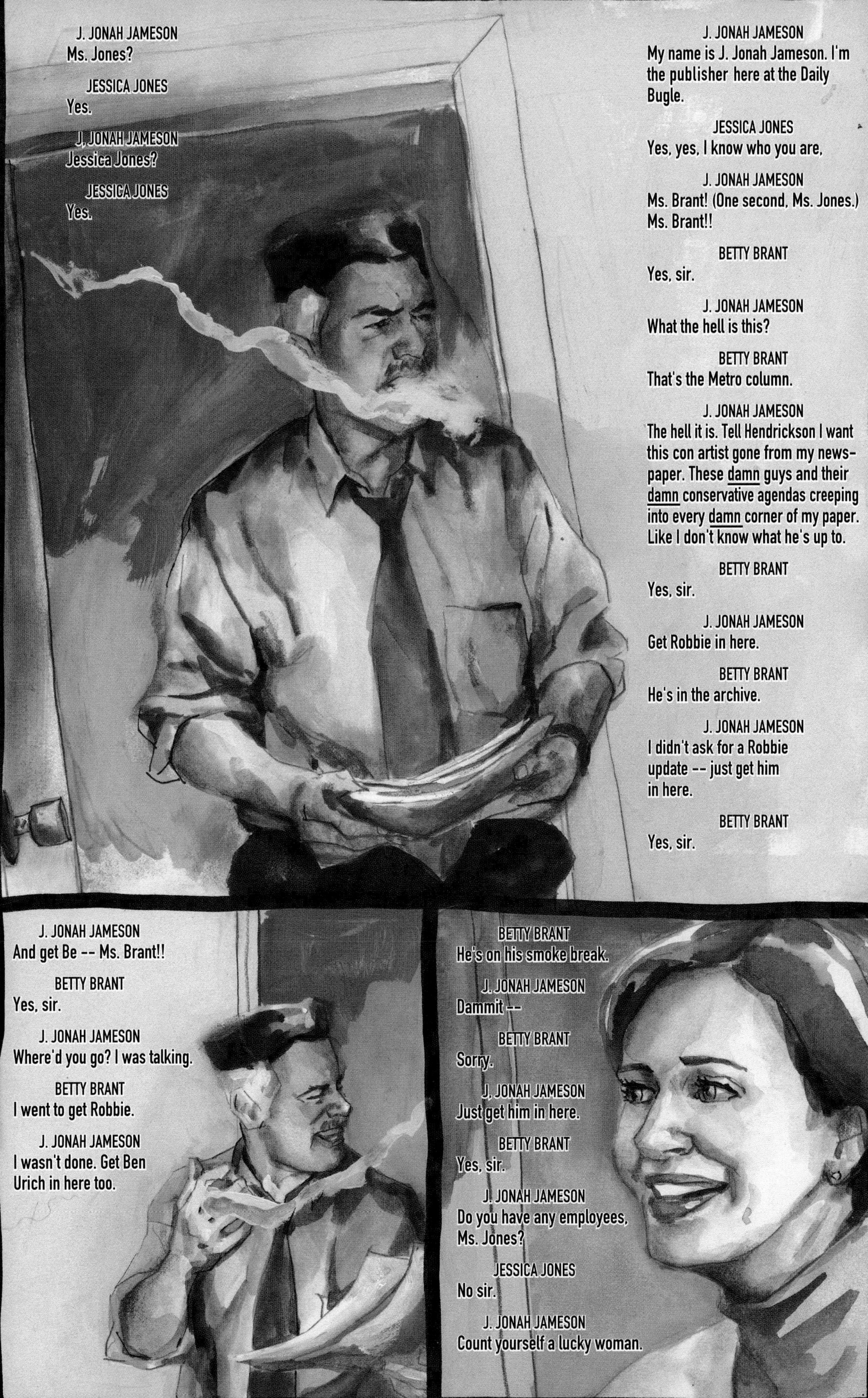
J. JONAH JAMESON
Ms. Jones?
JESSICA JONES
Yes.
J. JONAH JAMESON
Jessica Jones?
JESSICA JONES
Yes.
J. JONAH JAMESON
My name is J. Jonah Jameson. I'm the publisher here at the Daily Bugle.
JESSICA JONES
Yes, yes, I know who you are.
J. JONAH JAMESON
Ms. Brant! (One second, Ms. Jones.) Ms. Brant!!
BETTY BRANT
Yes, sir.
J. JONAH JAMESON
What the hell is this?
BETTY BRANT
That's the Metro column.
J. JONAH JAMESON
The hell it is. Tell Hendrickson I want this con artist gone from my newspaper. These damn guys and their damn conservative agendas creeping into every damn corner of my paper. Like I don't know what he's up to.
BETTY BRANT
Yes, sir.
J. JONAH JAMESON
Get Robbie in here.
BETTY BRANT
He's in the archive.
J. JONAH JAMESON
I didn't ask for a Robbie update -- just get him in here.
BETTY BRANT
Yes, sir.
J. JONAH JAMESON
And get Be -- Ms. Brant!!
BETTY BRANT
Yes, sir.
J. JONAH JAMESON
Where'd you go? I was talking.
BETTY BRANT
I went to get Robbie.
J. JONAH JAMESON
I wasn't done. Get Ben Urich in here too.
BETTY BRANT
He's on his smoke break.
J. JONAH JAMESON
Dammit --
BETTY BRANT
Sorry.
J. JONAH JAMESON
Just get him in here.
BETTY BRANT
Yes, sir.
J. JONAH JAMESON
Do you have any employees, Ms. Jones?
JESSICA JONES
No sir.
J. JONAH JAMESON
Count yourself a lucky woman.

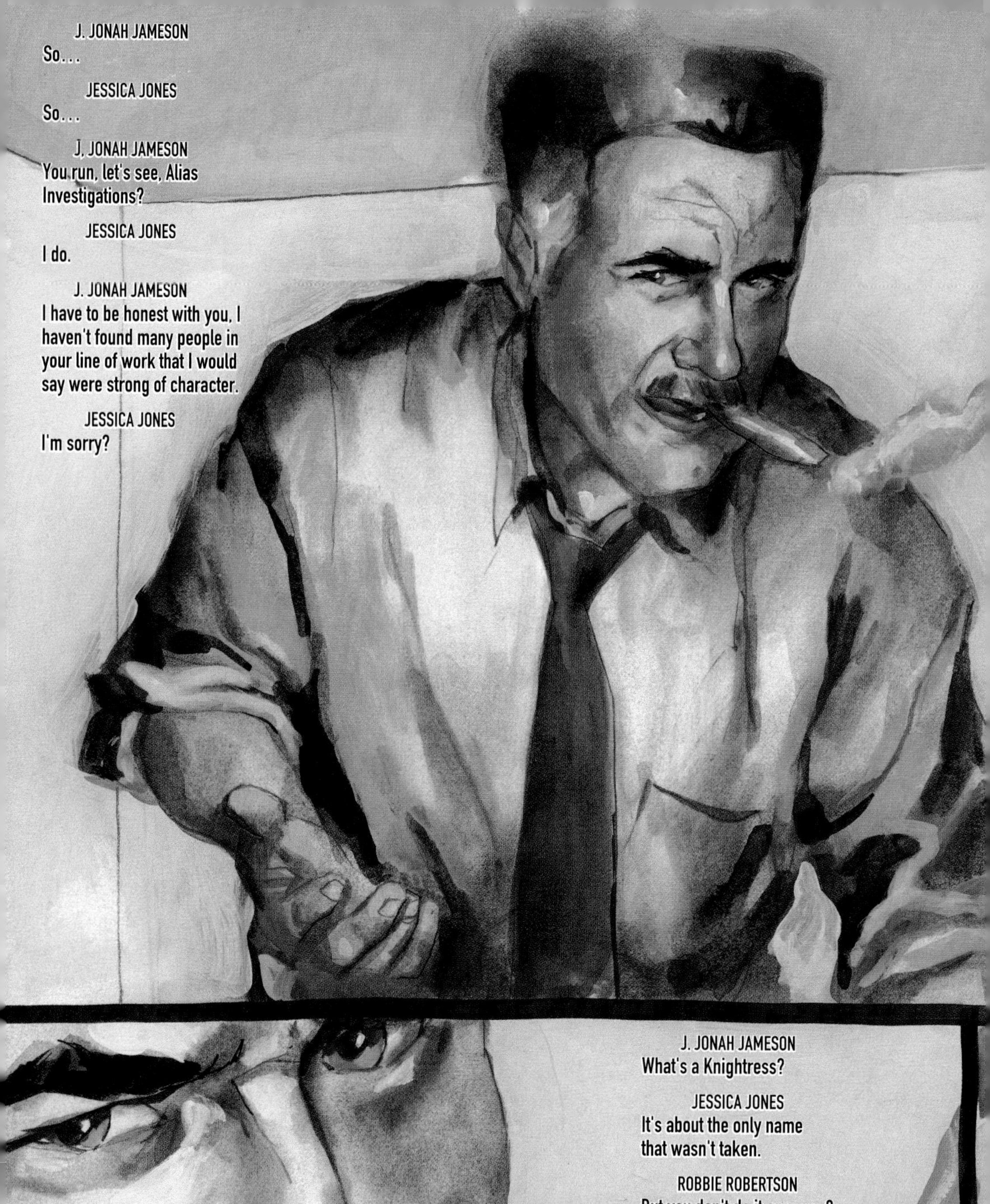
J. JONAH JAMESON
So...
JESSICA JONES
So...
J. JONAH JAMESON
You run, let's see, Alias Investigations?
JESSICA JONES
I do.
J. JONAH JAMESON
I have to be honest with you, I haven't found many people in your line of work that I would say were strong of character.
JESSICA JONES
I'm sorry?

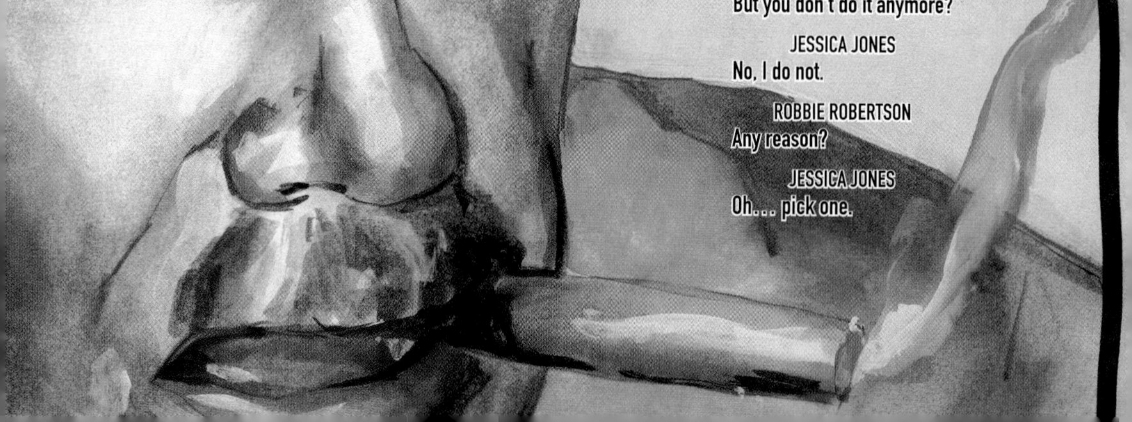
J. JONAH JAMESON
What's a Knightress?
JESSICA JONES
It's about the only name that wasn't taken.
ROBBIE ROBERTSON
But you don't do it anymore?
JESSICA JONES
No, I do not.
ROBBIE ROBERTSON
Any reason?
JESSICA JONES
Oh... pick one.

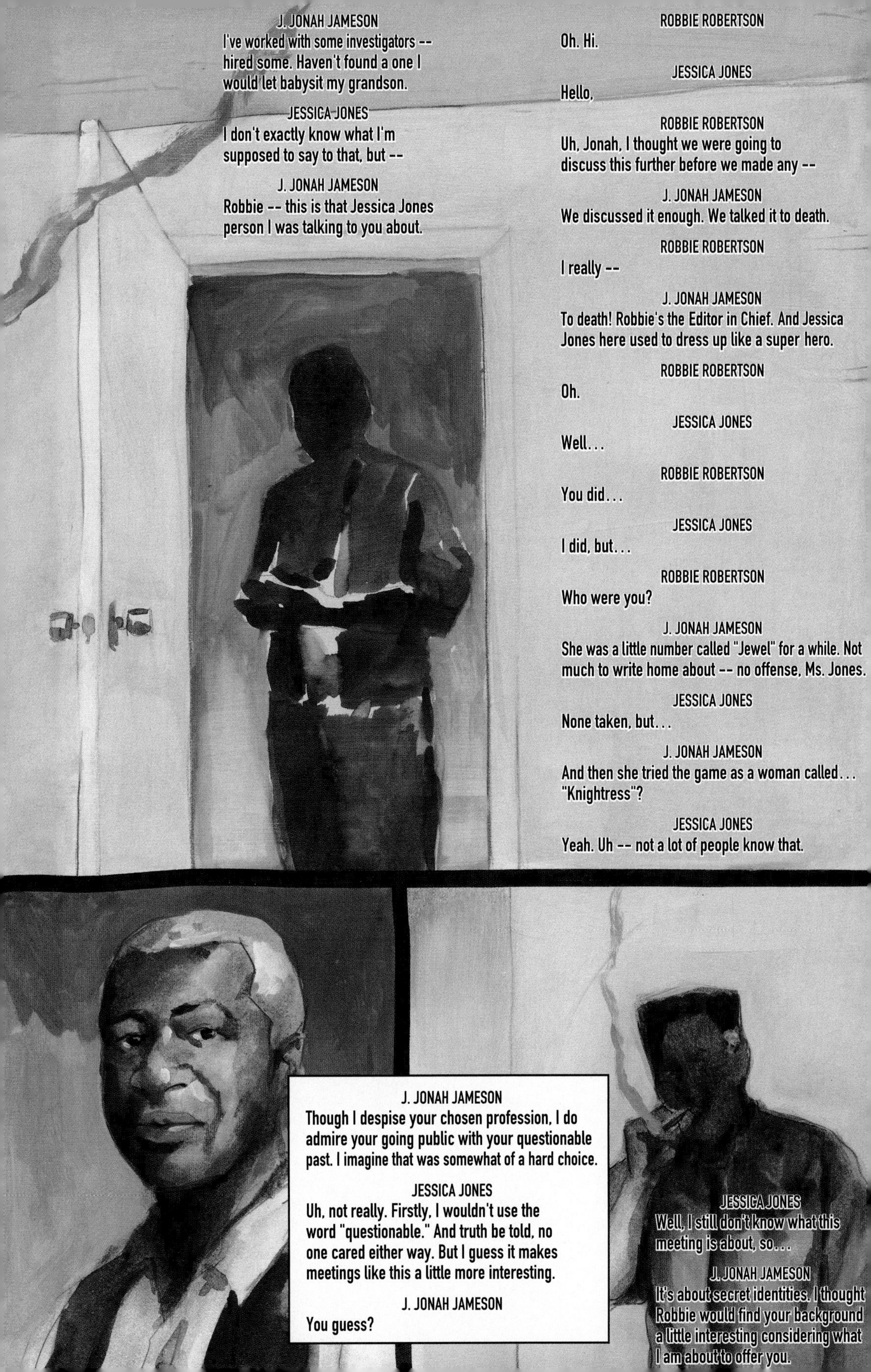

J. JONAH JAMESON
I've worked with some investigators -- hired some. Haven't found a one I would let babysit my grandson.
JESSICA JONES
I don't exactly know what I'm supposed to say to that, but --
J. JONAH JAMESON
Robbie -- this is that Jessica Jones person I was talking to you about.
ROBBIE ROBERTSON
Oh. Hi.
JESSICA JONES
Hello.
ROBBIE ROBERTSON
Uh, Jonah, I thought we were going to discuss this further before we made any --
J. JONAH JAMESON
We discussed it enough. We talked it to death.
ROBBIE ROBERTSON
I really --
J. JONAH JAMESON
To death! Robbie's the Editor in Chief. And Jessica Jones here used to dress up like a super hero.
ROBBIE ROBERTSON
Oh.
JESSICA JONES
Well...
ROBBIE ROBERTSON
You did...
JESSICA JONES
I did, but...
ROBBIE ROBERTSON
Who were you?
J. JONAH JAMESON
She was a little number called "Jewel" for a while. Not much to write home about -- no offense, Ms. Jones.
JESSICA JONES
None taken, but...
J. JONAH JAMESON
And then she tried the game as a woman called... "Knightress"?
JESSICA JONES
Yeah. Uh -- not a lot of people know that.
J. JONAH JAMESON
Though I despise your chosen profession, I do admire your going public with your questionable past. I imagine that was somewhat of a hard choice.
JESSICA JONES
Uh, not really. Firstly, I wouldn't use the word "questionable." And truth be told, no one cared either way. But I guess it makes meetings like this a little more interesting.
J. JONAH JAMESON
You guess?
JESSICA JONES
Well, I still don't know what this meeting is about, so...
J. JONAH JAMESON
It's about secret identities. I thought Robbie would find your background a little interesting considering what I am about to offer you.

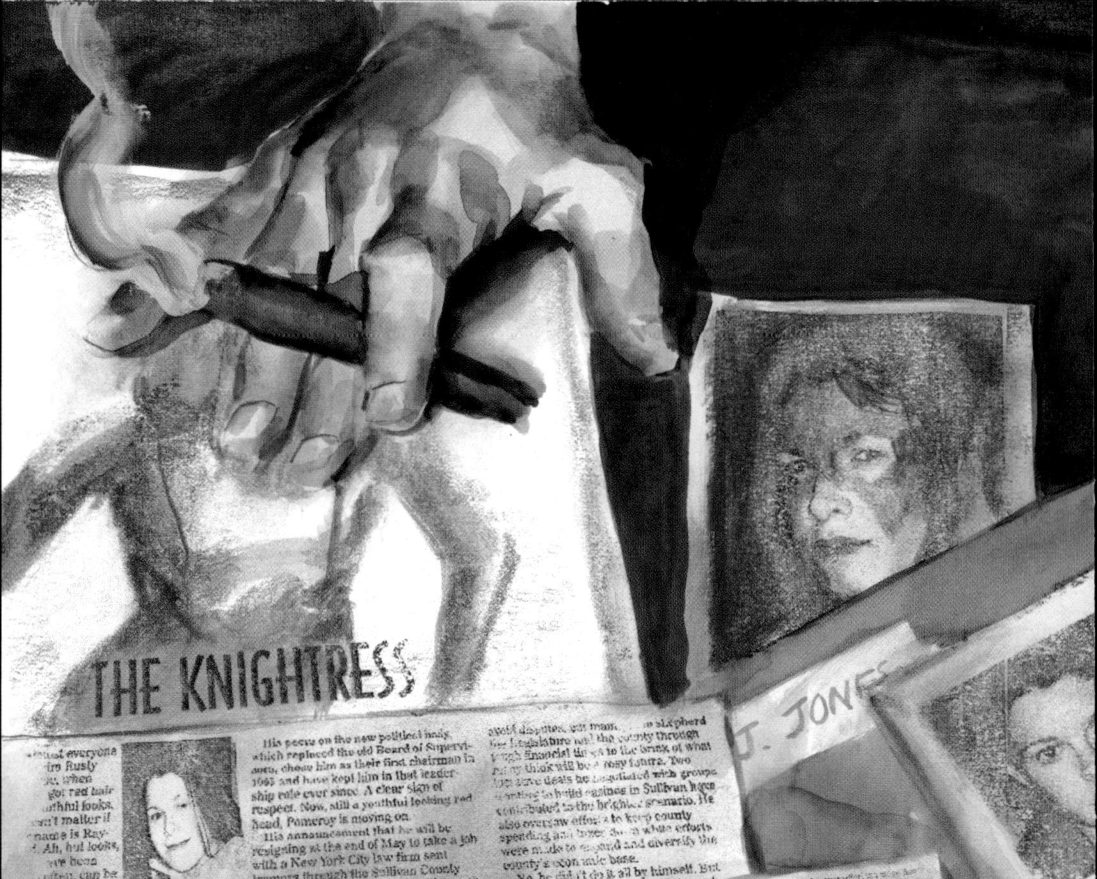
THE KNIGHTRESS
J. JONES

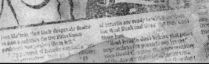

JESSICA JONES
Uh, what is that you have there?
Is that all about me?

J. JONAH JAMESON
Yes, it's your archive here
at the paper.

JESSICA JONES
My clippings?

J. JONAH JAMESON
Your clippings.

JESSICA JONES
Oh. I hadn't realized I made
the paper so many times.

J. JONAH JAMESON
Ms. Brant!

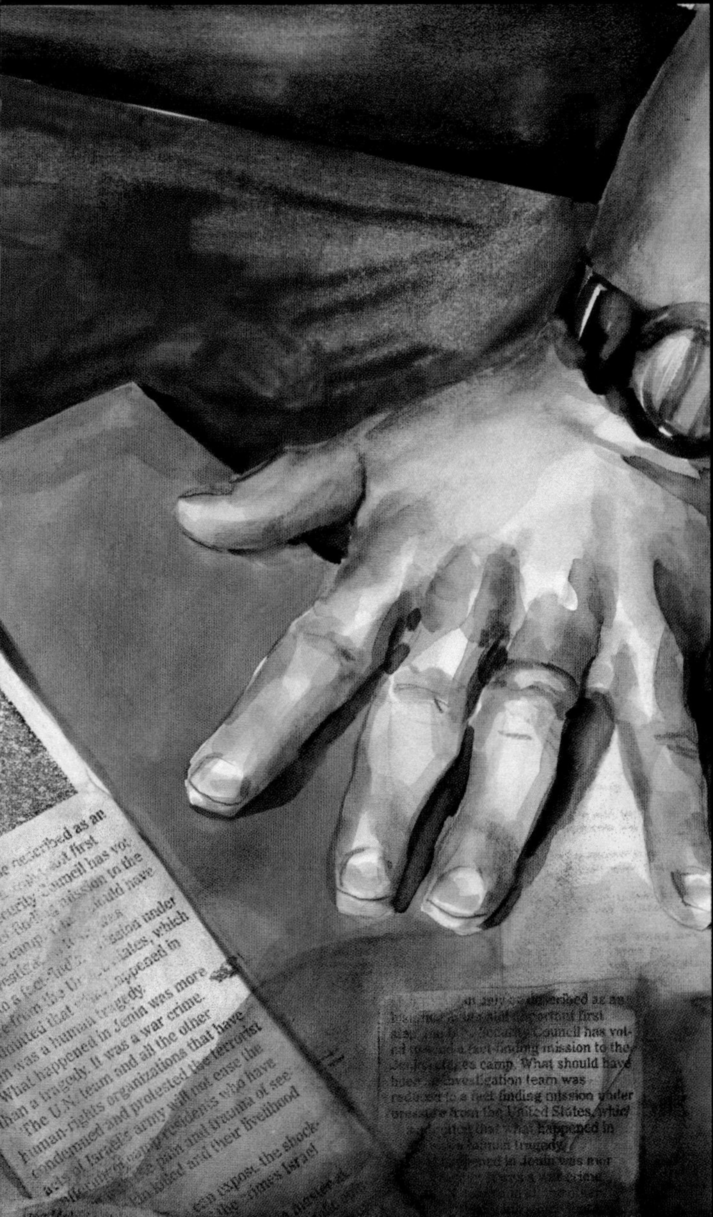

BETTY BRANT
Yes, sir.

J. JONAH JAMESON
Take this to Xerox and make a copy of it for Ms. Jones. Every paper.

BETTY BRANT
Yes, sir.

JESSICA JONES
Oh, uh, thanks.

J. JONAH JAMESON
Make yourself a little scrapbook. So, Ms. Jones, are the numbers on your web site correct?

JESSICA JONES
You mean my fees?

J. JONAH JAMESON
Yes.

JESSICA JONES
You want to hire me?

J. JONAH JAMESON.
Yes. I -- Ms. Brant!!

ROBBIE ROBERTSON
You just sent her to make copies.

J. JONAH JAMESON
Dammit! Where's Urich?

ROBBIE ROBERTSON
He's coming. Jonah, can we discuss this a little before --?

J. JONAH JAMESON
What we'd like to do, Ms. Jones, is hire you -- pay you your full wage and have one of my reporters follow you.

JESSICA JONES
Follow me where?

J. JONAH JAMESON
Ben, where were you?

BEN URICH
I didn't know you were --

J. JONAH JAMESON
Sit down. Say hi to Jessica Jones.

BEN URICH
Why is that name familiar?

J. JONAH JAMESON
You can do the niceys later. Jessica is a private investigator. The Daily Bugle is hiring her to find out who Spider-Man really is.

JESSICA JONES
Uh -- what?

J. JONAH JAMESON
Jessica here is going to crack his world in half and you are going to follow her while she does it.

JESSICA JONES
Well, I...

J. JONAH JAMESON
What we're hoping for is a series of articles. A real conversation piece to spread over days -- but hey! If all it is is a big red headline -- then all it is is a big red headline.

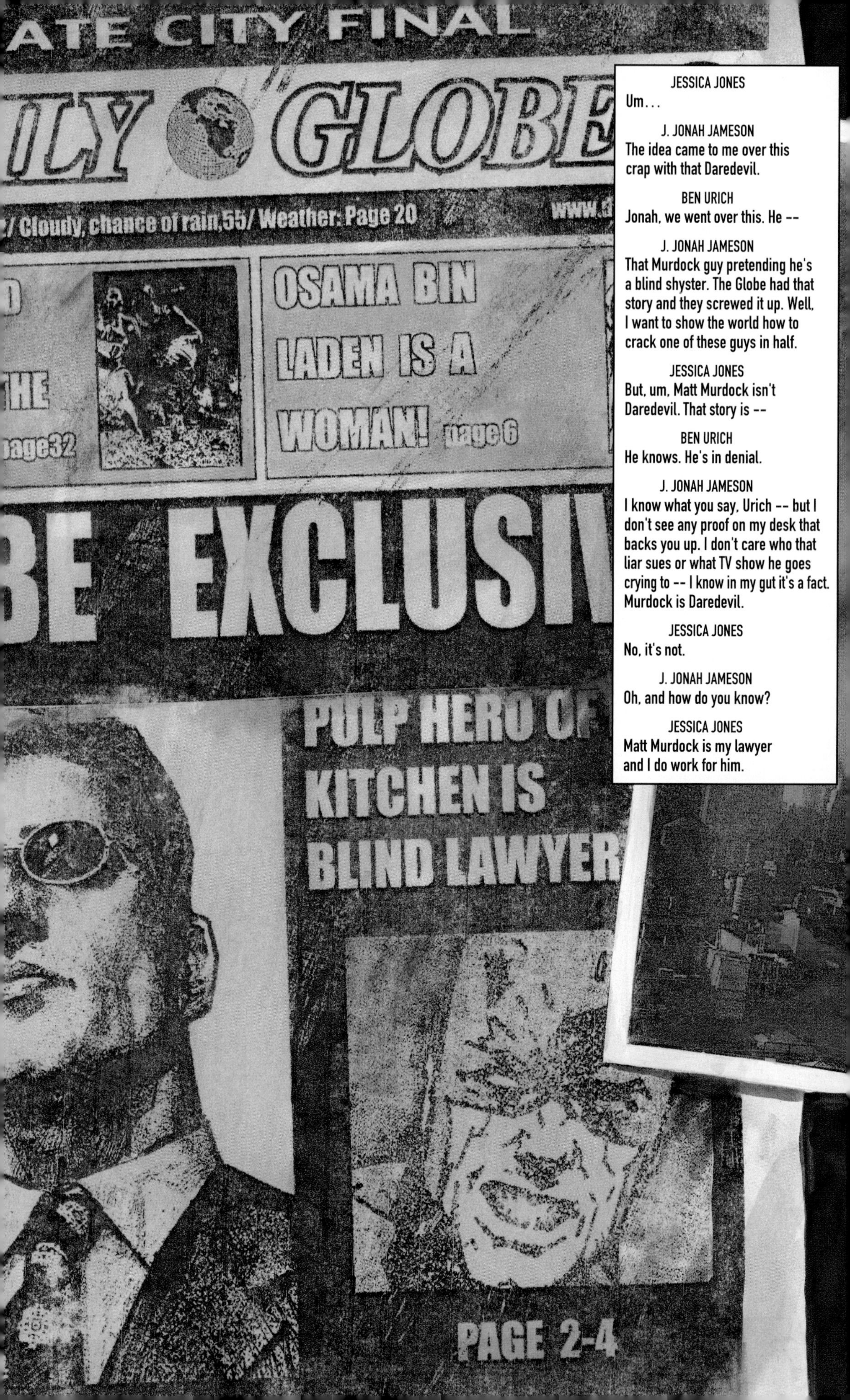
ATE CITY FINAL
LY GLOBE
/ Cloudy, chance of rain,55/ Weather: Page 20
OSAMA BIN LADEN IS A WOMAN! page 6
page32
BE EXCLUSIV
PULP HERO OF KITCHEN IS BLIND LAWYER
PAGE 2-4

JESSICA JONES
Um...

J. JONAH JAMESON
The idea came to me over this crap with that Daredevil.

BEN URICH
Jonah, we went over this. He --

J. JONAH JAMESON
That Murdock guy pretending he's a blind shyster. The Globe had that story and they screwed it up. Well, I want to show the world how to crack one of these guys in half.

JESSICA JONES
But, um, Matt Murdock isn't Daredevil. That story is --

BEN URICH
He knows. He's in denial.

J. JONAH JAMESON
I know what you say, Urich -- but I don't see any proof on my desk that backs you up. I don't care who that liar sues or what TV show he goes crying to -- I know in my gut it's a fact. Murdock is Daredevil.

JESSICA JONES
No, it's not.

J. JONAH JAMESON
Oh, and how do you know?

JESSICA JONES
Matt Murdock is my lawyer and I do work for him.

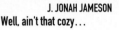

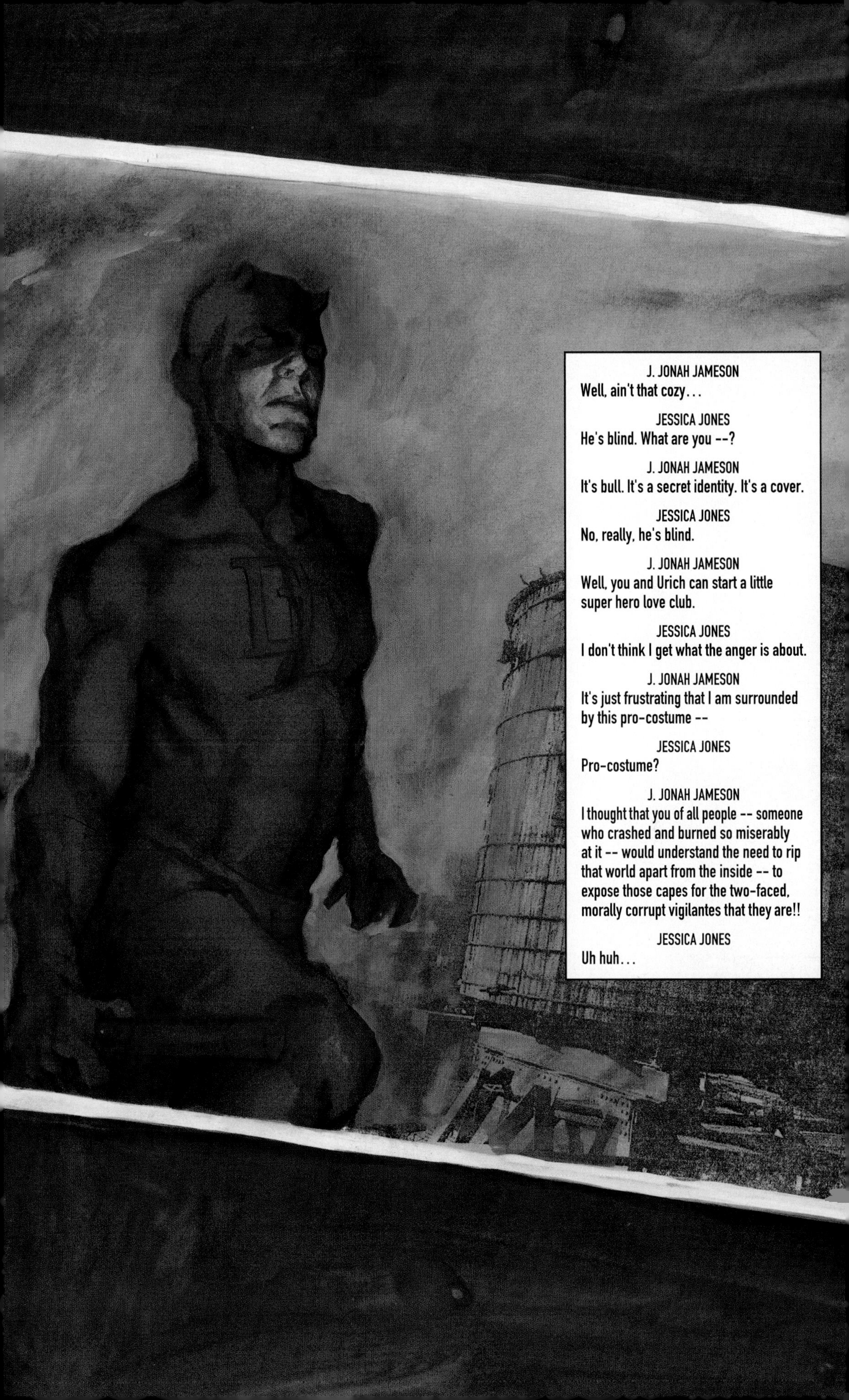

J. JONAH JAMESON
Well, ain't that cozy...

JESSICA JONES
He's blind. What are you --?

J. JONAH JAMESON
It's bull. It's a secret identity. It's a cover.

JESSICA JONES
No, really, he's blind.

J. JONAH JAMESON
Well, you and Urich can start a little super hero love club.

JESSICA JONES
I don't think I get what the anger is about.

J. JONAH JAMESON
It's just frustrating that I am surrounded by this pro-costume --

JESSICA JONES
Pro-costume?

J. JONAH JAMESON
I thought that you of all people -- someone who crashed and burned so miserably at it -- would understand the need to rip that world apart from the inside -- to expose those capes for the two-faced, morally corrupt vigilantes that they are!!

JESSICA JONES
Uh huh...

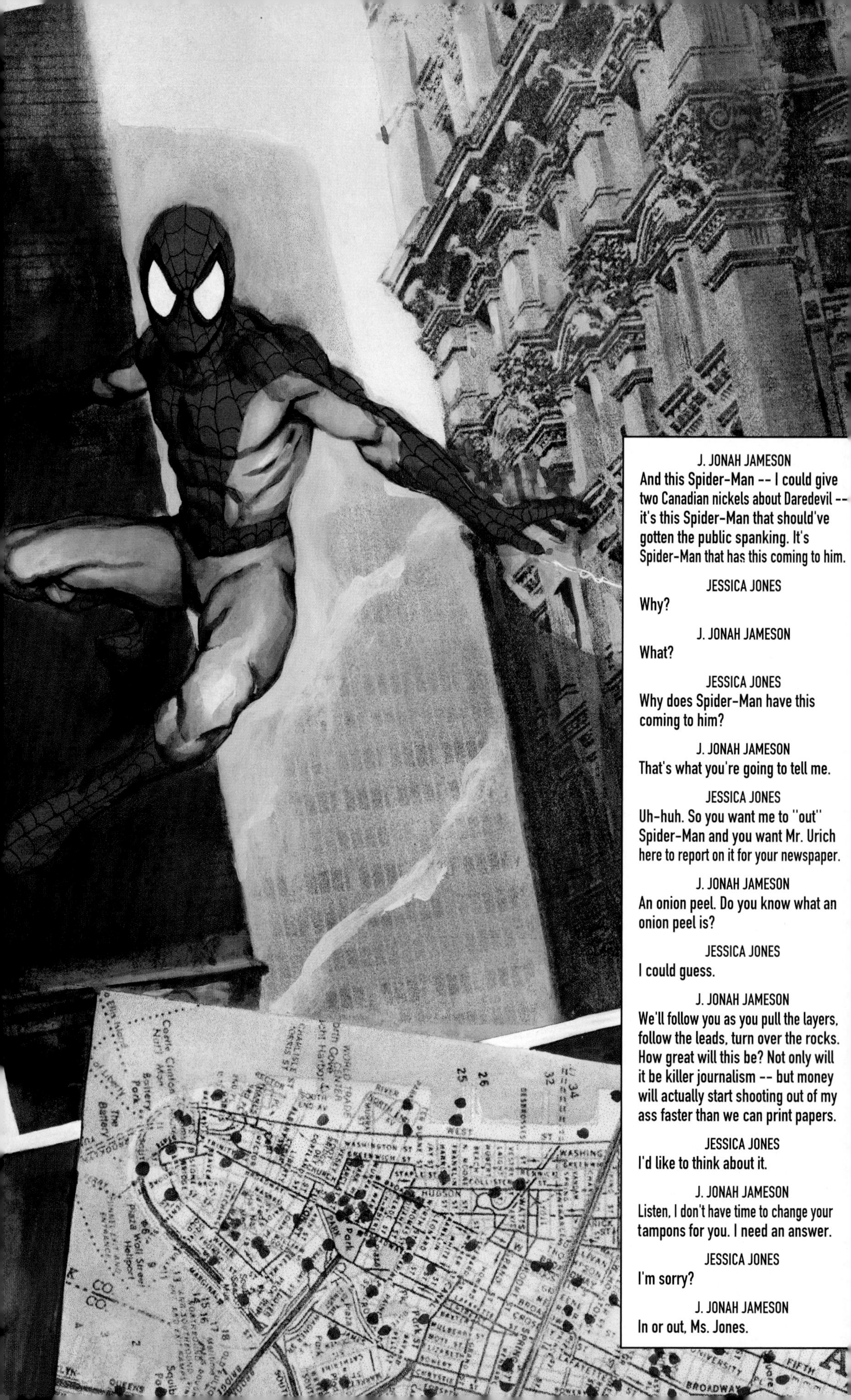
WASHINGTON ST
HUDSON
BROADWAY

J. JONAH JAMESON
And this Spider-Man -- I could give two Canadian nickels about Daredevil -- it's this Spider-Man that should've gotten the public spanking. It's Spider-Man that has this coming to him.

JESSICA JONES
Why?

J. JONAH JAMESON
What?

JESSICA JONES
Why does Spider-Man have this coming to him?

J. JONAH JAMESON
That's what you're going to tell me.

JESSICA JONES
Uh-huh. So you want me to "out" Spider-Man and you want Mr. Urich here to report on it for your newspaper.

J. JONAH JAMESON
An onion peel. Do you know what an onion peel is?

JESSICA JONES
I could guess.

J. JONAH JAMESON
We'll follow you as you pull the layers, follow the leads, turn over the rocks. How great will this be? Not only will it be killer journalism -- but money will actually start shooting out of my ass faster than we can print papers.

JESSICA JONES
I'd like to think about it.

J. JONAH JAMESON
Listen, I don't have time to change your tampons for you. I need an answer.

JESSICA JONES
I'm sorry?

J. JONAH JAMESON
In or out, Ms. Jones.

JESSICA JONES
Well, these kinds of investigations are rather unique.

J. JONAH JAMESON
Don't toss my salad -- how much are we talking?

JESSICA JONES
Hard to say. I don't even know where I am going to begin.

J. JONAH JAMESON
Ms. Brant!!

BETTY BRANT
Here -- here -- I was making the copies.

J. JONAH JAMESON
Where's the Spider-Man map?

BETTY BRANT
It's right there.

J. JONAH JAMESON
Right where?

BETTY BRANT
Right under your elbow.

J. JONAH JAMESON
Oh...

JESSICA JONES
Map? Map?

J. JONAH JAMESON
We've taken the liberty of compiling a list and a chart of frequent Spider-Man sightings. Places where he is repeatedly seen. See? Empire State University, Queens...

JESSICA JONES
So, I'm not the first investigator you've had on this.

J. JONAH JAMESON
It's a pet project -- as I said -- renewed by this Daredevil news. Here are some pictures that Parker kid took a couple of years back. You can see -- see? You can see some of the same buildings in the background. I think it's Soho.

JESSICA JONES
What happened the last time you tried this?

J. JONAH JAMESON
I'll be blunt with you, Jones. I'm offering you fame and fortune. The kind you weren't able to put together on your own -- even in any of your silly little "identities." One would imagine that off the fumes of a story like this you'll be up to your elbows in "sneaky work" till the cows come home. So, last time, are you in or --?

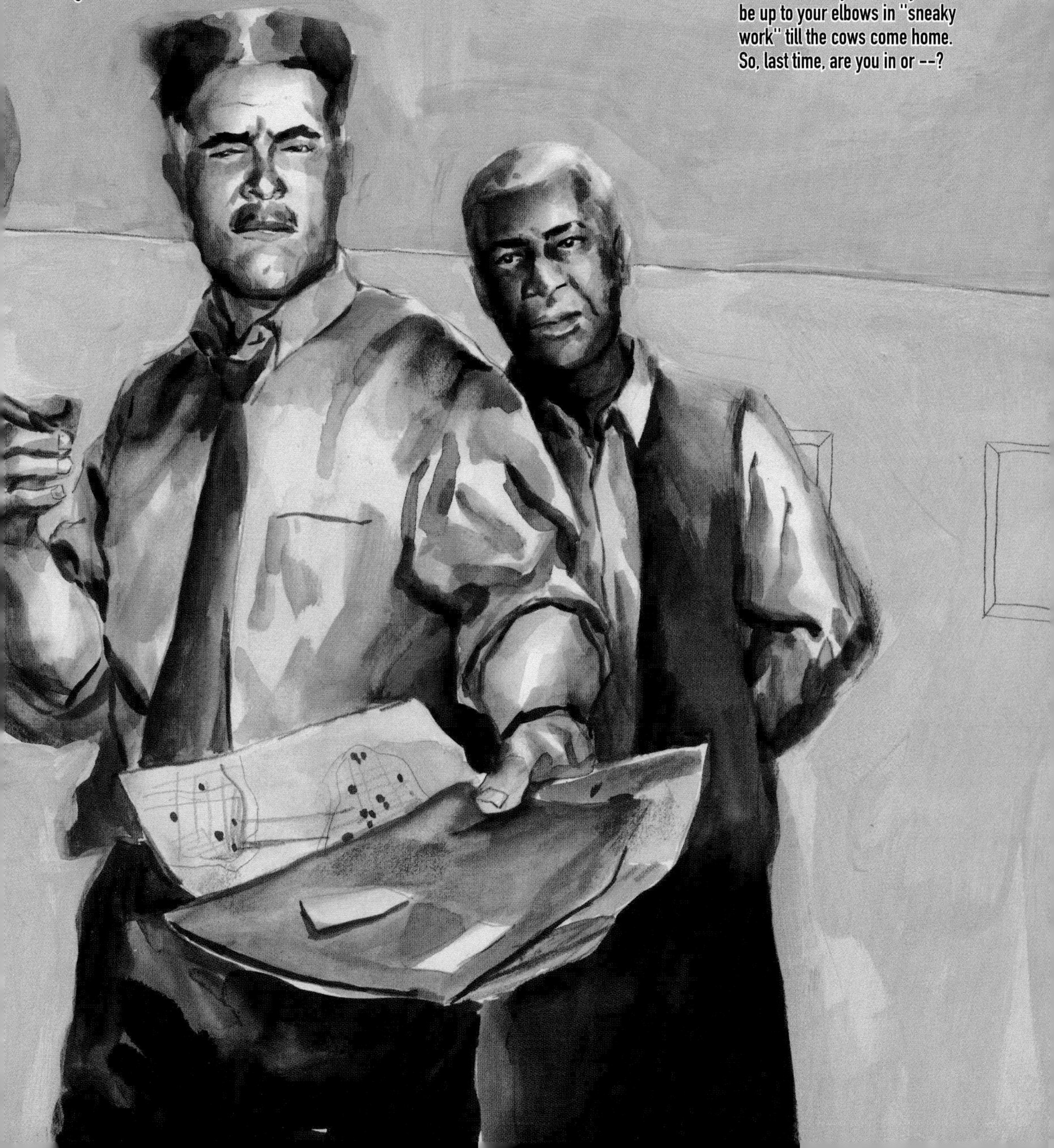

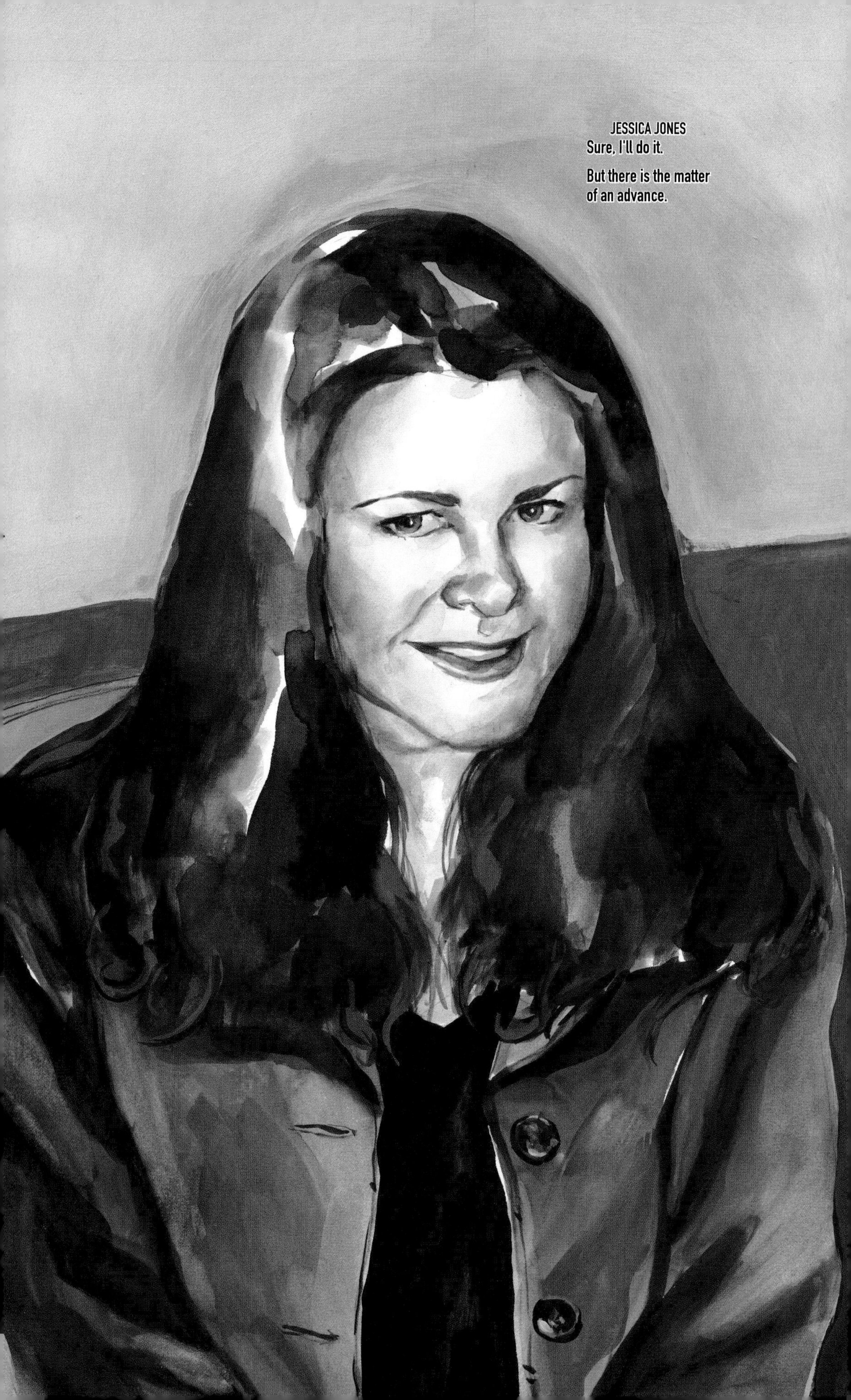
JESSICA JONES
Sure, I'll do it.
But there is the matter of an advance.

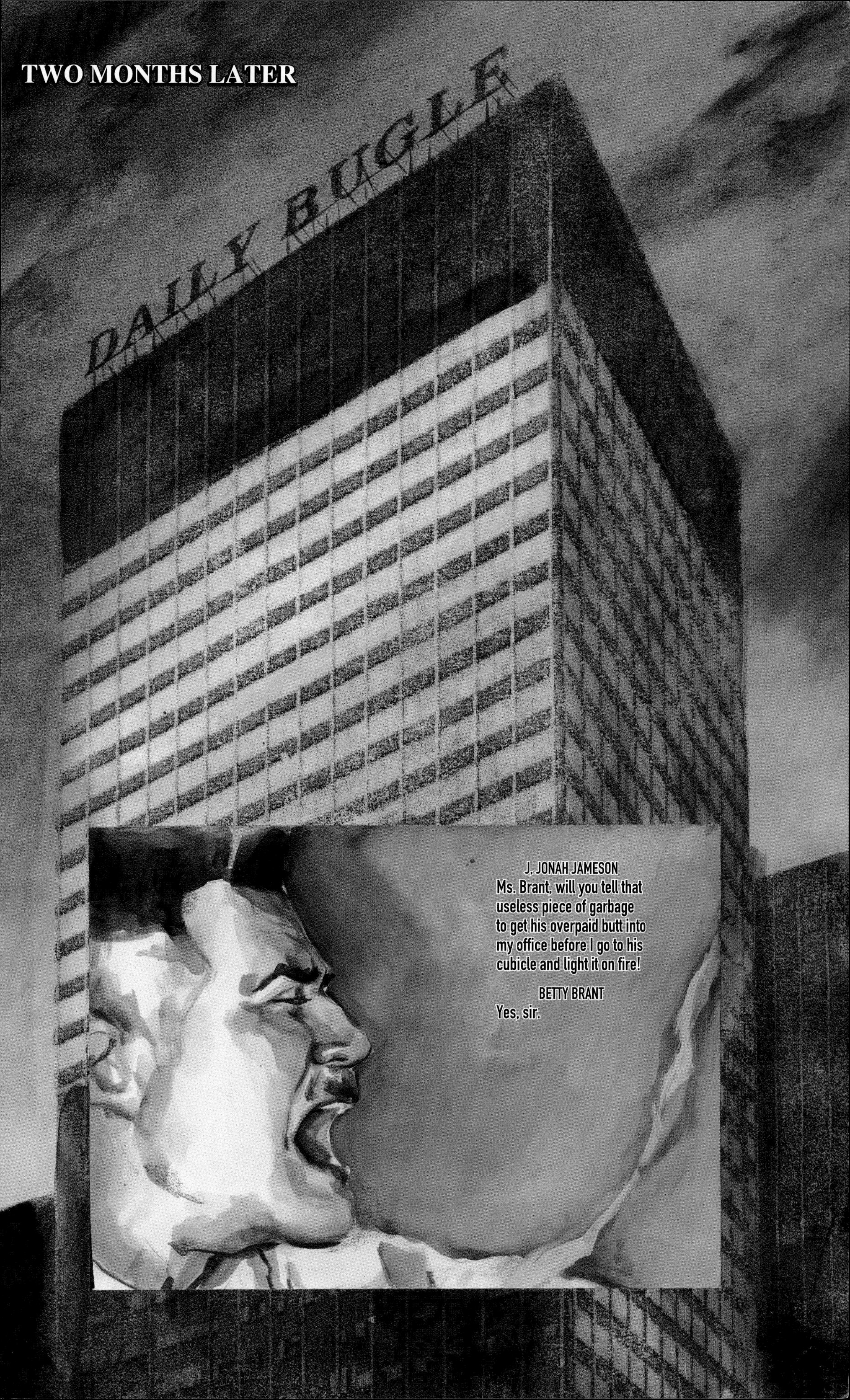
TWO MONTHS LATER
DAILY BUGLE
J. JONAH JAMESON
Ms. Brant, will you tell that useless piece of garbage to get his overpaid butt into my office before I go to his cubicle and light it on fire!
BETTY BRANT
Yes, sir.

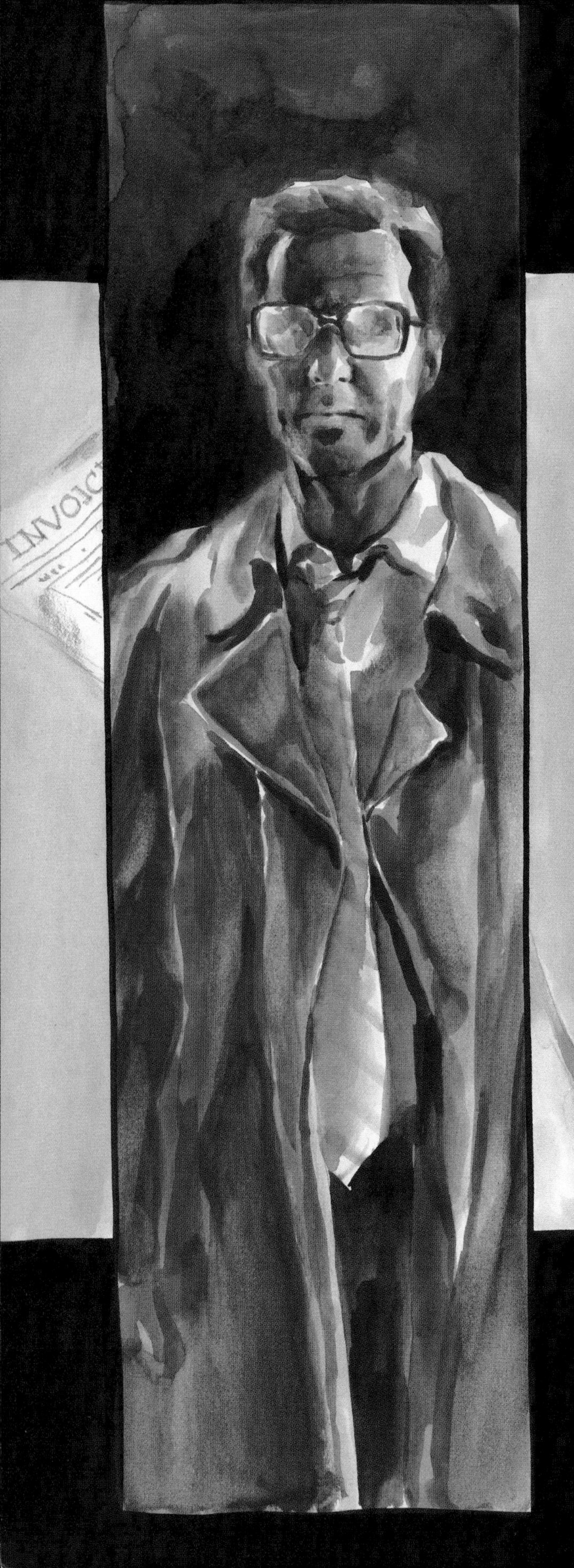
INVOIC

J. JONAH JAMESON
What is this?

BEN URICH
I don't know -- what is that?

J. JONAH JAMESON
It's Jessica's invoices for the last three weeks.

BEN URICH
Well I told you , Jonah --

J. JONAH JAMESON
What is this?!!

BEN URICH
Jonah -- I'm not in charge of invoicing -- I don't. . .

J. JONAH JAMESON
What kind of crap are you pulling?

BEN URICH
Me?

J. JONAH JAMESON
Ms. Black from accounting red-flagged this -- this -- this. . . What the hell is "Mercy's Kitchen"?

BEN URICH
Oh -- uh -- that's that soup kitchen in Hell's Kitchen that she has been --

J. JONAH JAMESON
Soup kitchen in Hell's kitchen?

BEN URICH
Yes. Yeah -- she's been working there for the last three weeks. She's been --

J. JONAH JAMESON
Working there, why?

BEN URICH
Said she had it on a good source that one of the regulars at the kitchen is Spider-Man. She said --

J. JONAH JAMESON
One of the drunken bums who comes into the --

BEN URICH
She said that she planned on gaining the trust of the regulars in hope of finding out who, and --

J. JONAH JAMESON
She serves them lunch?

BEN URICH
Yes.

J. JONAH JAMESON
And what do you do. . . ?

BEN URICH
I --

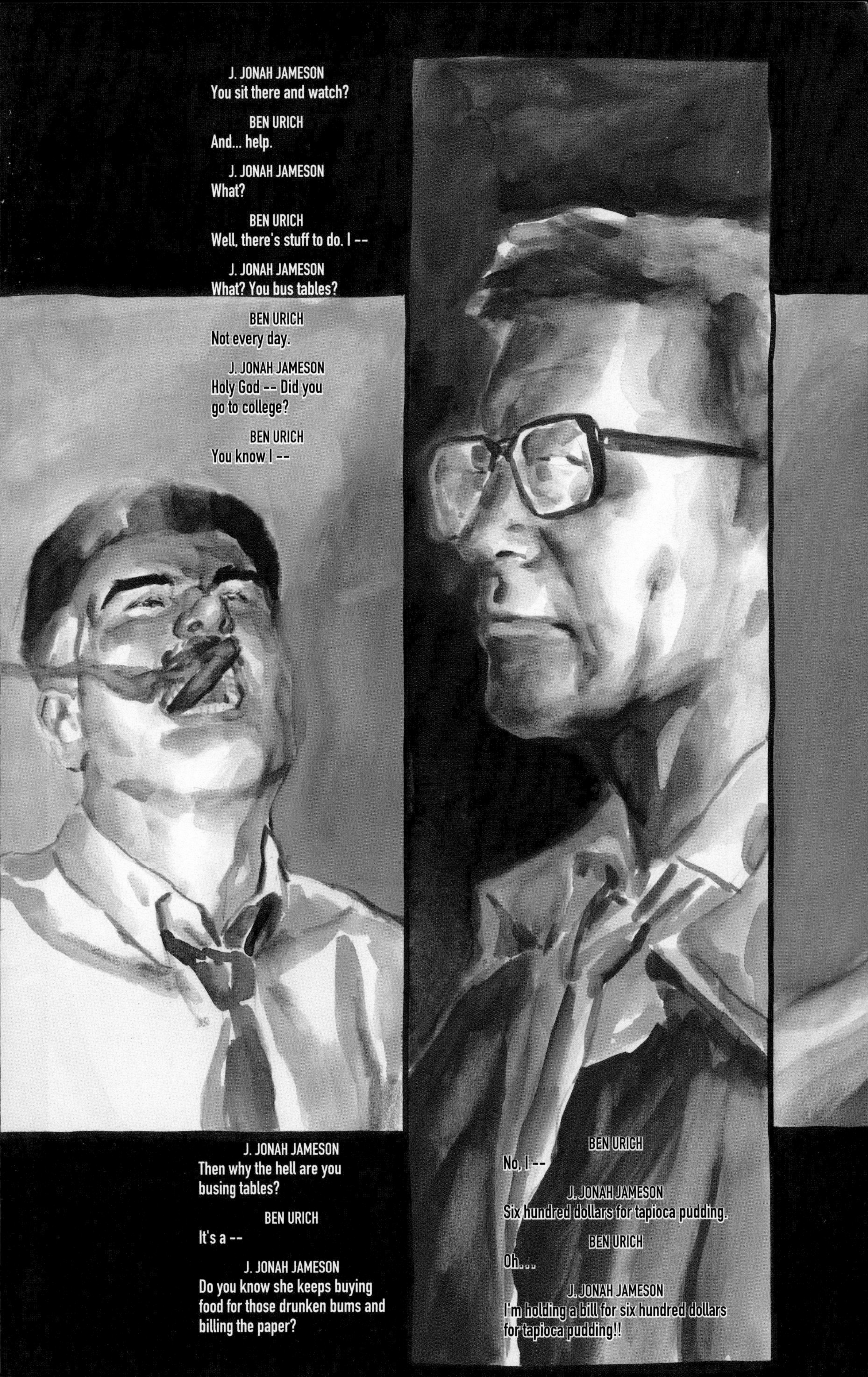
J. JONAH JAMESON
You sit there and watch?
BEN URICH
And... help.
J. JONAH JAMESON
What?
BEN URICH
Well, there's stuff to do. I --
J. JONAH JAMESON
What? You bus tables?
BEN URICH
Not every day.
J. JONAH JAMESON
Holy God -- Did you go to college?
BEN URICH
You know I --
J. JONAH JAMESON
Then why the hell are you busing tables?
BEN URICH
It's a --
J. JONAH JAMESON
Do you know she keeps buying food for those drunken bums and billing the paper?
BEN URICH
No, I --
J. JONAH JAMESON
Six hundred dollars for tapioca pudding.
BEN URICH
Oh...
J. JONAH JAMESON
I'm holding a bill for six hundred dollars for tapioca pudding!!

J. JONAH JAMESON
For the first time in my decades-long career as a -- She's buying pudding for drunks and trying to get me to pay for it --

BEN URICH
Well, she did say expenses.

J. JONAH JAMESON
Phone calls and paperclips are expenses!!! This is pudding!!

BEN URICH
I didn't know she was billing it to you.

J. JONAH JAMESON
Well, she is!! Two hundred dollars an hour, all day every day!! For her to serve pudding to meth addicts -- and one of my best reporters bussing tables!

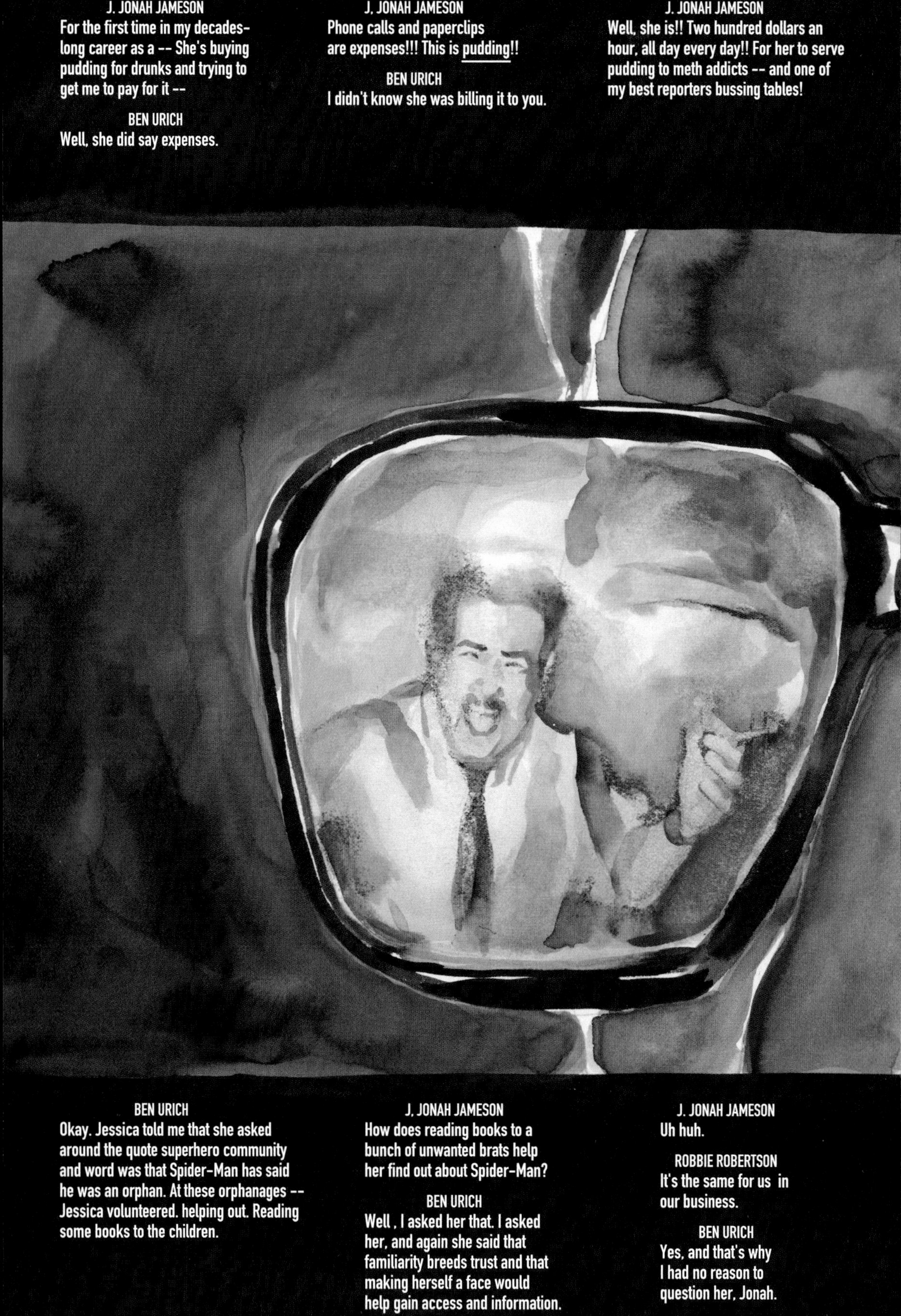

BEN URICH
Okay. Jessica told me that she asked around the quote superhero community and word was that Spider-Man has said he was an orphan. At these orphanages -- Jessica volunteered. helping out. Reading some books to the children.

J. JONAH JAMESON
How does reading books to a bunch of unwanted brats help her find out about Spider-Man?

BEN URICH
Well , I asked her that. I asked her, and again she said that familiarity breeds trust and that making herself a face would help gain access and information.

J. JONAH JAMESON
Uh huh.

ROBBIE ROBERTSON
It's the same for us in our business.

BEN URICH
Yes, and that's why I had no reason to question her, Jonah.

BEN URICH
Thanks --

J. JONAH JAMESON
Shut up! Give me the report so far --

BEN URICH
Didn't she send some kind of --

J. JONAH JAMESON
Give me your notes, Urich!!

BEN URICH
Okay, Okay. Here -- uh -- well, soon after you hired her we made the rounds to a handful of orphanages. Three orphanages. St. Alexis' of 49th, The Tony Stark Foundation Home for Wayward --

J. JONAH JAMESON
Come on --

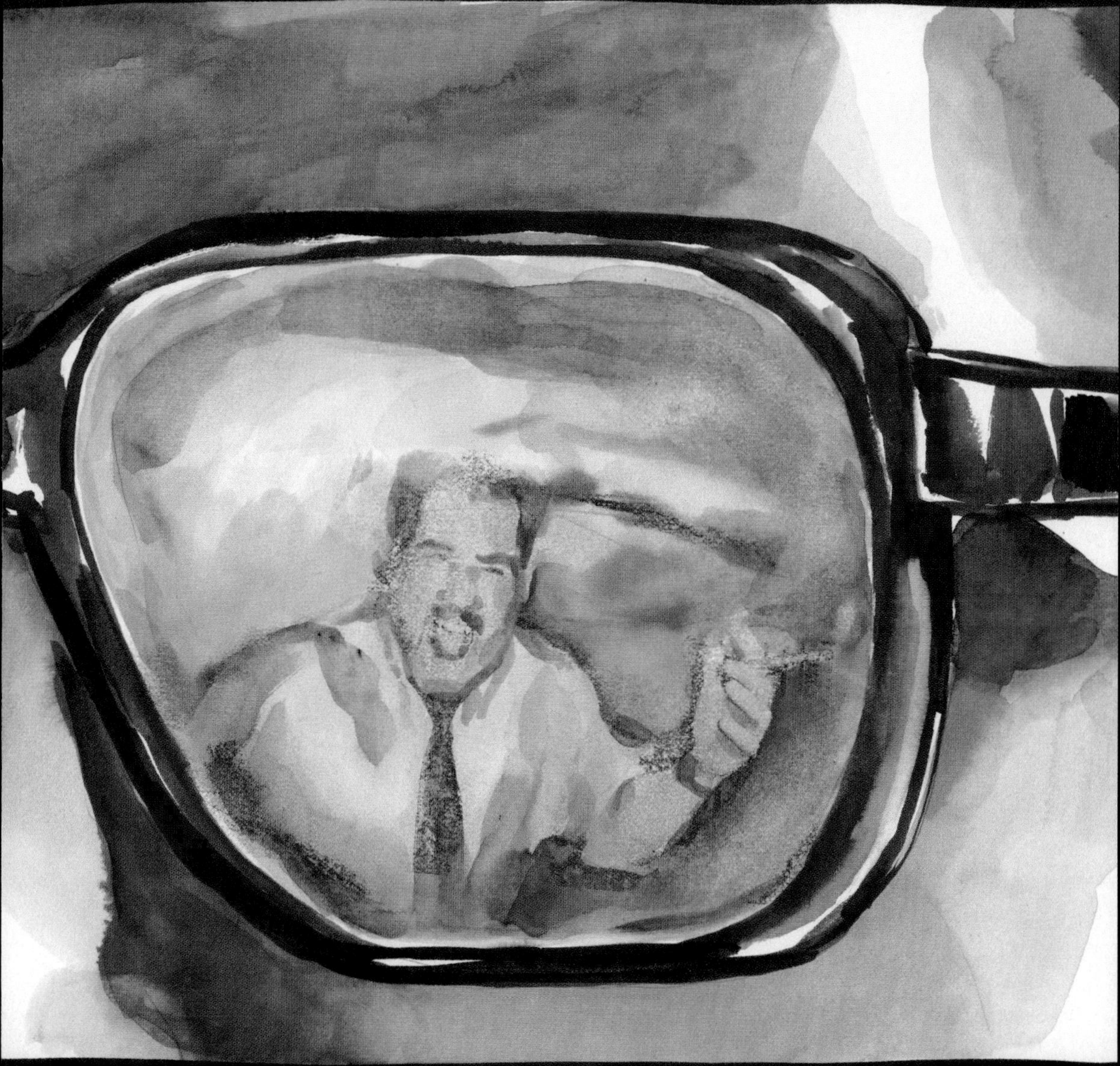

J. JONAH JAMESON
I have a bill here. She bought the kids cupcakes for a week at one of these --

BEN URICH
Then it was on to St. Catherine's Hospital where Jessica said she had a tip that one of the orderlies was Spider-Man. She said it was well known among

J. JONAH JAMESON
So she volunteered at the hospital.

BEN URICH
The AIDS ward.

J. JONAH JAMESON
Pssss...

BEN URICH
And for the last few weeks she's been at the soup kitchen...

J. JONAH JAMESON
Damn it, Urich!

BEN URICH
What?

J. JONAH JAMESON
She's scamming us!!

BEN URICH
How is she --

J. JONAH JAMESON
AIDS patients, orphans, winos!!
Volunteering at two hundred
dollars an hour!

BEN URICH
I --

J. JONAH JAMESON
Were you ever there when she got
one of these little "tips" of hers?

BEN URICH
The actual tip? No. It was after --

J. JONAH JAMESON
Did you ever see any of her
so called super hero pals?

BEN URICH
Uh -- no.

J. JONAH JAMESON
No?

BEN URICH
No.

J. JONAH JAMESON
You stupid, WORTHLESS,
WASTE OF --

ROBBIE ROBERTSON
Jonah!

J. JONAH JAMESON
Dammit! She scammed us!
A damn scam artist!

ROBBIE ROBERTSON
Jonah --

BEN URICH
Well maybe if --

J. JONAH JAMESON
What??!!

BEN URICH
Nothing.

ROBBIE ROBERTSON
What Ben was going to say is --
that maybe when you hired her if
you hadn't insulted every single
facet of her life --

J. JONAH JAMESON
What?

ROBBIE ROBERTSON
Jonah. You...!

J. JONAH JAMESON
What did I say?

ROBBIE ROBERTSON
You said that superheroes
deserve to be --

J. JONAH JAMESON
I say that in the paper
every freaking day.

ROBBIE ROBERTSON
You said that private investigators
are pieces of --

J. JONAH JAMESON
They are! She knows that.
Doesn't mean she can steal
from me --

ROBBIE ROBERTSON
Jonah --

J. JONAH JAMESON
Stole money out of me --

ROBBIE ROBERTSON
Jonah, you can't prove that.

J. JONAH JAMESON
What?

ROBBIE ROBERTSON
They are legitimate --

J. JONAH JAMESON
Shut up!

ROBBIE ROBERTSON
Legitimate claims --

J. JONAH JAMESON
Well, I'm not buying
this pudding.

ROBBIE ROBERTSON
You signed a contract with
the woman.

J. JONAH JAMESON
Ms. Brant!! Get in here!!

ROBBIE ROBERTSON
You signed a contract --

J. JONAH JAMESON
You know what, Ben? You write
your damn story -- you tell
the world what this lying --

ROBBIE ROBERTSON
That she what? Fed the homeless,
read to orphans, and cared for
AIDS patients?

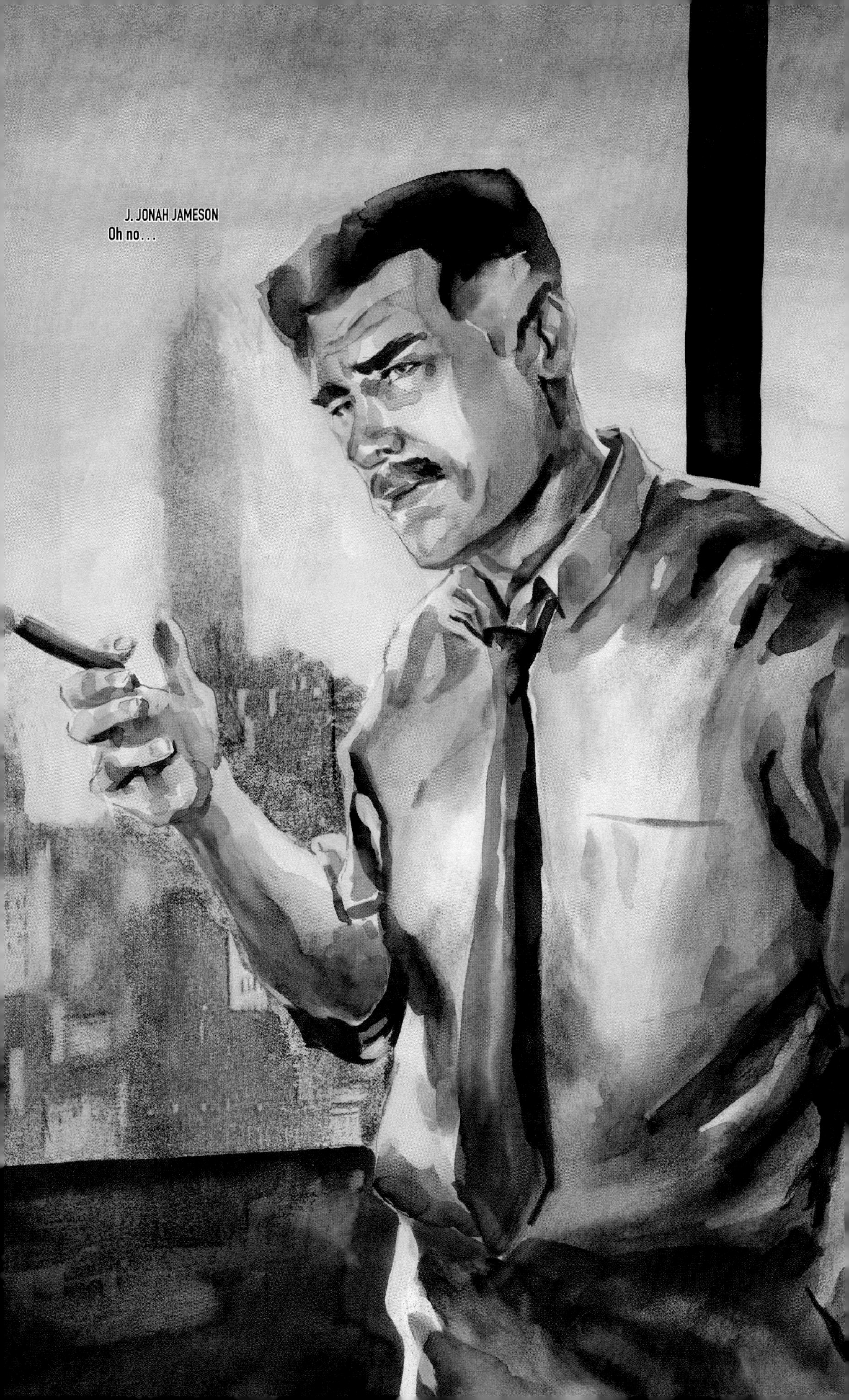
J. JONAH JAMESON
Oh no...

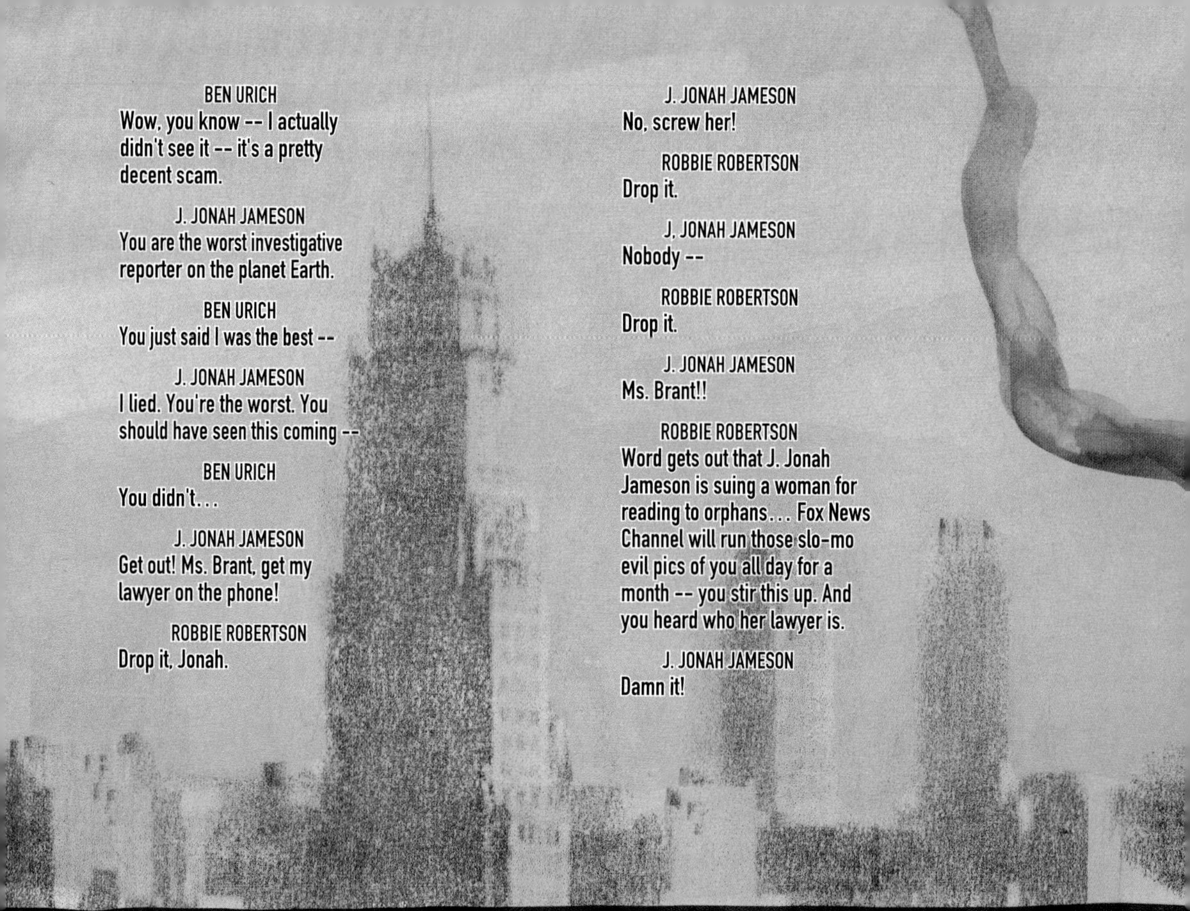
BEN URICH
Wow, you know -- I actually didn't see it -- it's a pretty decent scam.
J. JONAH JAMESON
You are the worst investigative reporter on the planet Earth.
BEN URICH
You just said I was the best --
J. JONAH JAMESON
I lied. You're the worst. You should have seen this coming --
BEN URICH
You didn't...
J. JONAH JAMESON
Get out! Ms. Brant, get my lawyer on the phone!
ROBBIE ROBERTSON
Drop it, Jonah.
J. JONAH JAMESON
No, screw her!
ROBBIE ROBERTSON
Drop it.
J. JONAH JAMESON
Nobody --
ROBBIE ROBERTSON
Drop it.
J. JONAH JAMESON
Ms. Brant!!
ROBBIE ROBERTSON
Word gets out that J. Jonah Jameson is suing a woman for reading to orphans... Fox News Channel will run those slo-mo evil pics of you all day for a month -- you stir this up. And you heard who her lawyer is.
J. JONAH JAMESON
Damn it!

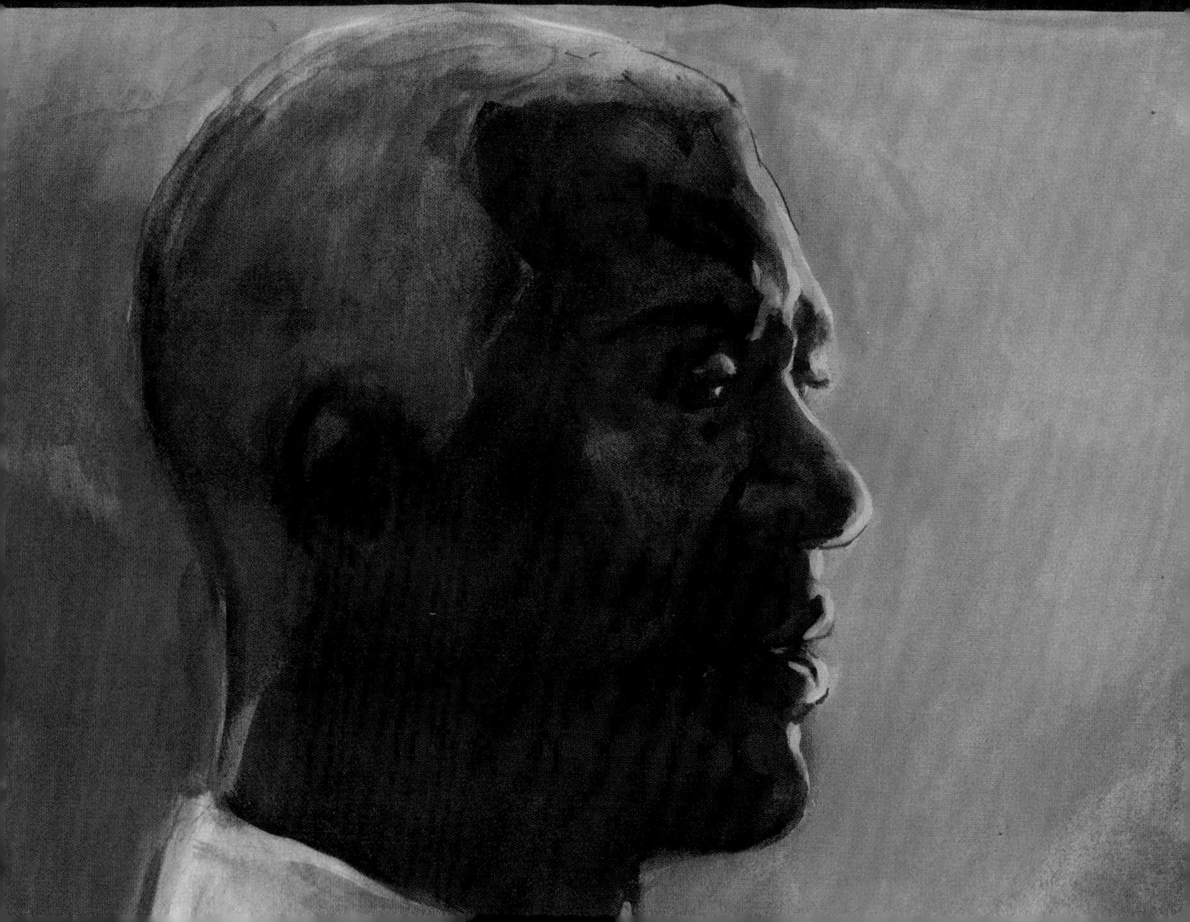

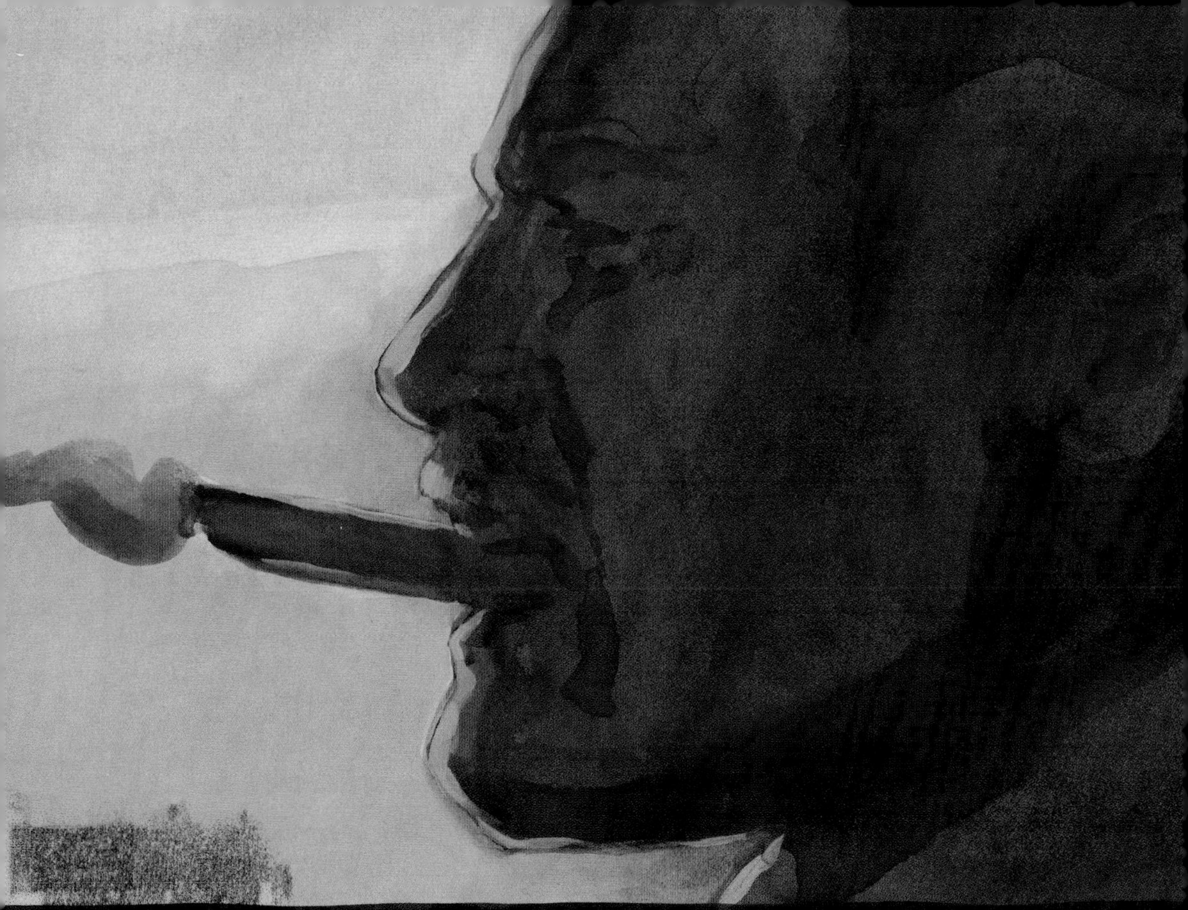

ROBBIE ROBERTSON
Drop it.

J. JONAH JAMESON
Damn it!

ROBBIE ROBERTSON
Just chalk it up --

J. JONAH JAMESON
Damn super heroes --
every time.

ROBBIE ROBERTSON
All right, I'm going home.

J. JONAH JAMESON
Ms. Brant, get me that woman's
telephone number -- oh here
it is -- I got it! Never mind!

ROBBIE ROBERTSON
Jonah...

J. JONAH JAMESON
Oh no! Oh no! the least I get
to do -- the least I get to do
is let her know I know and
that the jig is up!

ROBBIE ROBERTSON
I don't think --

J. JONAH JAMESON
It's her machine. Doesn't
even have the guts to --
Ms. Jones, this is J. Jonah
Jameson, publisher of
the Daily Bugle.

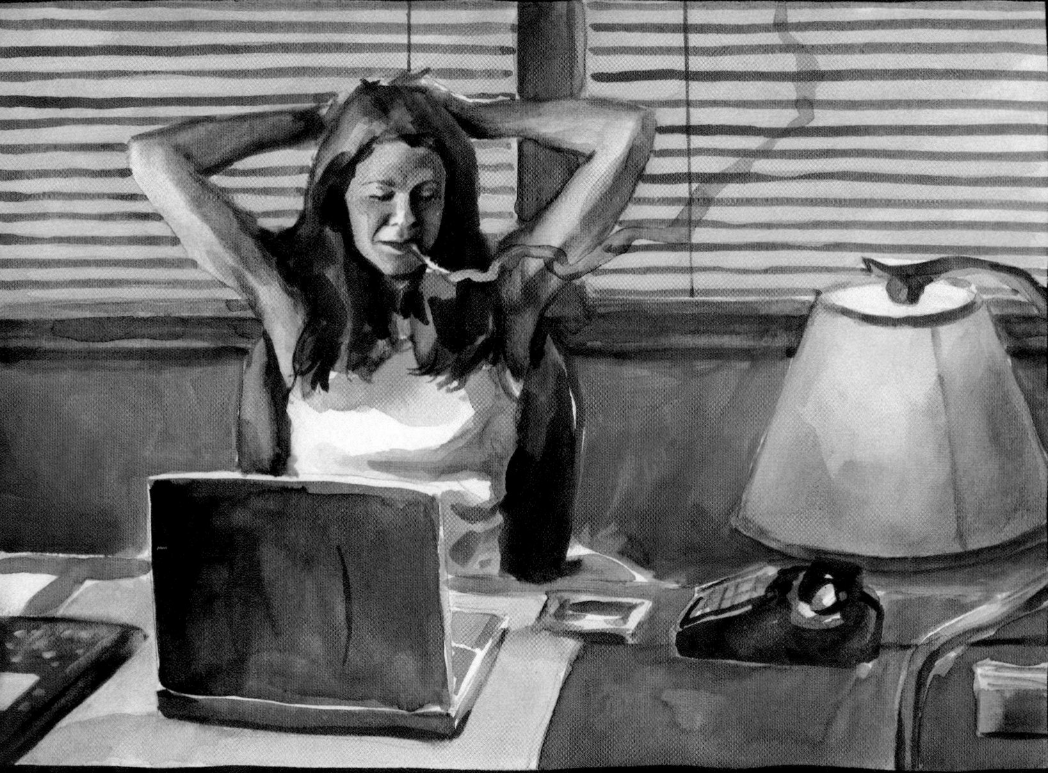

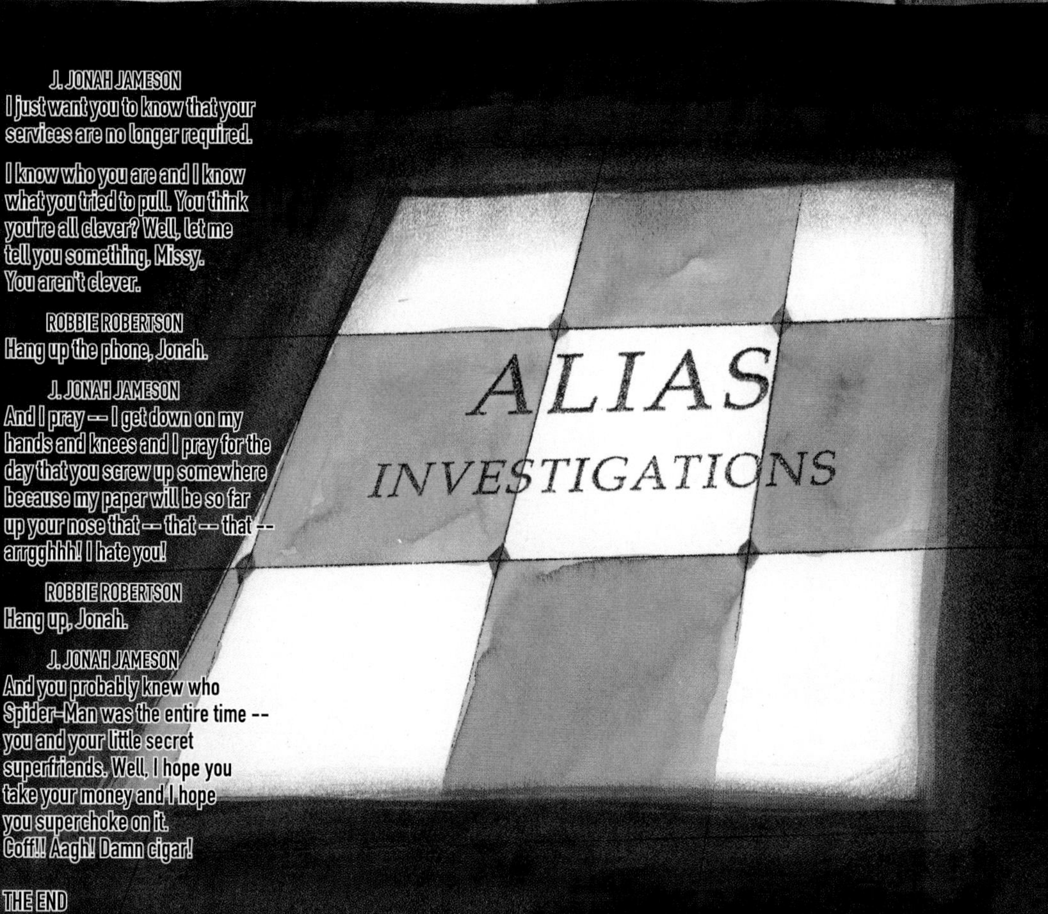

J. JONAH JAMESON
I just want you to know that your services are no longer required.
I know who you are and I know what you tried to pull. You think you're all clever? Well, let me tell you something, Missy. You aren't clever.
ROBBIE ROBERTSON
Hang up the phone, Jonah.
J. JONAH JAMESON
And I pray -- I get down on my hands and knees and I pray for the day that you screw up somewhere because my paper will be so far up your nose that -- that -- that -- arrgghhh! I hate you!
ROBBIE ROBERTSON
Hang up, Jonah.
J. JONAH JAMESON
And you probably knew who Spider-Man was the entire time -- you and your little secret superfriends. Well, I hope you take your money and I hope you superchoke on it. Coff!! Aagh! Damn cigar!
THE END
ALIAS
INVESTIGATIONS

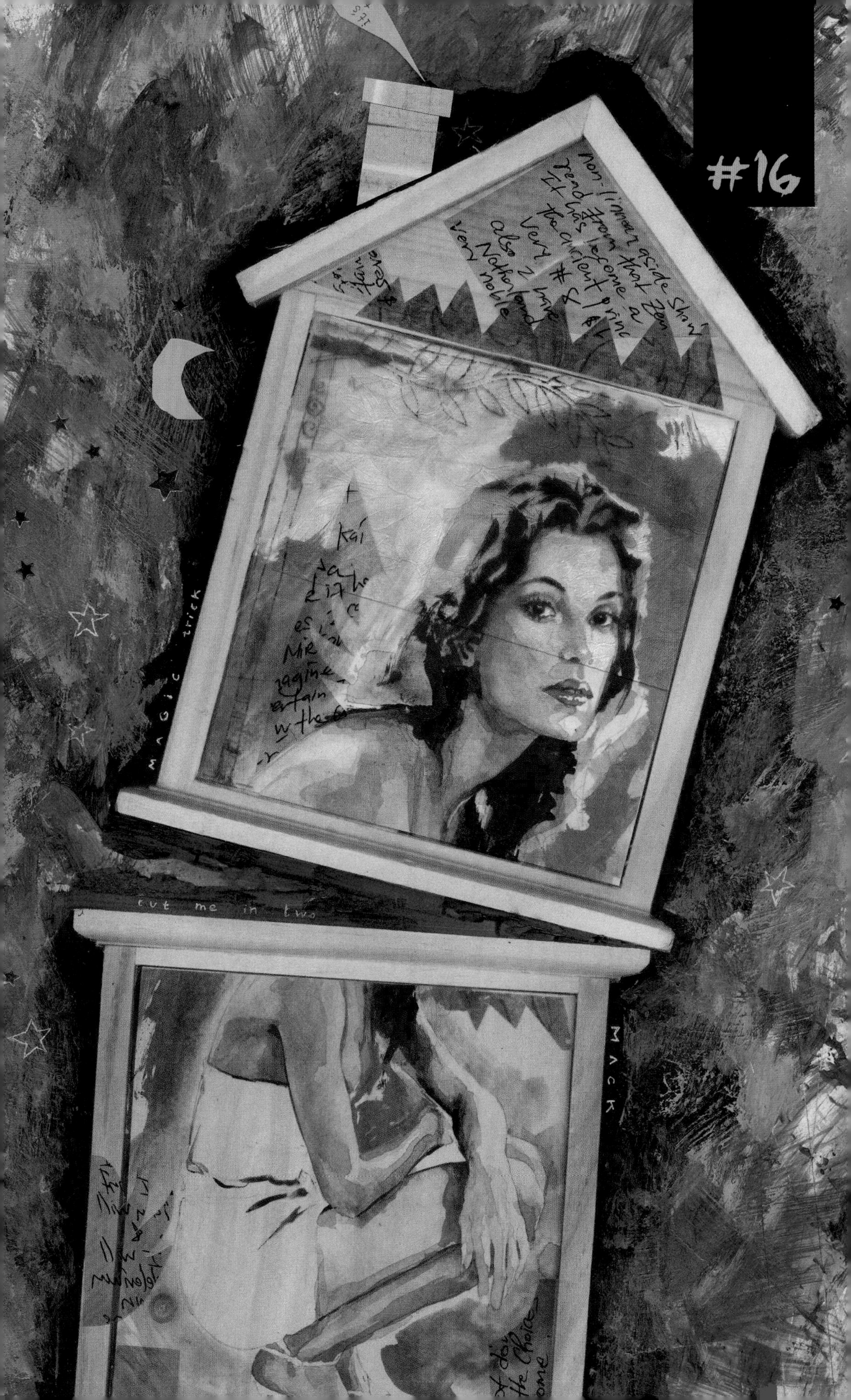

#16
MAGIC trick
cut me in two
MACK

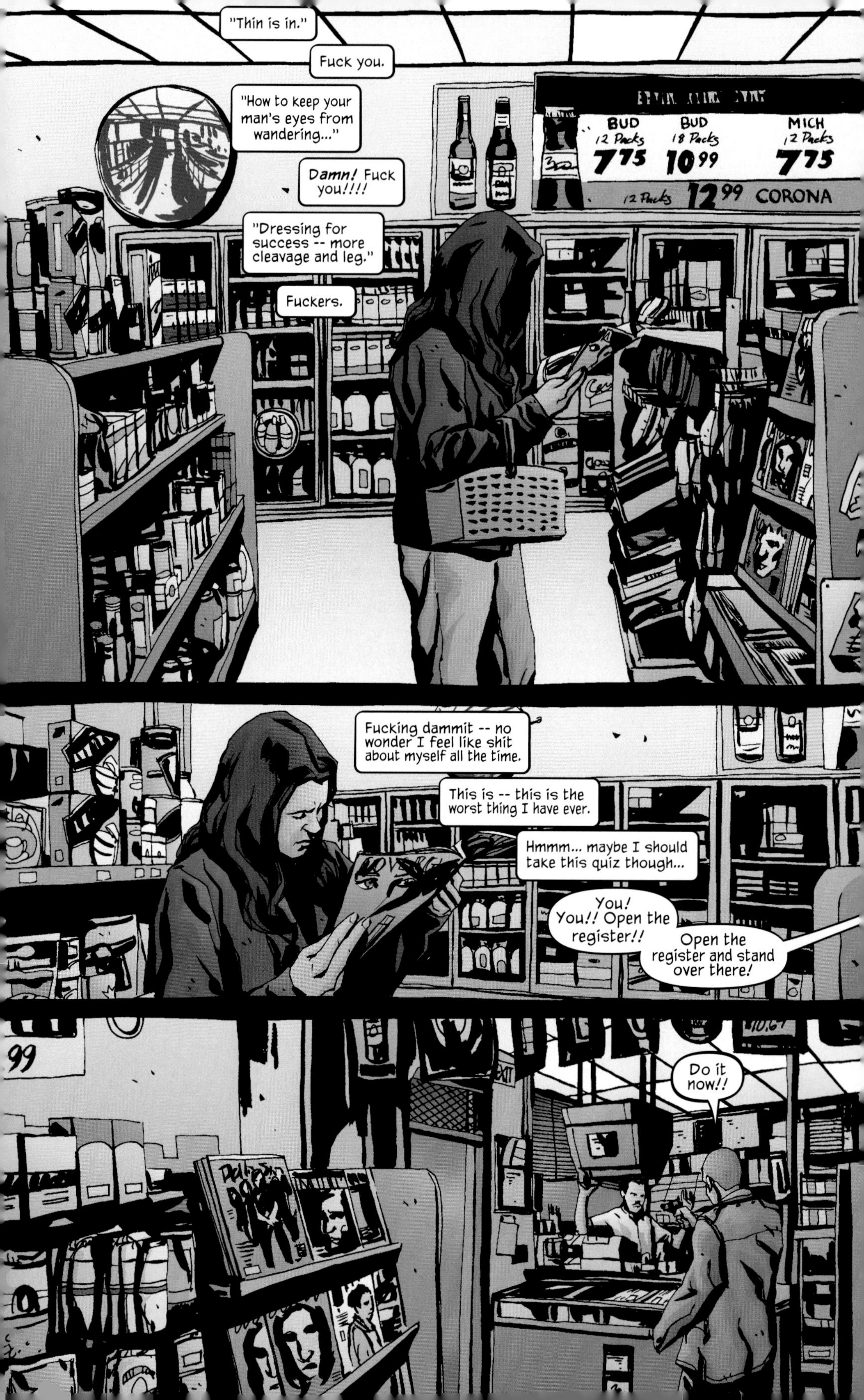
"Thin is in."
Fuck you.
"How to keep your man's eyes from wandering..."
Damn! Fuck you!!!!
"Dressing for success -- more cleavage and leg."
Fuckers.
BUD 12 Packs 7.75
BUD 18 Packs 10.99
MICH 12 Packs 7.75
12 Packs 12.99 CORONA
Fucking dammit -- no wonder I feel like shit about myself all the time.
This is -- this is the worst thing I have ever.
Hmmm... maybe I should take this quiz though...
You! You!! Open the register!!
Open the register and stand over there!
Do it now!!

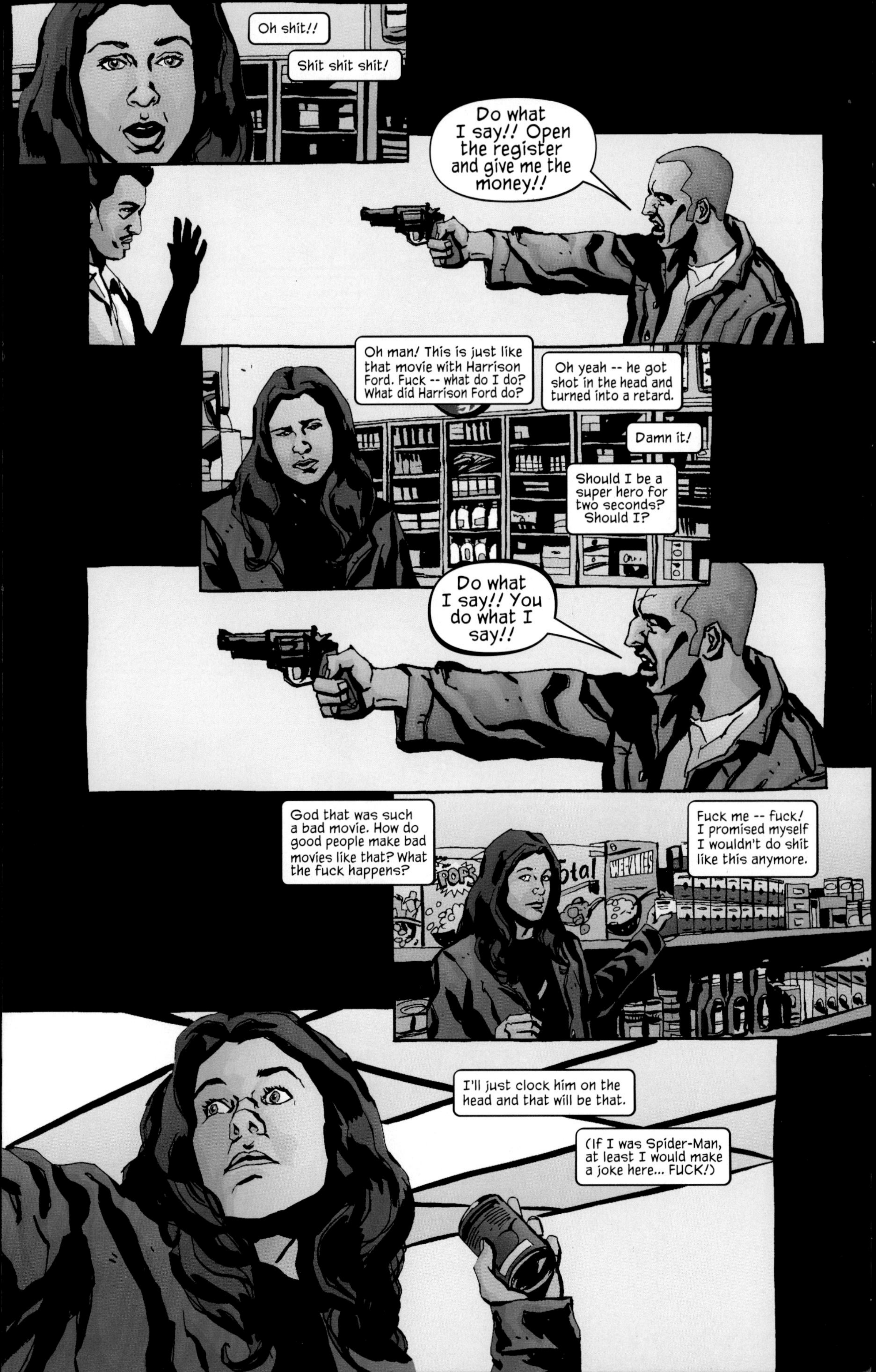

Oh shit!!
Shit shit shit!
Do what I say!! Open the register and give me the money!!
Oh man! This is just like that movie with Harrison Ford. Fuck -- what do I do? What did Harrison Ford do?
Oh yeah -- he got shot in the head and turned into a retard.
Damn it!
Should I be a super hero for two seconds? Should I?
Do what I say!! You do what I say!!
God that was such a bad movie. How do good people make bad movies like that? What the fuck happens?
Fuck me -- fuck! I promised myself I wouldn't do shit like this anymore.
I'll just clock him on the head and that will be that.
(If I was Spider-Man, at least I would make a joke here... FUCK!)

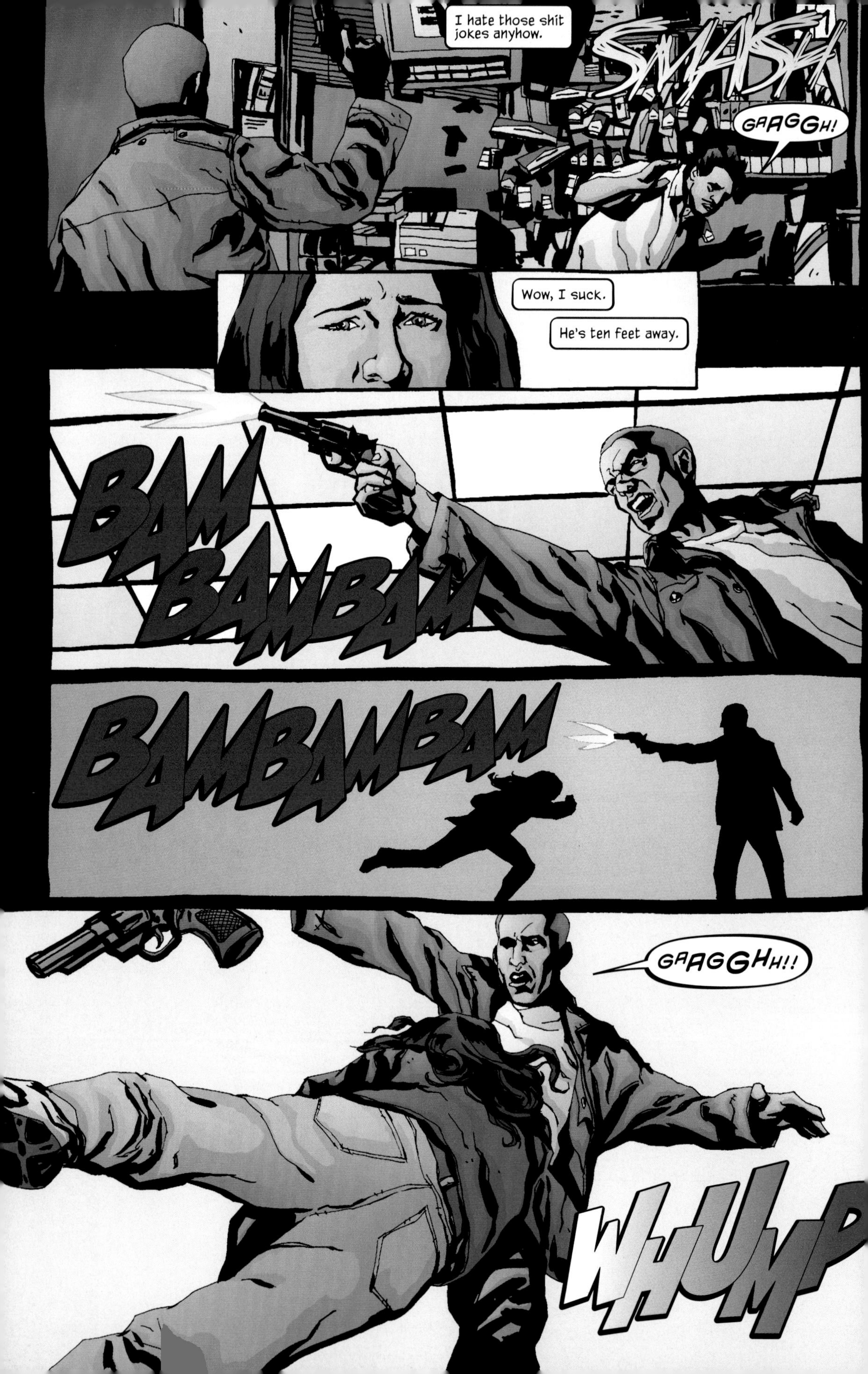
I hate those shit jokes anyhow.
SMASH
GAAGGH!
Wow, I suck.
He's ten feet away.
BAM BAMBAM
BAMBAMBAM
GAAGGHH!!
WHUMP

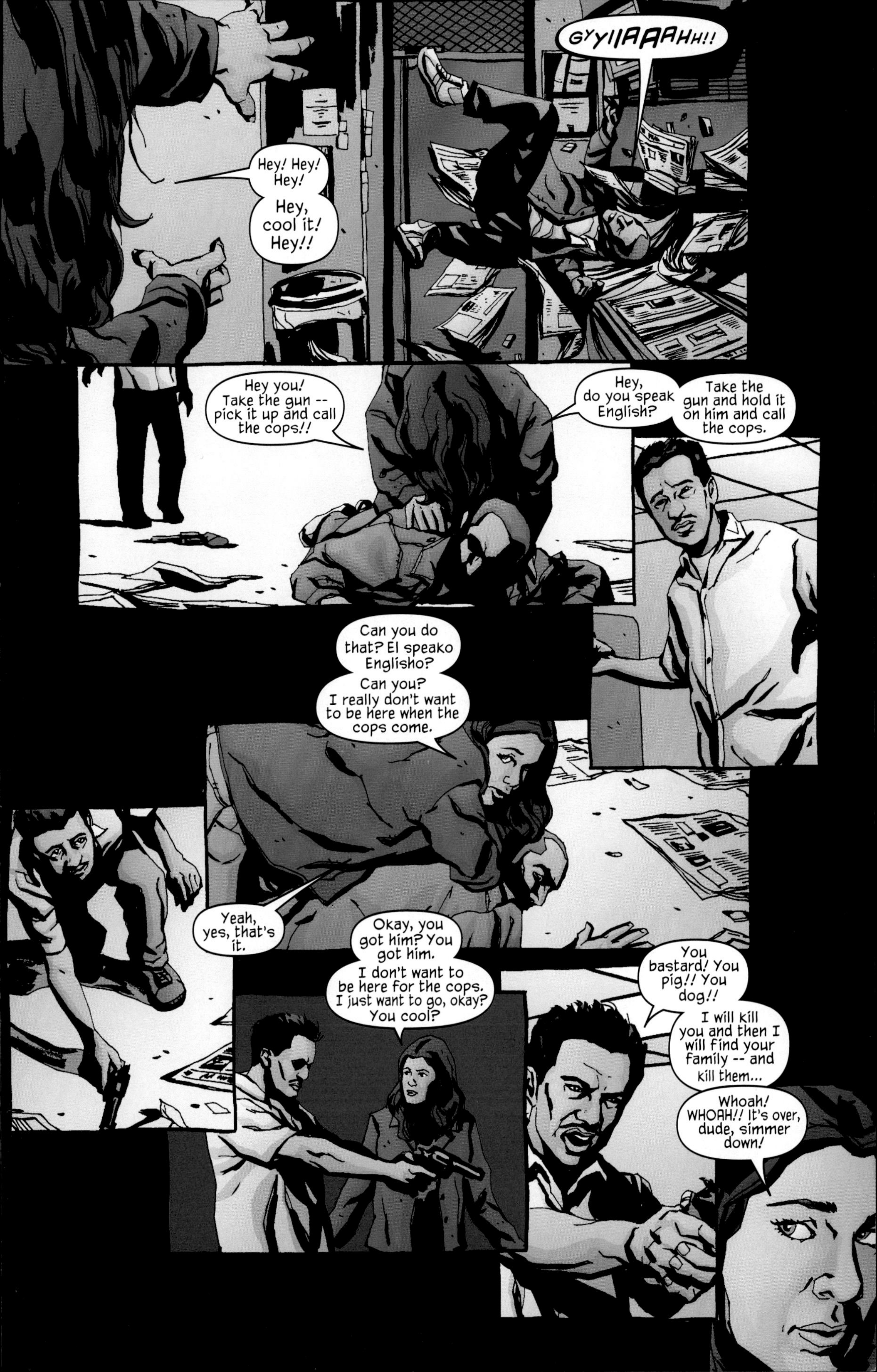
GYYIIAAAHH!!
Hey! Hey! Hey!
Hey, cool it! Hey!!
Hey you! Take the gun -- pick it up and call the cops!!
Hey, do you speak English?
Take the gun and hold it on him and call the cops.
Can you do that? El speako Englisho?
Can you? I really don't want to be here when the cops come.
Yeah, yes, that's it.
Okay, you got him? You got him.
I don't want to be here for the cops. I just want to go, okay? You cool?
You bastard! You pig!! You dog!!
I will kill you and then I will find your family -- and kill them...
Whoah! WHOAH!! It's over, dude, simmer down!

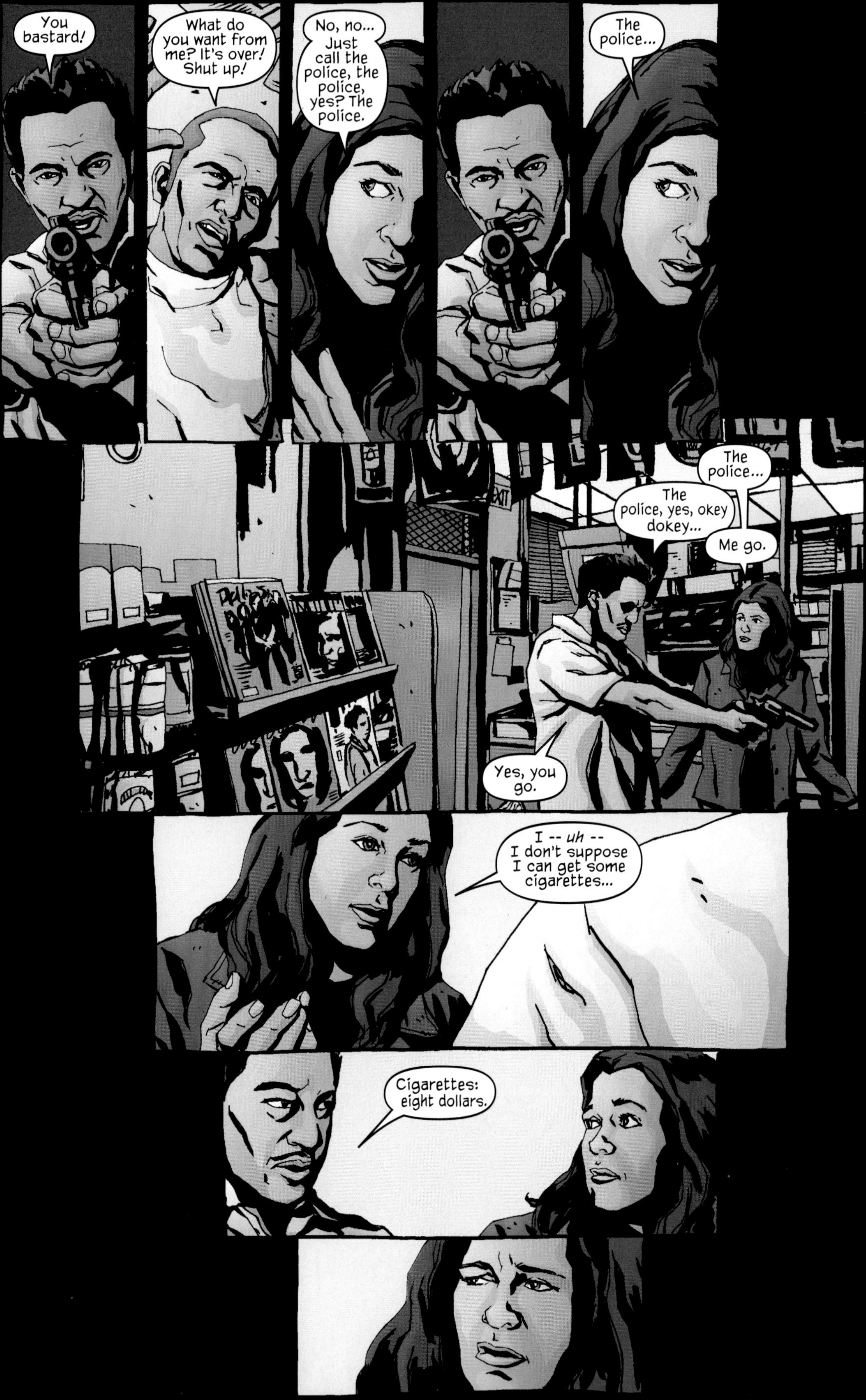
You bastard!
What do you want from me? It's over! Shut up!
No, no... Just call the police, the police, yes? The police.
The police...
The police, yes, okey dokey...
The police...
Me go.
Yes, you go.
I -- *uh* -- I don't suppose I can get some cigarettes...
Cigarettes: eight dollars.

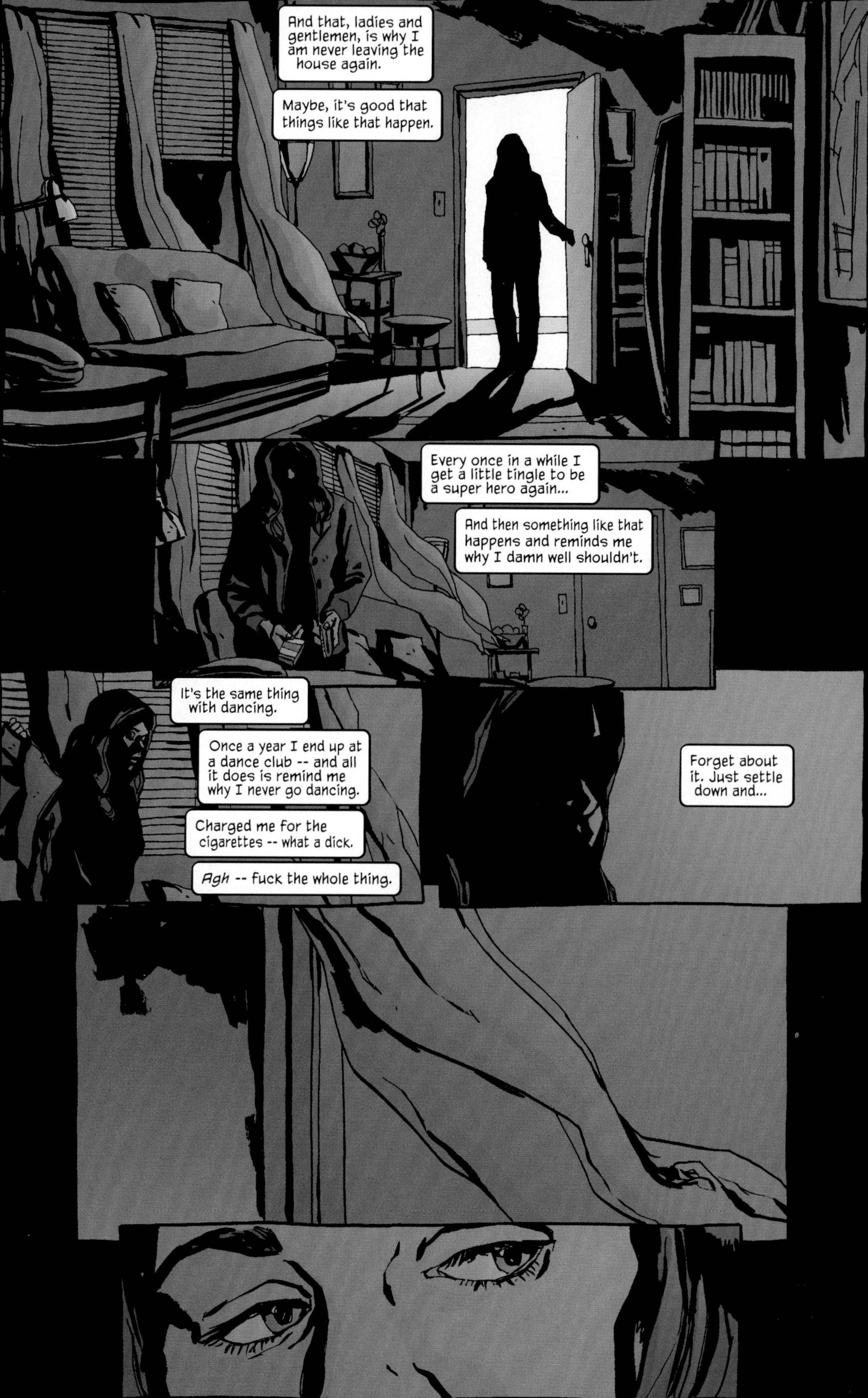
And that, ladies and gentlemen, is why I am never leaving the house again.
Maybe, it's good that things like that happen.
Every once in a while I get a little tingle to be a super hero again...
And then something like that happens and reminds me why I damn well shouldn't.
It's the same thing with dancing.
Once a year I end up at a dance club -- and all it does is remind me why I never go dancing.
Charged me for the cigarettes -- what a dick.
Agh -- fuck the whole thing.
Forget about it. Just settle down and...

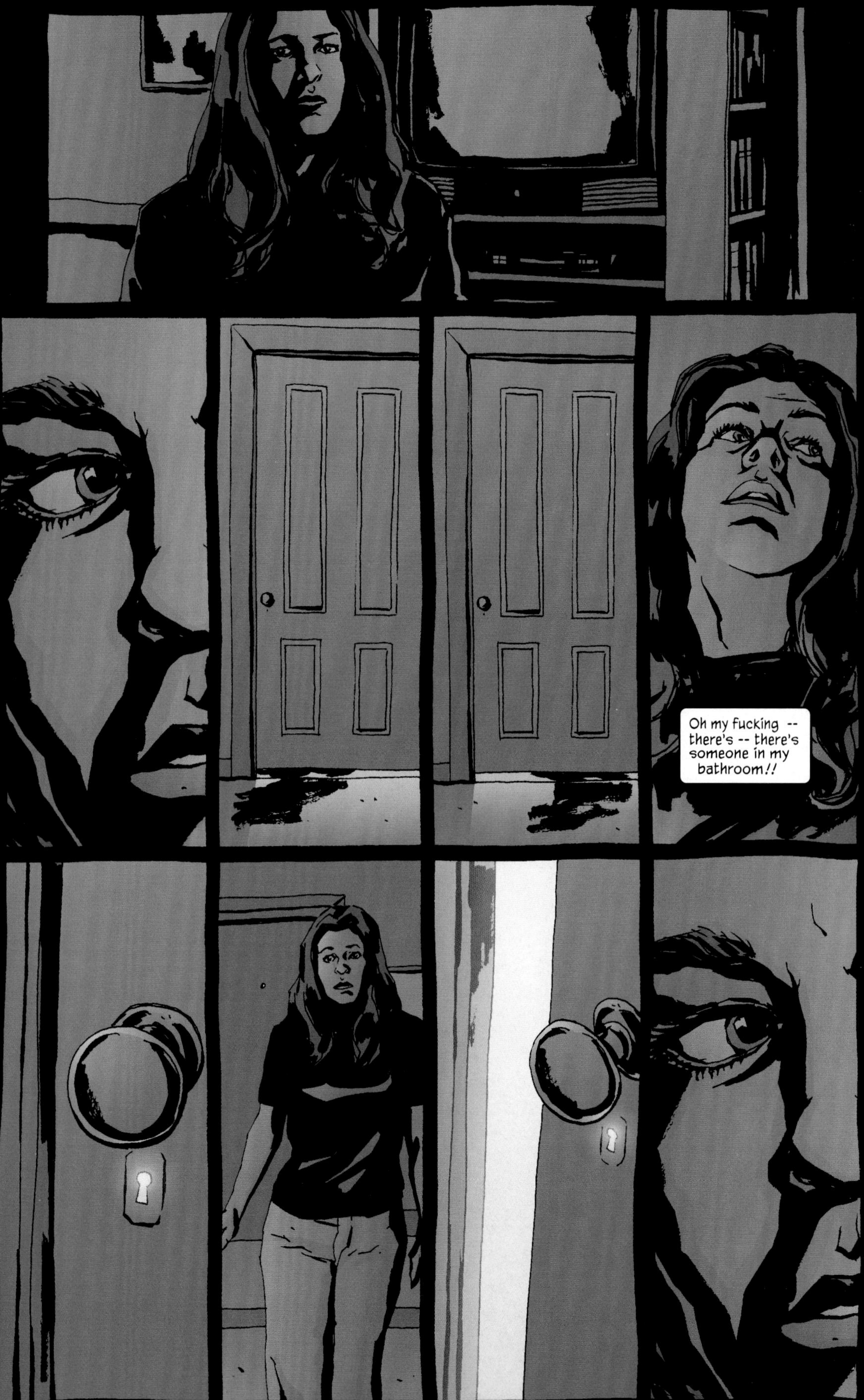
Oh my fucking -- there's -- there's someone in my bathroom!!

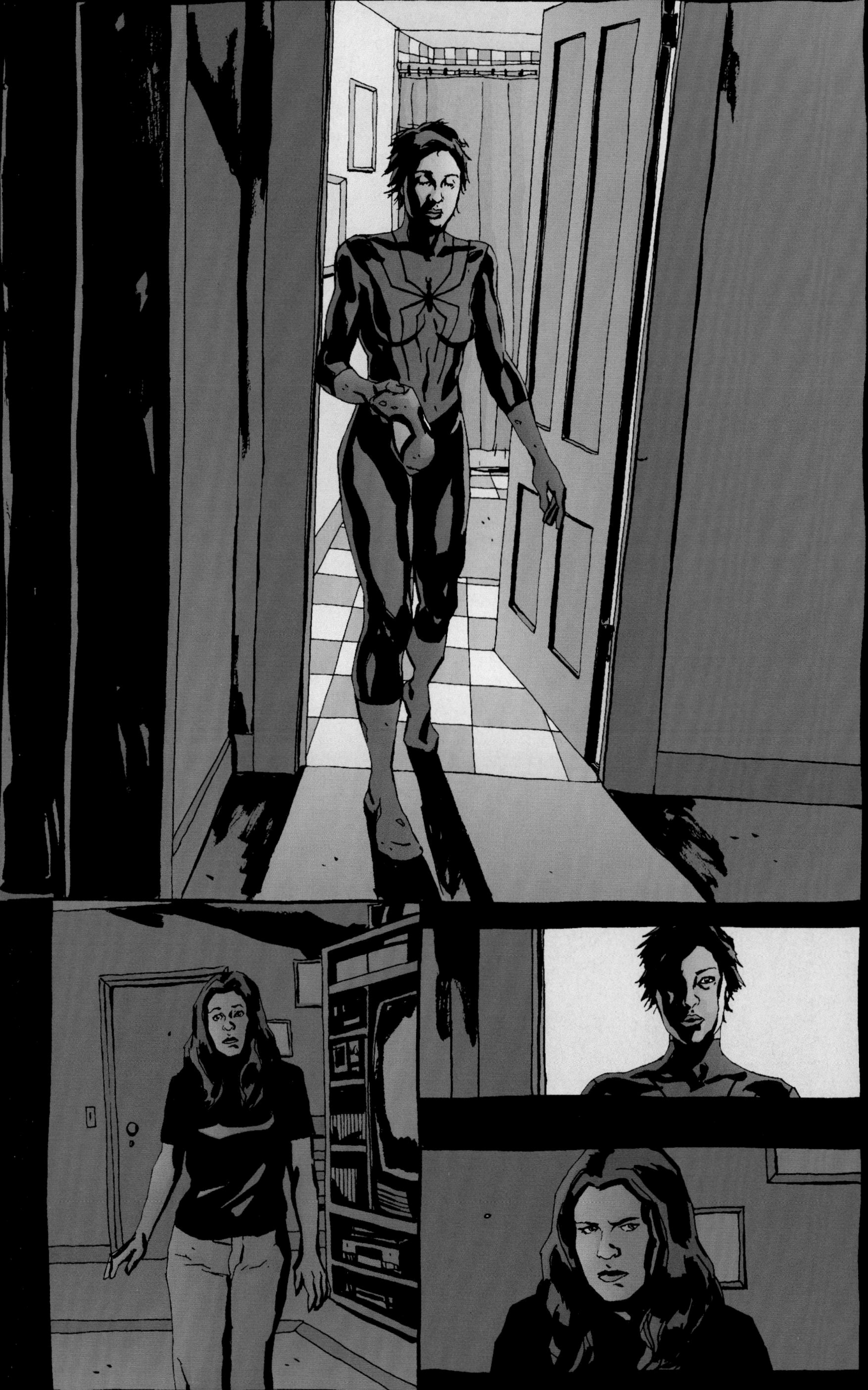

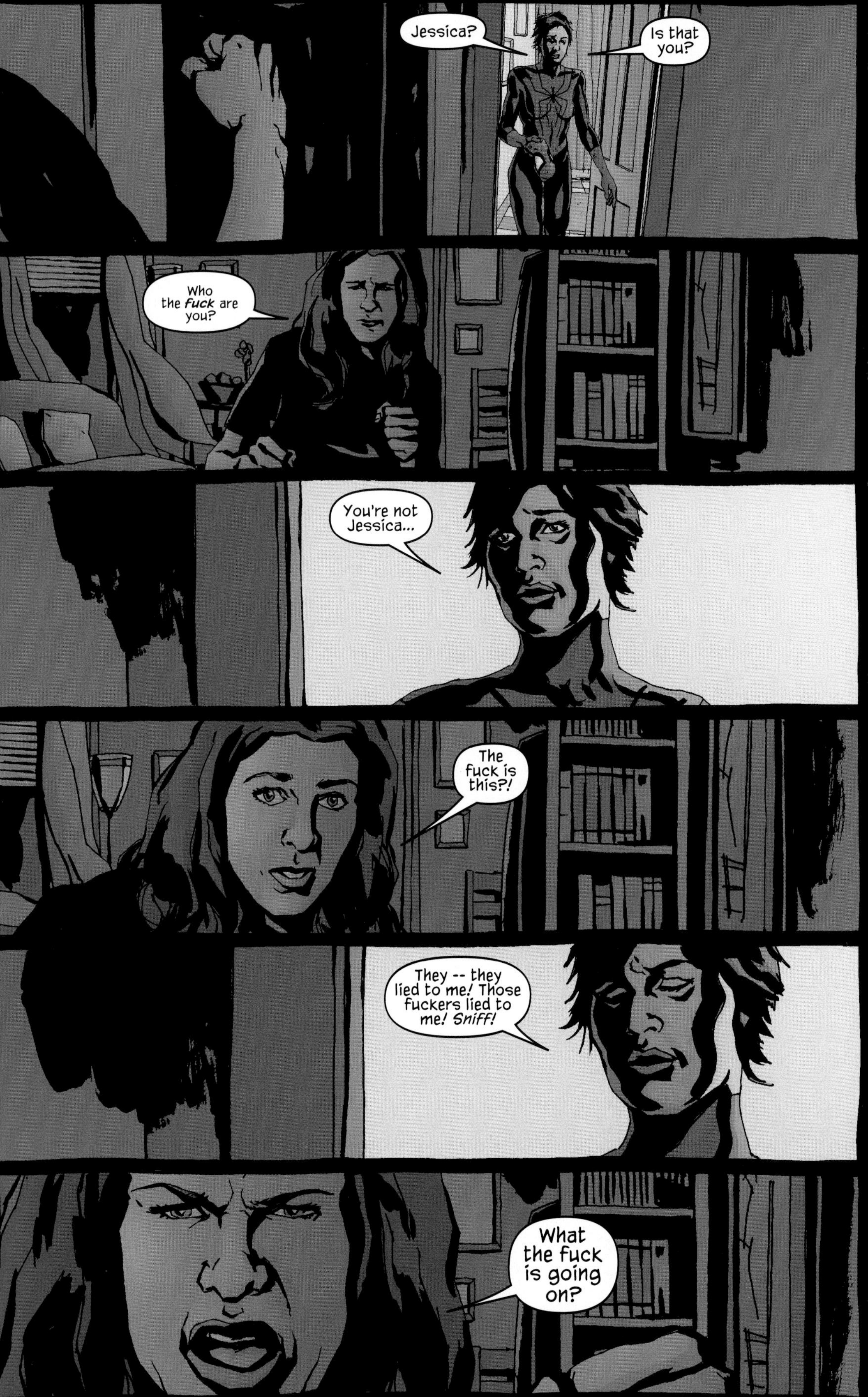
Jessica?
Is that you?
Who the *fuck* are you?
You're not Jessica...
The fuck is this?!
They -- they lied to me! Those fuckers lied to me! *Sniff!*
What the fuck is going on?

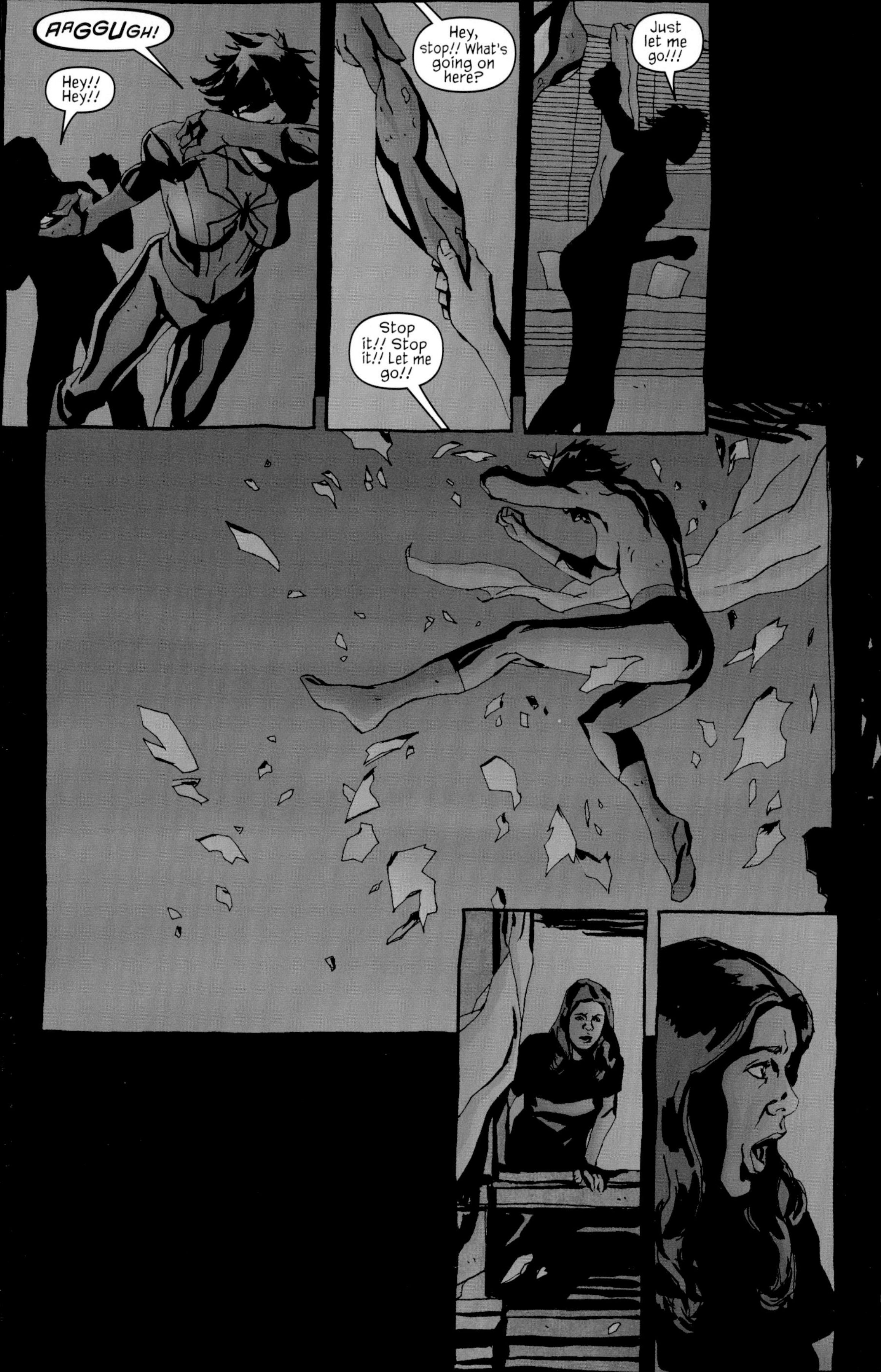
AAGGUGH!
Hey!! Hey!!
Hey, stop!! What's going on here?
Stop it!! Stop it!! Let me go!!
Just let me go!!!

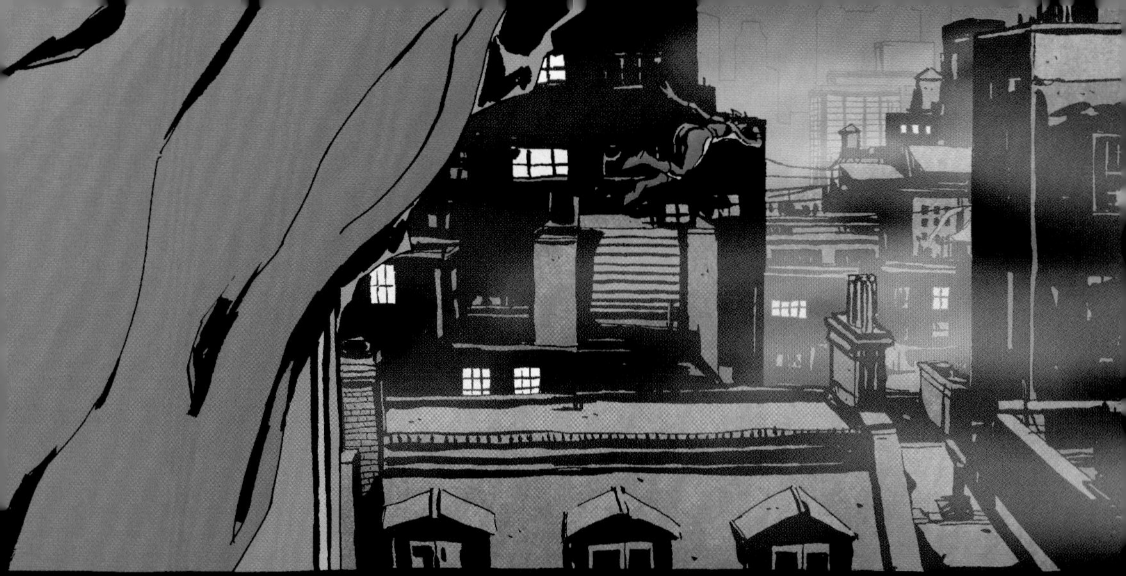

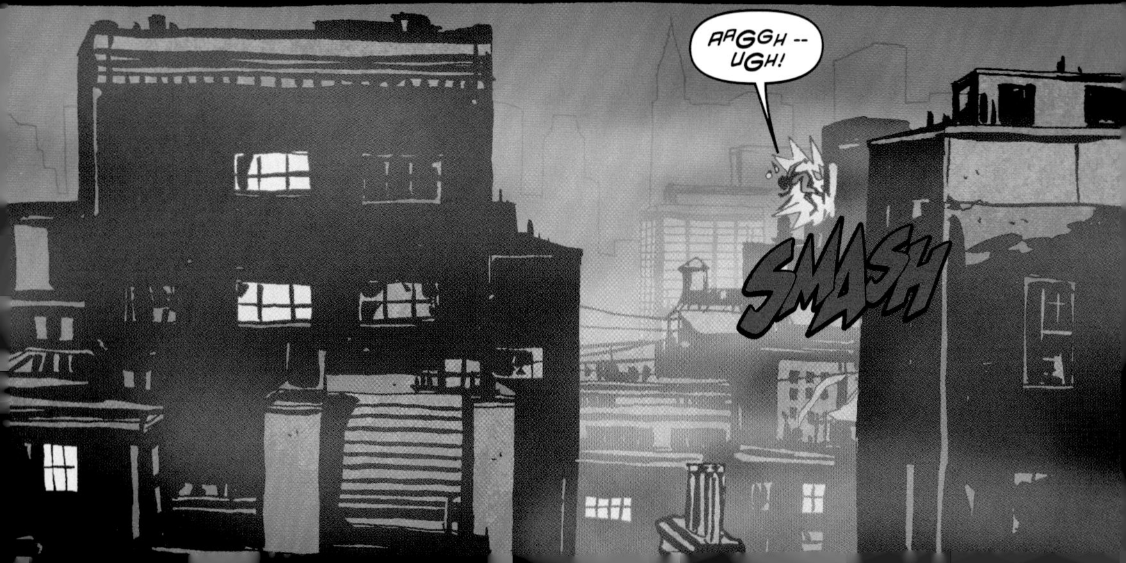
AAGGH -- UGH!
SMASH

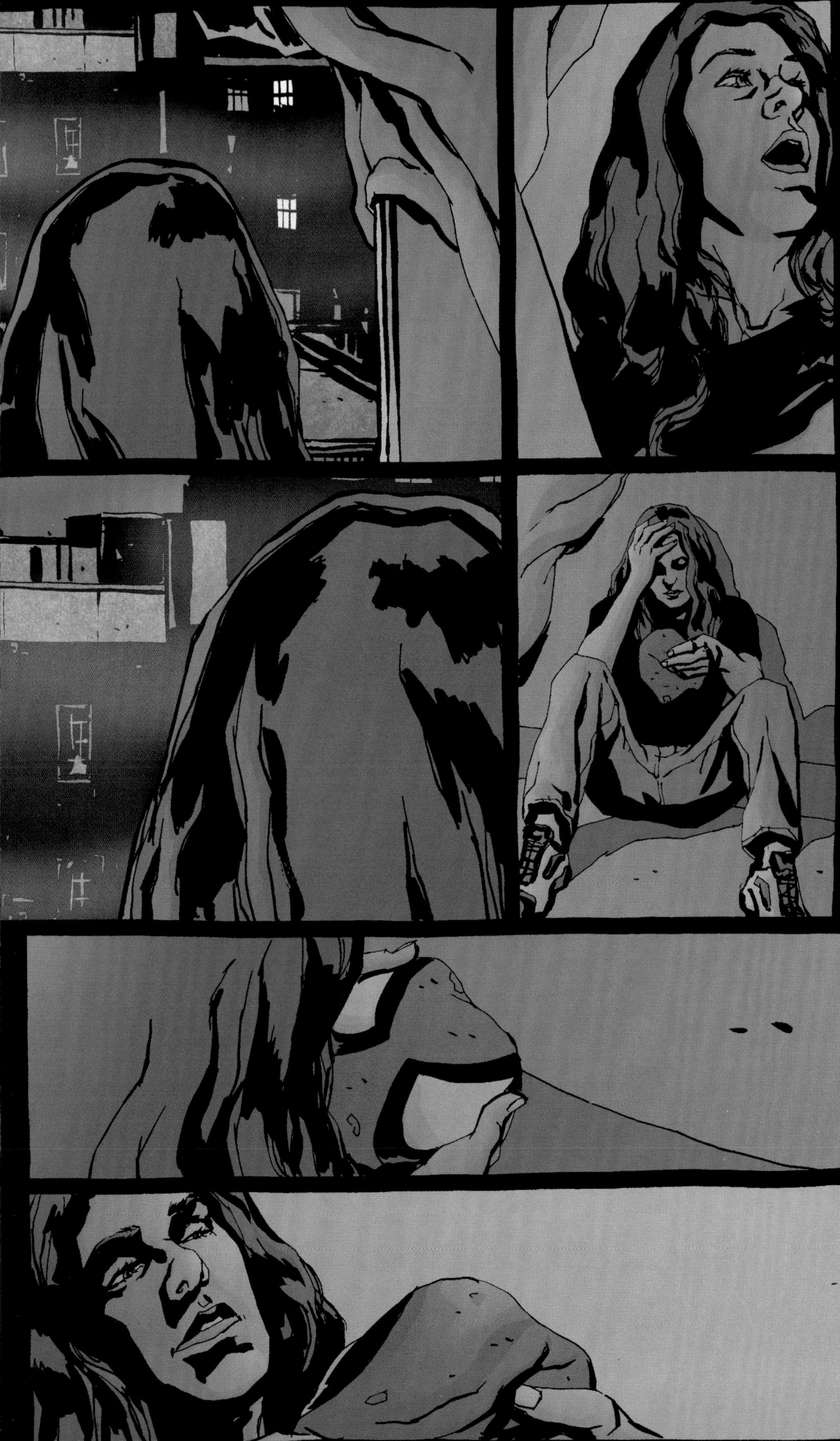

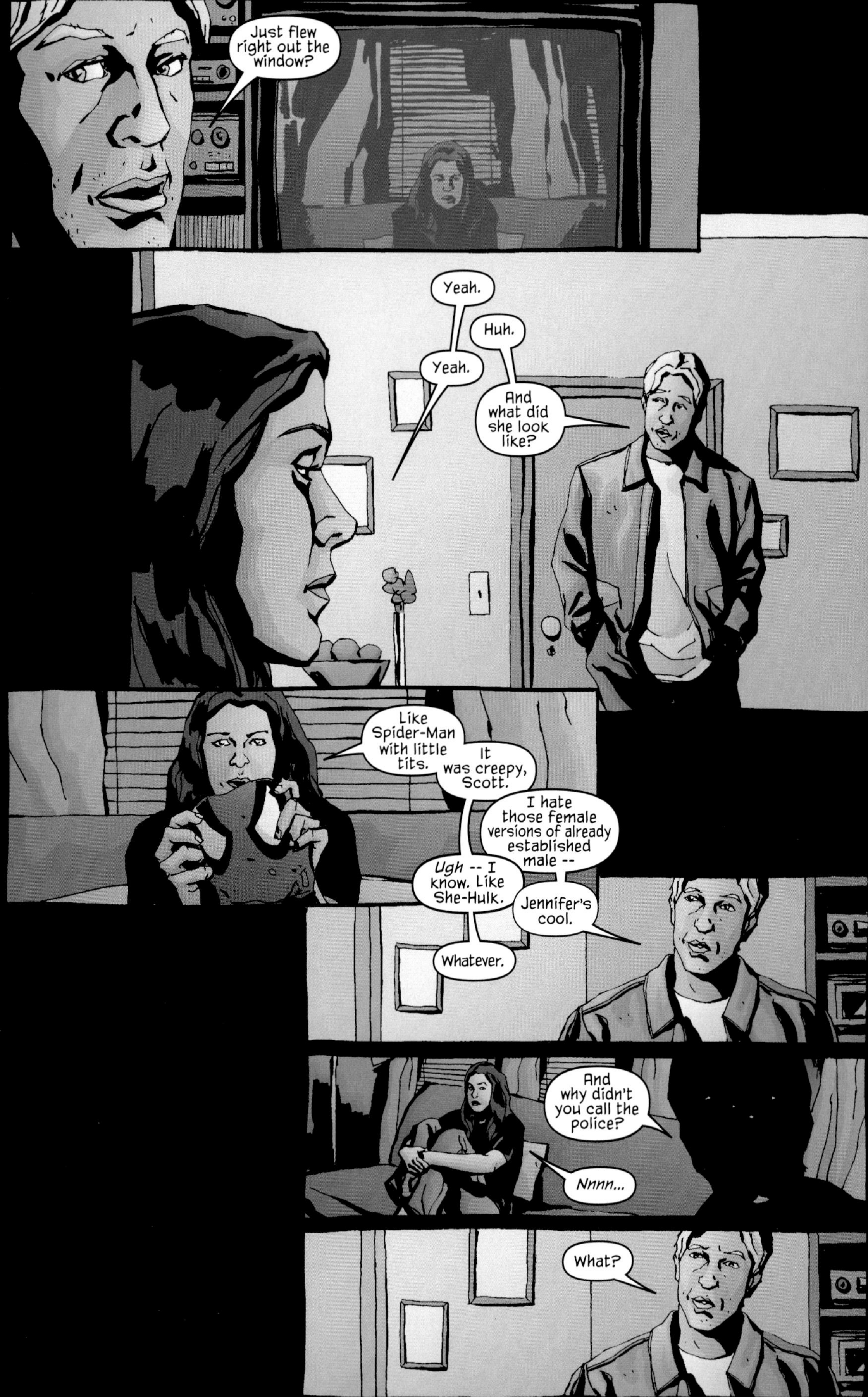

Just flew right out the window?
Yeah.
Huh.
Yeah.
And what did she look like?
Like Spider-Man with little tits.
It was creepy, Scott.
I hate those female versions of already established male --
Ugh -- I know. Like She-Hulk.
Jennifer's cool.
Whatever.
And why didn't you call the police?
Nnnn...
What?

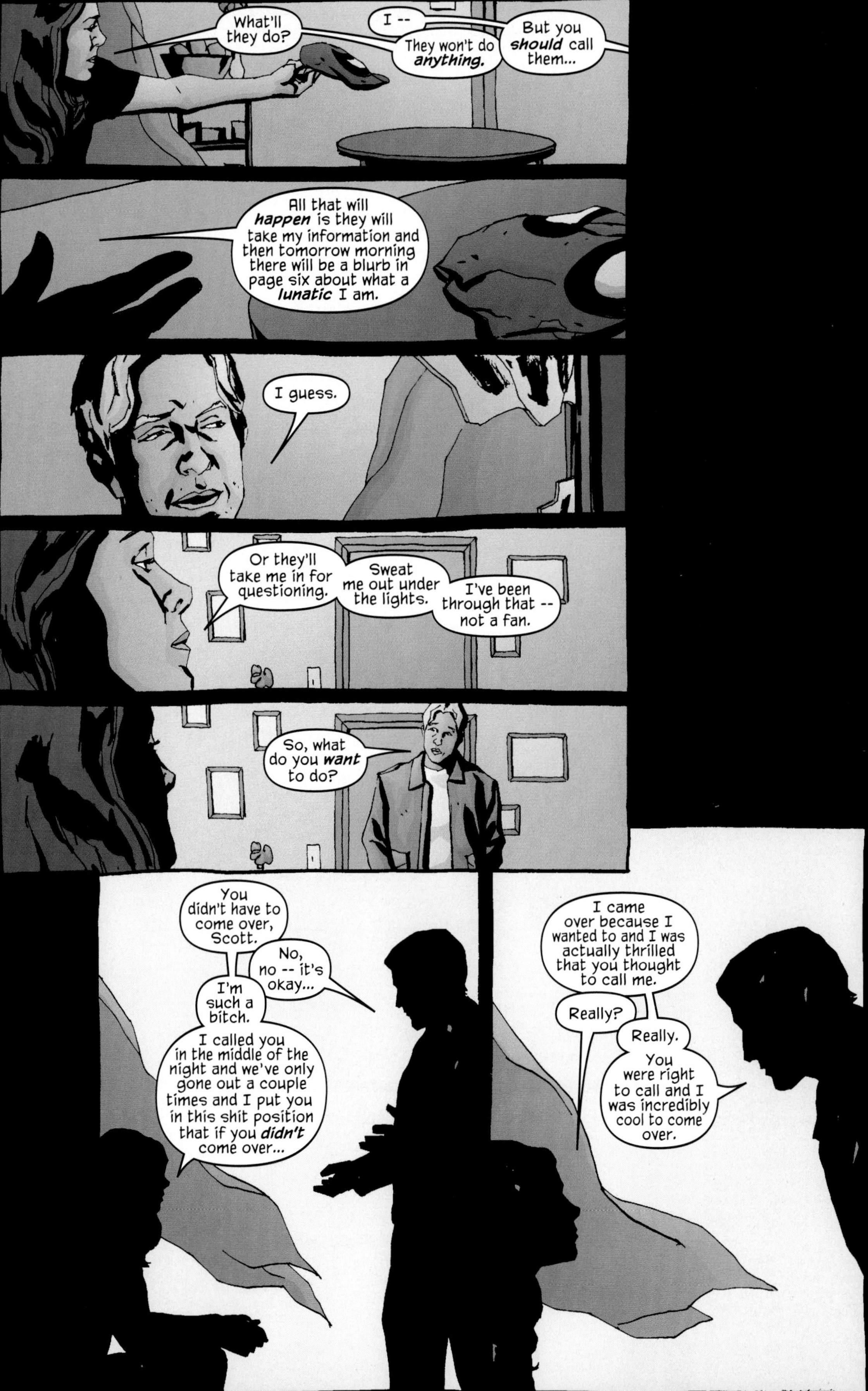
What'll they do?
I --
They won't do *anything.*
But you *should* call them...
All that will *happen* is they will take my information and then tomorrow morning there will be a blurb in page six about what a *lunatic* I am.
I guess.
Or they'll take me in for questioning.
Sweat me out under the lights.
I've been through that -- not a fan.
So, what do you *want* to do?
You didn't have to come over, Scott.
No, no -- it's okay...
I'm such a bitch.
I called you in the middle of the night and we've only gone out a couple times and I put you in this shit position that if you *didn't* come over...
I came over because I wanted to and I was actually thrilled that you thought to call me.
Really?
Really.
You were right to call and I was incredibly cool to come over.

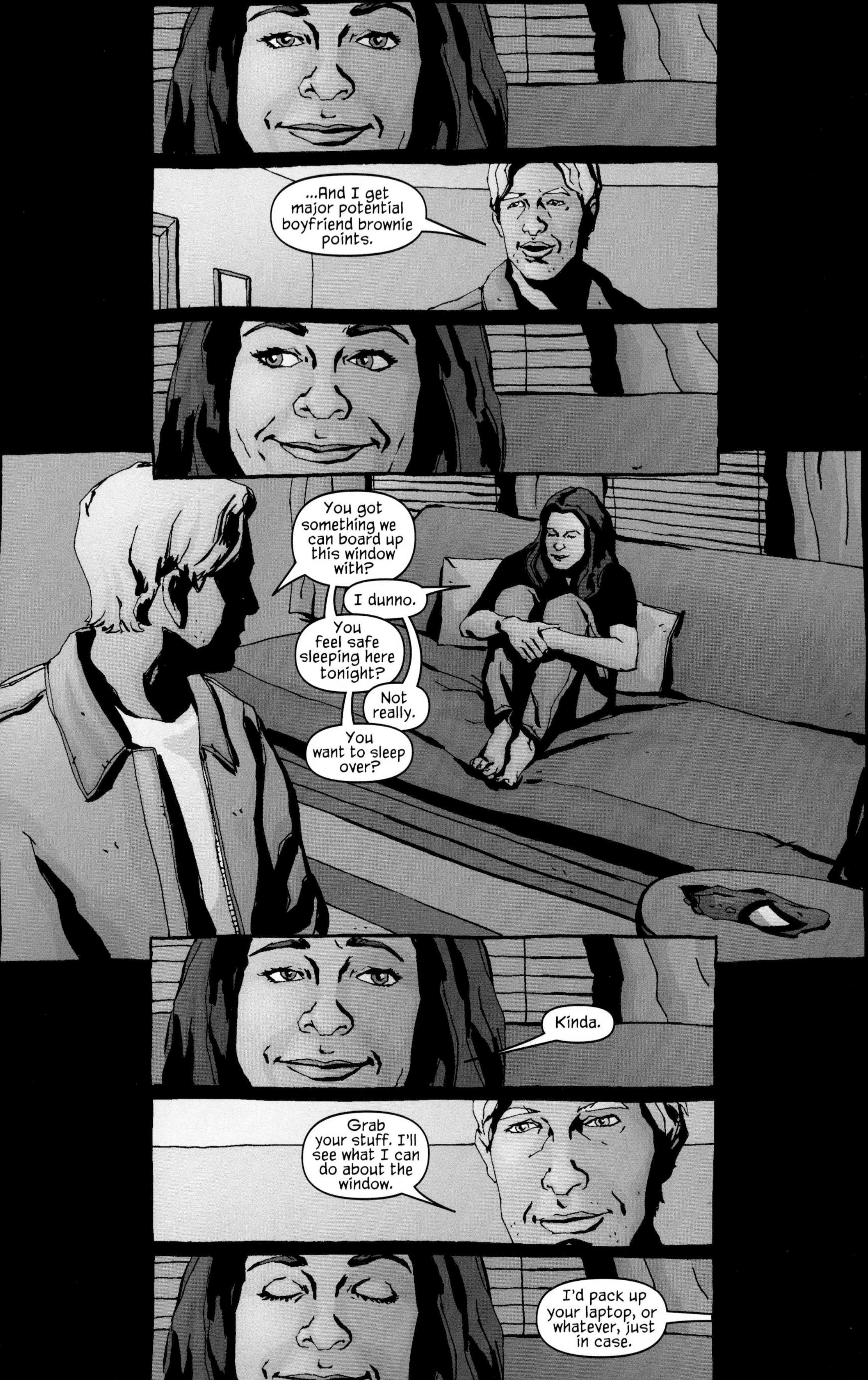
...And I get major potential boyfriend brownie points.
You got something we can board up this window with?
I dunno.
You feel safe sleeping here tonight?
Not really.
You want to sleep over?
Kinda.
Grab your stuff. I'll see what I can do about the window.
I'd pack up your laptop, or whatever, just in case.

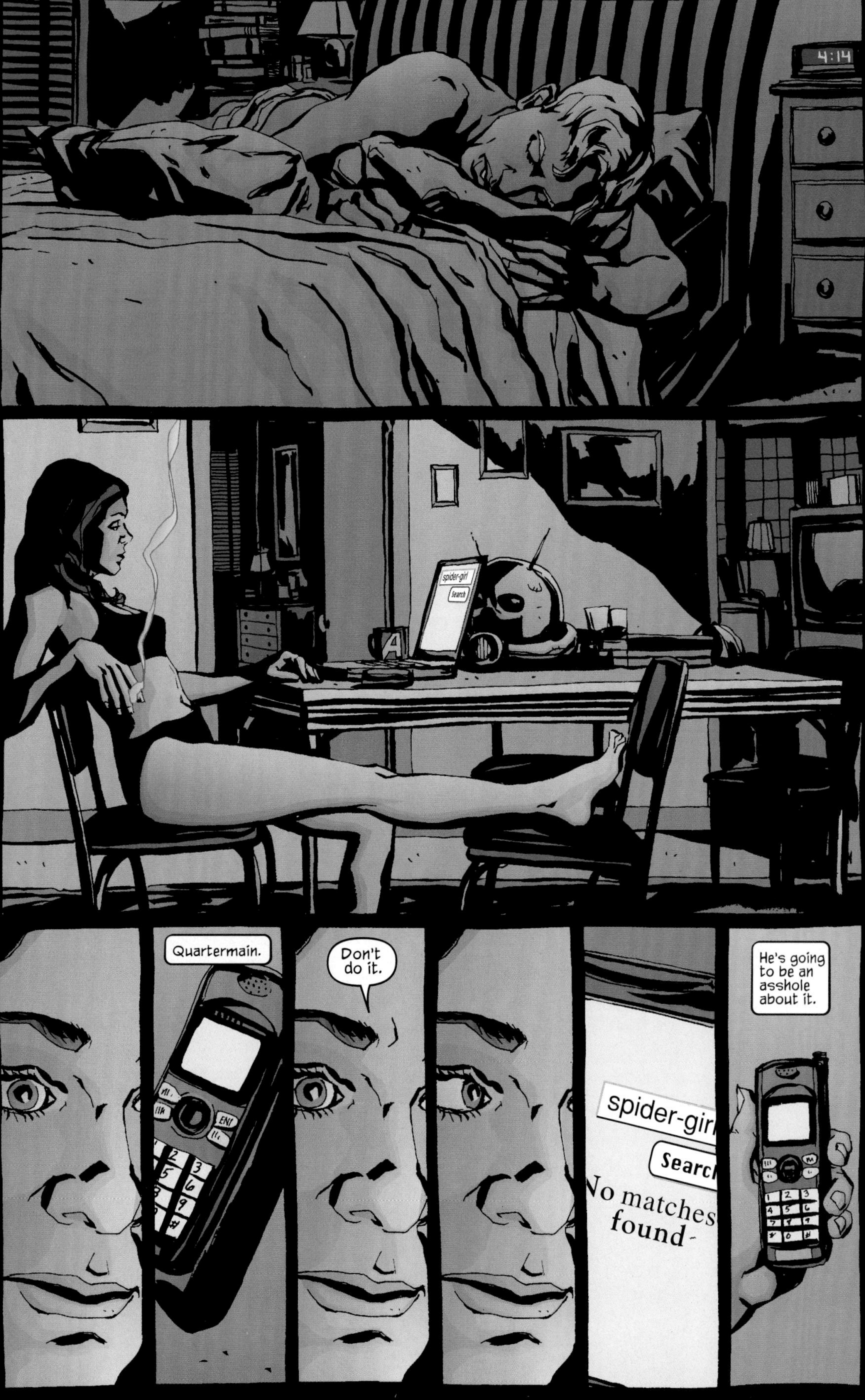
4:14
spider-girl
Search
Quartermain.
Don't do it.
spider-girl
Search
No matches found
He's going to be an asshole about it.

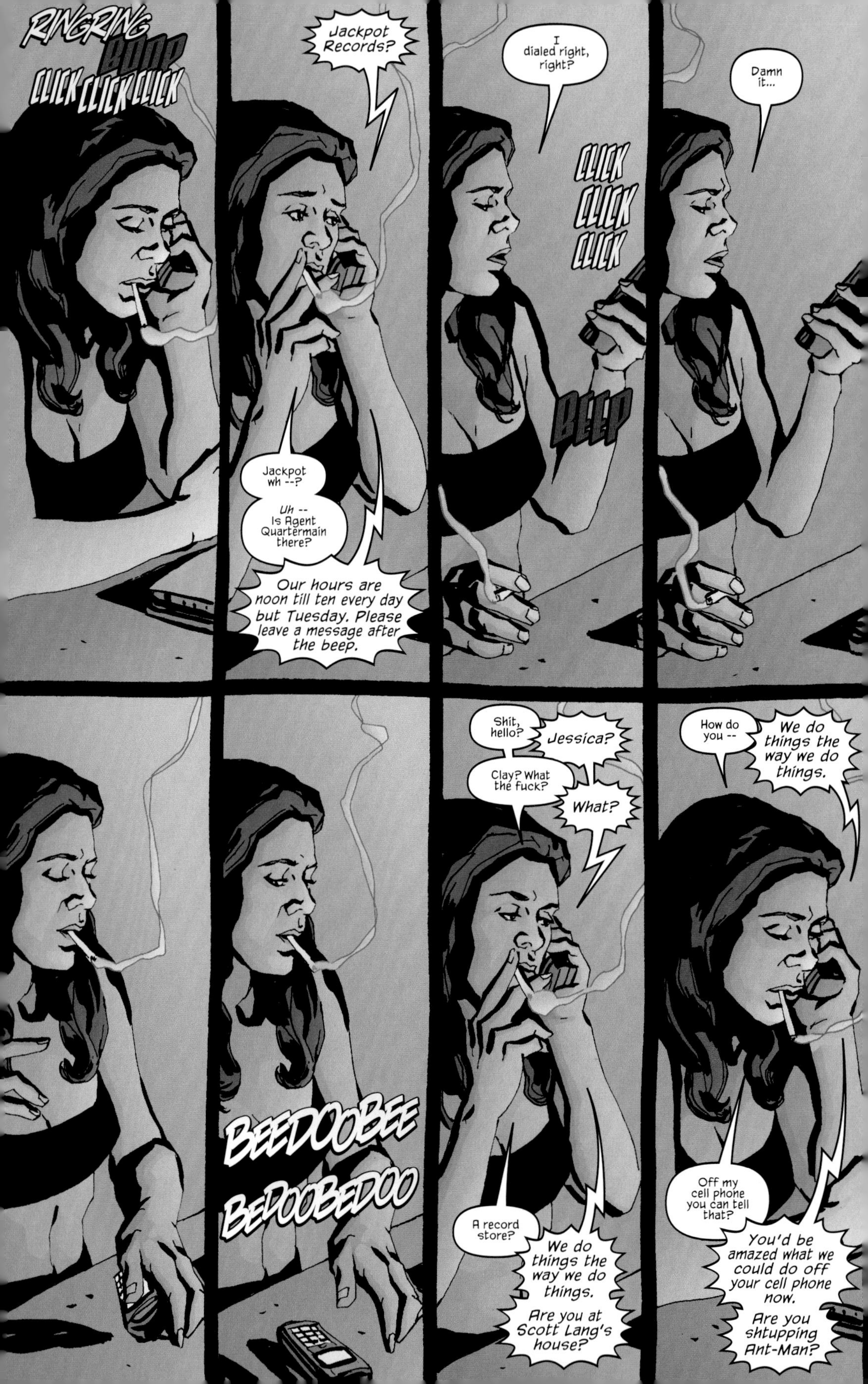
RINGRING
BOOP
CLICK CLICK CLICK
Jackpot Records?
Jackpot wh --?
Uh -- Is Agent Quartermain there?
Our hours are noon till ten every day but Tuesday. Please leave a message after the beep.
I dialed right, right?
CLICK CLICK CLICK
BEEP
Damn it...
BEEDOOBEE
BEDOOBEDOO
Shit, hello?
Jessica?
Clay? What the fuck?
What?
A record store?
We do things the way we do things.
Are you at Scott Lang's house?
How do you --
We do things the way we do things.
Off my cell phone you can tell that?
You'd be amazed what we could do off your cell phone now.
Are you shtupping Ant-Man?

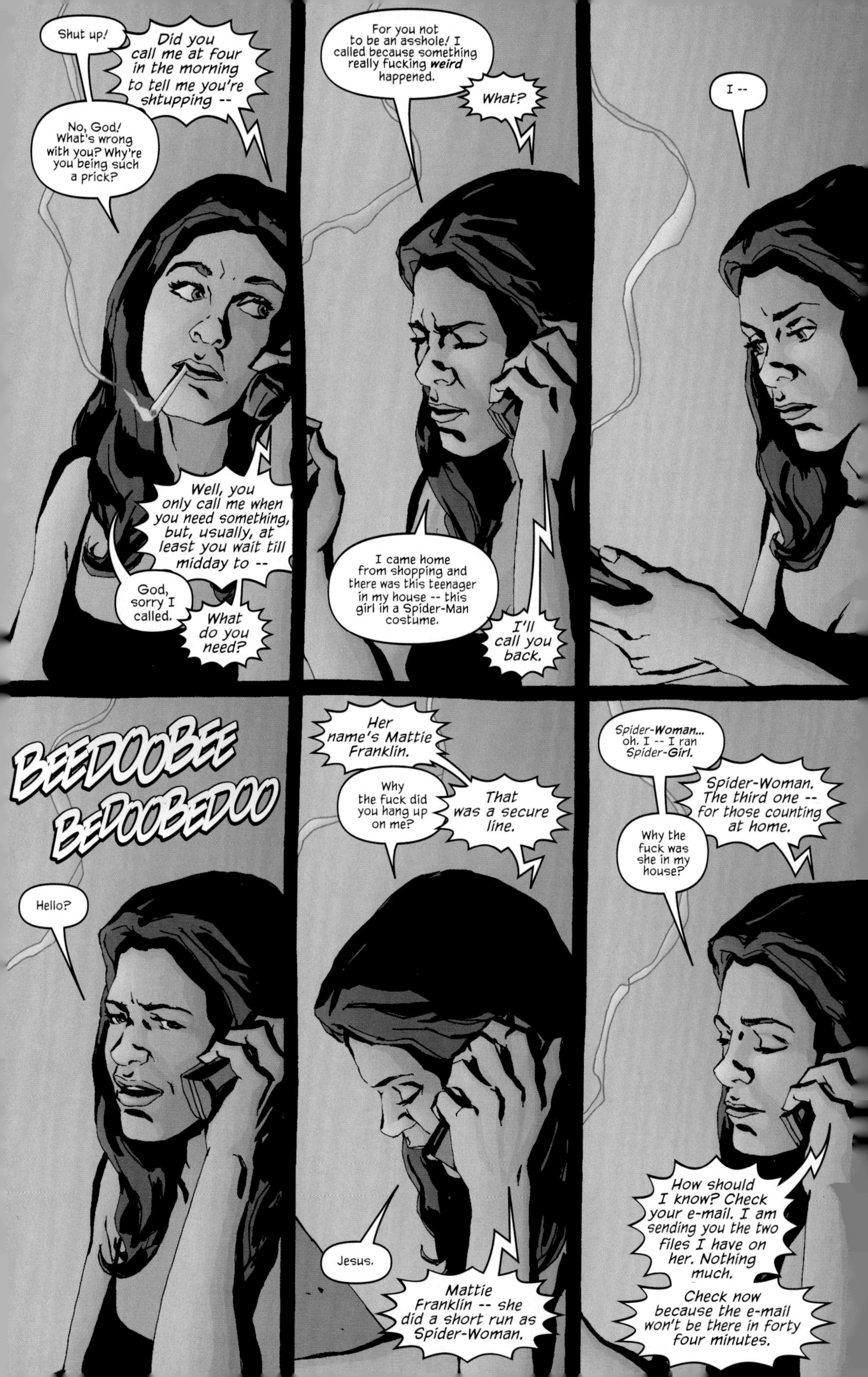
Did you call me at four in the morning to tell me you're shtupping --
Shut up!
No, God! What's wrong with you? Why're you being such a prick?
Well, you only call me when you need something, but, usually, at least you wait till midday to --
God, sorry I called.
What do you need?
For you not to be an asshole! I called because something really fucking **weird** happened.
What?
I came home from shopping and there was this teenager in my house -- this girl in a Spider-Man costume.
I'll call you back.
I --
BEEDOOBEE BEDOOBEDOO
Hello?
Why the fuck did you hang up on me?
That was a secure line.
Her name's Mattie Franklin.
Jesus.
Mattie Franklin -- she did a short run as Spider-Woman.
Spider-**Woman**... oh. I -- I ran Spider-**Girl.**
Spider-Woman. The third one -- for those counting at home.
Why the fuck was she in my house?
How should I know? Check your e-mail. I am sending you the two files I have on her. Nothing much.
Check now because the e-mail won't be there in forty four minutes.

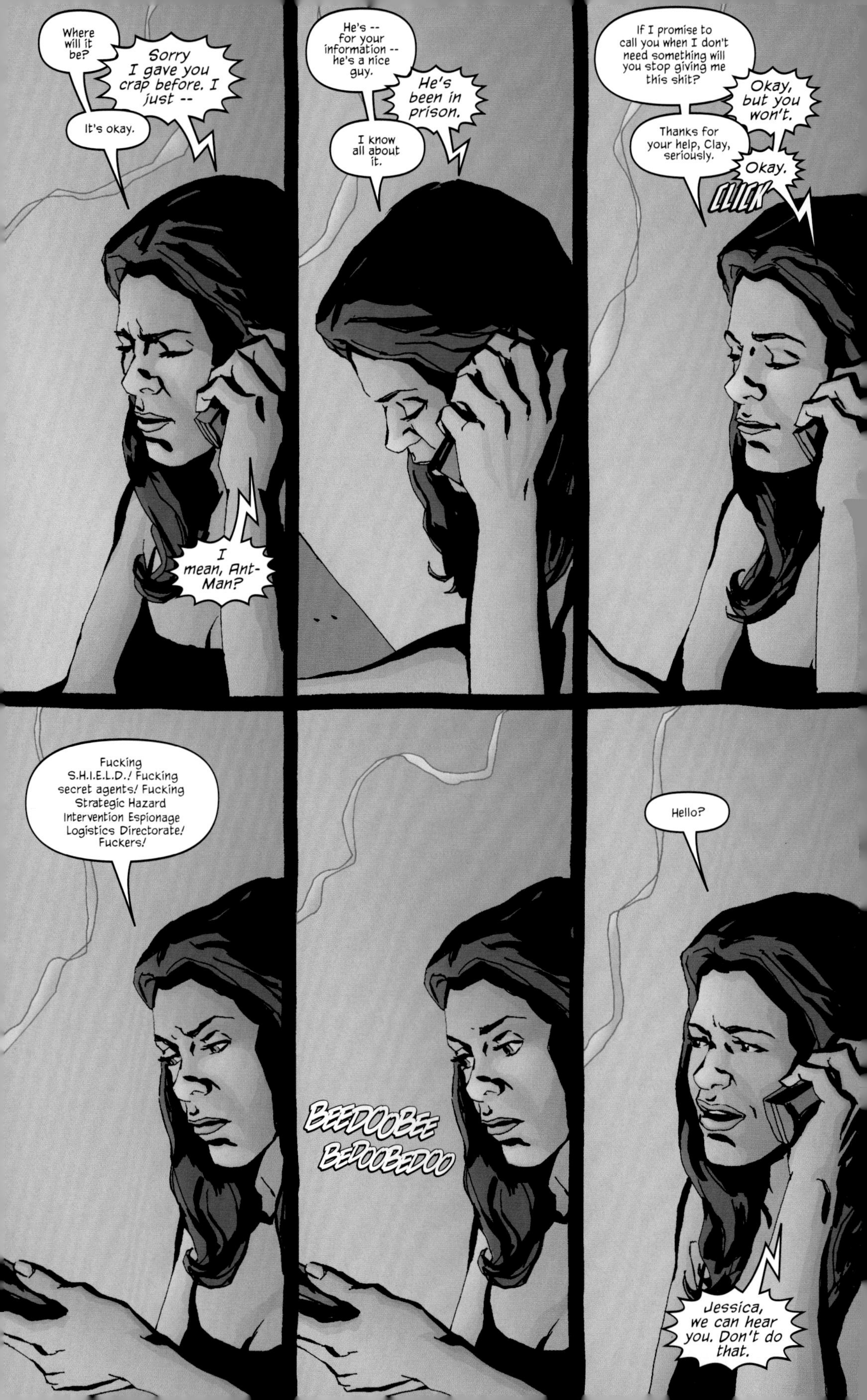

Where will it be?
Sorry I gave you crap before. I just --
It's okay.
I mean, Ant-Man?
He's -- for your information -- he's a nice guy.
He's been in prison.
I know all about it.
If I promise to call you when I don't need something will you stop giving me this shit?
Okay, but you won't.
Thanks for your help, Clay, seriously.
Okay.
CLICK
Fucking S.H.I.E.L.D.! Fucking secret agents! Fucking Strategic Hazard Intervention Espionage Logistics Directorate! Fuckers!
BEEDOOBEE BEDOOBEDOO
Hello?
Jessica, we can hear you. Don't do that.

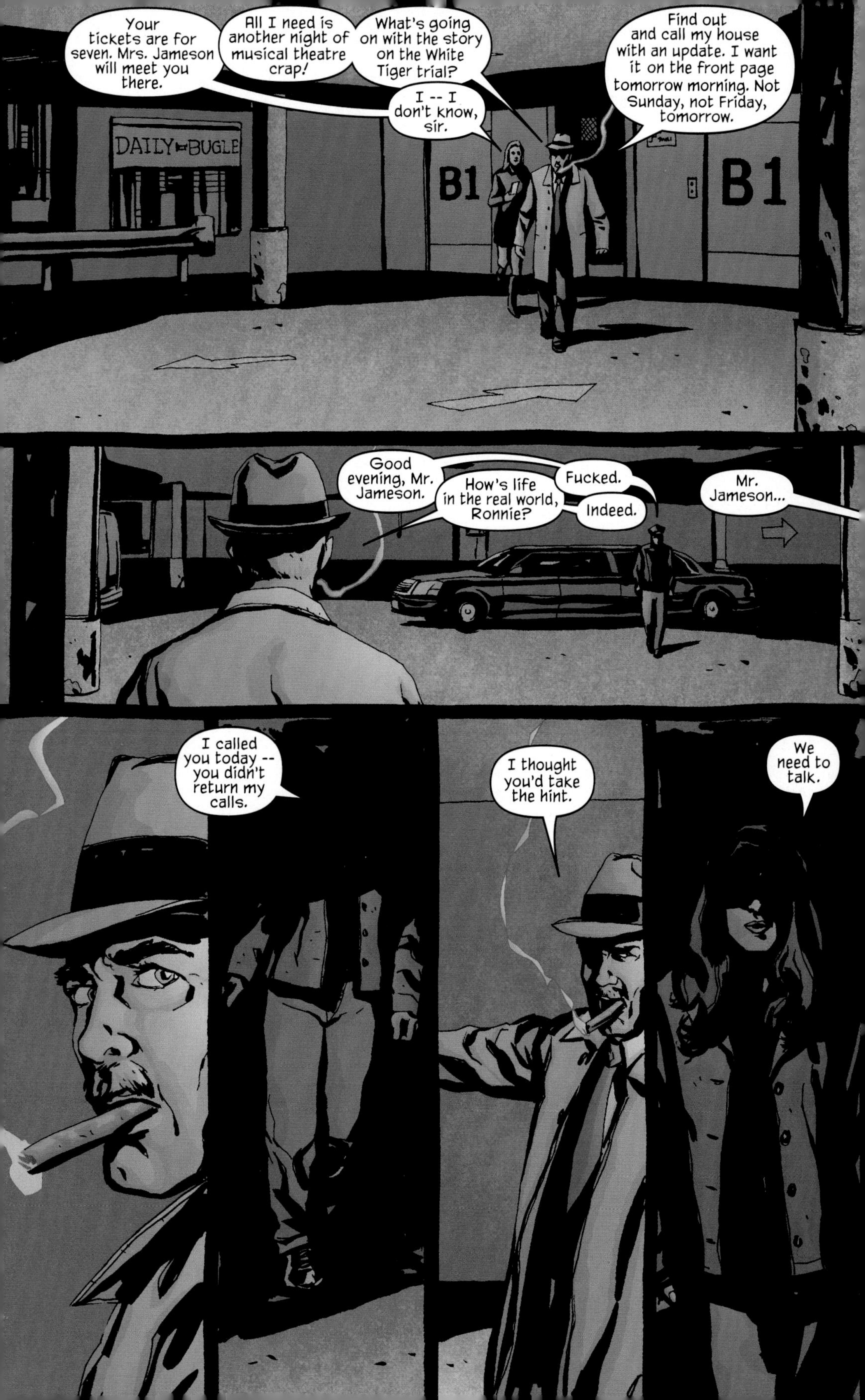

Your tickets are for seven. Mrs. Jameson will meet you there.
All I need is another night of musical theatre crap!
What's going on with the story on the White Tiger trial?
I -- I don't know, sir.
Find out and call my house with an update. I want it on the front page tomorrow morning. Not Sunday, not Friday, tomorrow.
DAILY BUGLE
B1
B1
Good evening, Mr. Jameson.
How's life in the real world, Ronnie?
Fucked.
Indeed.
Mr. Jameson...
I called you today -- you didn't return my calls.
I thought you'd take the hint.
We need to talk.

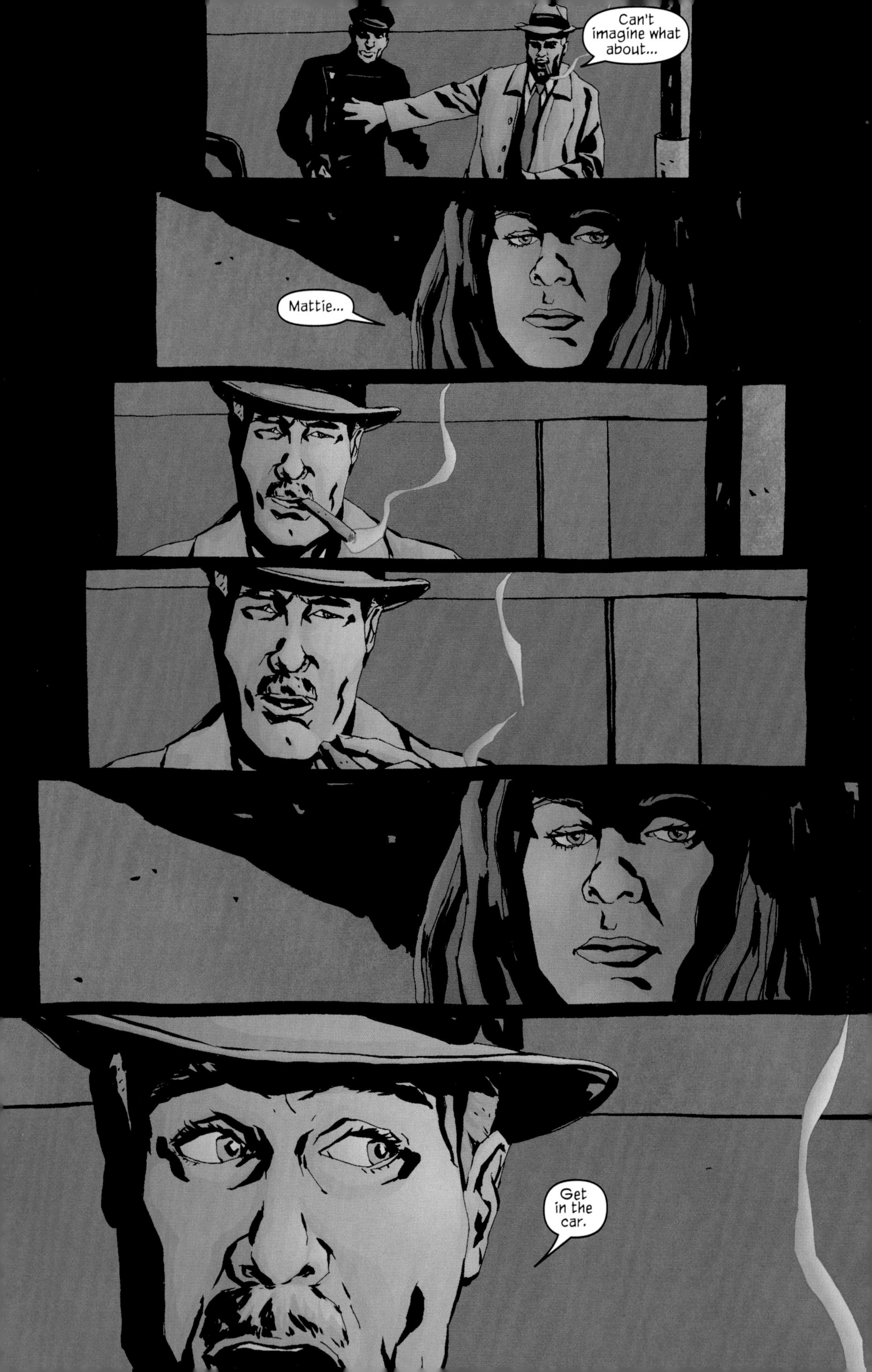
Can't imagine what about...
Mattie...
Get in the car.

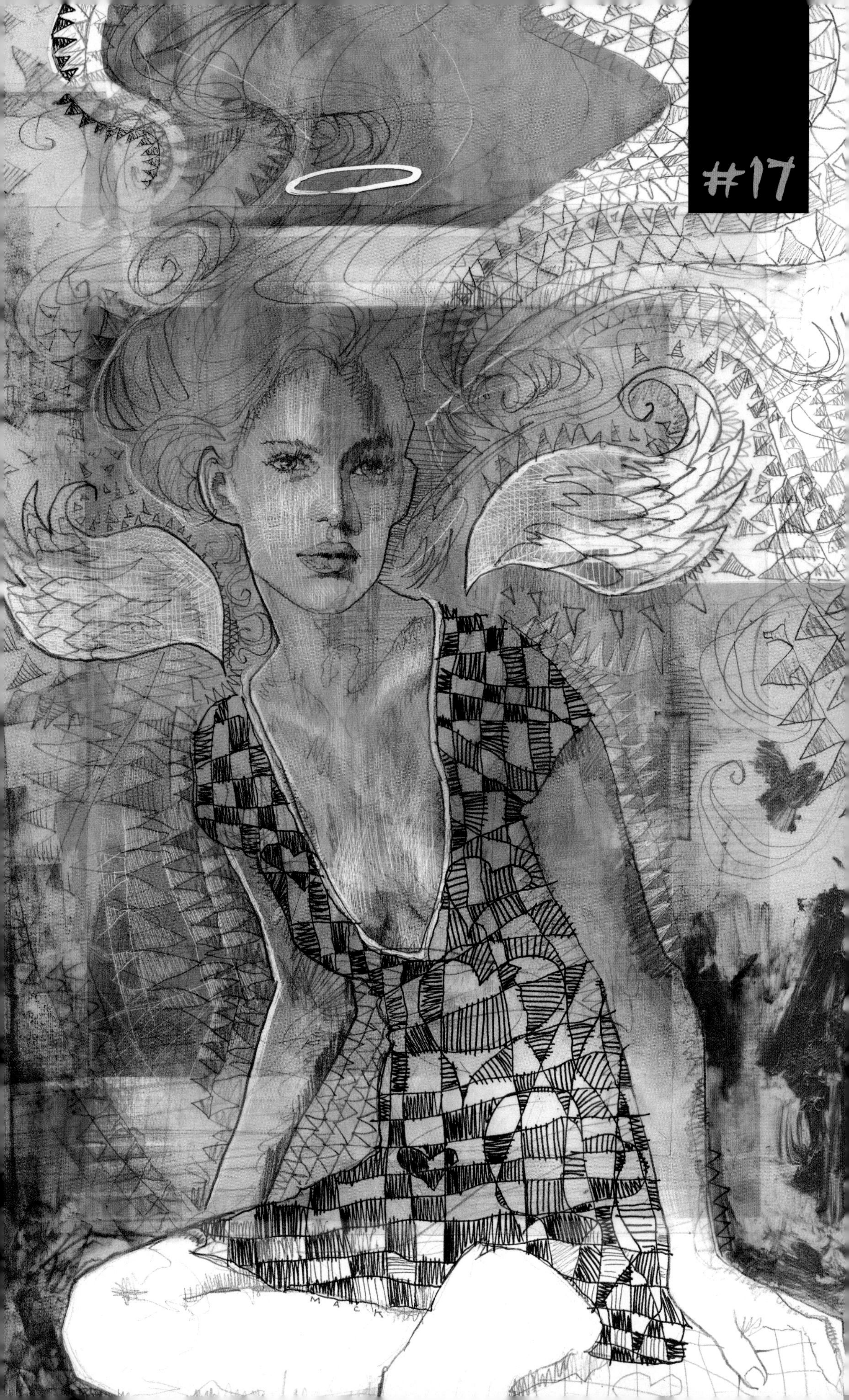
#17
MACK

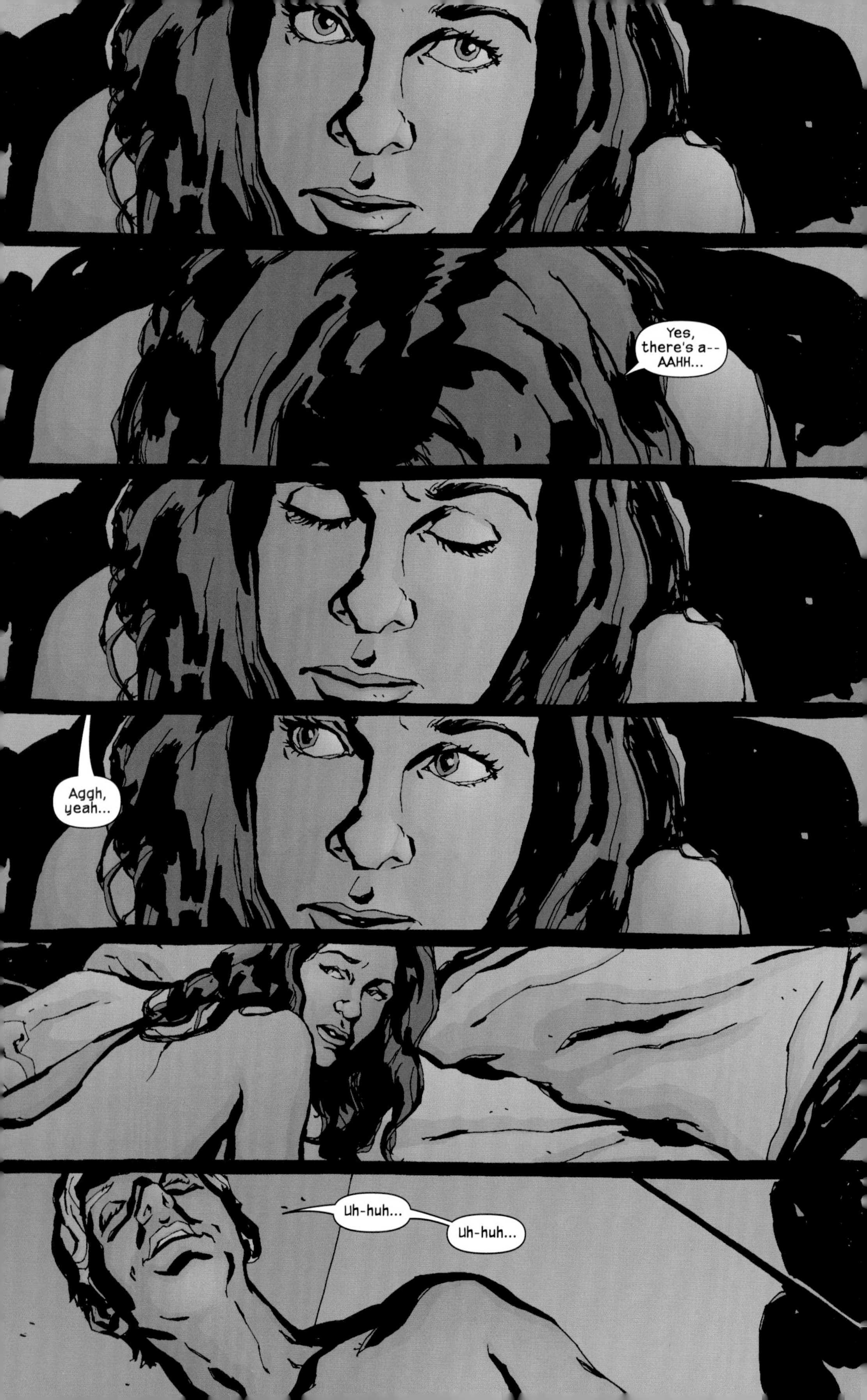
Yes, there's a-- AAHH...
Aggh, yeah...
Uh-huh...
Uh-huh...

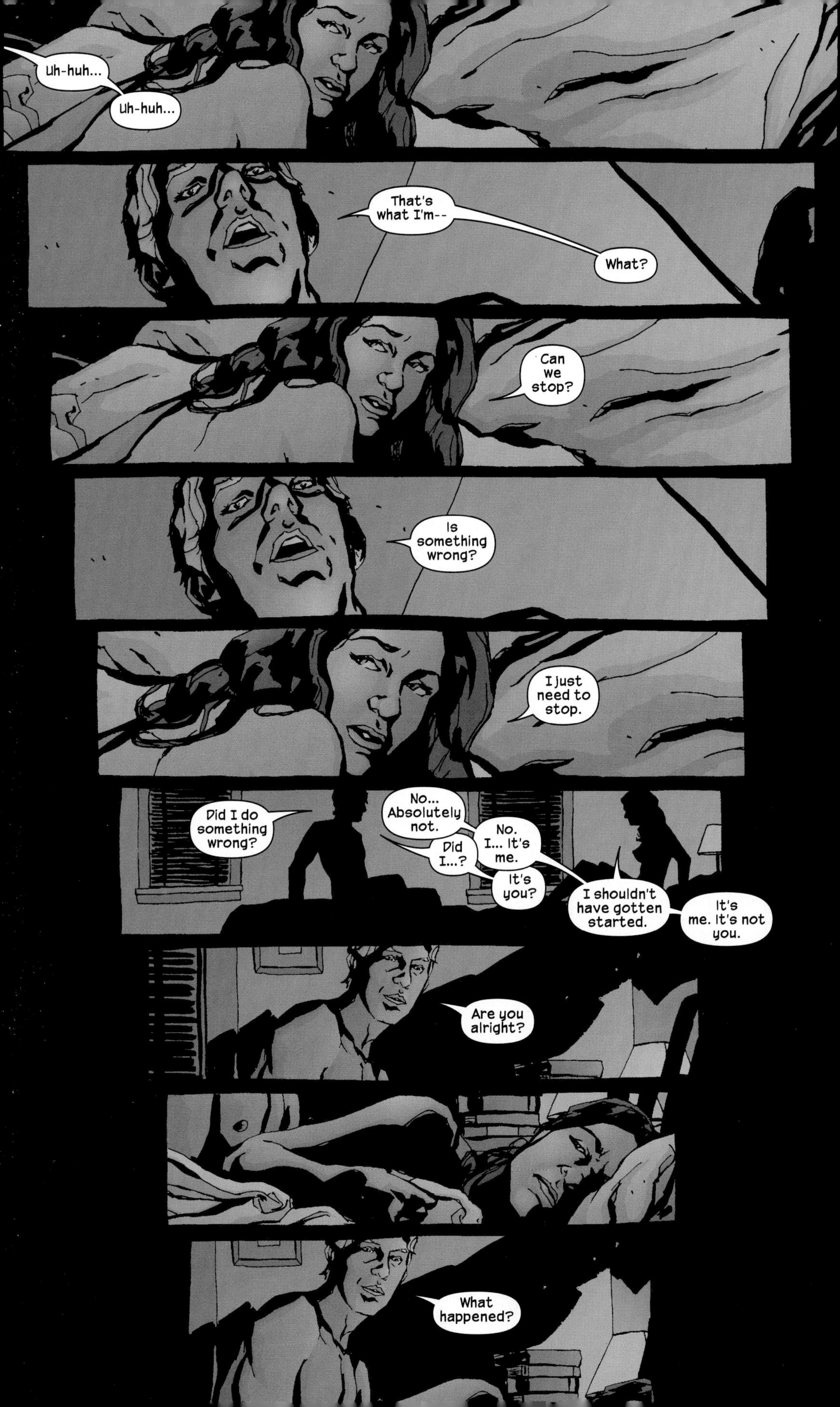
Uh-huh...
Uh-huh...
That's what I'm--
What?
Can we stop?
Is something wrong?
I just need to stop.
Did I do something wrong?
No... Absolutely not.
Did I...?
No. I... It's me.
It's you?
I shouldn't have gotten started.
It's me. It's not you.
Are you alright?
What happened?

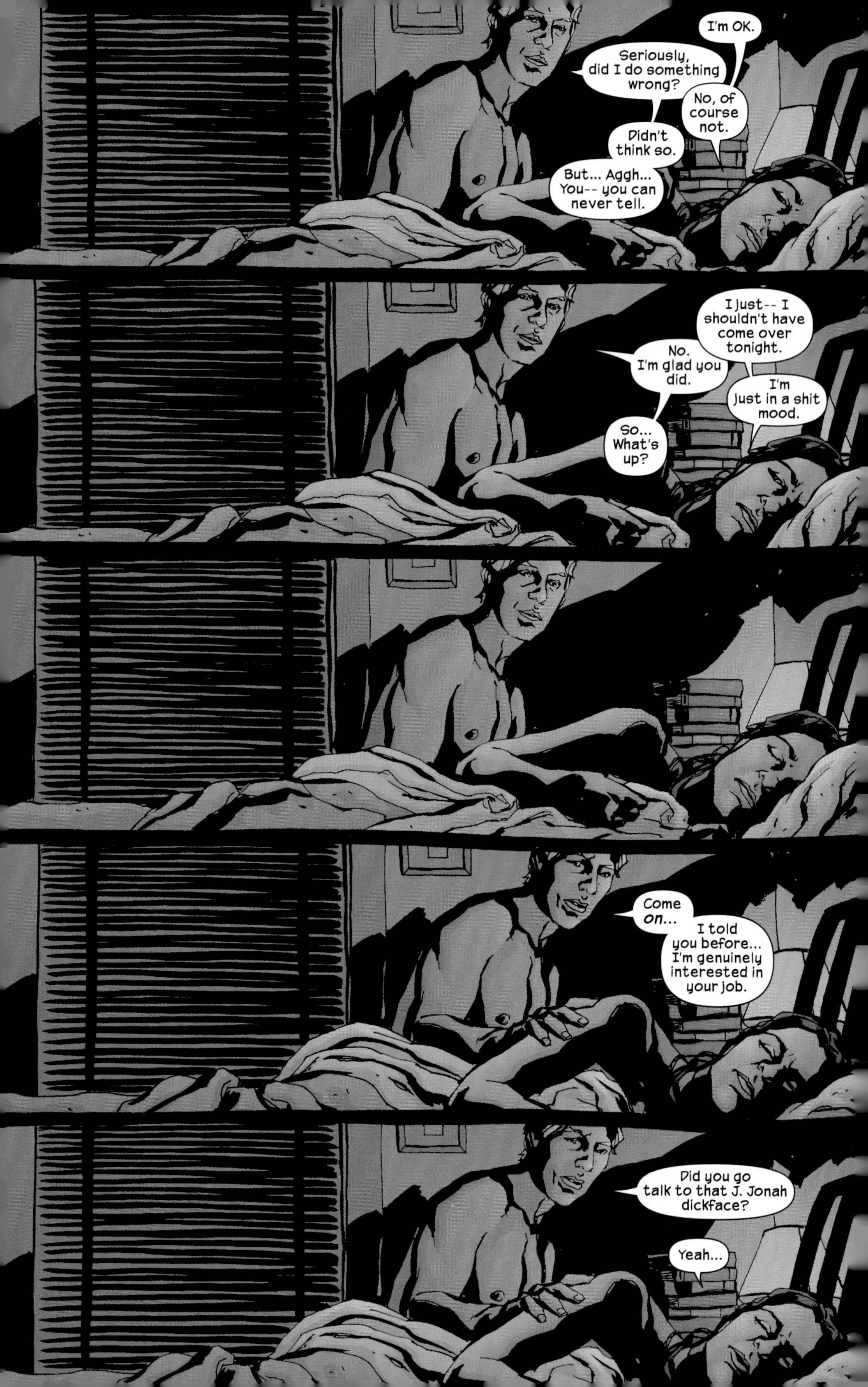
Seriously, did I do something wrong?
I'm OK.
No, of course not.
Didn't think so.
But... Aggh... You-- you can never tell.
I just-- I shouldn't have come over tonight.
No. I'm glad you did.
I'm just in a shit mood.
So... What's up?
Come *on*...
I told you before... I'm genuinely interested in your job.
Did you go talk to that J. Jonah dickface?
Yeah...

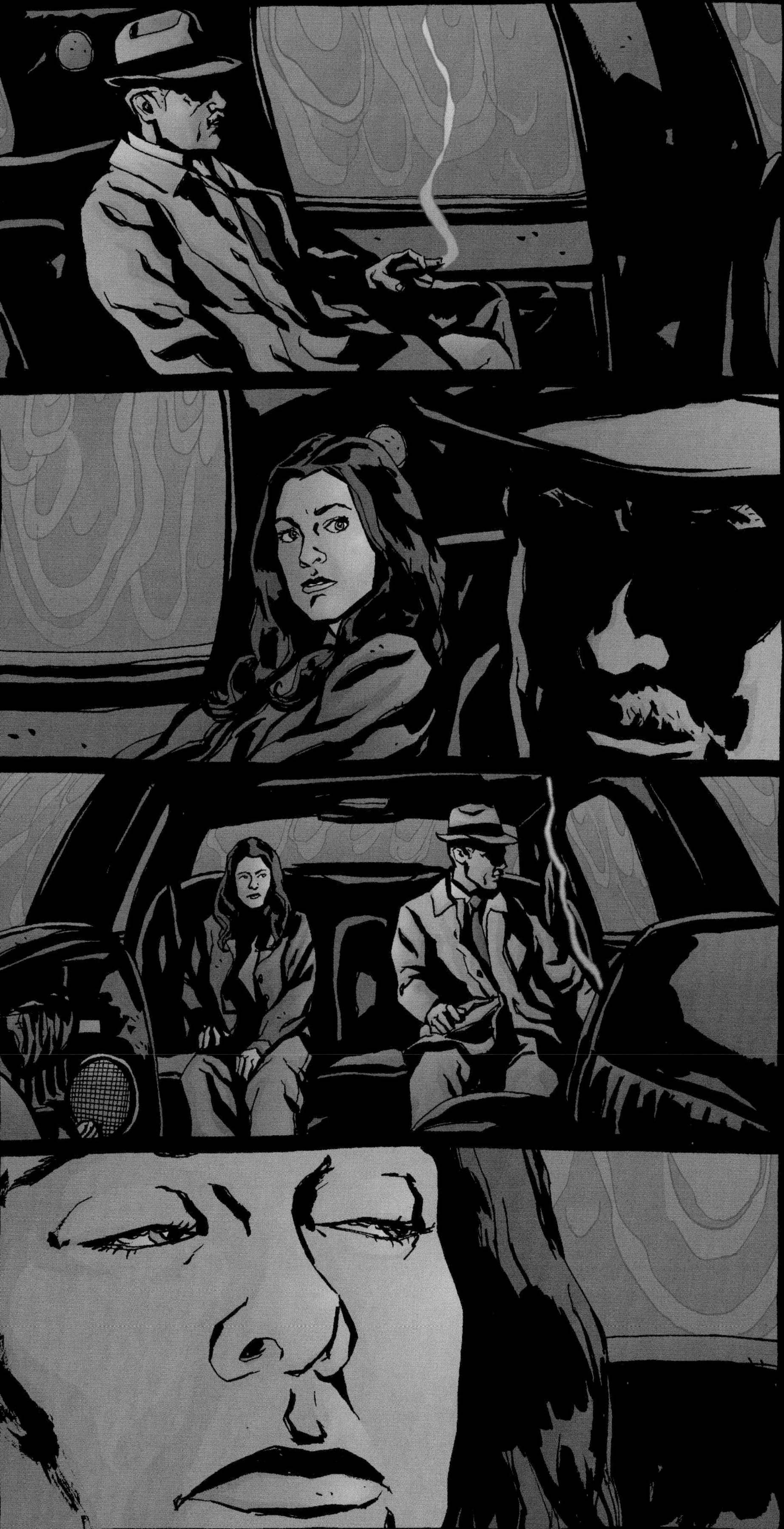

We're sitting there in his limo.

And I'm waiting... waiting for a response from him.

And nothing.

He just sits there. Which is the exact opposite of what he was like the last time I met him when he wouldn't shut his fucking mouth.

And then I start reminding myself how much I don't want to be sitting here with this piece of garbage.

All I hear in my head is: This guy hates you.

And this isn't like my usual self-loathing paranoia. No.

I have it on tape. On my answering machine. Him wishing I would drop dead.

This guy-- this rich, asshole scumbag.

He's everything that's wrong with journalism in America. Guy with a clear agenda and he uses his Daily Bugle as a forum to express it instead of reporting the facts.

Disgusting.

I'm sitting there thinking... this piece of garbage.

And believe me, if this was about him... Fuck 'im!

But it's not. It's about a girl.

It's about some girl I know nothing about named Mattie Franklin. A girl that he somehow took responsibility for who is now in some kind of trouble.

And I sat there in silence.

And I didn't know what else to do.

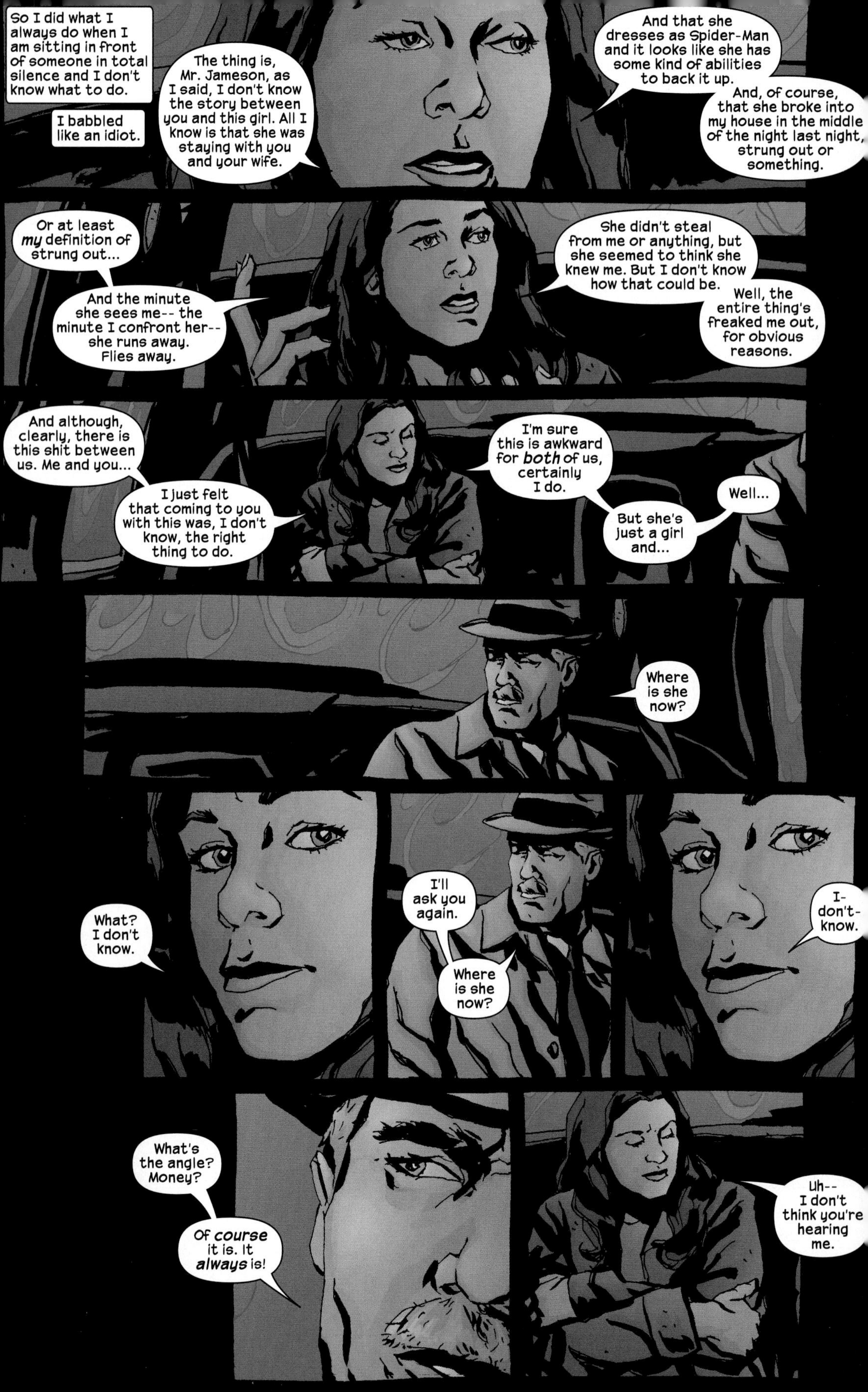
So I did what I always do when I am sitting in front of someone in total silence and I don't know what to do.
I babbled like an idiot.
The thing is, Mr. Jameson, as I said, I don't know the story between you and this girl. All I know is that she was staying with you and your wife.
And that she dresses as Spider-Man and it looks like she has some kind of abilities to back it up.
And, of course, that she broke into my house in the middle of the night last night, strung out or something.
Or at least *my* definition of strung out...
And the minute she sees me-- the minute I confront her-- she runs away. Flies away.
She didn't steal from me or anything, but she seemed to think she knew me. But I don't know how that could be.
Well, the entire thing's freaked me out, for obvious reasons.
And although, clearly, there is this shit between us. Me and you...
I just felt that coming to you with this was, I don't know, the right thing to do.
I'm sure this is awkward for *both* of us, certainly I do.
But she's just a girl and...
Well...
Where is she now?
What? I don't know.
I'll ask you again.
Where is she now?
I- don't- know.
What's the angle? Money?
Of *course* it is. It *always* is!
Uh-- I don't think you're hearing me.

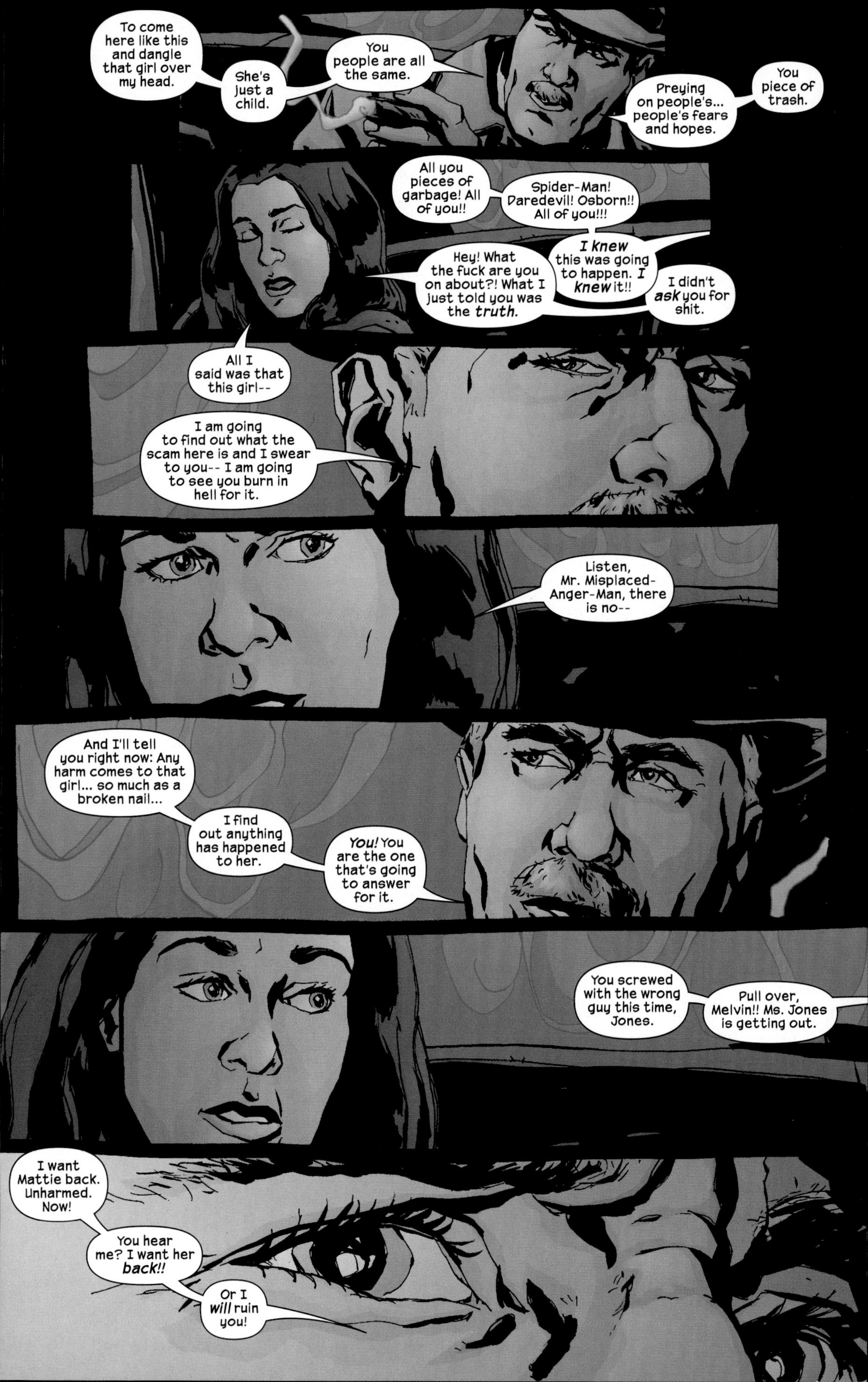
To come here like this and dangle that girl over my head.
She's just a child.
You people are all the same.
Preying on people's... people's fears and hopes.
You piece of trash.
All you pieces of garbage! All of you!!
Spider-Man! Daredevil! Osborn!! All of you!!!
Hey! What the fuck are you on about?! What I just told you was the *truth.*
I knew this was going to happen. *I knew* it!!
I didn't *ask* you for shit.
All I said was that this girl--
I am going to find out what the scam here is and I swear to you-- I am going to see you burn in hell for it.
Listen, Mr. Misplaced-Anger-Man, there is no--
And I'll tell you right now: Any harm comes to that girl... so much as a broken nail...
I find out anything has happened to her.
You! You are the one that's going to answer for it.
You screwed with the wrong guy this time, Jones.
Pull over, Melvin!! Ms. Jones is getting out.
I want Mattie back. Unharmed. Now!
You hear me? I want her *back!!*
Or I *will* ruin you!

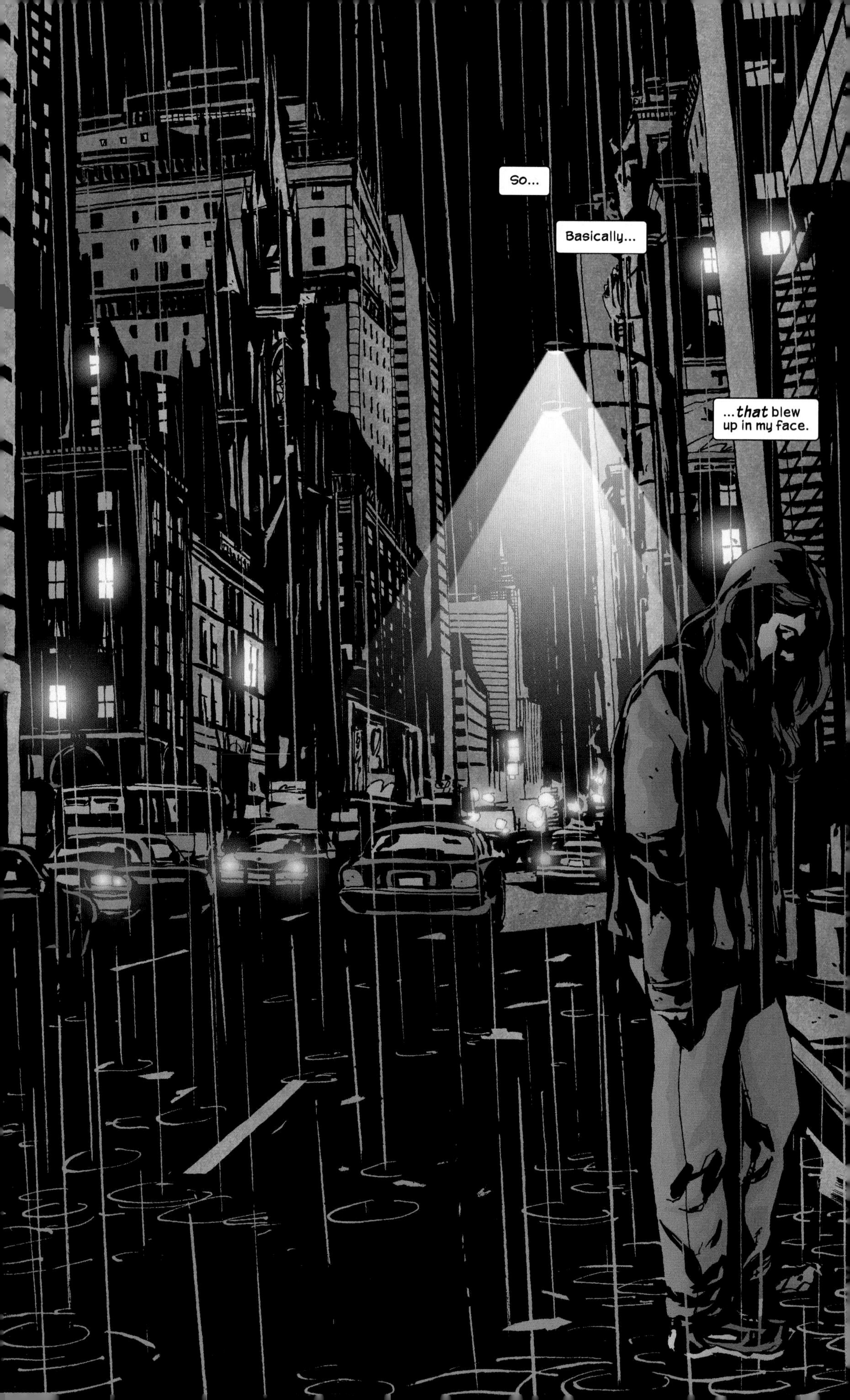
So...
Basically...
...*that* blew up in my face.

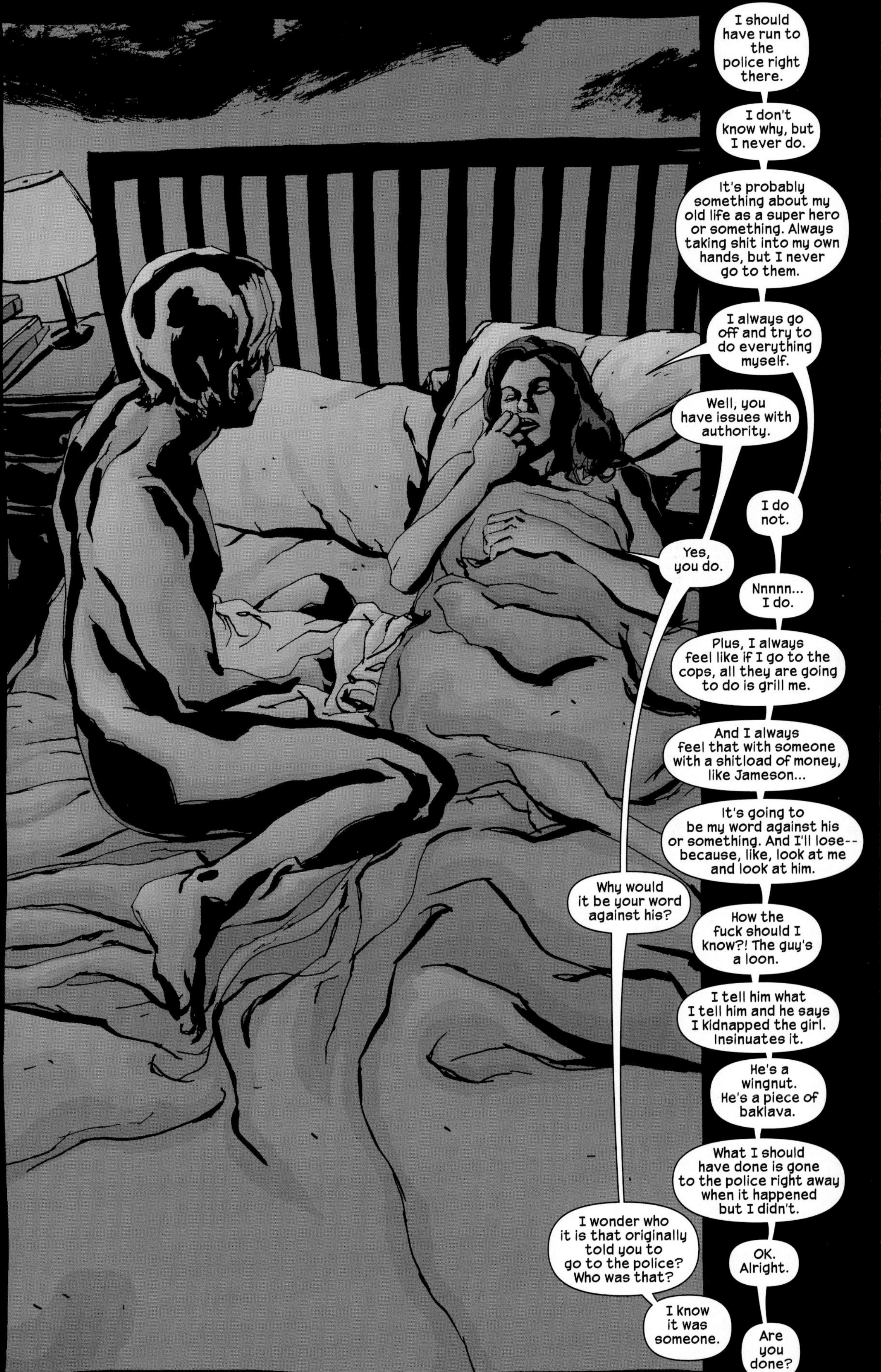

I should have run to the police right there.
I don't know why, but I never do.
It's probably something about my old life as a super hero or something. Always taking shit into my own hands, but I never go to them.
I always go off and try to do everything myself.
Well, you have issues with authority.
I do not.
Yes, you do.
Nnnnn... I do.
Plus, I always feel like if I go to the cops, all they are going to do is grill me.
And I always feel that with someone with a shitload of money, like Jameson...
It's going to be my word against his or something. And I'll lose-- because, like, look at me and look at him.
Why would it be your word against his?
How the fuck should I know?! The guy's a loon.
I tell him what I tell him and he says I kidnapped the girl. Insinuates it.
He's a wingnut. He's a piece of baklava.
What I should have done is gone to the police right away when it happened but I didn't.
I wonder who it is that originally told you to go to the police? Who was that?
OK. Alright.
I know it was someone.
Are you done?

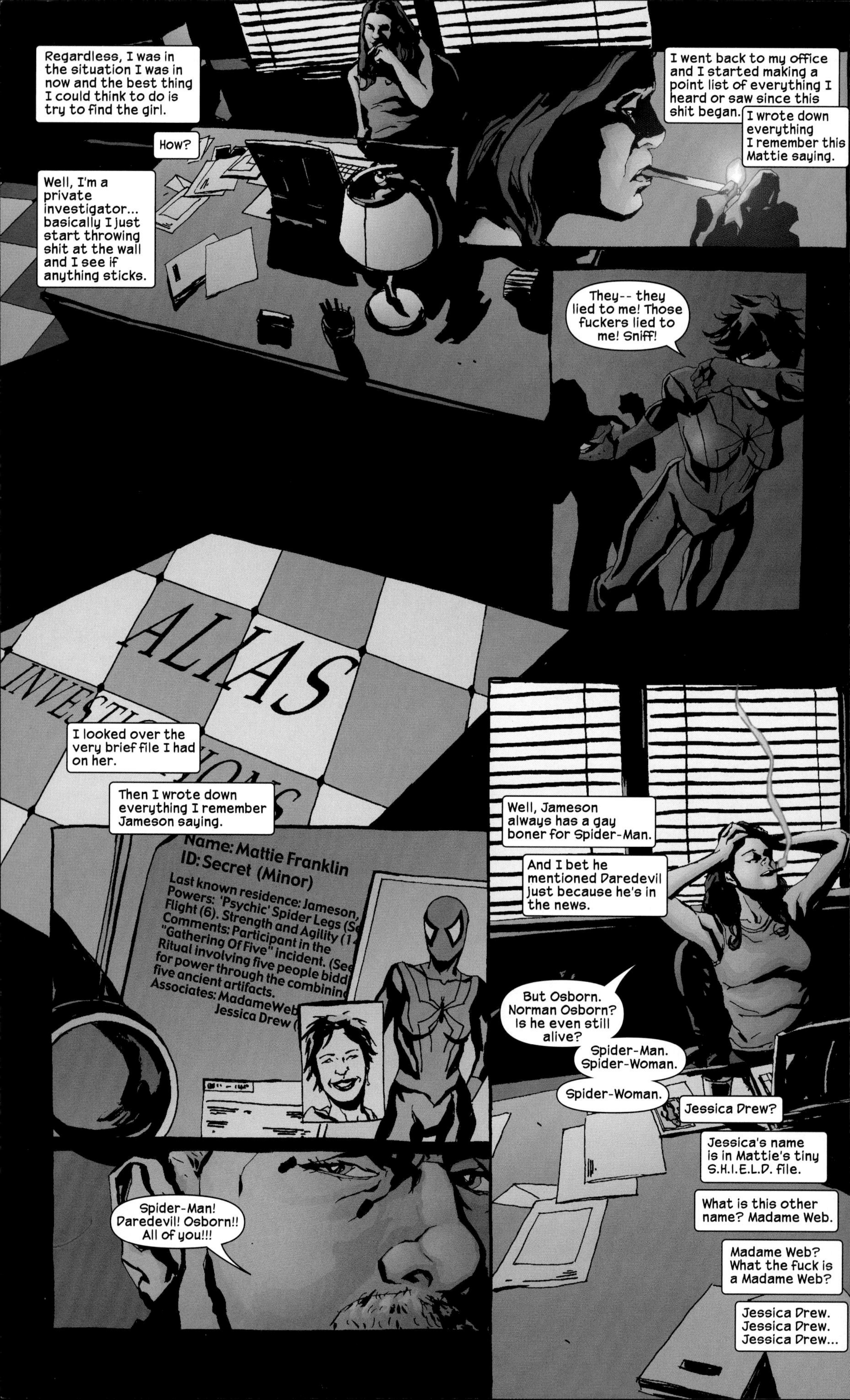
Regardless, I was in the situation I was in now and the best thing I could think to do is try to find the girl.
How?
Well, I'm a private investigator... basically I just start throwing shit at the wall and I see if anything sticks.
I went back to my office and I started making a point list of everything I heard or saw since this shit began.
I wrote down everything I remember this Mattie saying.
They-- they lied to me! Those fuckers lied to me! Sniff!
ALIAS
INVESTIGATIONS
I looked over the very brief file I had on her.
Then I wrote down everything I remember Jameson saying.
Name: Mattie Franklin
ID: Secret (Minor)
Last known residence: Jameson,
Powers: "Psychic" Spider Legs (Se
Flight (6). Strength and Agility (1
Comments: Participant in the
"Gathering Of Five" incident. (See
Ritual involving five people bidd
for power through the combinin
five ancient artifacts.
Associates: MadameWeb
Jessica Drew (
Spider-Man! Daredevil! Osborn!! All of you!!!
Well, Jameson always has a gay boner for Spider-Man.
And I bet he mentioned Daredevil just because he's in the news.
But Osborn. Norman Osborn? Is he even still alive?
Spider-Man. Spider-Woman.
Spider-Woman.
Jessica Drew?
Jessica's name is in Mattie's tiny S.H.I.E.L.D. file.
What is this other name? Madame Web.
Madame Web? What the fuck is a Madame Web?
Jessica Drew. Jessica Drew. Jessica Drew...

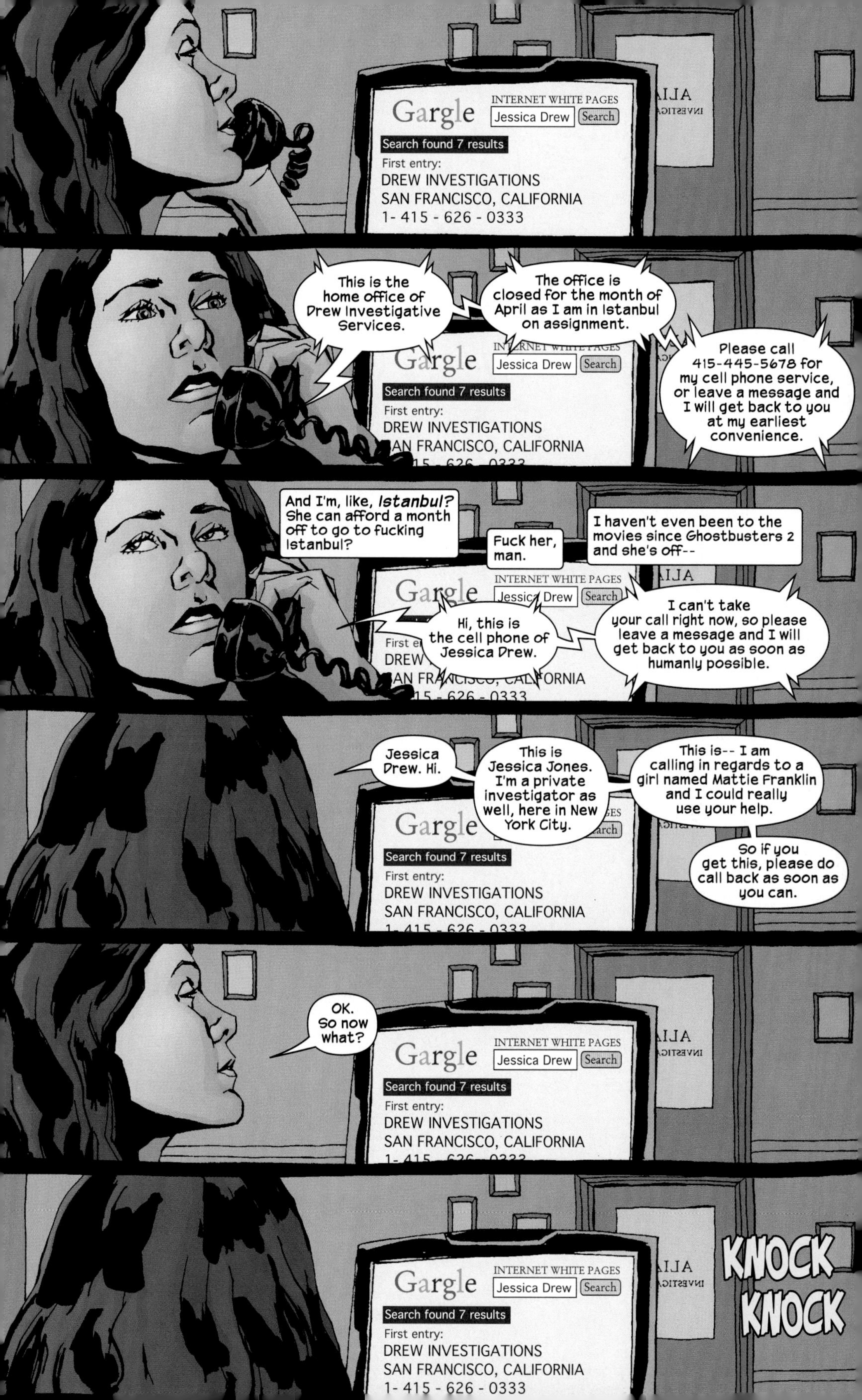

Gargle
INTERNET WHITE PAGES
Jessica Drew
Search
Search found 7 results
First entry:
DREW INVESTIGATIONS
SAN FRANCISCO, CALIFORNIA
1- 415 - 626 - 0333
This is the home office of Drew Investigative Services.
The office is closed for the month of April as I am in Istanbul on assignment.
Please call 415-445-5678 for my cell phone service, or leave a message and I will get back to you at my earliest convenience.
And I'm, like, *Istanbul?* She can afford a month off to go to fucking Istanbul?
Fuck her, man.
I haven't even been to the movies since Ghostbusters 2 and she's off--
Hi, this is the cell phone of Jessica Drew.
I can't take your call right now, so please leave a message and I will get back to you as soon as humanly possible.
Jessica Drew. Hi.
This is Jessica Jones. I'm a private investigator as well, here in New York City.
This is-- I am calling in regards to a girl named Mattie Franklin and I could really use your help.
So if you get this, please do call back as soon as you can.
OK. So now what?
KNOCK
KNOCK

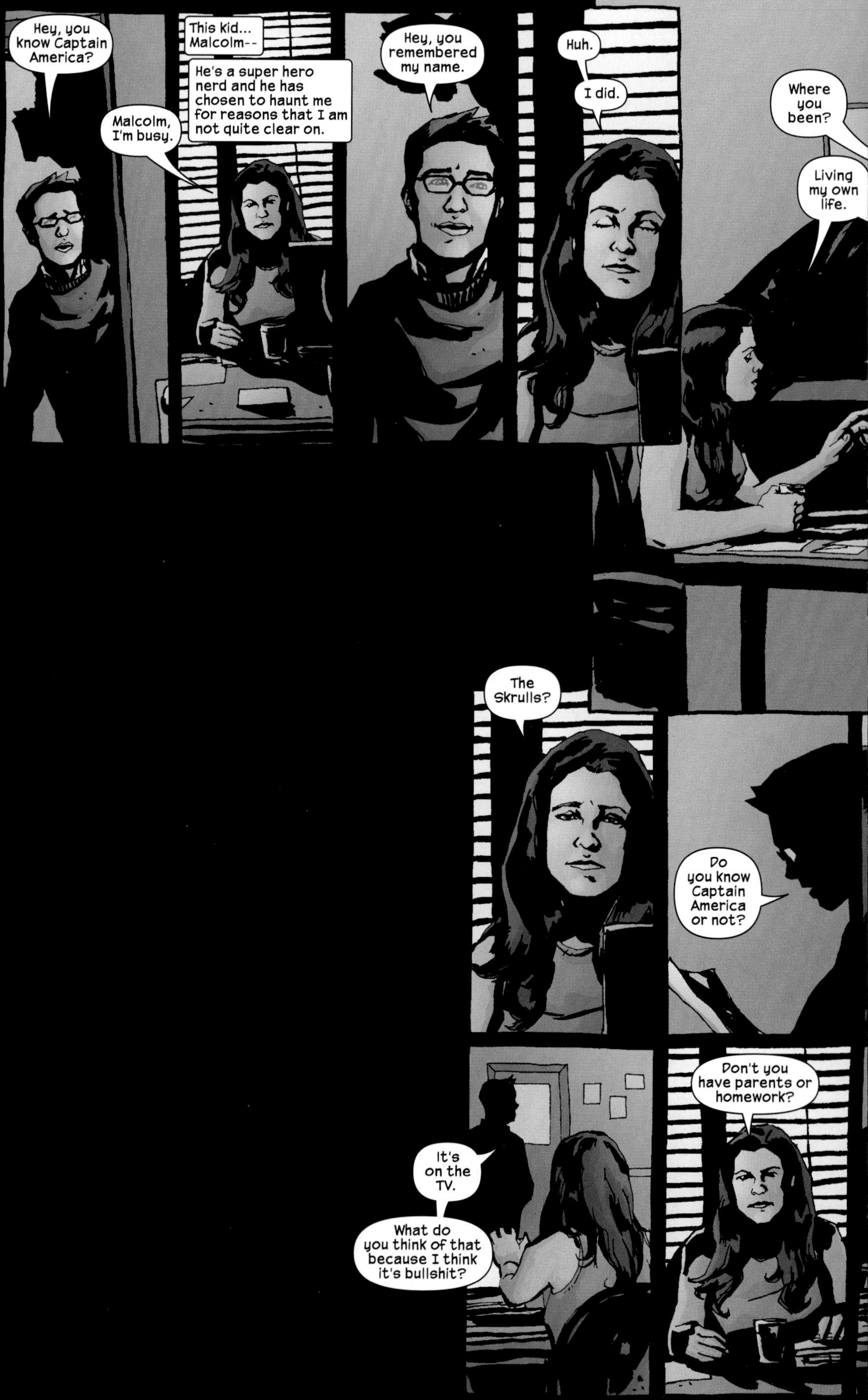

Hey, you know Captain America?
Malcolm, I'm busy.
This kid... Malcolm--
He's a super hero nerd and he has chosen to haunt me for reasons that I am not quite clear on.
Hey, you remembered my name.
Huh.
I did.
Where you been?
Living my own life.
The Skrulls?
Do you know Captain America or not?
It's on the TV.
What do you think of that because I think it's bullshit?
Don't you have parents or homework?

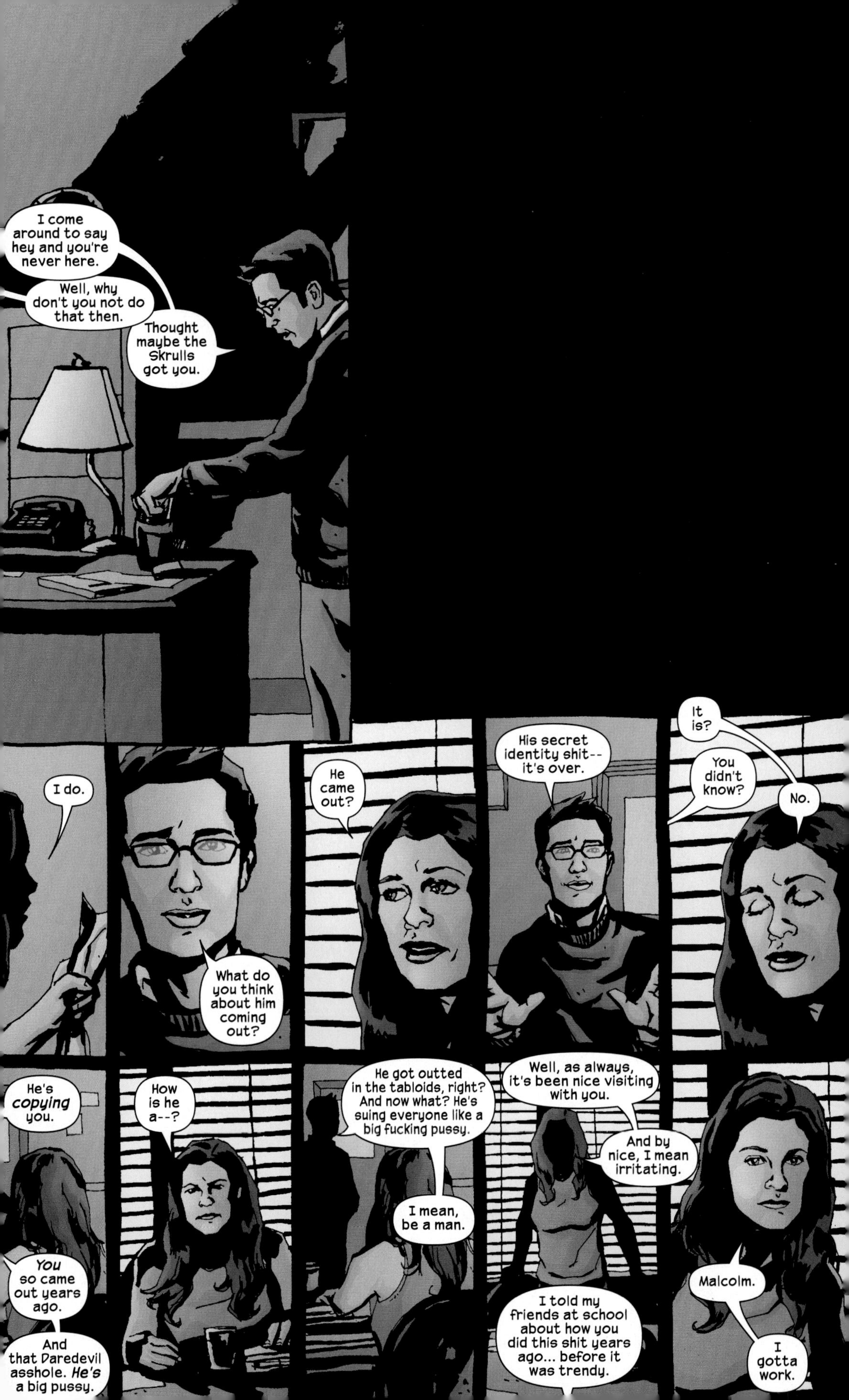

I come around to say hey and you're never here.
Well, why don't you not do that then.
Thought maybe the Skrulls got you.
I do.
What do you think about him coming out?
He came out?
His secret identity shit-- it's over.
It is?
You didn't know?
No.
He's *copying* you.
You so came out years ago.
And that Daredevil asshole. *He's* a big pussy.
How is he a--?
He got outted in the tabloids, right? And now what? He's suing everyone like a big fucking pussy.
I mean, be a man.
Well, as always, it's been nice visiting with you.
And by nice, I mean irritating.
I told my friends at school about how you did this shit years ago... before it was trendy.
Malcolm.
I gotta work.

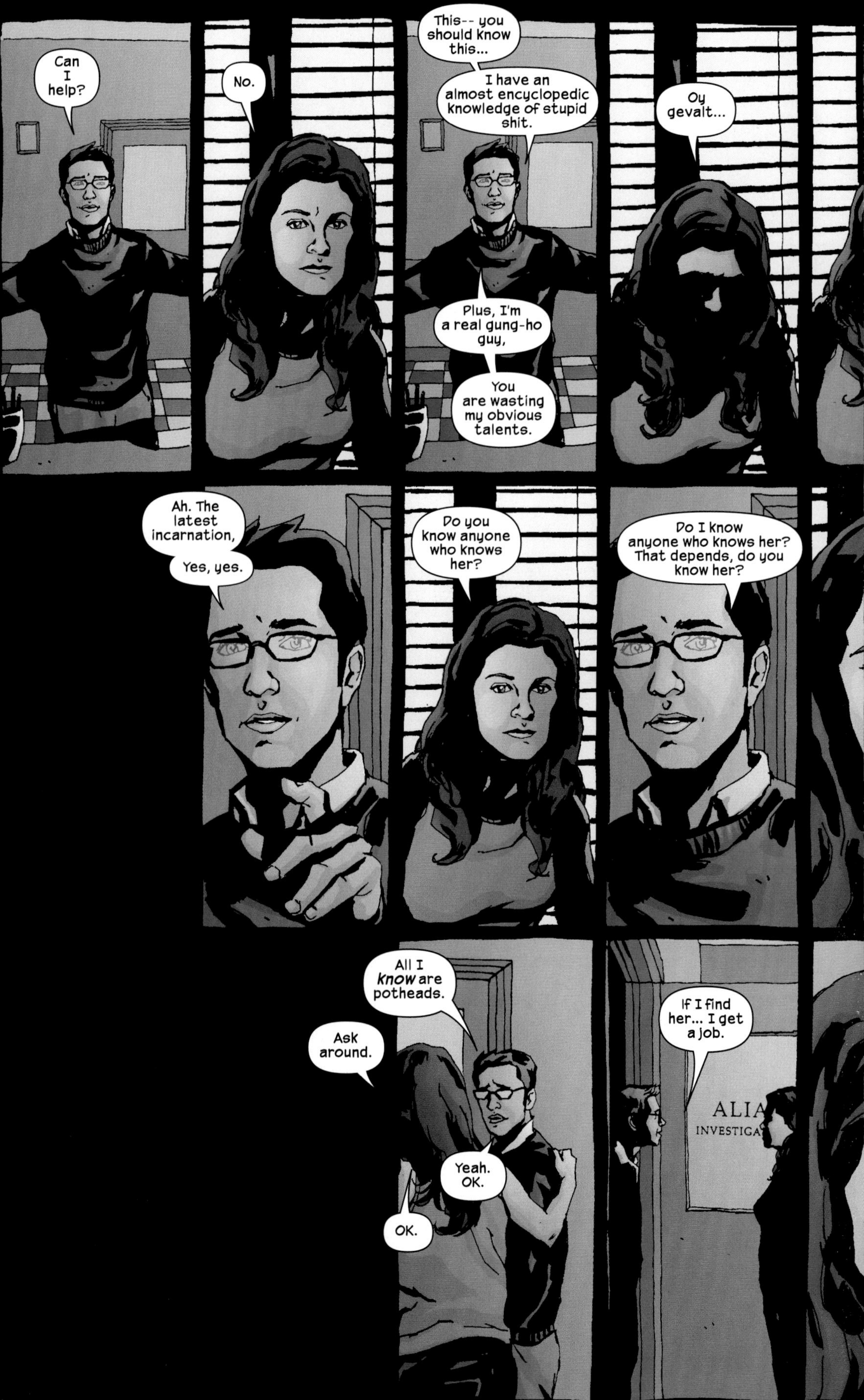
Can I help?
No.
This-- you should know this...
I have an almost encyclopedic knowledge of stupid shit.
Plus, I'm a real gung-ho guy,
You are wasting my obvious talents.
Oy gevalt...
Ah. The latest incarnation,
Yes, yes.
Do you know anyone who knows her?
Do I know anyone who knows her? That depends, do you know her?
All I *know* are potheads.
Ask around.
Yeah. OK.
OK.
If I find her... I get a job.
ALIA
INVESTIGA

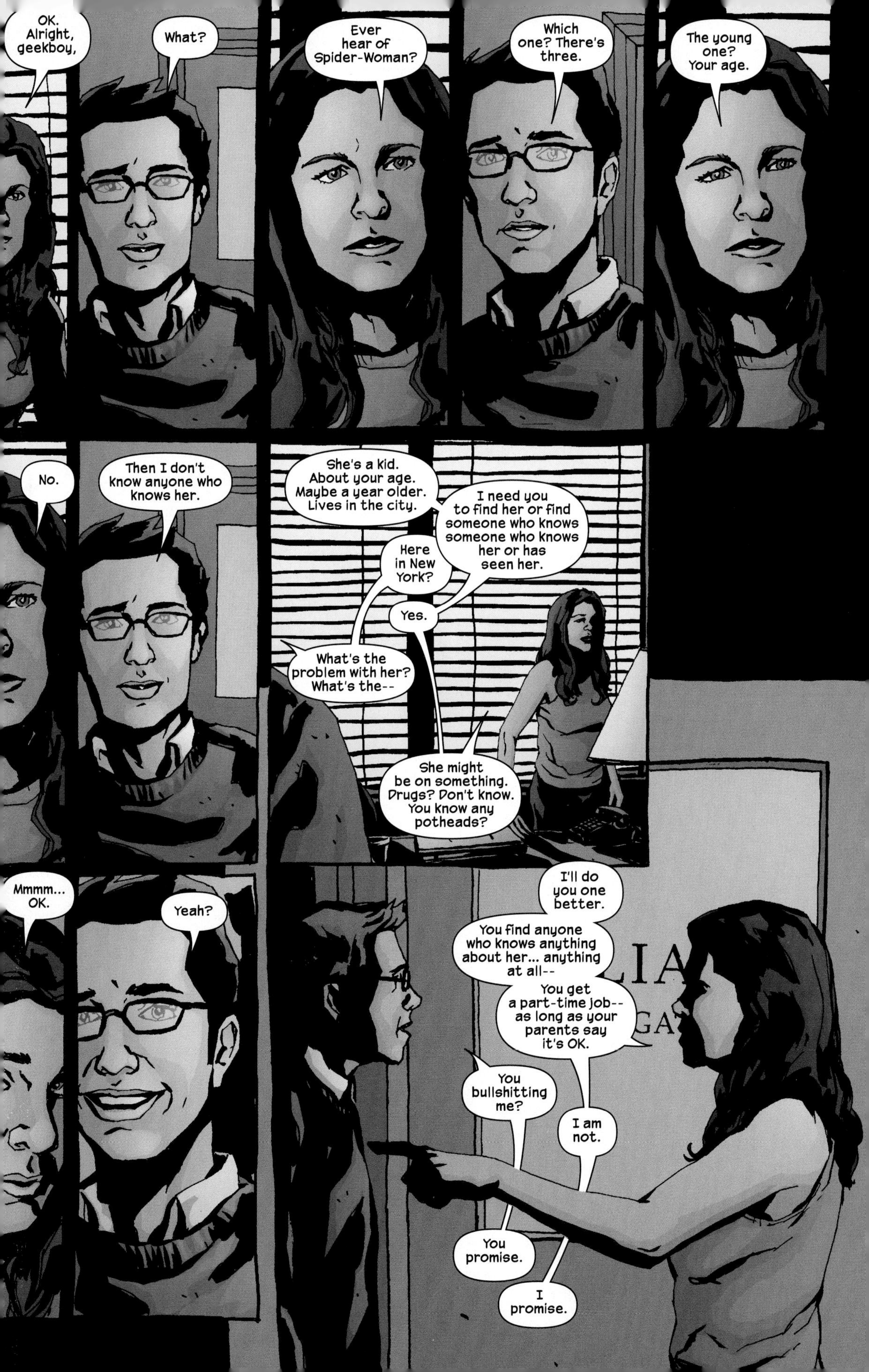
OK. Alright, geekboy,
What?
Ever hear of Spider-Woman?
Which one? There's three.
The young one? Your age.
No.
Then I don't know anyone who knows her.
She's a kid. About your age. Maybe a year older. Lives in the city.
I need you to find her or find someone who knows someone who knows her or has seen her.
Here in New York?
Yes.
What's the problem with her? What's the--
She might be on something. Drugs? Don't know. You know any potheads?
Mmmm... OK.
Yeah?
I'll do you one better.
You find anyone who knows anything about her... anything at all--
You get a part-time job-- as long as your parents say it's OK.
You bullshitting me?
I am not.
You promise.
I promise.

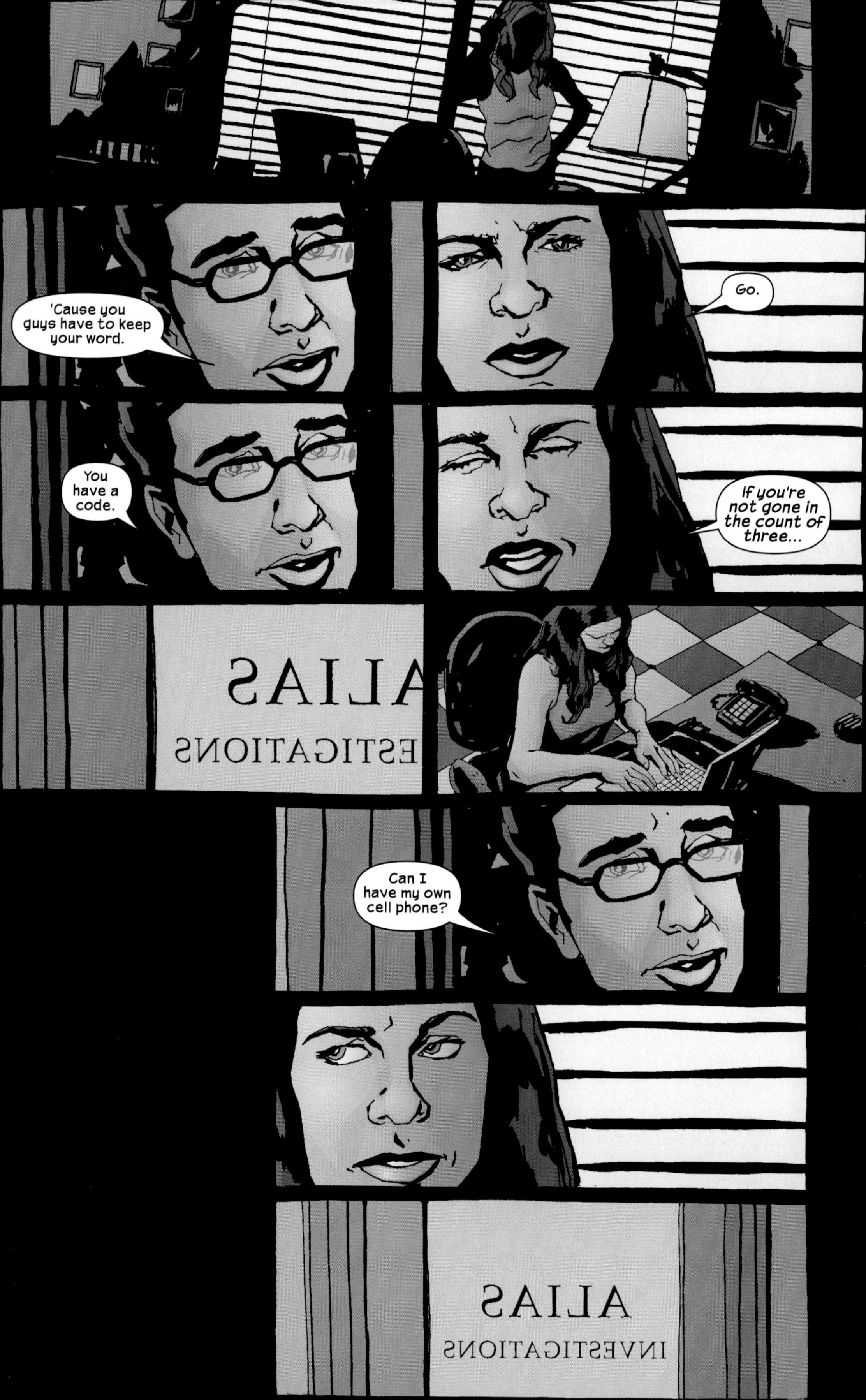
'Cause you guys have to keep your word.
Go.
You have a code.
If you're not gone in the count of three...
ALIAS
ESTIGATIONS
Can I have my own cell phone?
ALIAS
INVESTIGATIONS

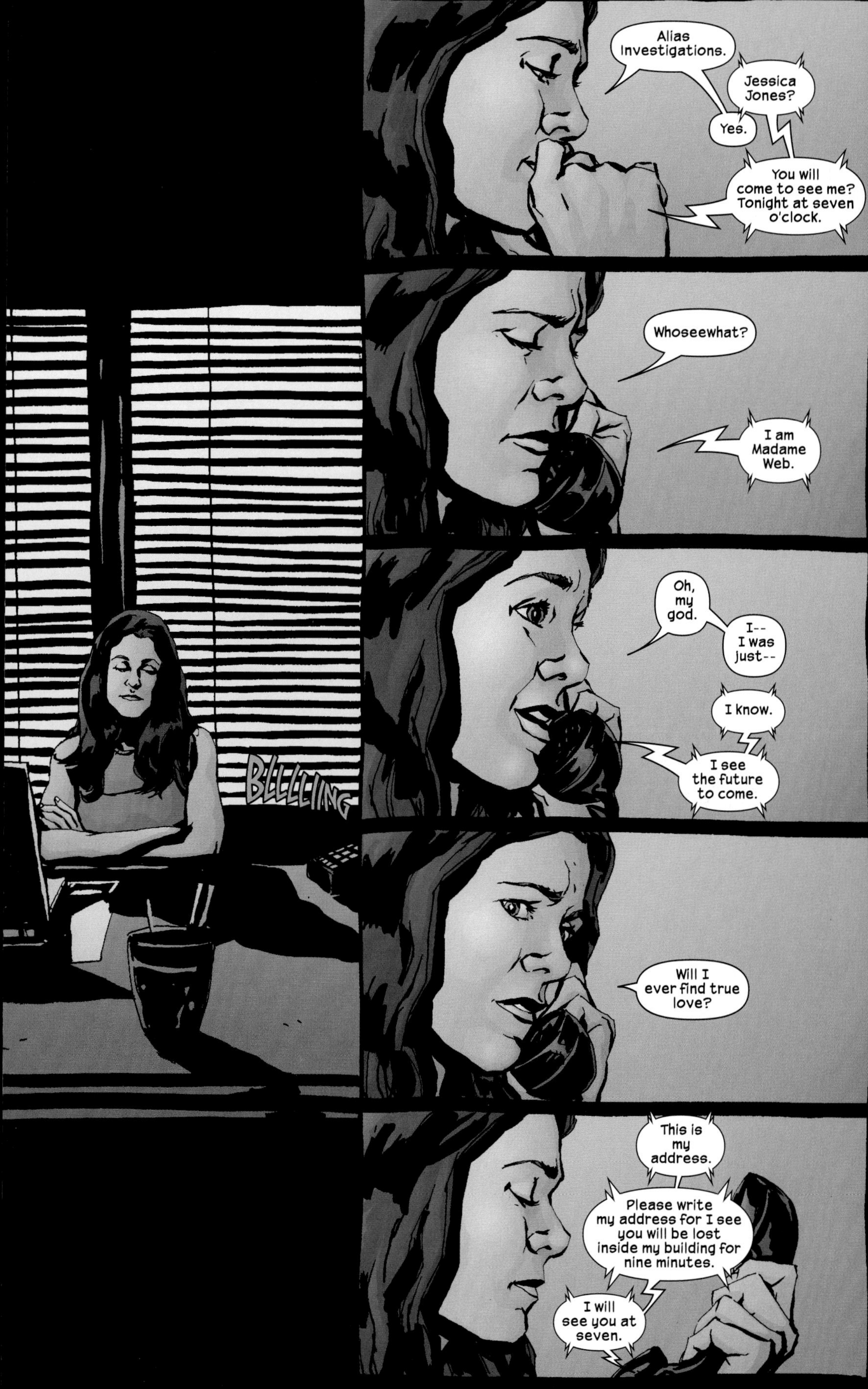
BLLLLING
Alias Investigations.
Jessica Jones?
Yes.
You will come to see me? Tonight at seven o'clock.
Whoseewhat?
I am Madame Web.
Oh, my god.
I-- I was just--
I know.
I see the future to come.
Will I ever find true love?
This is my address.
Please write my address for I see you will be lost inside my building for nine minutes.
I will see you at seven.

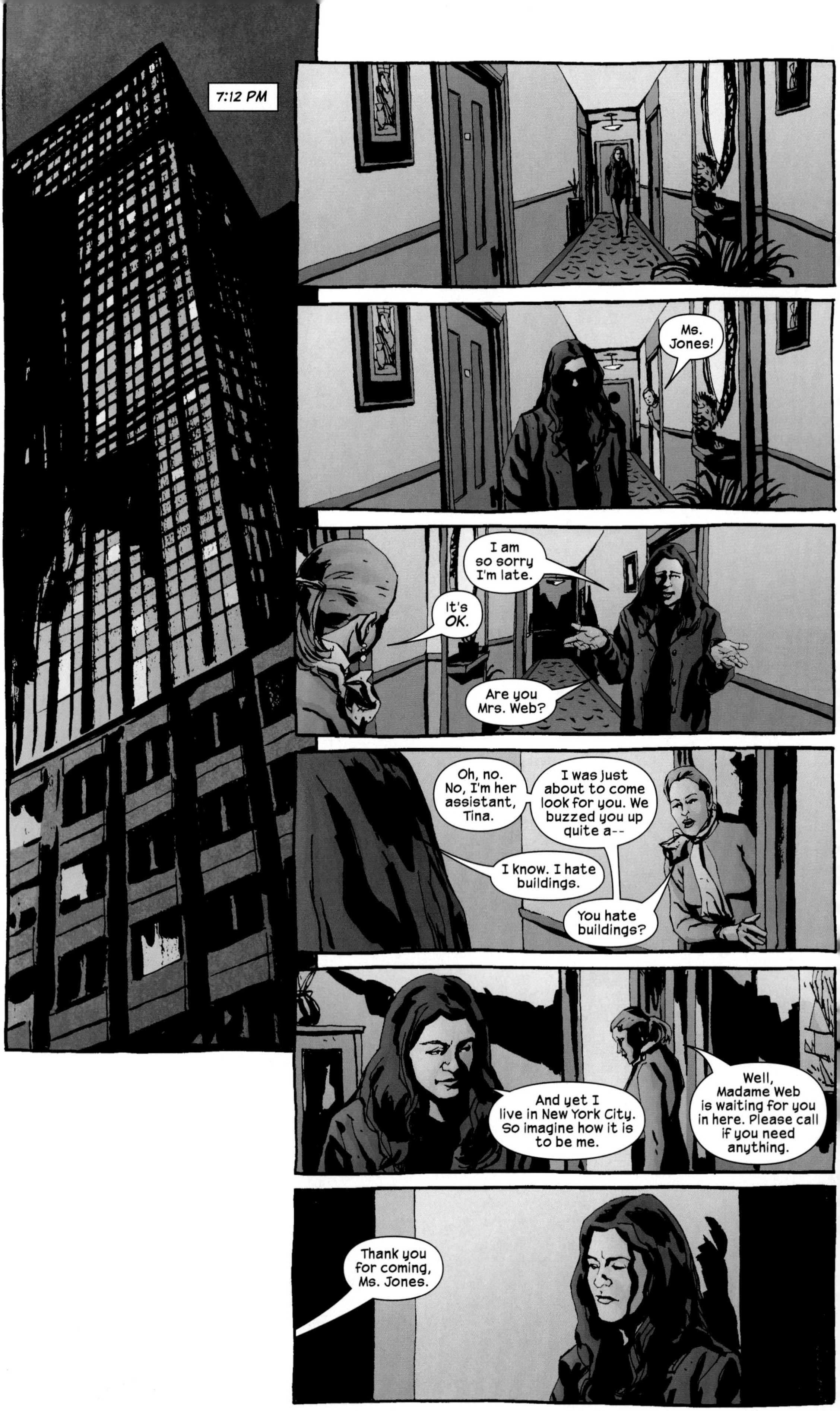
7:12 PM
Ms. Jones!
I am so sorry I'm late.
It's OK.
Are you Mrs. Web?
Oh, no. No, I'm her assistant, Tina.
I was just about to come look for you. We buzzed you up quite a--
I know. I hate buildings.
You hate buildings?
And yet I live in New York City. So imagine how it is to be me.
Well, Madame Web is waiting for you in here. Please call if you need anything.
Thank you for coming, Ms. Jones.

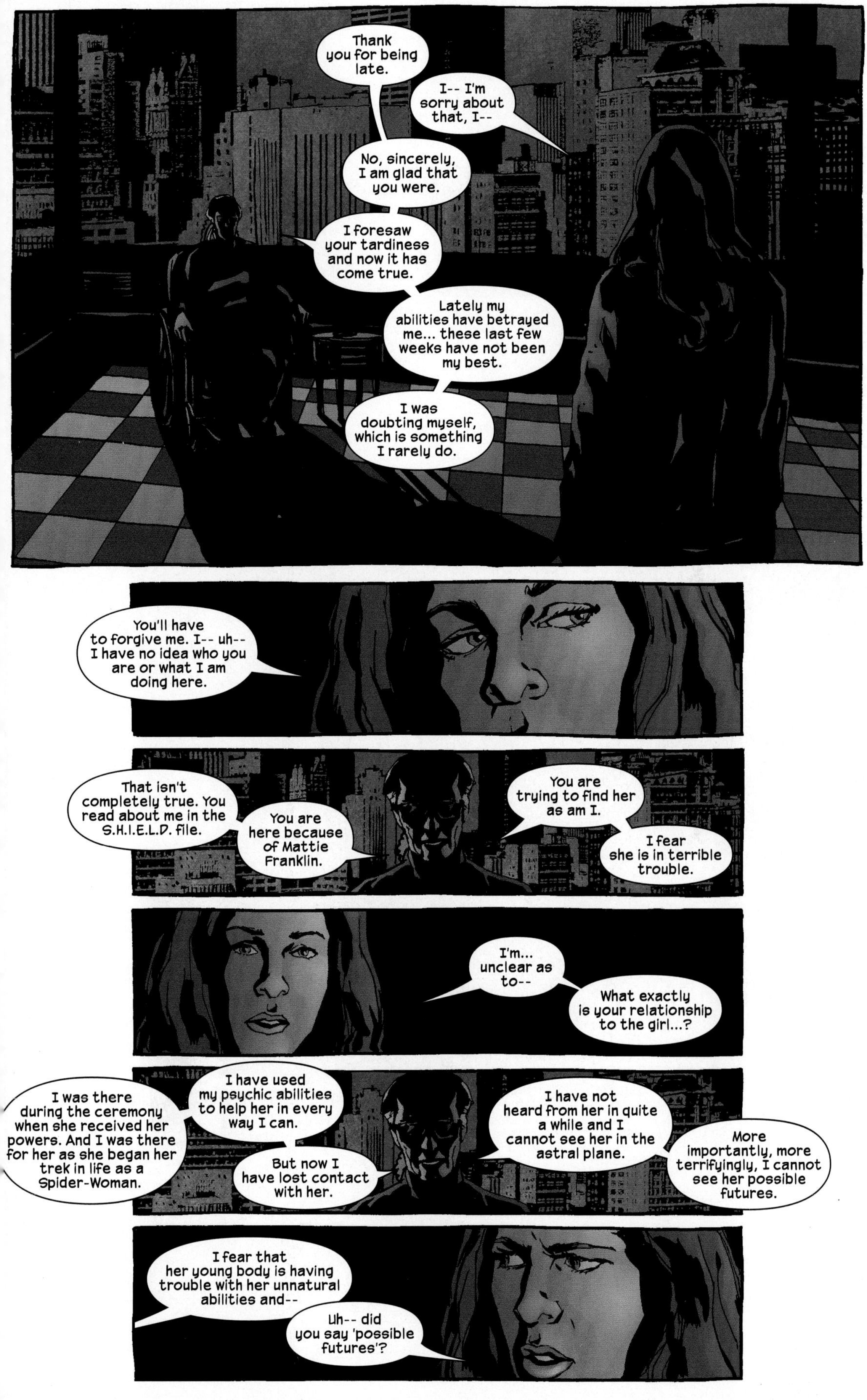
Thank you for being late.
I-- I'm sorry about that, I--
No, sincerely, I am glad that you were.
I foresaw your tardiness and now it has come true.
Lately my abilities have betrayed me... these last few weeks have not been my best.
I was doubting myself, which is something I rarely do.
You'll have to forgive me. I-- uh-- I have no idea who you are or what I am doing here.
That isn't completely true. You read about me in the S.H.I.E.L.D. file.
You are here because of Mattie Franklin.
You are trying to find her as am I.
I fear she is in terrible trouble.
I'm... unclear as to--
What exactly is your relationship to the girl...?
I was there during the ceremony when she received her powers. And I was there for her as she began her trek in life as a Spider-Woman.
I have used my psychic abilities to help her in every way I can.
But now I have lost contact with her.
I have not heard from her in quite a while and I cannot see her in the astral plane.
More importantly, more terrifyingly, I cannot see her possible futures.
I fear that her young body is having trouble with her unnatural abilities and--
Uh-- did you say 'possible futures'?

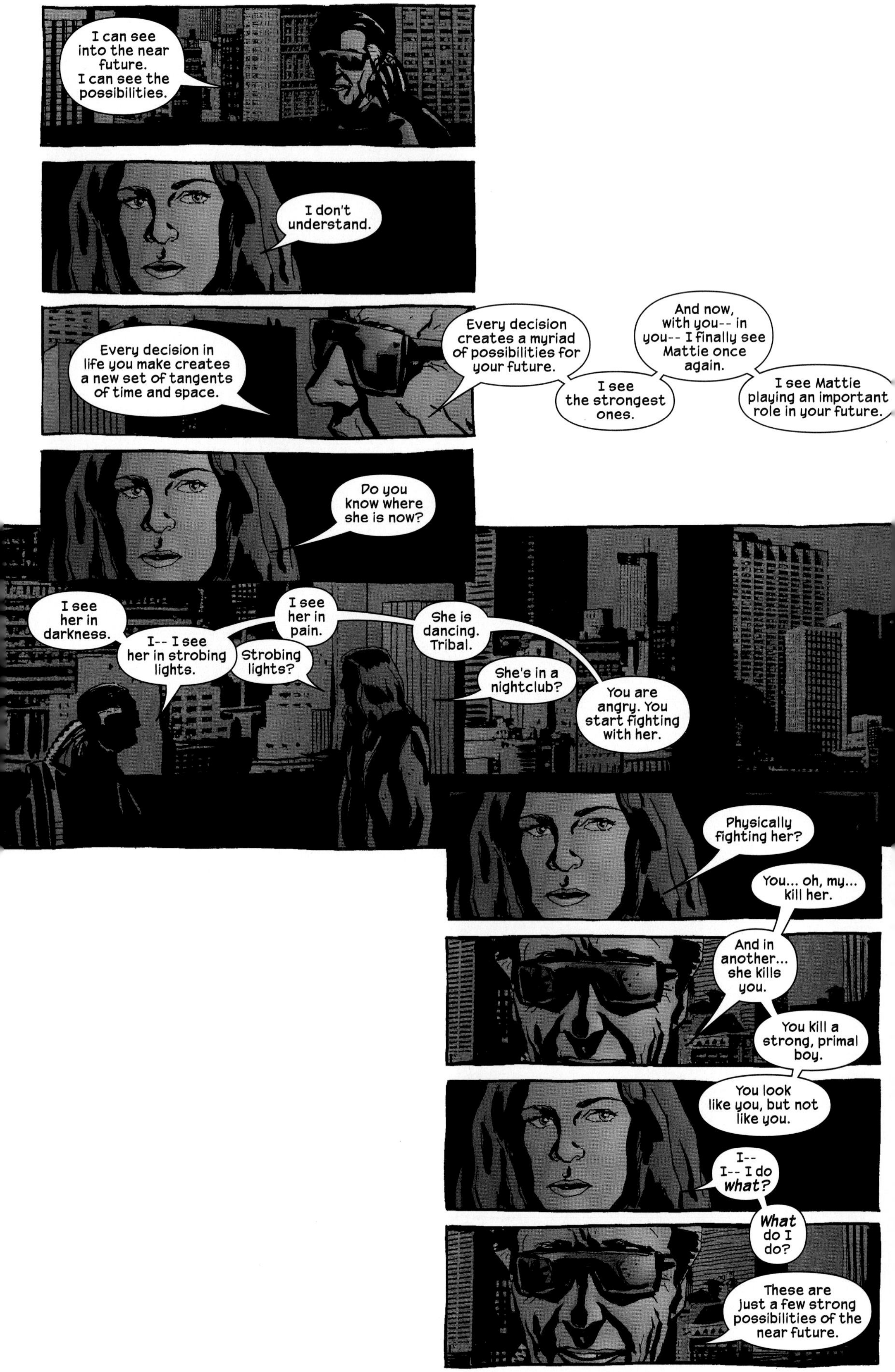
I can see into the near future. I can see the possibilities.
I don't understand.
Every decision in life you make creates a new set of tangents of time and space.
Every decision creates a myriad of possibilities for your future.
I see the strongest ones.
And now, with you-- in you-- I finally see Mattie once again.
I see Mattie playing an important role in your future.
Do you know where she is now?
I see her in darkness.
I see her in pain.
I-- I see her in strobing lights.
Strobing lights?
She is dancing. Tribal.
She's in a nightclub?
You are angry. You start fighting with her.
Physically fighting her?
You... oh, my... kill her.
And in another... she kills you.
You kill a strong, primal boy.
You look like you, but not like you.
I-- I-- I do *what?*
What do I do?
These are just a few strong possibilities of the near future.

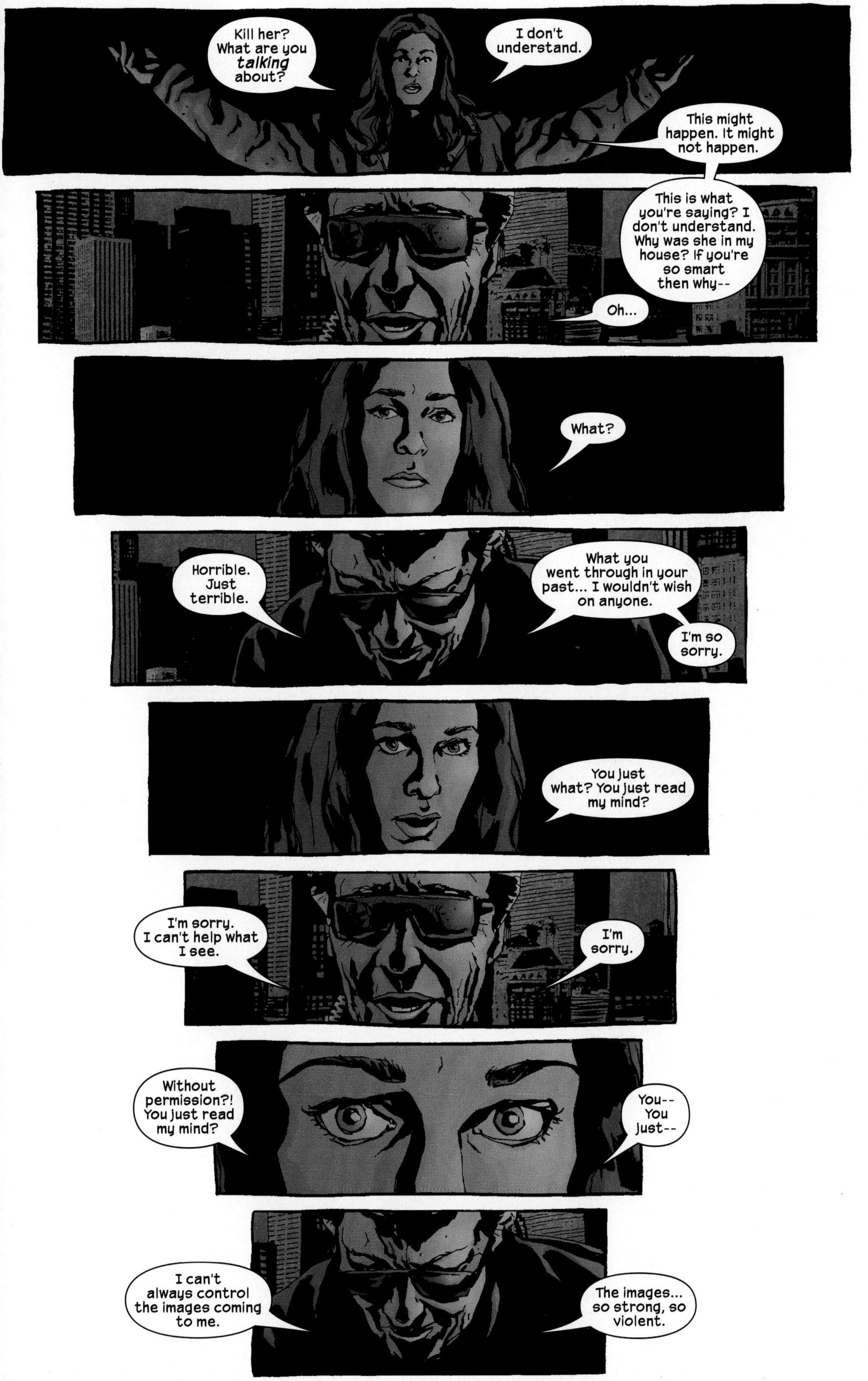
Kill her? What are you *talking* about?
I don't understand.
This might happen. It might not happen.
This is what you're saying? I don't understand. Why was she in my house? If you're so smart then why--
Oh...
What?
Horrible. Just terrible.
What you went through in your past... I wouldn't wish on anyone.
I'm so sorry.
You just what? You just read my mind?
I'm sorry. I can't help what I see.
I'm sorry.
Without permission?! You just read my mind?
You-- You just--
I can't always control the images coming to me.
The images... so strong, so violent.

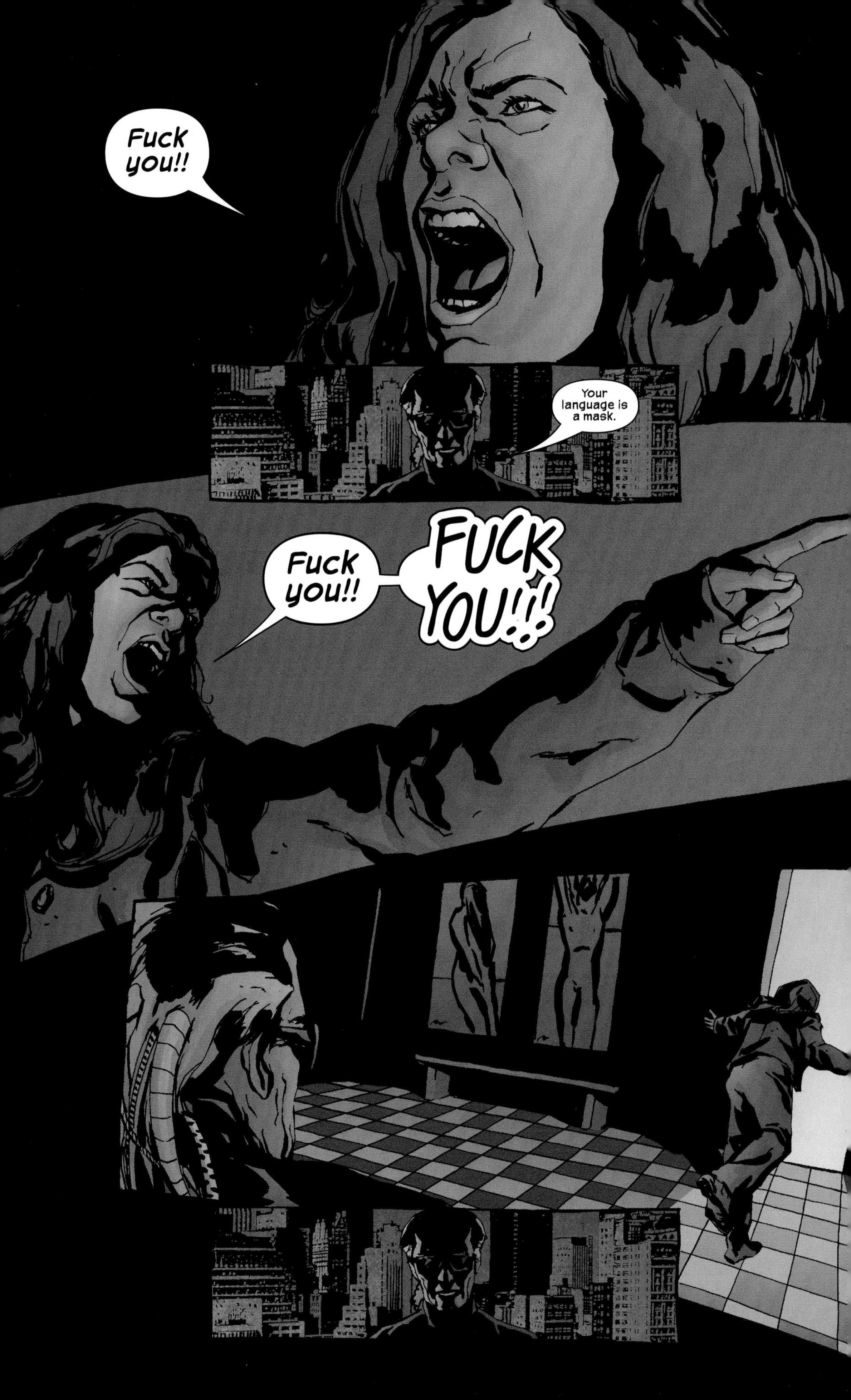
Fuck you!!
Your language is a mask.
Fuck you!!
FUCK YOU!!!

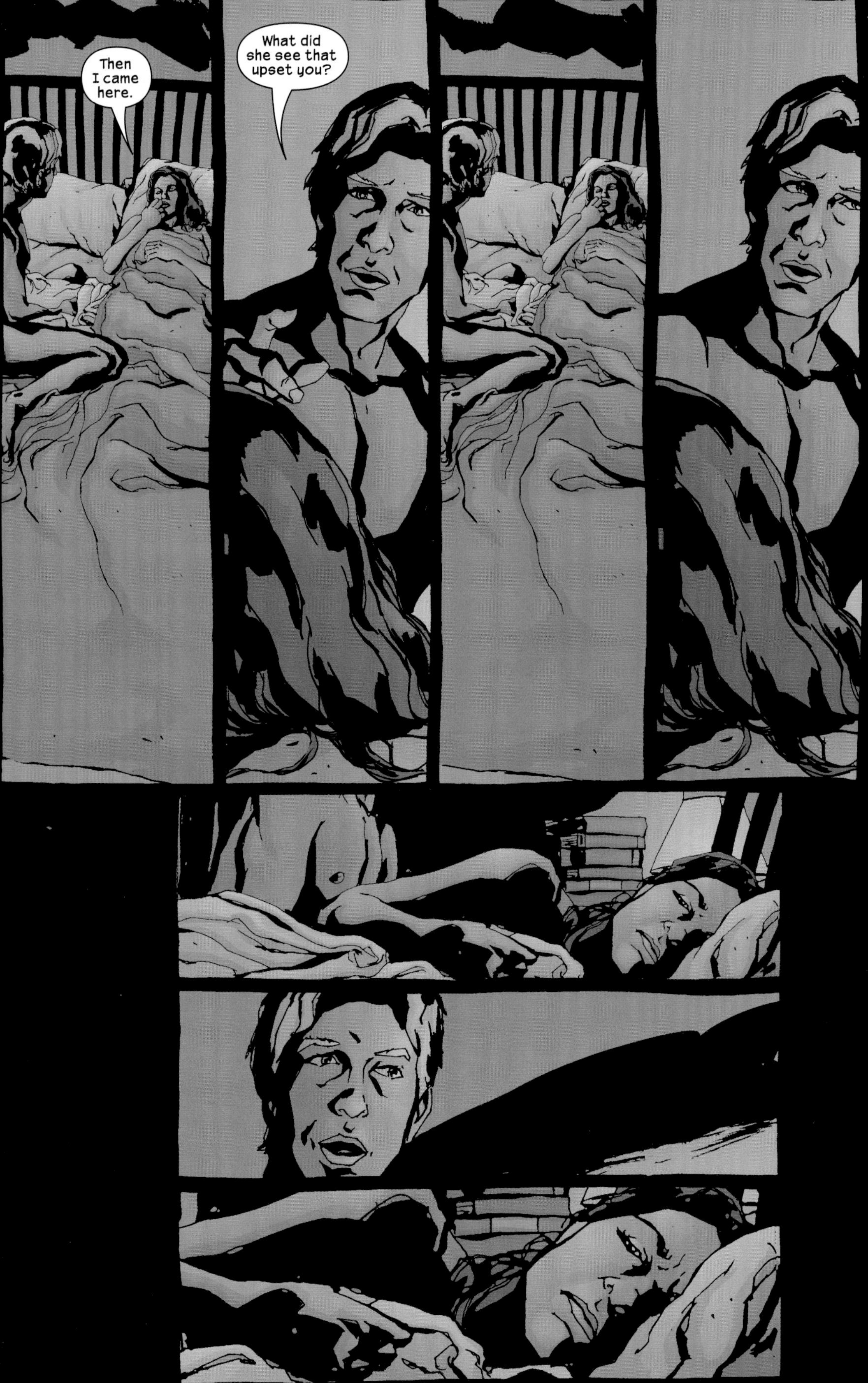
Then I came here.
What did she see that upset you?

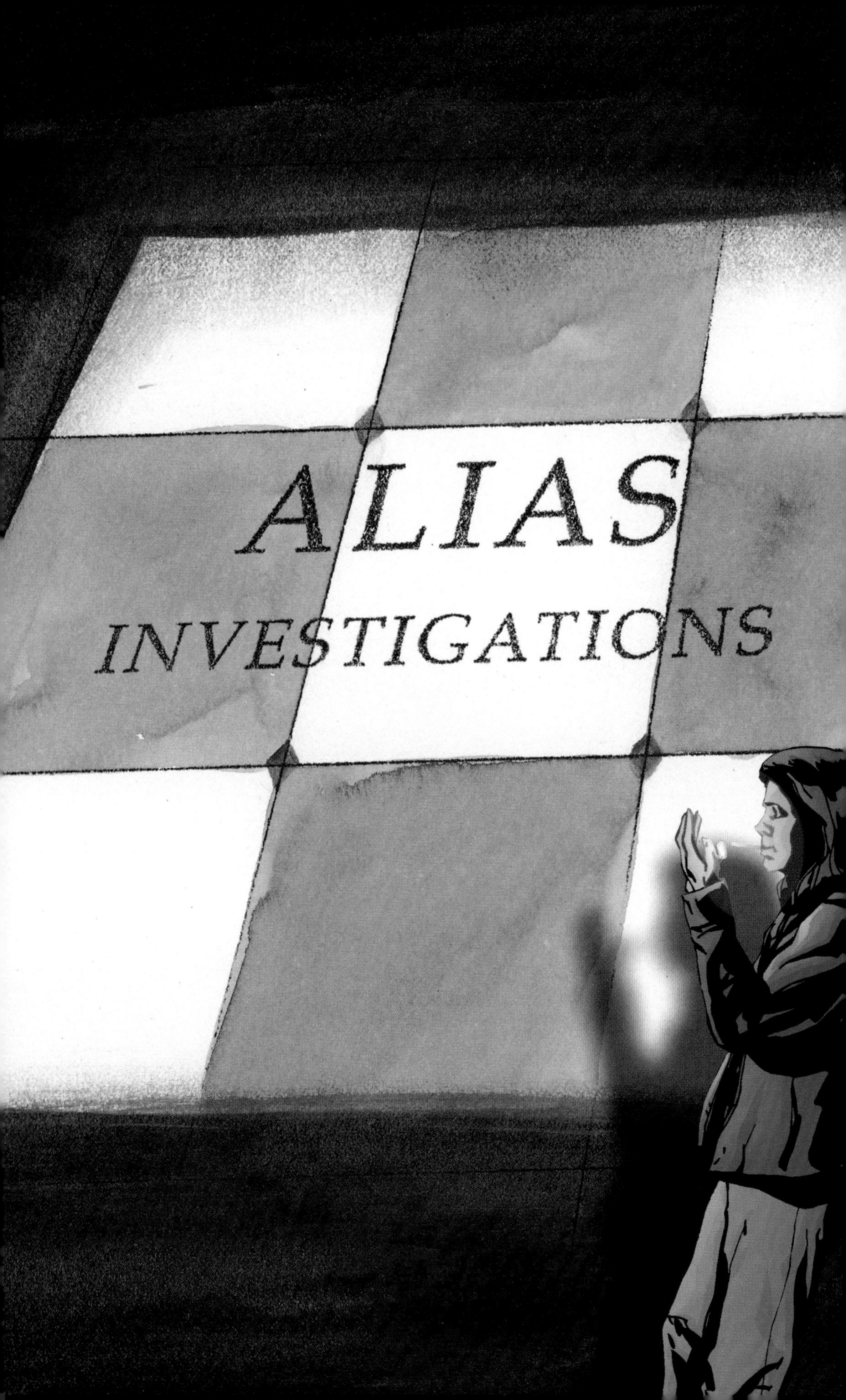
ALIAS
INVESTIGATIONS

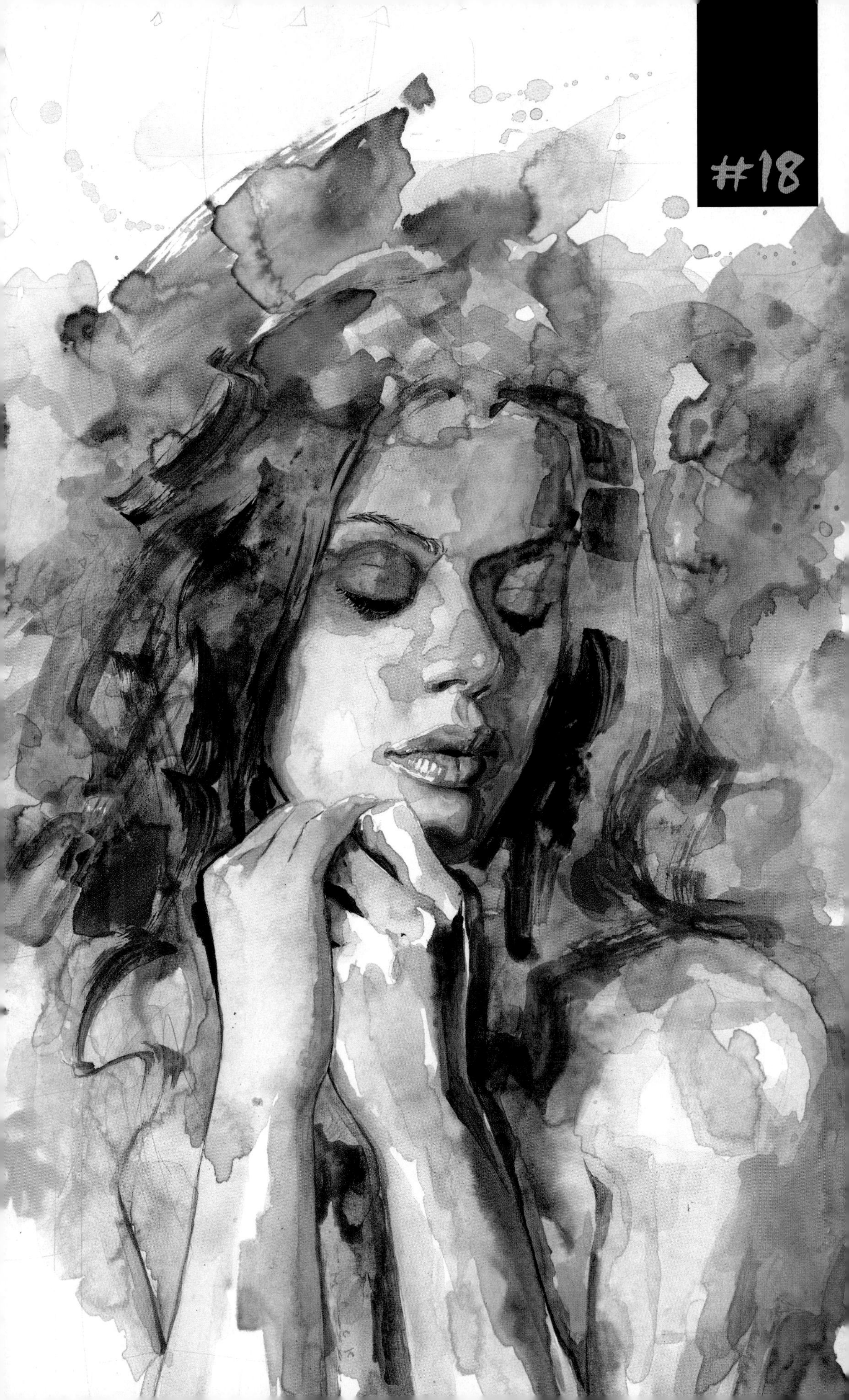
#18

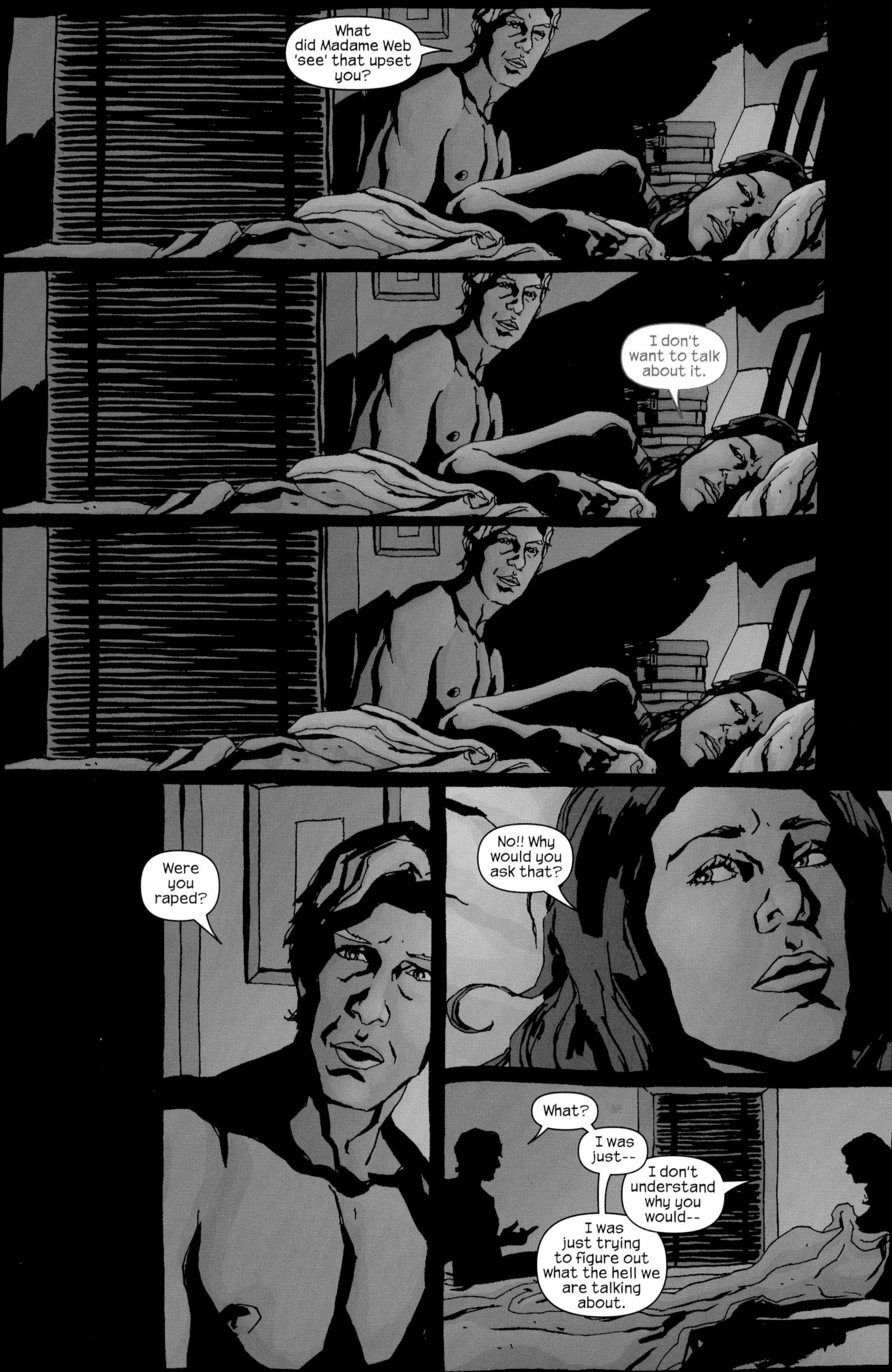
What did Madame Web 'see' that upset you?
I don't want to talk about it.
Were you raped?
No!! Why would you ask that?
What?
I was just--
I don't understand why you would--
I was just trying to figure out what the hell we are talking about.

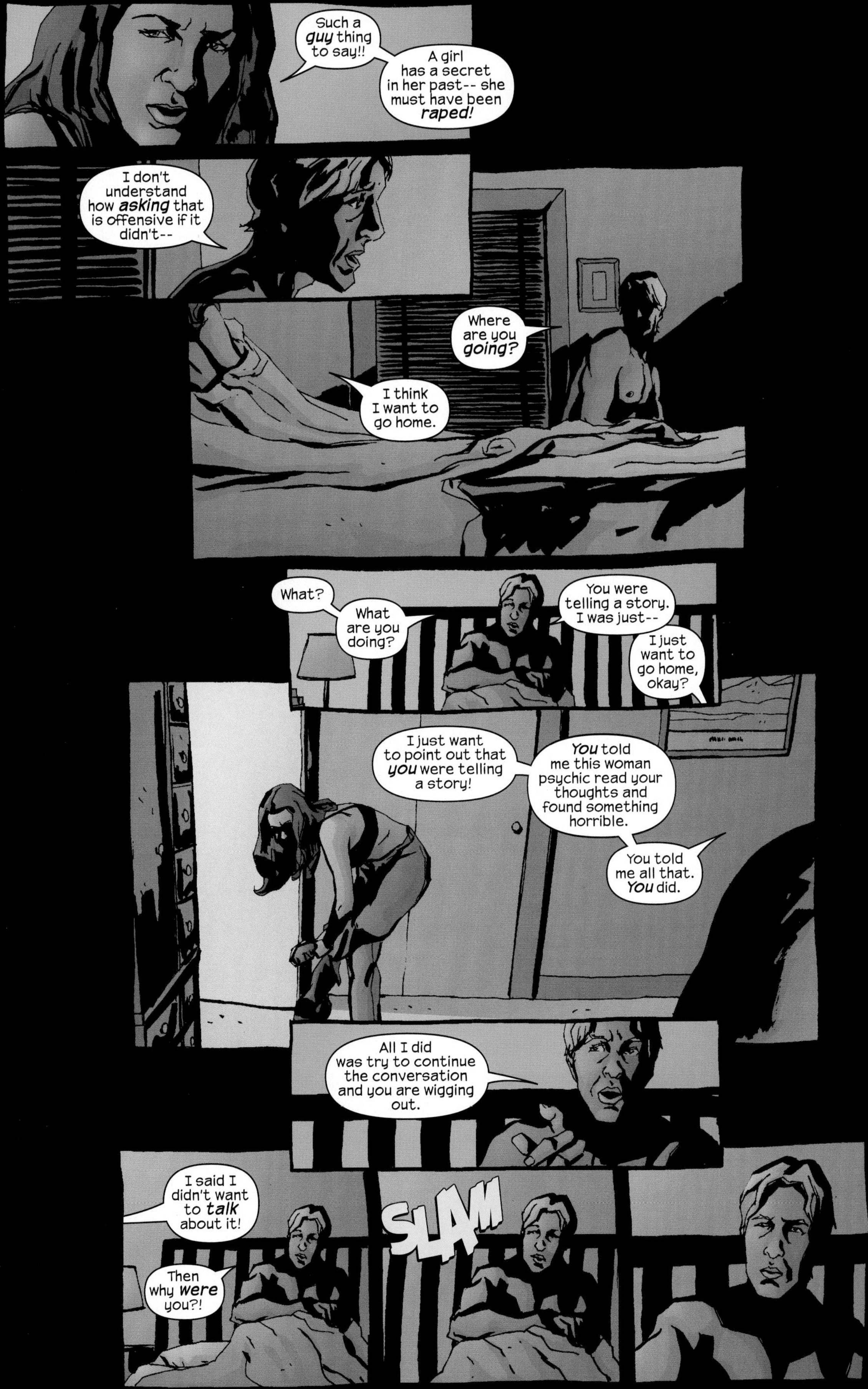
Such a guy thing to say!!
A girl has a secret in her past-- she must have been raped!
I don't understand how asking that is offensive if it didn't--
Where are you going?
I think I want to go home.
What?
What are you doing?
You were telling a story. I was just--
I just want to go home, okay?
I just want to point out that you were telling a story!
You told me this woman psychic read your thoughts and found something horrible.
You told me all that. You did.
All I did was try to continue the conversation and you are wigging out.
I said I didn't want to talk about it!
Then why were you?!
SLAM

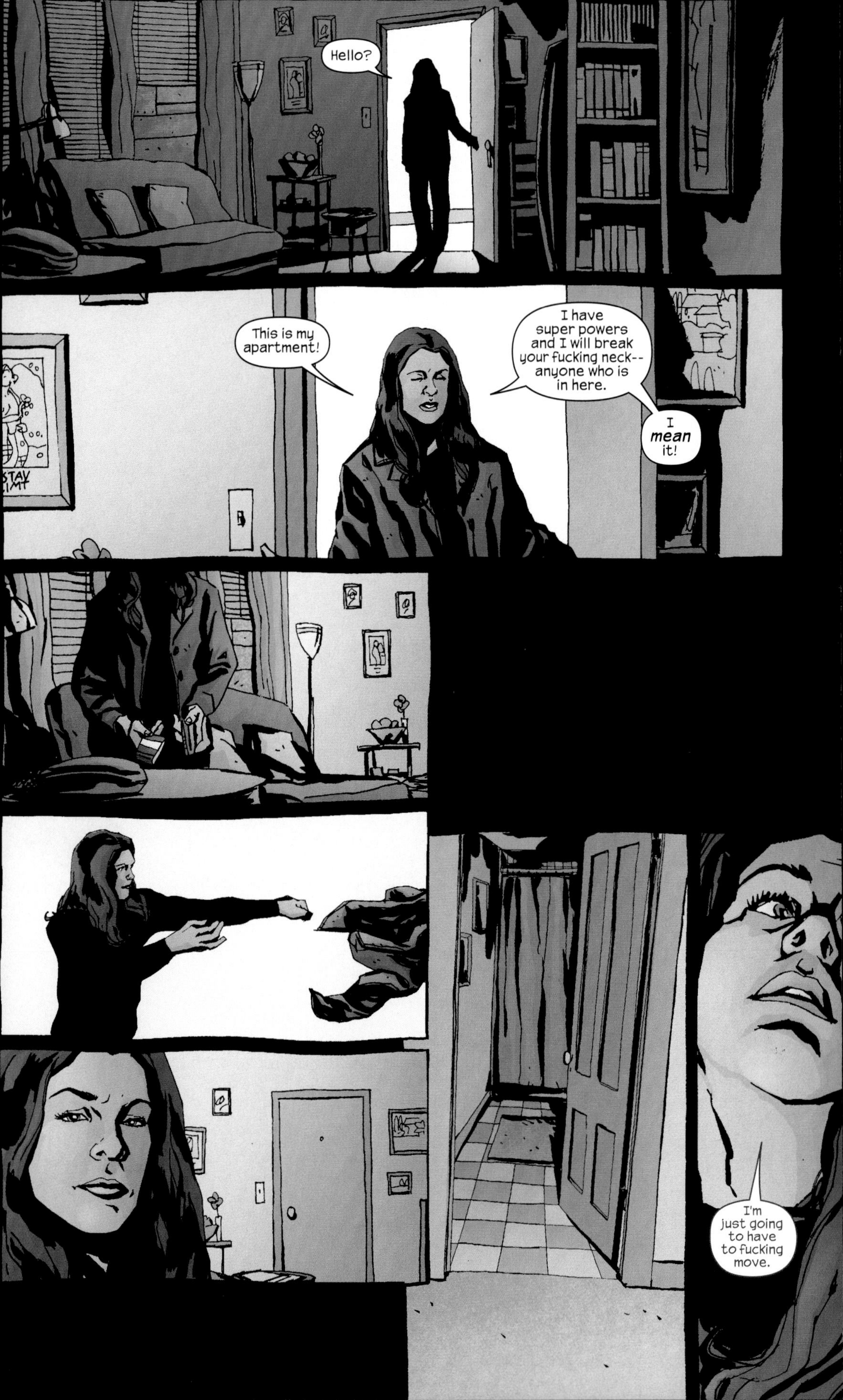
Hello?
This is my apartment!
I have super powers and I will break your fucking neck-- anyone who is in here.
I *mean* it!
STAY
I'm just going to have to fucking move.

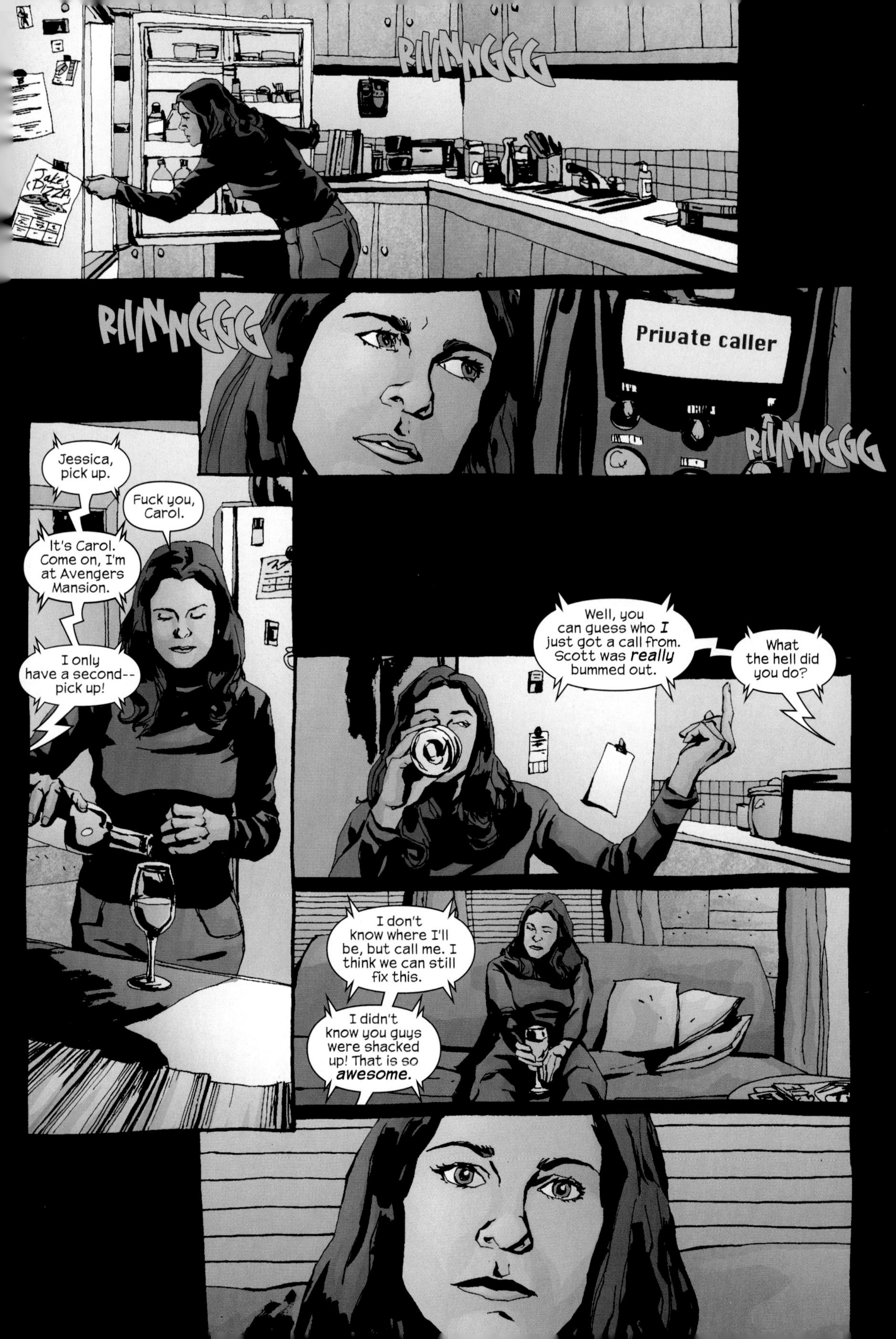
RIIINNGGG
Jake's PIZZA
RIIINNGGG
Private caller
RIIINNGGG
Jessica, pick up.
Fuck you, Carol.
It's Carol. Come on, I'm at Avengers Mansion.
I only have a second-- pick up!
Well, you can guess who I just got a call from. Scott was really bummed out.
What the hell did you do?
I don't know where I'll be, but call me. I think we can still fix this.
I didn't know you guys were shacked up! That is so awesome.

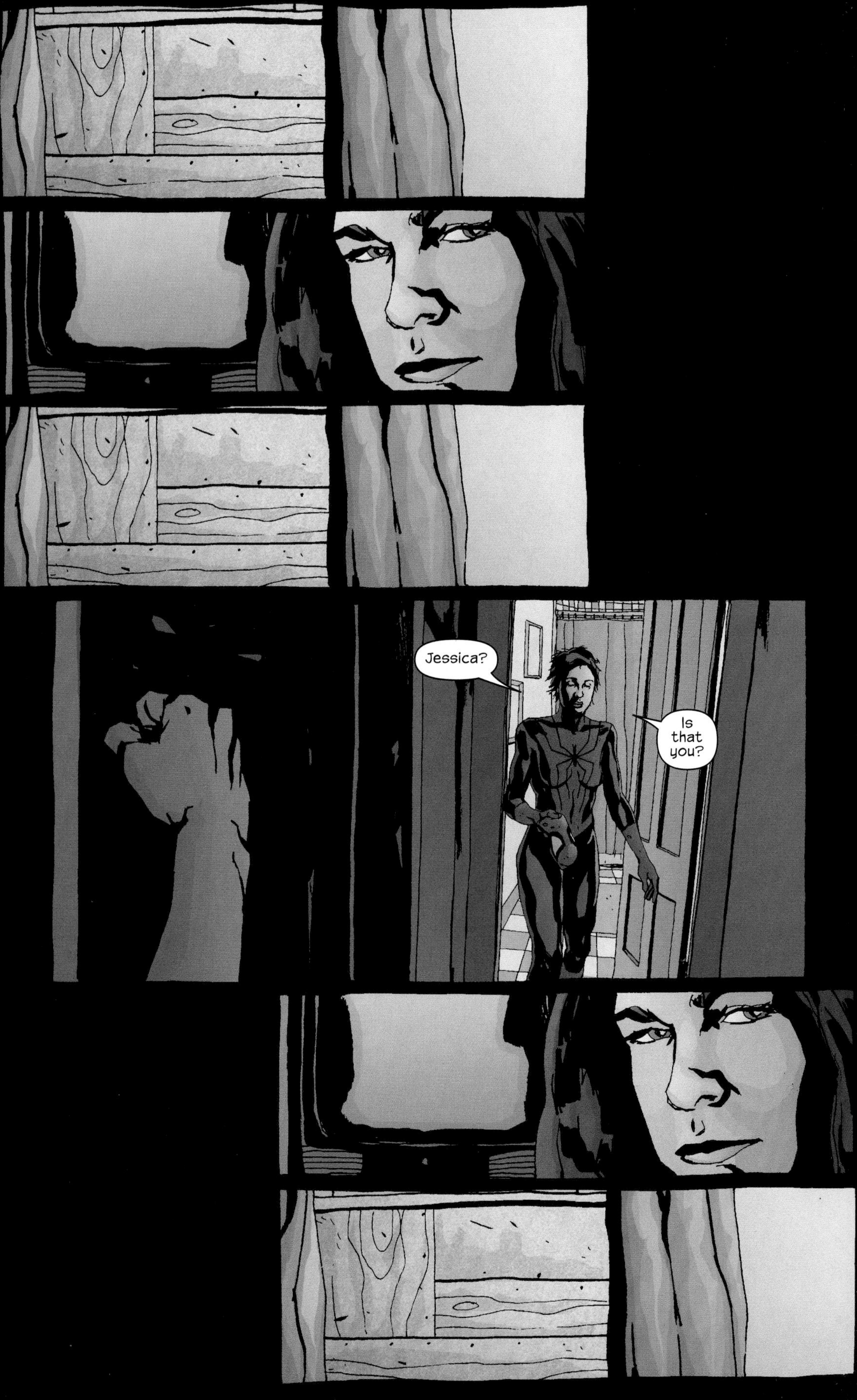
Jessica?
Is that you?

Didn't set my alarm. Fell asleep on my couch like an asshole.

Thank God I got up in time to shower and get over to my actually paying job this month.

I don't usually bodyguard-- even though a lot of P.I.s do. I don't like to do it. It's grunt work. Mindless bullshit.

But for my attorney, Matt Murdock, I'll do it. He's certainly been there for me enough times-- and he's going through a real bunch of crap now.

The tabloids outted him as Daredevil. Can you believe that shit? They just outted him. "The man without fear" outted as a blind Hell's Kitchen lawyer.

("Man without fear"-- I had nothing that cool in my flying days.)

They outted him, but he is publicly standing up to it. He's denying the whole thing and suing the shit out of everybody.

Good for him. Fuck the assholes.

So he needs me, and a couple of others like Luke Cage, to hang around the office, walk him to work.

We're supposed to keep an eye out for any of Daredevil's asshole butt-buddy rogue's gallery who might come around looking for some mindless payback-- but none of them have shown up.

All we end up doing all day is pushing the media away from him.

But he asks me to be here-- I'm here. Hate taking his money but he won't let me ***not*** take it.

And I need it.

He has it and I need it.

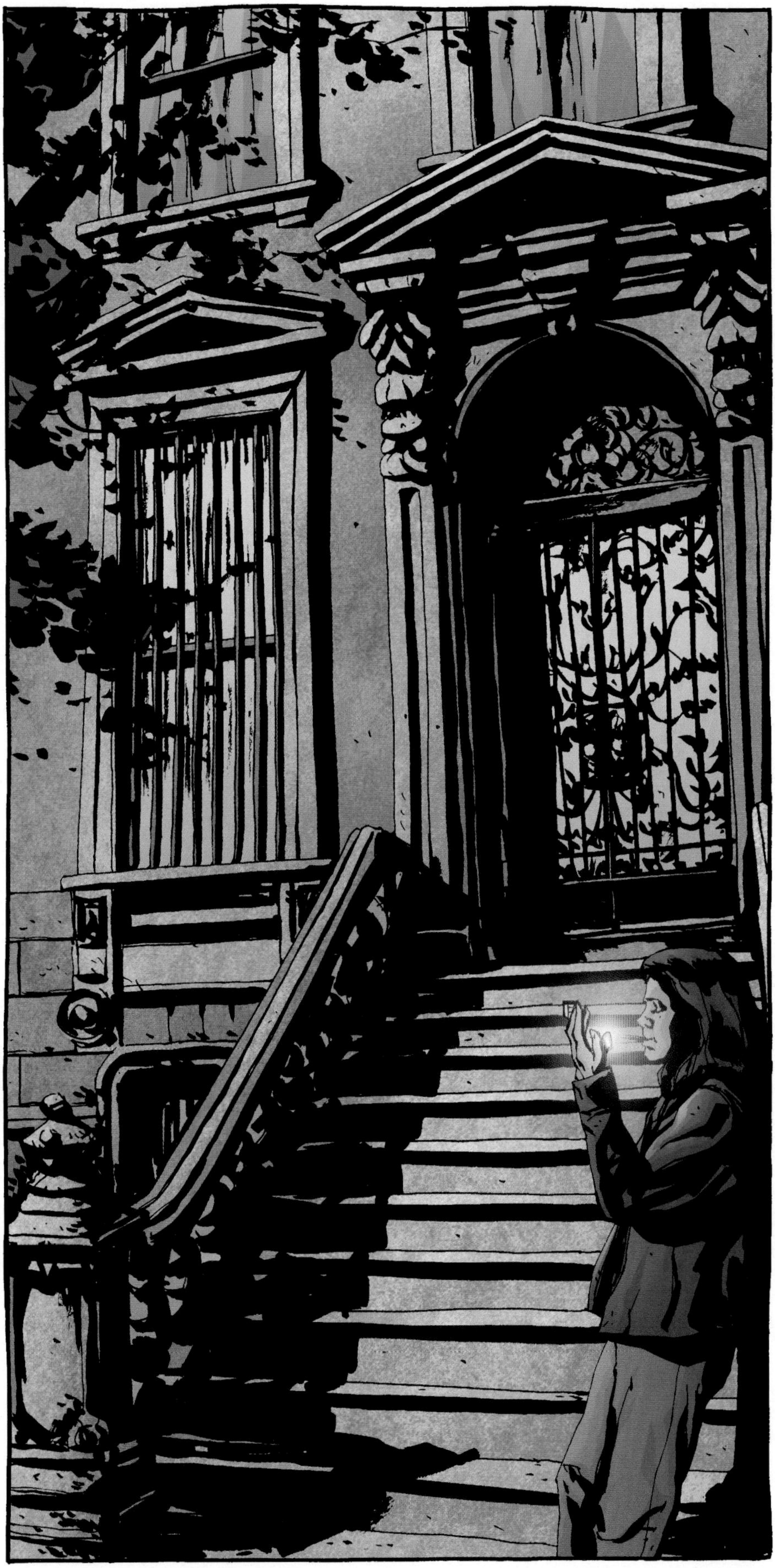

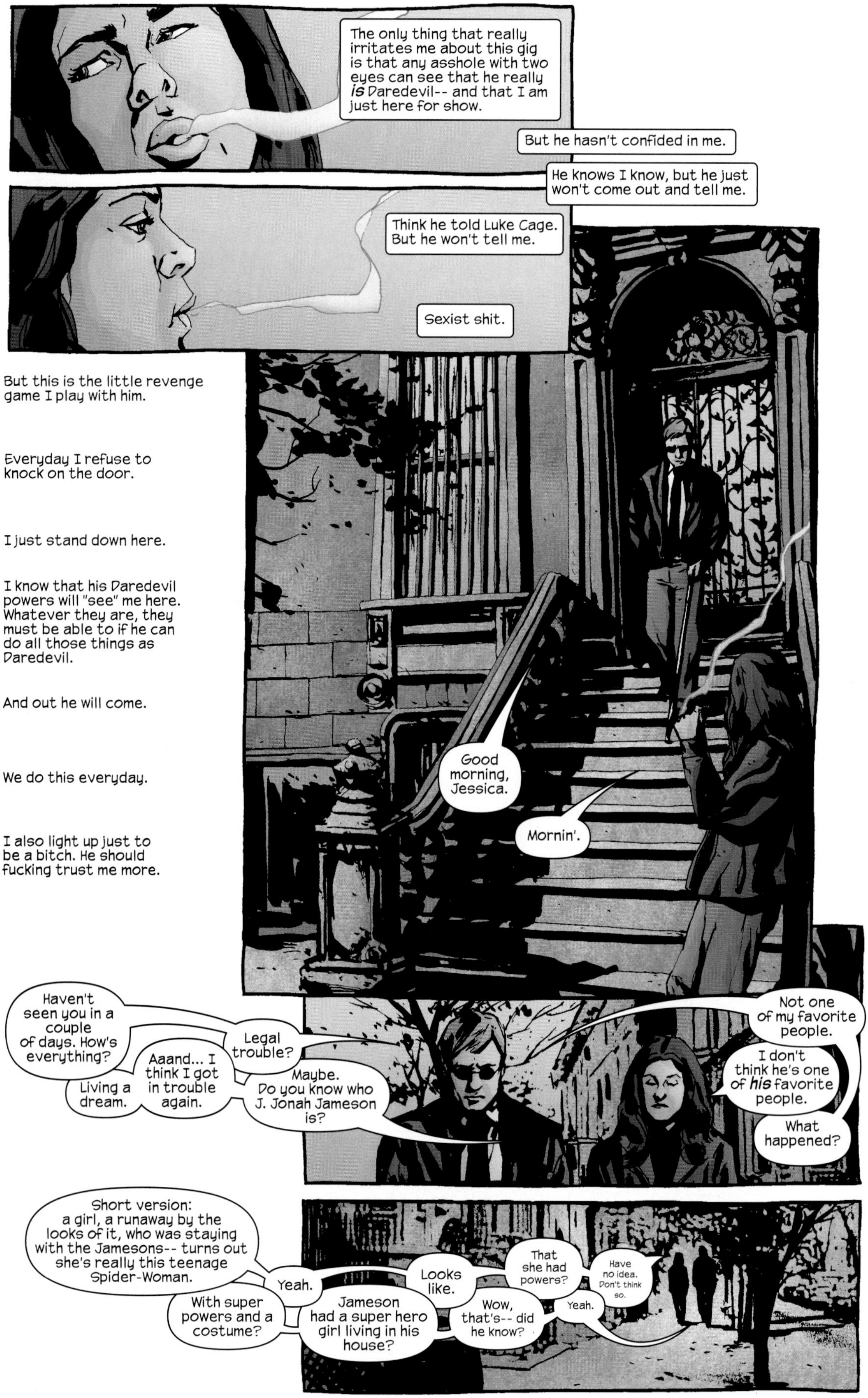

The only thing that really irritates me about this gig is that any asshole with two eyes can see that he really *is* Daredevil-- and that I am just here for show.
But he hasn't confided in me.
He knows I know, but he just won't come out and tell me.
Think he told Luke Cage. But he won't tell me.
Sexist shit.
But this is the little revenge game I play with him.
Everyday I refuse to knock on the door.
I just stand down here.
I know that his Daredevil powers will "see" me here. Whatever they are, they must be able to if he can do all those things as Daredevil.
And out he will come.
We do this everyday.
I also light up just to be a bitch. He should fucking trust me more.
Good morning, Jessica.
Mornin'.
Haven't seen you in a couple of days. How's everything?
Living a dream.
Aaand... I think I got in trouble again.
Legal trouble?
Maybe. Do you know who J. Jonah Jameson is?
Not one of my favorite people.
I don't think he's one of *his* favorite people.
What happened?
Short version: a girl, a runaway by the looks of it, who was staying with the Jamesons-- turns out she's really this teenage Spider-Woman.
With super powers and a costume?
Yeah.
Jameson had a super hero girl living in his house?
Looks like.
Wow, that's-- did he know?
That she had powers?
Yeah.
Have no idea. Don't think so.

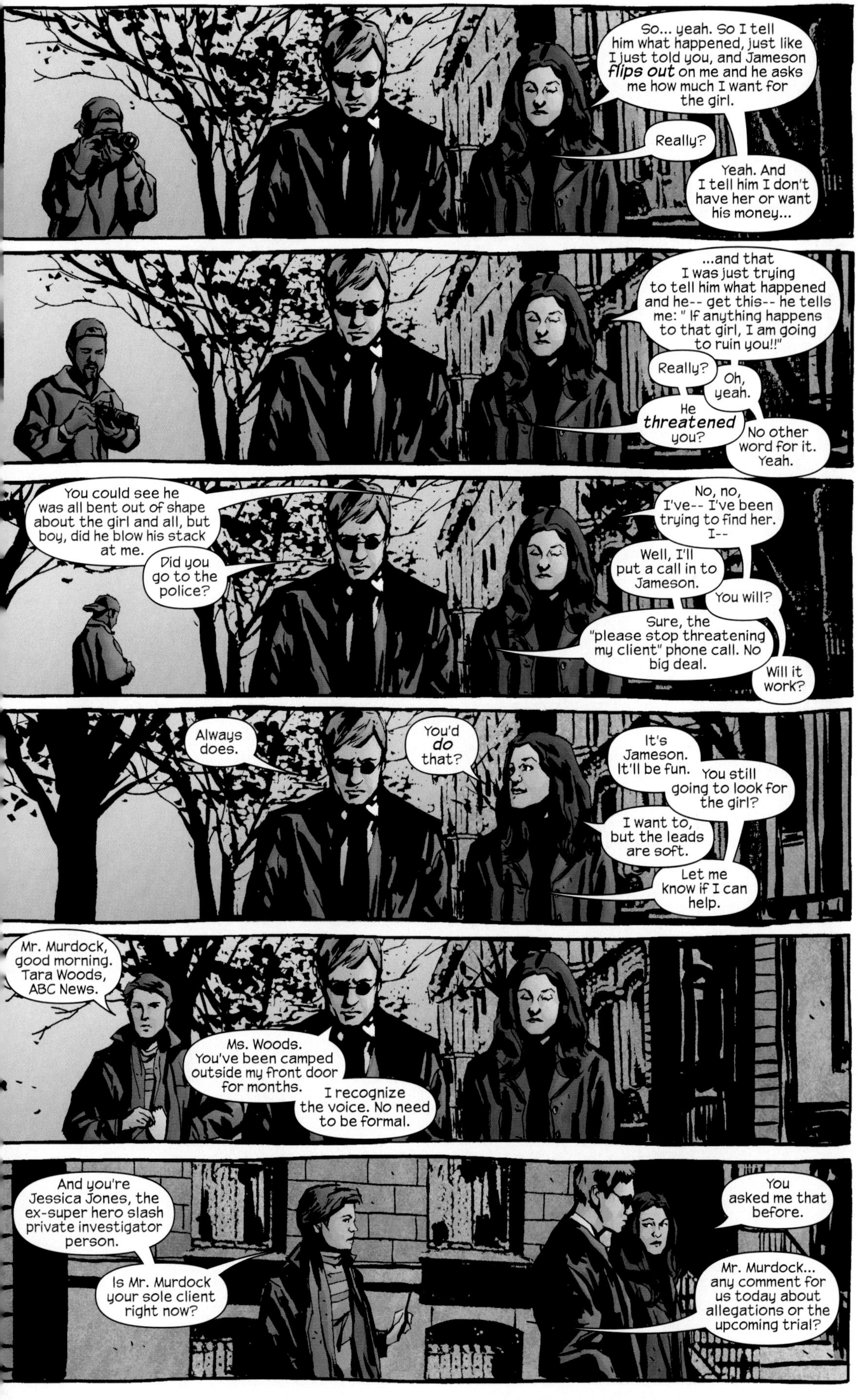
So... yeah. So I tell him what happened, just like I just told you, and Jameson *flips out* on me and he asks me how much I want for the girl.
Really?
Yeah. And I tell him I don't have her or want his money...
...and that I was just trying to tell him what happened and he-- get this-- he tells me: " If anything happens to that girl, I am going to ruin you!!"
Really?
Oh, yeah.
He *threatened* you?
No other word for it. Yeah.
You could see he was all bent out of shape about the girl and all, but boy, did he blow his stack at me.
Did you go to the police?
No, no, I've-- I've been trying to find her. I--
Well, I'll put a call in to Jameson.
You will?
Sure, the "please stop threatening my client" phone call. No big deal.
Will it work?
Always does.
You'd *do* that?
It's Jameson. It'll be fun.
You still going to look for the girl?
I want to, but the leads are soft.
Let me know if I can help.
Mr. Murdock, good morning. Tara Woods, ABC News.
Ms. Woods. You've been camped outside my front door for months.
I recognize the voice. No need to be formal.
And you're Jessica Jones, the ex-super hero slash private investigator person.
Is Mr. Murdock your sole client right now?
You asked me that before.
Mr. Murdock... any comment for us today about allegations or the upcoming trial?

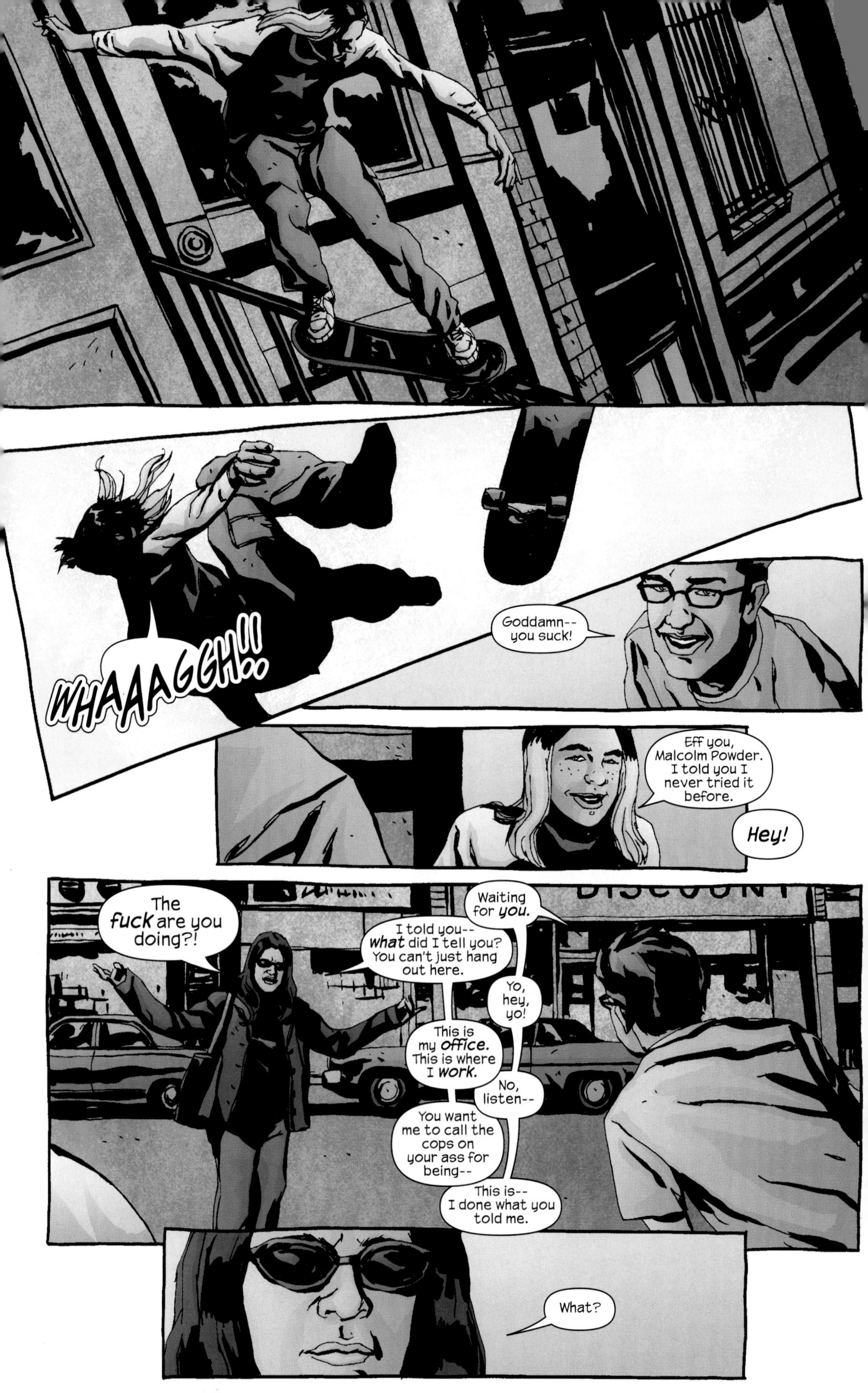
WHAAAGGH!!
Goddamn-- you suck!
Eff you, Malcolm Powder. I told you I never tried it before.
Hey!
The fuck are you doing?!
Waiting for you.
I told you-- what did I tell you? You can't just hang out here.
Yo, hey, yo!
This is my office. This is where I work.
No, listen--
You want me to call the cops on your ass for being--
This is-- I done what you told me.
What?

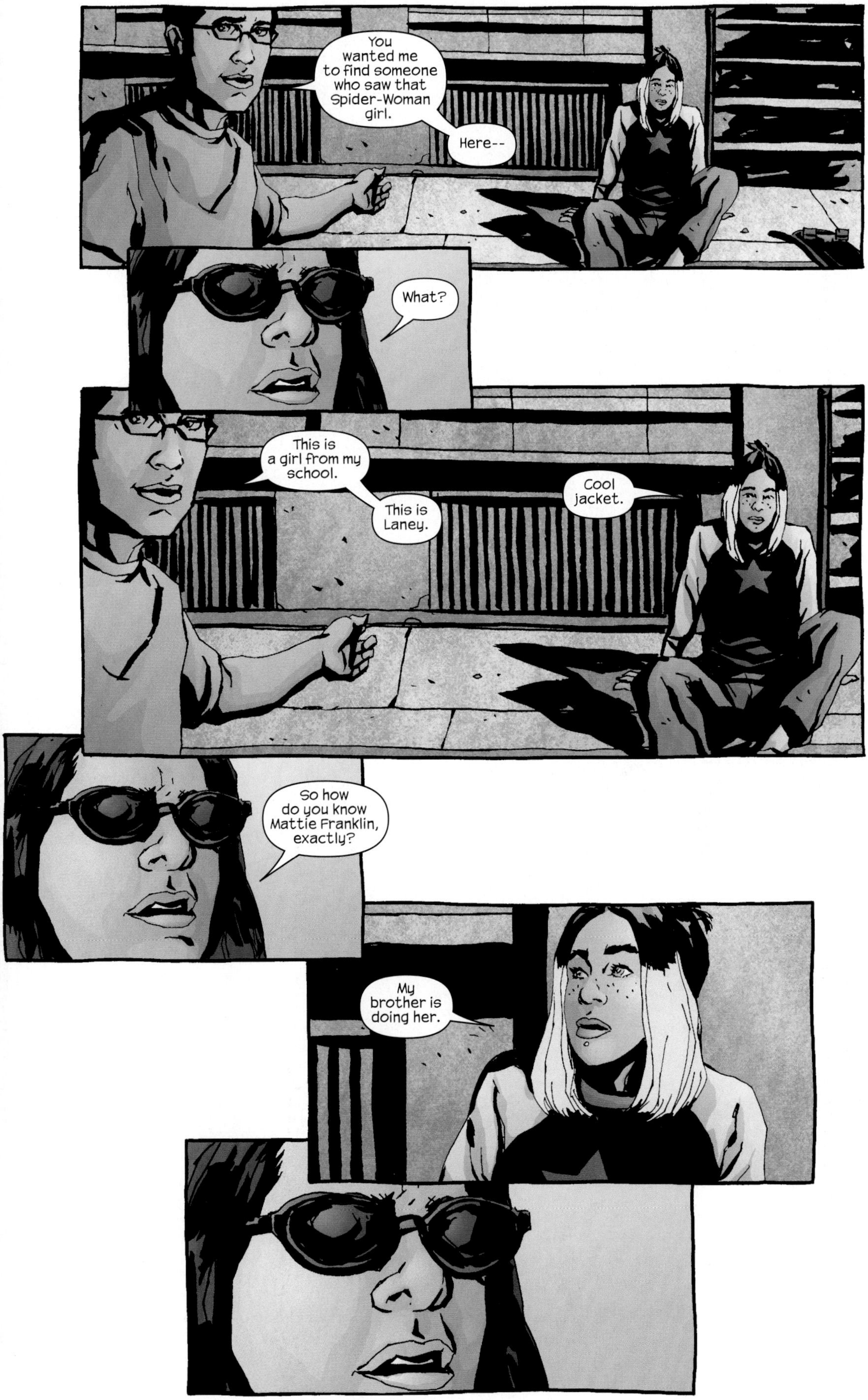
You wanted me to find someone who saw that Spider-Woman girl.
Here--
What?
This is a girl from my school.
This is Laney.
Cool jacket.
So how do you know Mattie Franklin, exactly?
My brother is doing her.

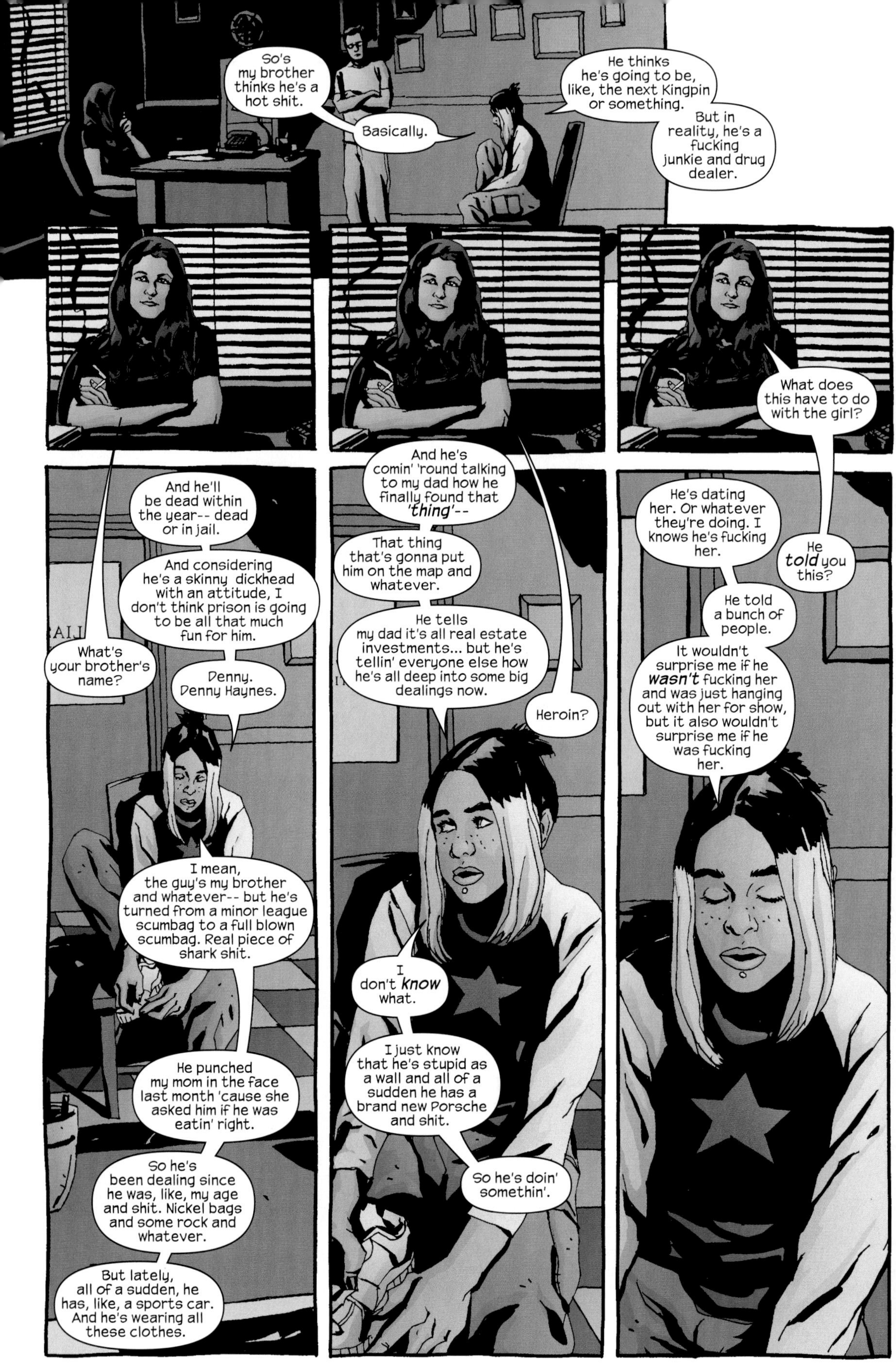
So's my brother thinks he's a hot shit.
Basically.
He thinks he's going to be, like, the next Kingpin or something.
But in reality, he's a fucking junkie and drug dealer.
What does this have to do with the girl?
And he'll be dead within the year-- dead or in jail.
And considering he's a skinny dickhead with an attitude, I don't think prison is going to be all that much fun for him.
What's your brother's name?
Denny. Denny Haynes.
I mean, the guy's my brother and whatever-- but he's turned from a minor league scumbag to a full blown scumbag. Real piece of shark shit.
He punched my mom in the face last month 'cause she asked him if he was eatin' right.
So he's been dealing since he was, like, my age and shit. Nickel bags and some rock and whatever.
But lately, all of a sudden, he has, like, a sports car. And he's wearing all these clothes.
And he's comin' 'round talking to my dad how he finally found that 'thing'--
That thing that's gonna put him on the map and whatever.
He tells my dad it's all real estate investments... but he's tellin' everyone else how he's all deep into some big dealings now.
Heroin?
I don't know what.
I just know that he's stupid as a wall and all of a sudden he has a brand new Porsche and shit.
So he's doin' somethin'.
He's dating her. Or whatever they're doing. I knows he's fucking her.
He told you this?
He told a bunch of people.
It wouldn't surprise me if he wasn't fucking her and was just hanging out with her for show, but it also wouldn't surprise me if he was fucking her.

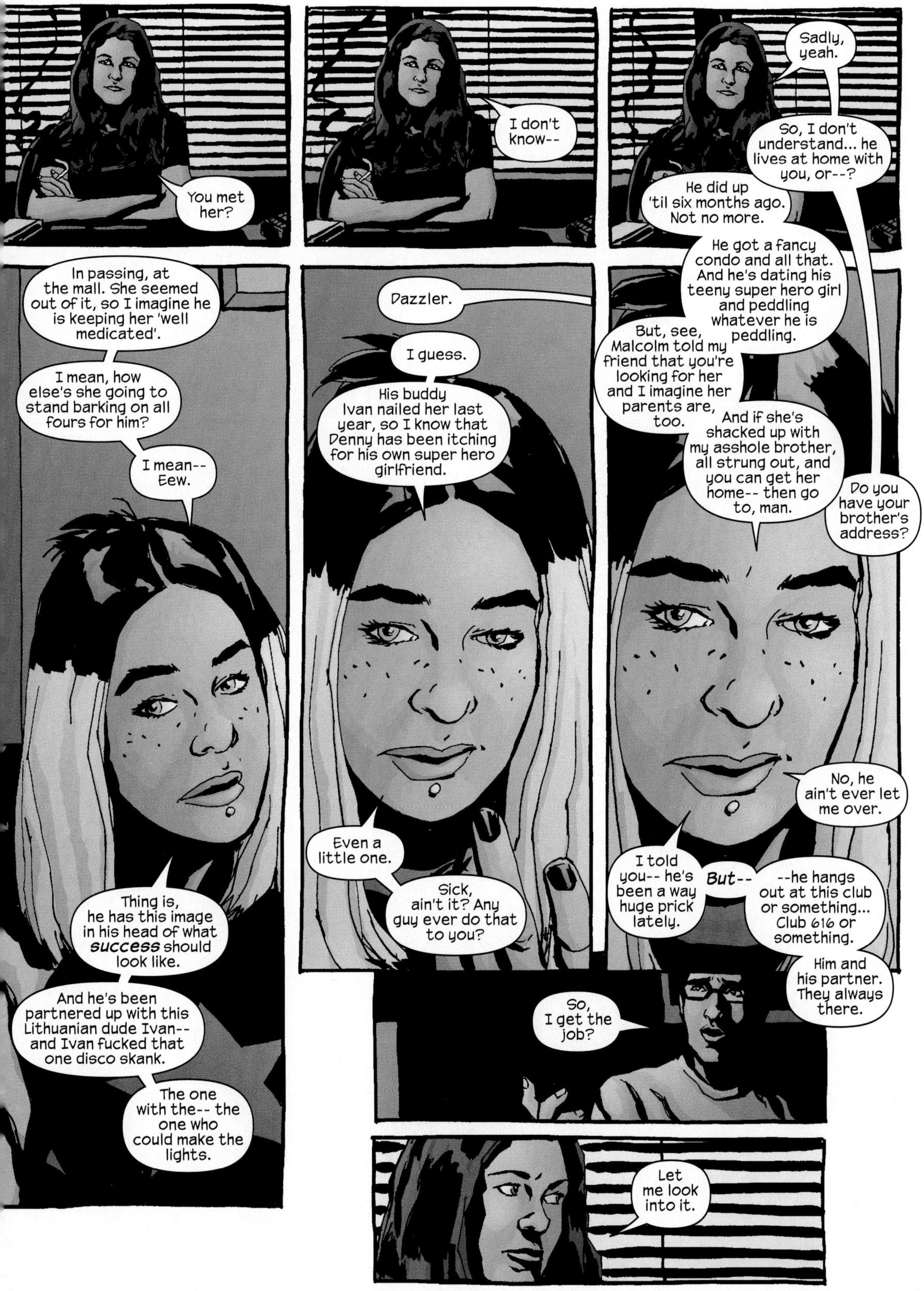
You met her?
I don't know--
Sadly, yeah.
So, I don't understand... he lives at home with you, or--?
He did up 'til six months ago. Not no more.
He got a fancy condo and all that. And he's dating his teeny super hero girl and peddling whatever he is peddling.
In passing, at the mall. She seemed out of it, so I imagine he is keeping her 'well medicated'.
I mean, how else's she going to stand barking on all fours for him?
I mean-- Eew.
Thing is, he has this image in his head of what *success* should look like.
And he's been partnered up with this Lithuanian dude Ivan-- and Ivan fucked that one disco skank.
The one with the-- the one who could make the lights.
Dazzler.
I guess.
His buddy Ivan nailed her last year, so I know that Denny has been itching for his own super hero girlfriend.
Even a little one.
Sick, ain't it? Any guy ever do that to you?
But, see, Malcolm told my friend that you're looking for her and I imagine her parents are, too.
And if she's shacked up with my asshole brother, all strung out, and you can get her home-- then go to, man.
Do you have your brother's address?
No, he ain't ever let me over.
I told you-- he's been a way huge prick lately.
But--
--he hangs out at this club or something... Club 616 or something.
Him and his partner. They always there.
So, I get the job?
Let me look into it.

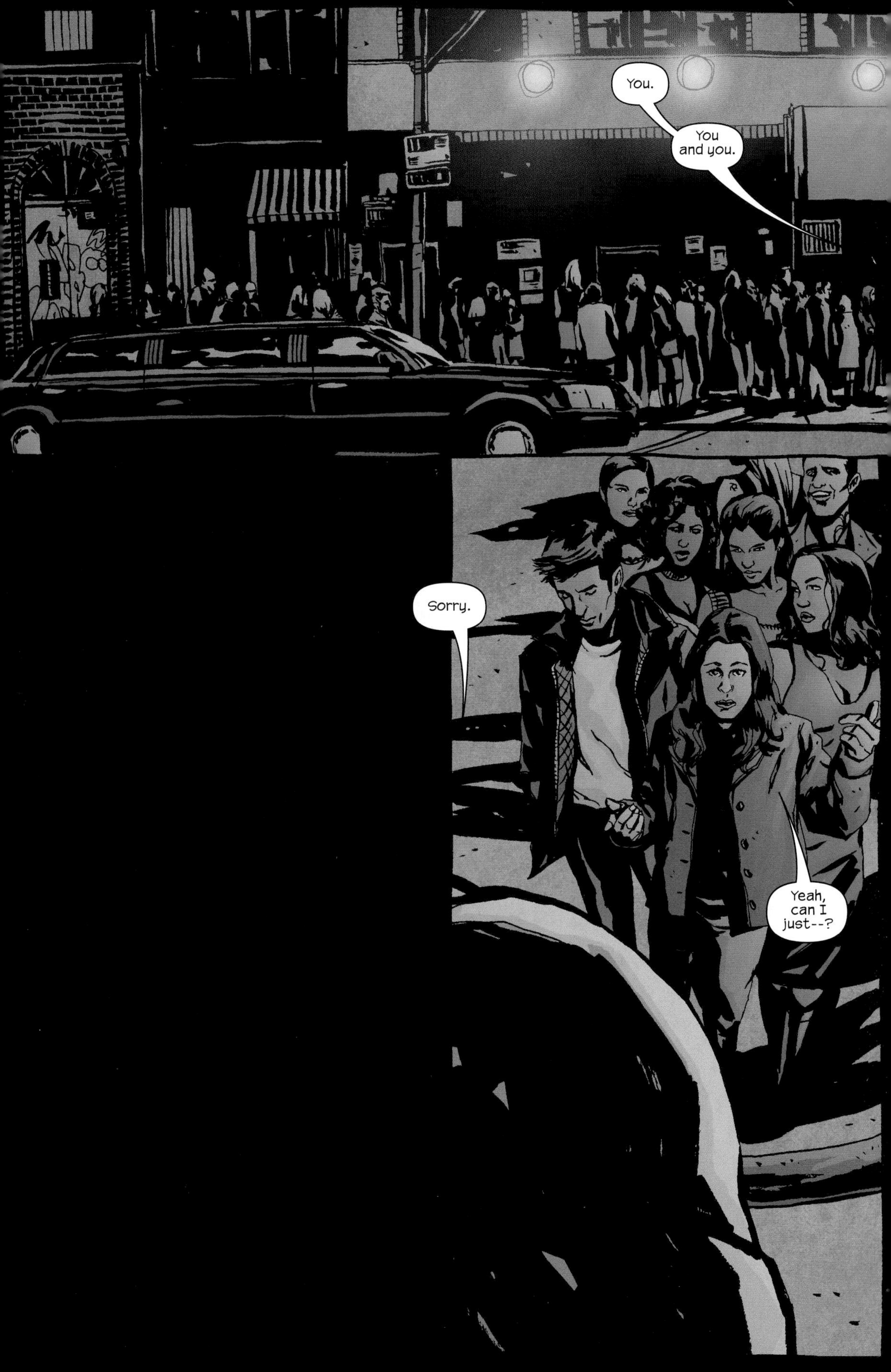
You.
You and you.
Sorry.
Yeah, can I just--?

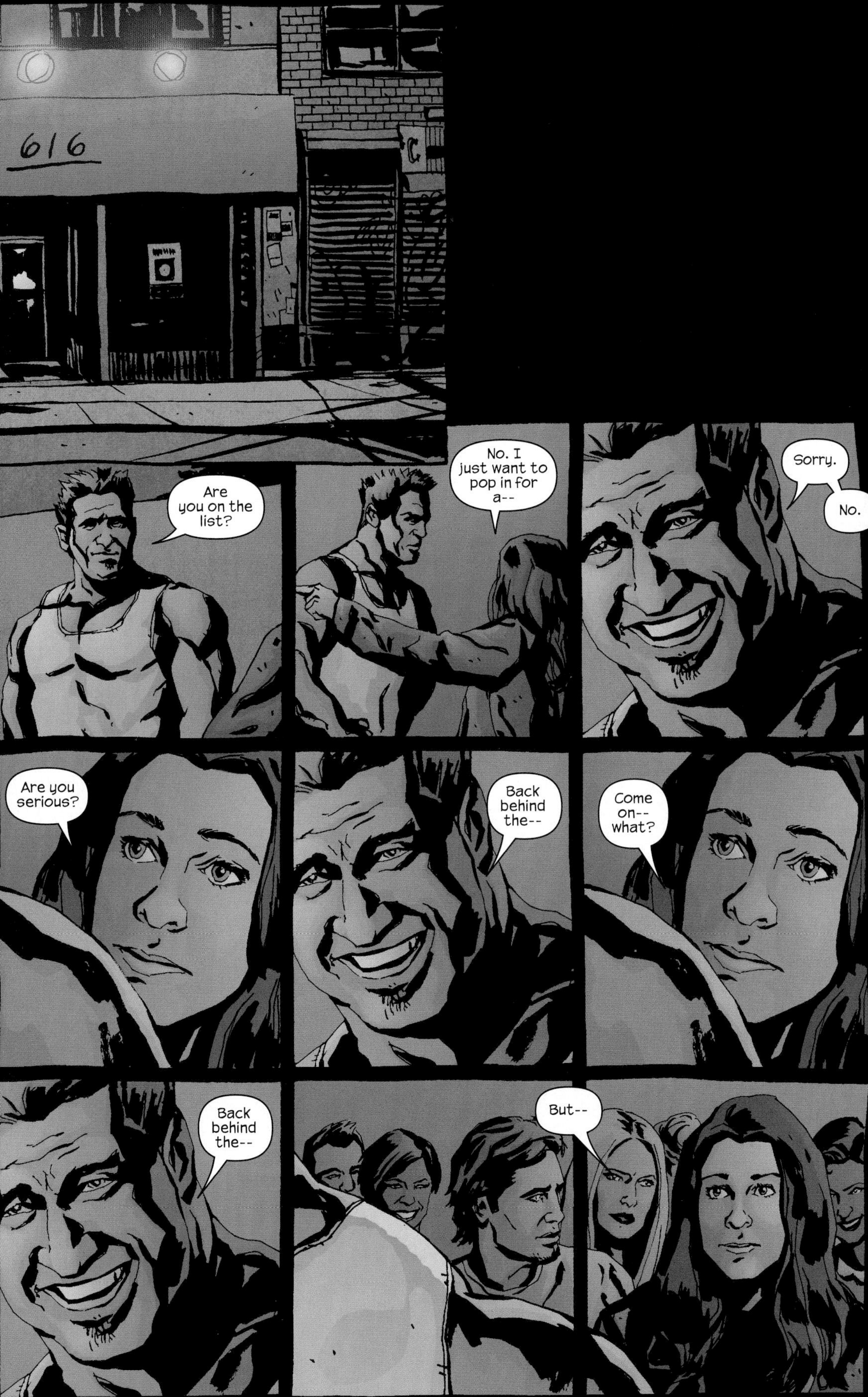
616
Are you on the list?
No. I just want to pop in for a--
Sorry.
No.
Are you serious?
Back behind the--
Come on-- what?
Back behind the--
But--

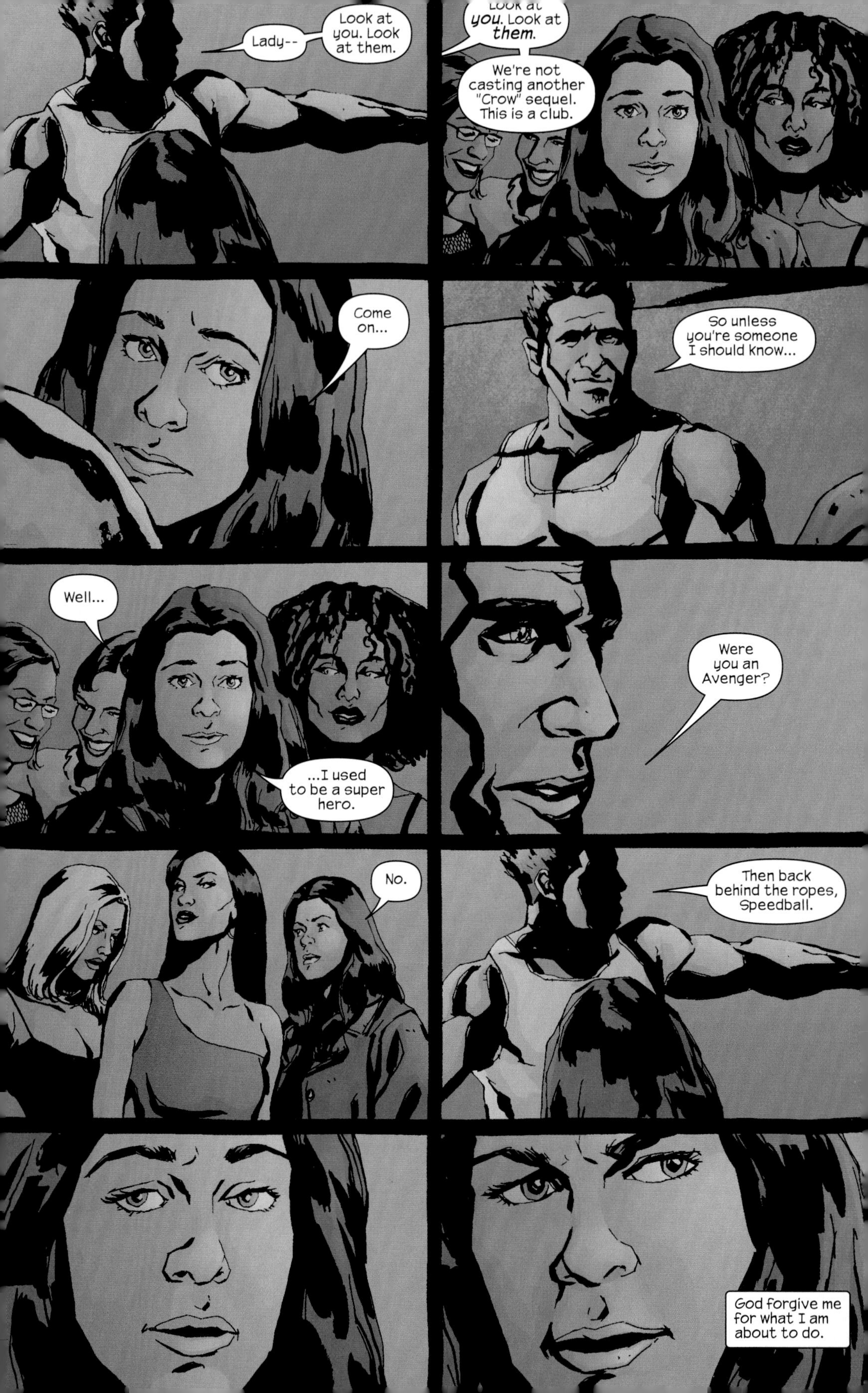
Lady--
Look at you. Look at them.
Look at you. Look at them.
We're not casting another "Crow" sequel. This is a club.
Come on...
So unless you're someone I should know...
Well...
...I used to be a super hero.
Were you an Avenger?
No.
Then back behind the ropes, Speedball.
God forgive me for what I am about to do.

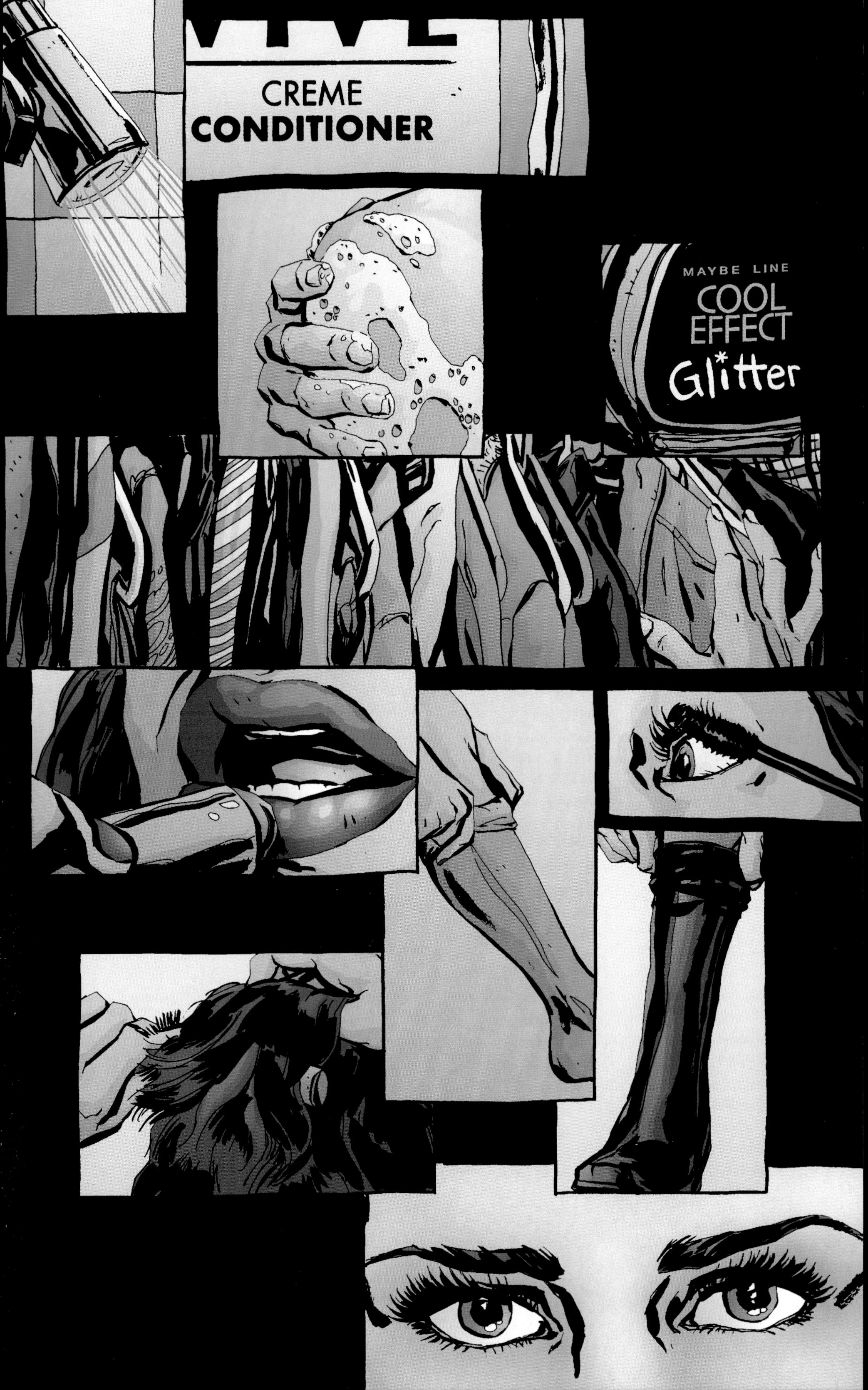
CREME
CONDITIONER
MAYBE LINE
COOL EFFECT
Glitter

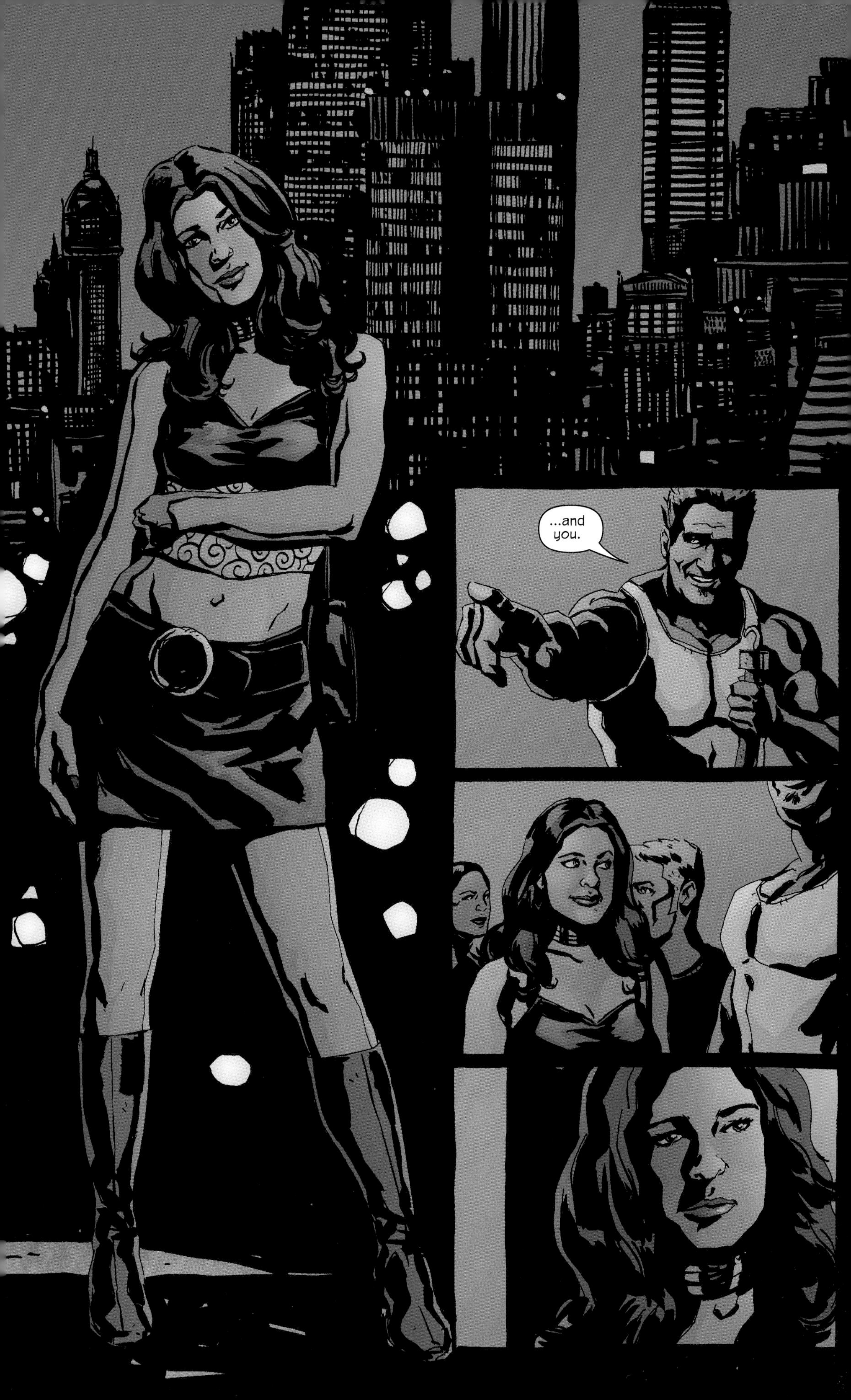
...and you.

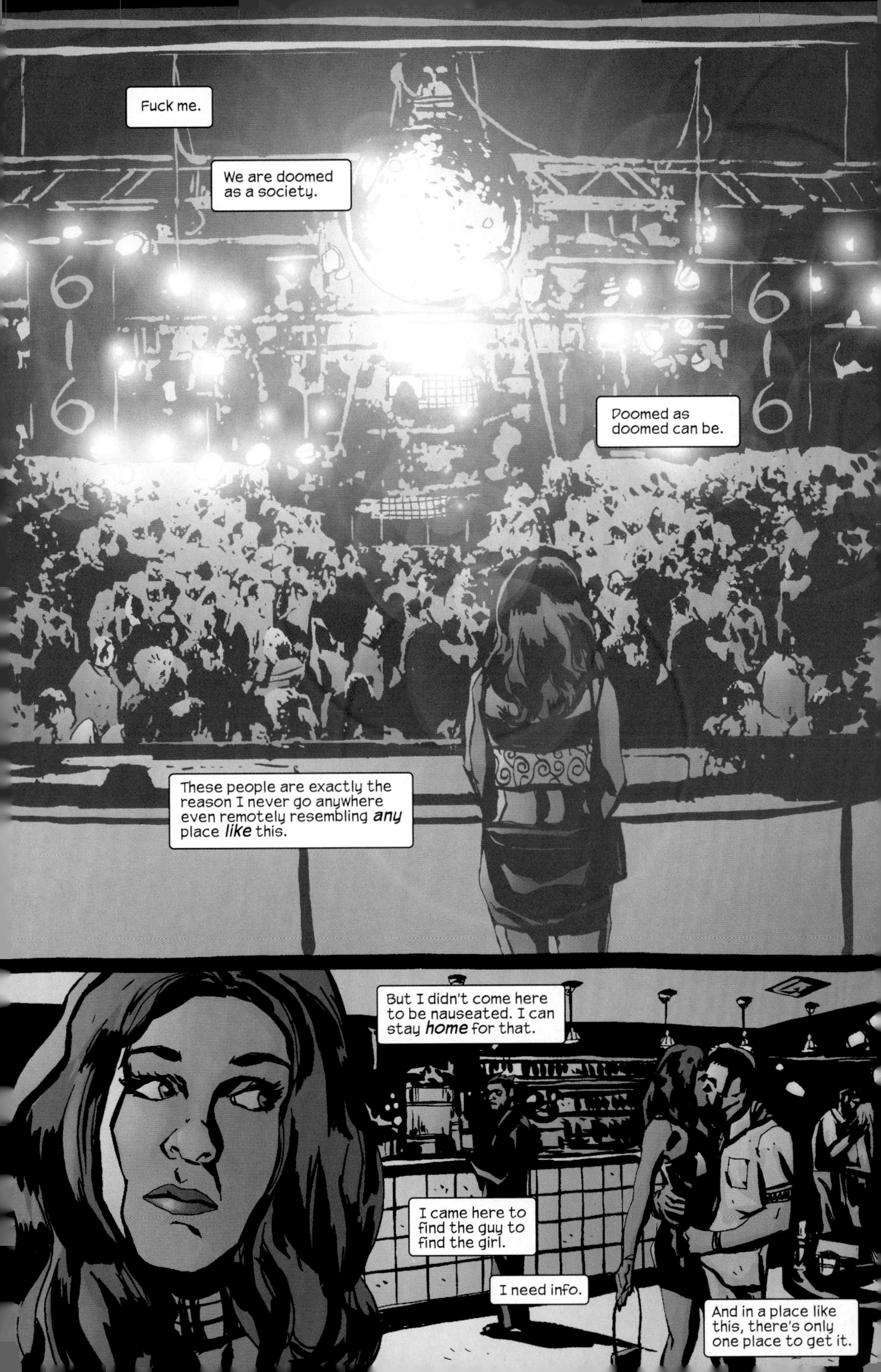

Fuck me.
We are doomed as a society.
Doomed as doomed can be.
These people are exactly the reason I never go anywhere even remotely resembling *any* place *like* this.
But I didn't come here to be nauseated. I can stay *home* for that.
I came here to find the guy to find the girl.
I need info.
And in a place like this, there's only one place to get it.

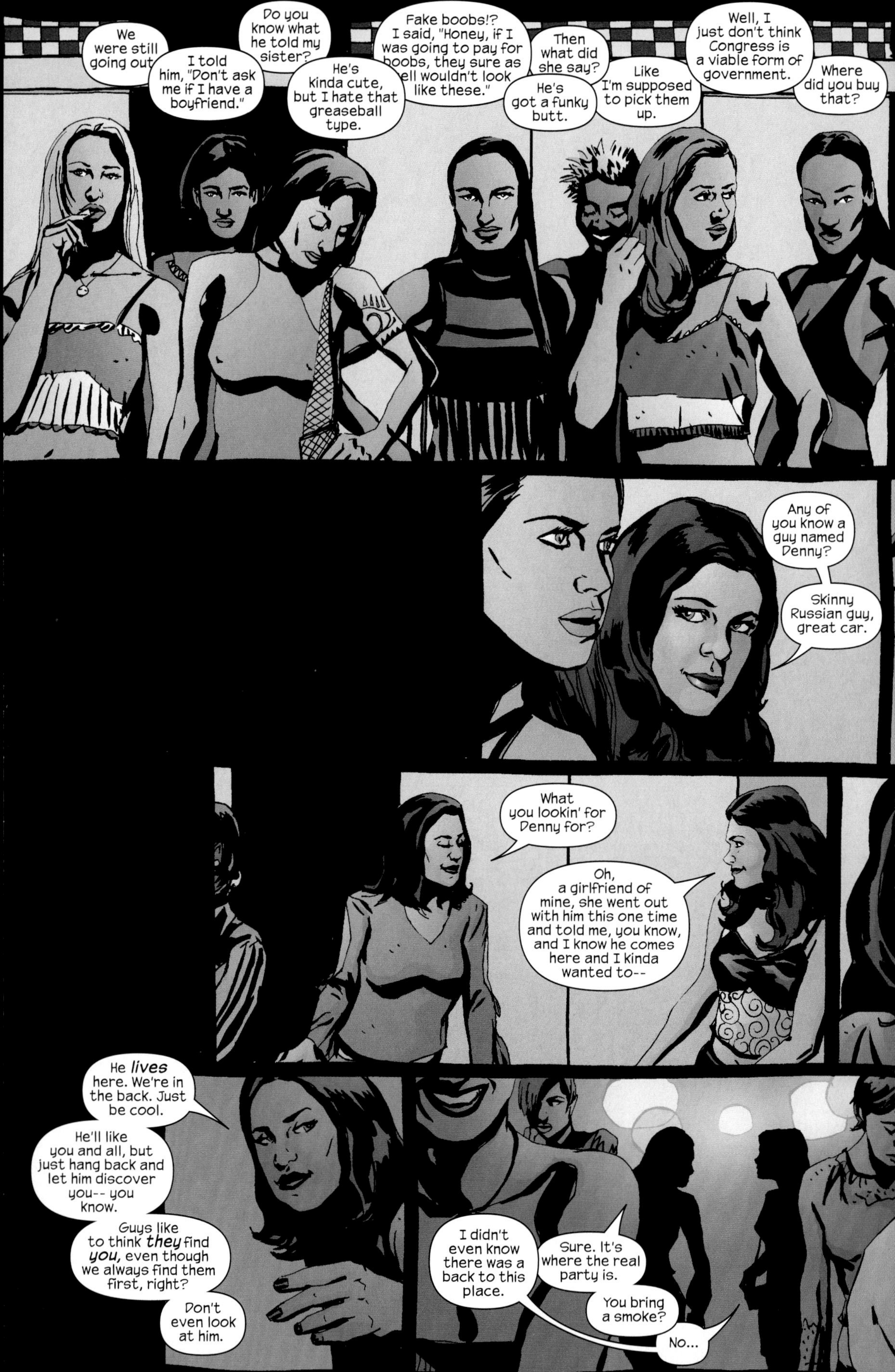
We were still going out
I told him, "Don't ask me if I have a boyfriend."
Do you know what he told my sister?
He's kinda cute, but I hate that greaseball type.
Fake boobs!? I said, "Honey, if I was going to pay for boobs, they sure as ell wouldn't look like these."
Then what did she say?
He's got a funky butt.
Like I'm supposed to pick them up.
Well, I just don't think Congress is a viable form of government.
Where did you buy that?
Any of you know a guy named Denny?
Skinny Russian guy, great car.
What you lookin' for Denny for?
Oh, a girlfriend of mine, she went out with him this one time and told me, you know, and I know he comes here and I kinda wanted to--
He *lives* here. We're in the back. Just be cool.
He'll like you and all, but just hang back and let him discover you-- you know.
Guys like to think ***they*** find ***you***, even though we always find them first, right?
Don't even look at him.
I didn't even know there was a back to this place.
Sure. It's where the real party is.
You bring a smoke?
No...

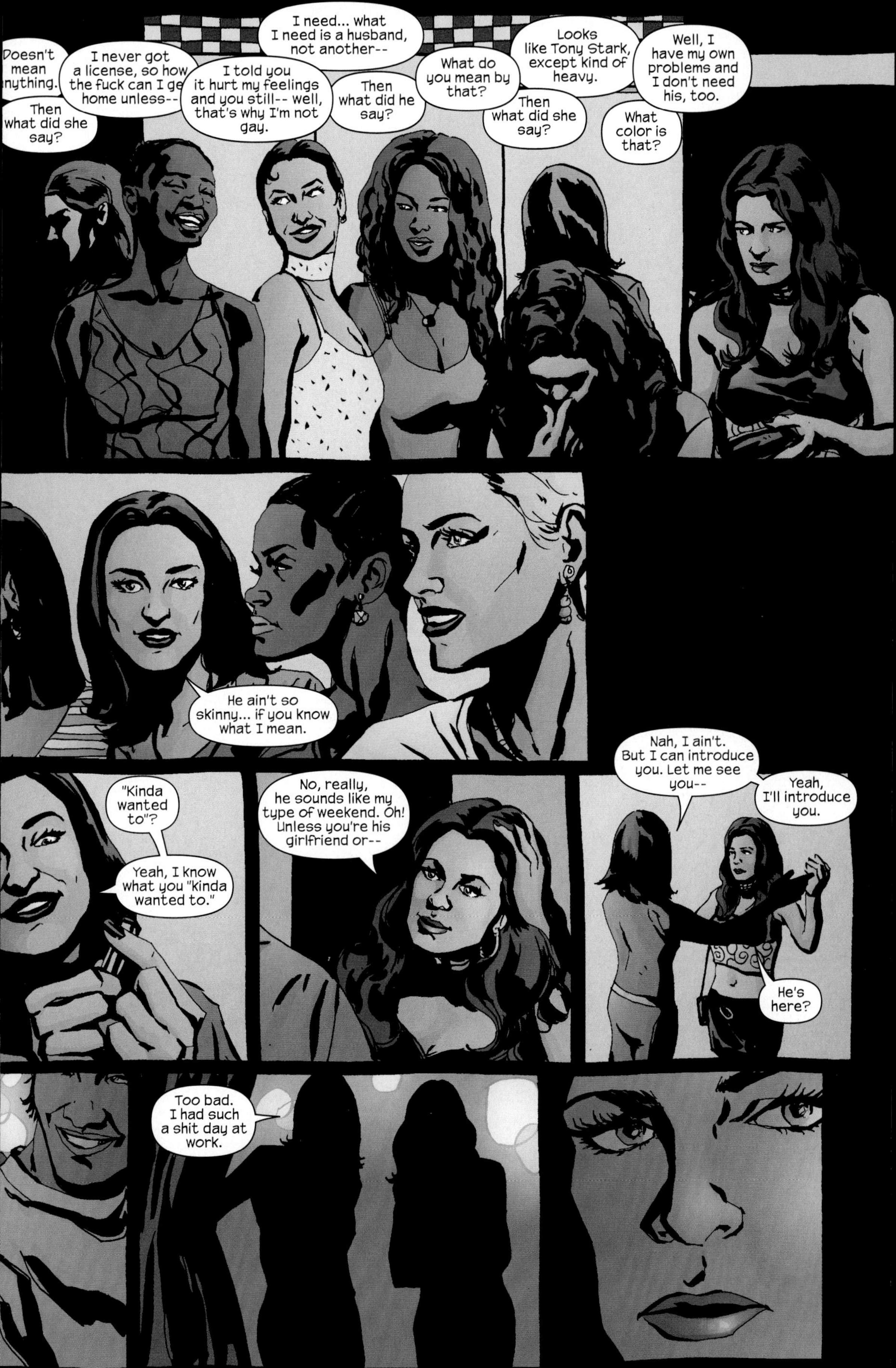
Doesn't mean nything.
Then what did she say?
I never got a license, so how the fuck can I ge home unless--
I need... what I need is a husband, not another--
I told you it hurt my feelings and you still-- well, that's why I'm not gay.
Then what did he say?
What do you mean by that?
Looks like Tony Stark, except kind of heavy.
Then what did she say?
Well, I have my own problems and I don't need his, too.
What color is that?
He ain't so skinny... if you know what I mean.
"Kinda wanted to"?
Yeah, I know what you "kinda wanted to."
No, really, he sounds like my type of weekend. Oh! Unless you're his girlfriend or--
Nah, I ain't. But I can introduce you. Let me see you--
Yeah, I'll introduce you.
He's here?
Too bad. I had such a shit day at work.

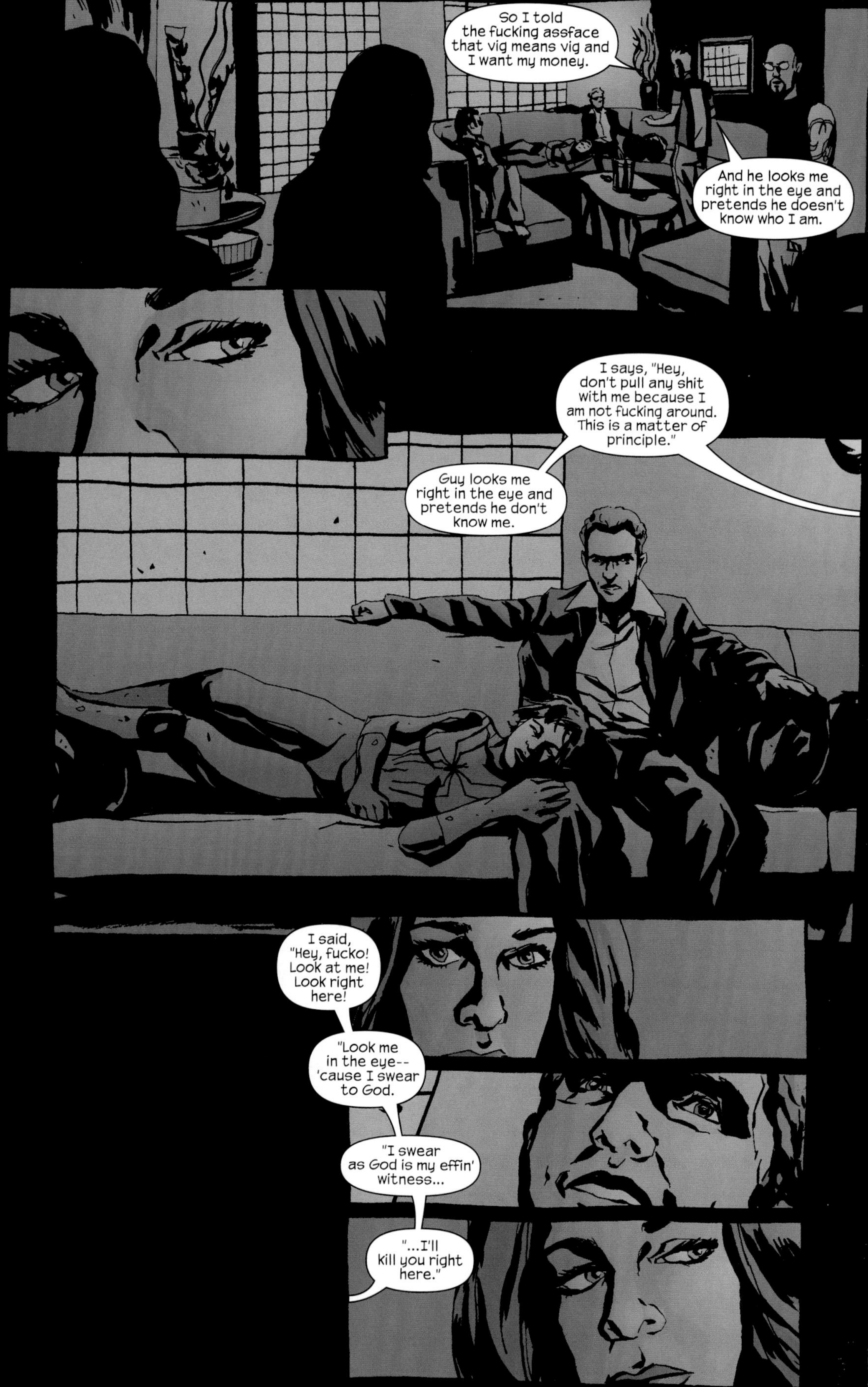
So I told the fucking assface that vig means vig and I want my money.
And he looks me right in the eye and pretends he doesn't know who I am.
I says, "Hey, don't pull any shit with me because I am not fucking around. This is a matter of principle."
Guy looks me right in the eye and pretends he don't know me.
I said, "Hey, fucko! Look at me! Look right here!
"Look me in the eye-- 'cause I swear to God.
"I swear as God is my effin' witness...
"...I'll kill you right here."

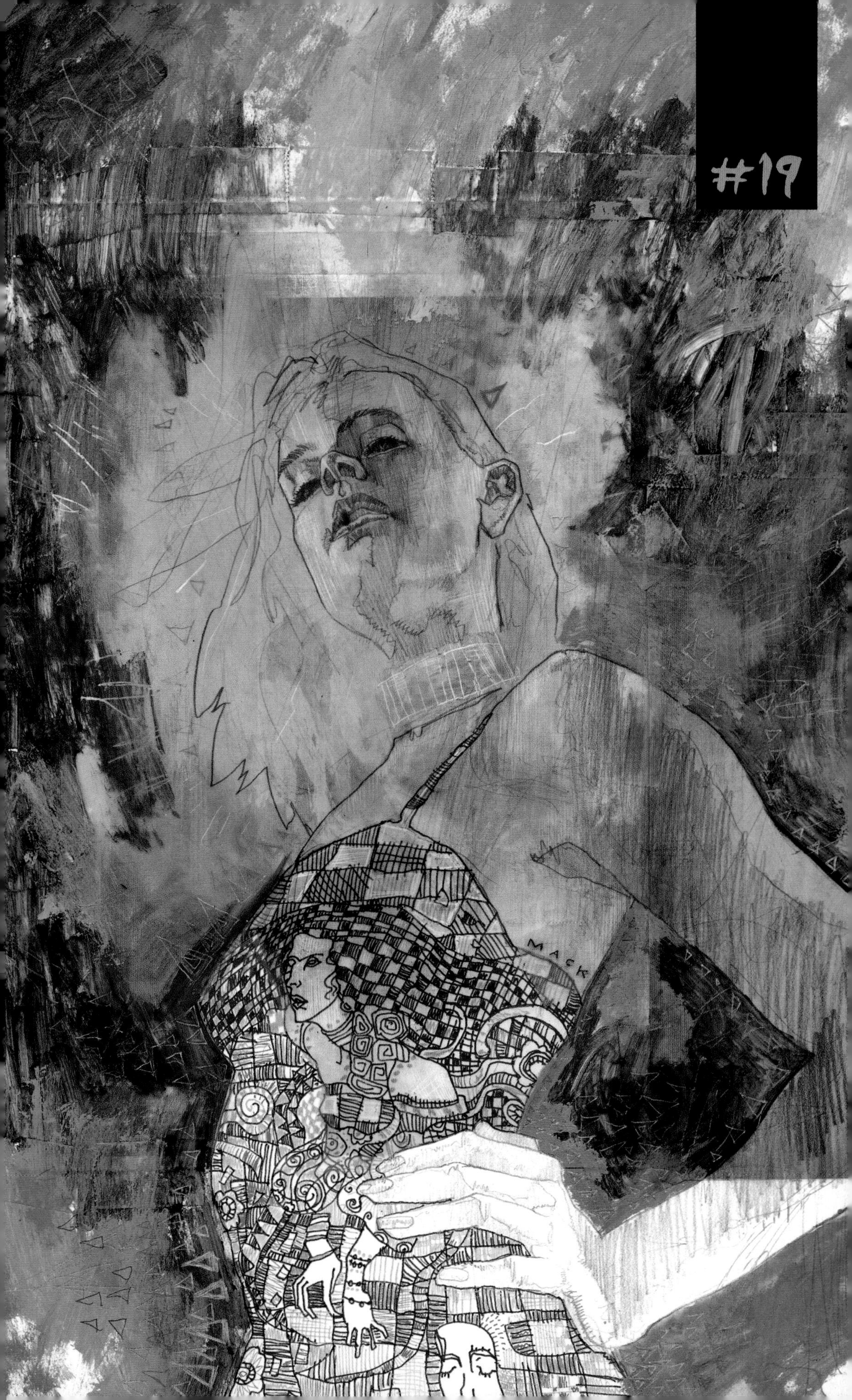
#19
MACK

It's her.

Mattie Franklin.

Spider-Woman.

It's her and she looks right at me.

Crap! I didn't expect her to be here. She's only a kid. This is a nightclub and she's only a kid.

I was looking for her boyfriend here-- get to him to get to her-- but here she is.

In costume? In a nightclub? What the fuck is going on here? What is she on?

She's looking right at me.

The jig is up. I'm going to have to grab her and run.

Fuck, though.

I don't know what the story is here-- I don't know who is who. If I just grab her and run, someone might get hurt.

Or these a-holes might come looking for her at the Jamesons', where she lives-- and I-- ugghh!!

I don't know what to do.

Jesus, she looks even worse than she did in my apartment a couple of days ago.

What is she on? Heroin?

I want to cry just from looking at her. She looks right at me, but-- is she so out of it she doesn't recognize me?

Maybe it's the outfit and incredibly whorish makeup I put on to get into this trendy fuckhole.

Mattie Franklin. It's hard to believe she's a super hero.

Kids shouldn't be super heroes-- look at her. God damn, on my worst day I never looked that bad.

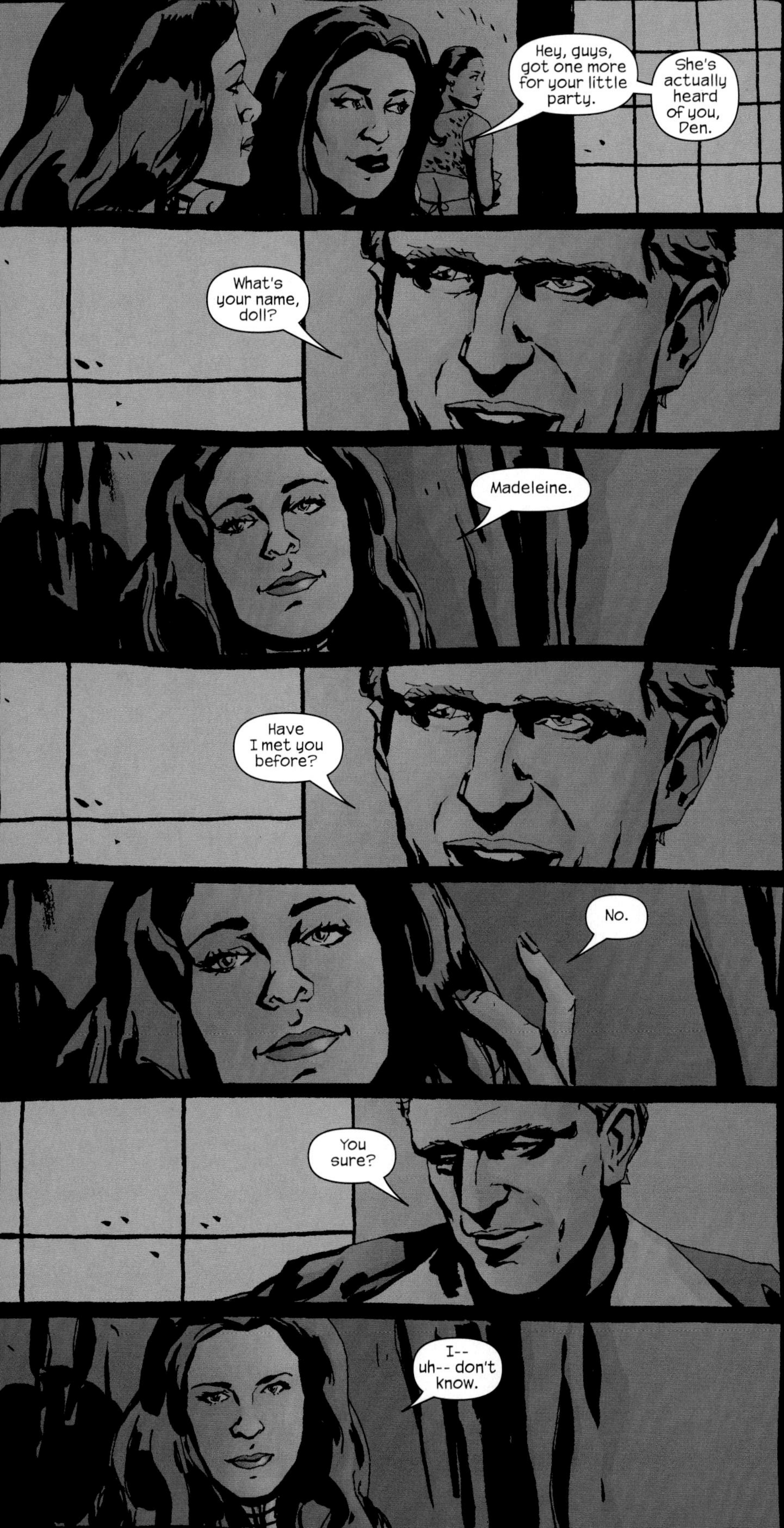
Hey, guys, got one more for your little party.
She's actually heard of you, Den.
What's your name, doll?
Madeleine.
Have I met you before?
No.
You sure?
I-- uh-- don't know.

The guy looks right at me. Denny Haynes. Fucker!

The guy I was looking for. Goes around telling everyone he's fucking a super hero and here he is. And he's got her-- what has he done to her?

He looks right at me and it hits me like a brick-- ***this*** is it.

This is what that psychic bitch Madame Web was babbling about.

She described this exact scene, and ***fuck!*** This is it! Fuck! ***Fuck!!***

What did she say? She said I will ***fight*** this girl. She said either I will ***die*** or ***she*** will die ***fighting.***

Someone here is going to ***die??!***

I don't want ***this!*** I don't want to ***fight*** her, and I sure as shit don't want to ***die.***

And I sure as shit don't want to kill a sixteen-year-old junkie super hero girl that doesn't even know where she is. Matt Murdock would kill me for doing this.

This isn't what I want. This isn't what I ***want*** in my life-- what the fuck am I ***doing*** here? I didn't have to do this! What the fuck am I thinking?

All the things I've done, and I'll be remembered as the broken-down super hero that killed a teenager in self-defense.

Matt Murdock. Why do I keep thinking about Matt Murdock? Oh, my God! I'm in love with Matt Murdock.

Fucker!!

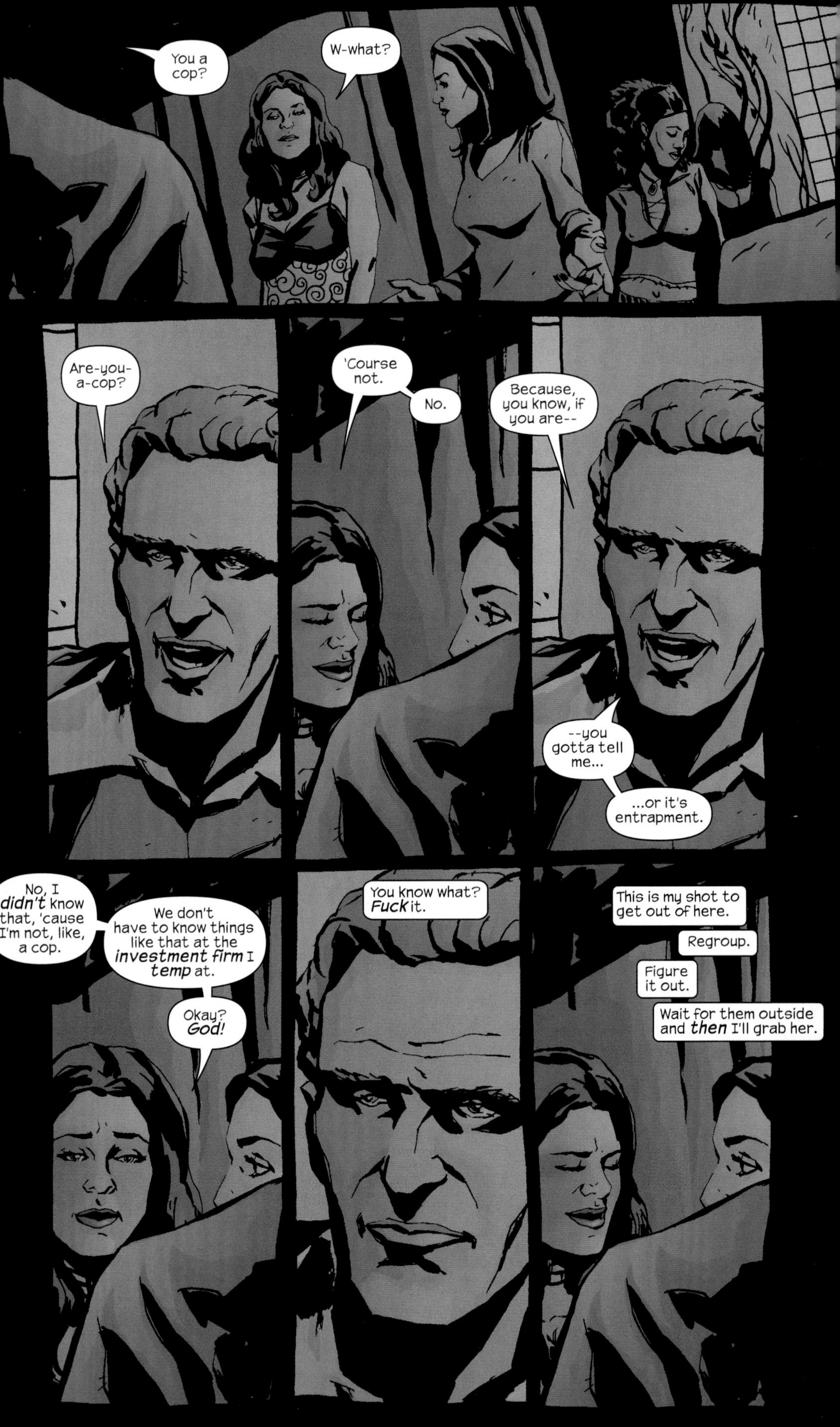
You a cop?
W-what?
Are-you-a-cop?
'Course not.
No.
Because, you know, if you are--
--you gotta tell me...
...or it's entrapment.
No, I *didn't* know that, 'cause I'm not, like, a cop.
We don't have to know things like that at the *investment firm* I *temp* at.
Okay? *God!*
You know what? *Fuck* it.
This is my shot to get out of here.
Regroup.
Figure it out.
Wait for them outside and *then* I'll grab her.

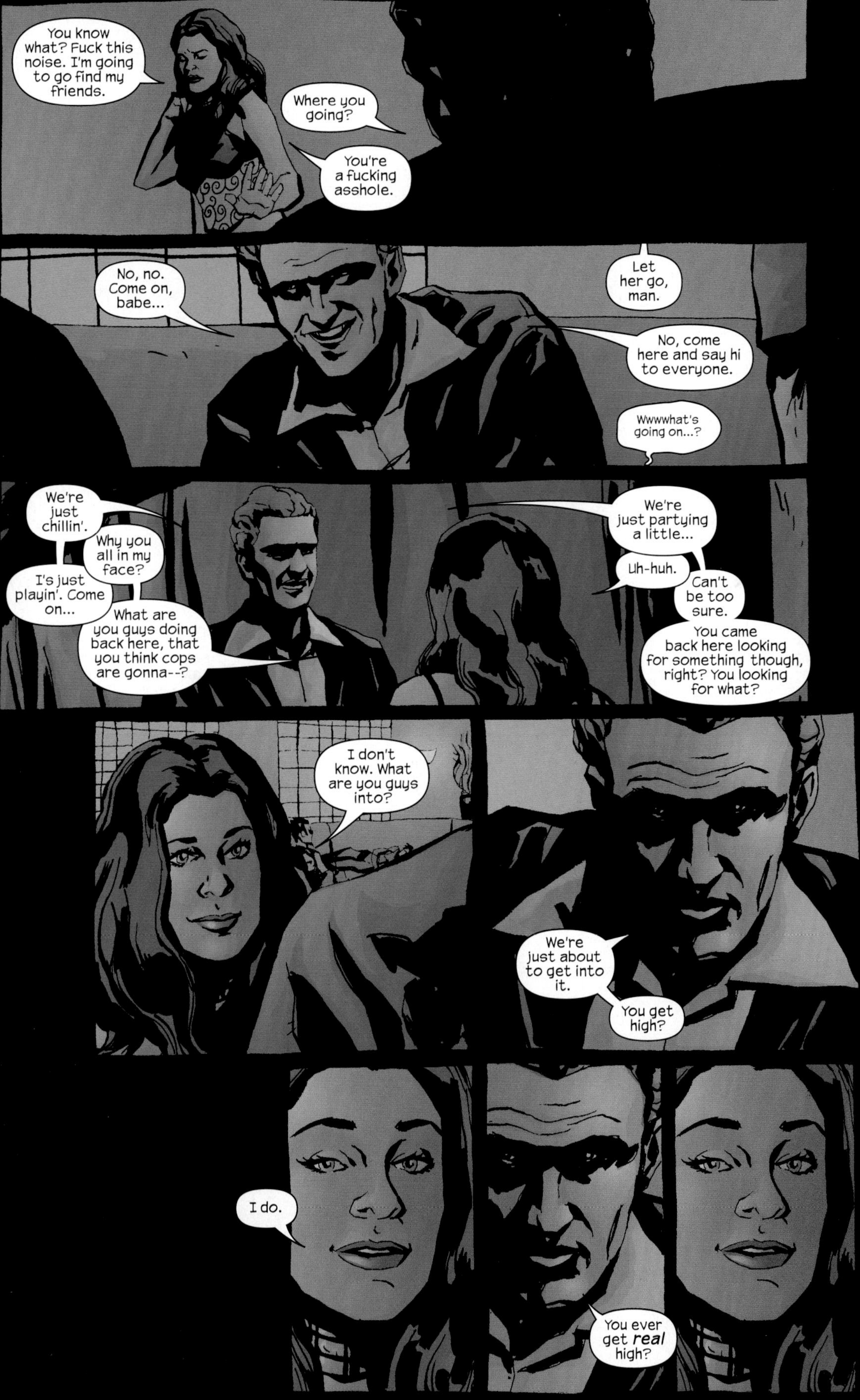

You know what? Fuck this noise. I'm going to go find my friends.
Where you going?
You're a fucking asshole.
No, no. Come on, babe...
Let her go, man.
No, come here and say hi to everyone.
Wwwwhat's going on...?
We're just chillin'.
Why you all in my face?
I's just playin'. Come on...
What are you guys doing back here, that you think cops are gonna--?
We're just partying a little...
Uh-huh.
Can't be too sure.
You came back here looking for something though, right? You looking for what?
I don't know. What are you guys into?
We're just about to get into it.
You get high?
I do.
You ever get *real* high?

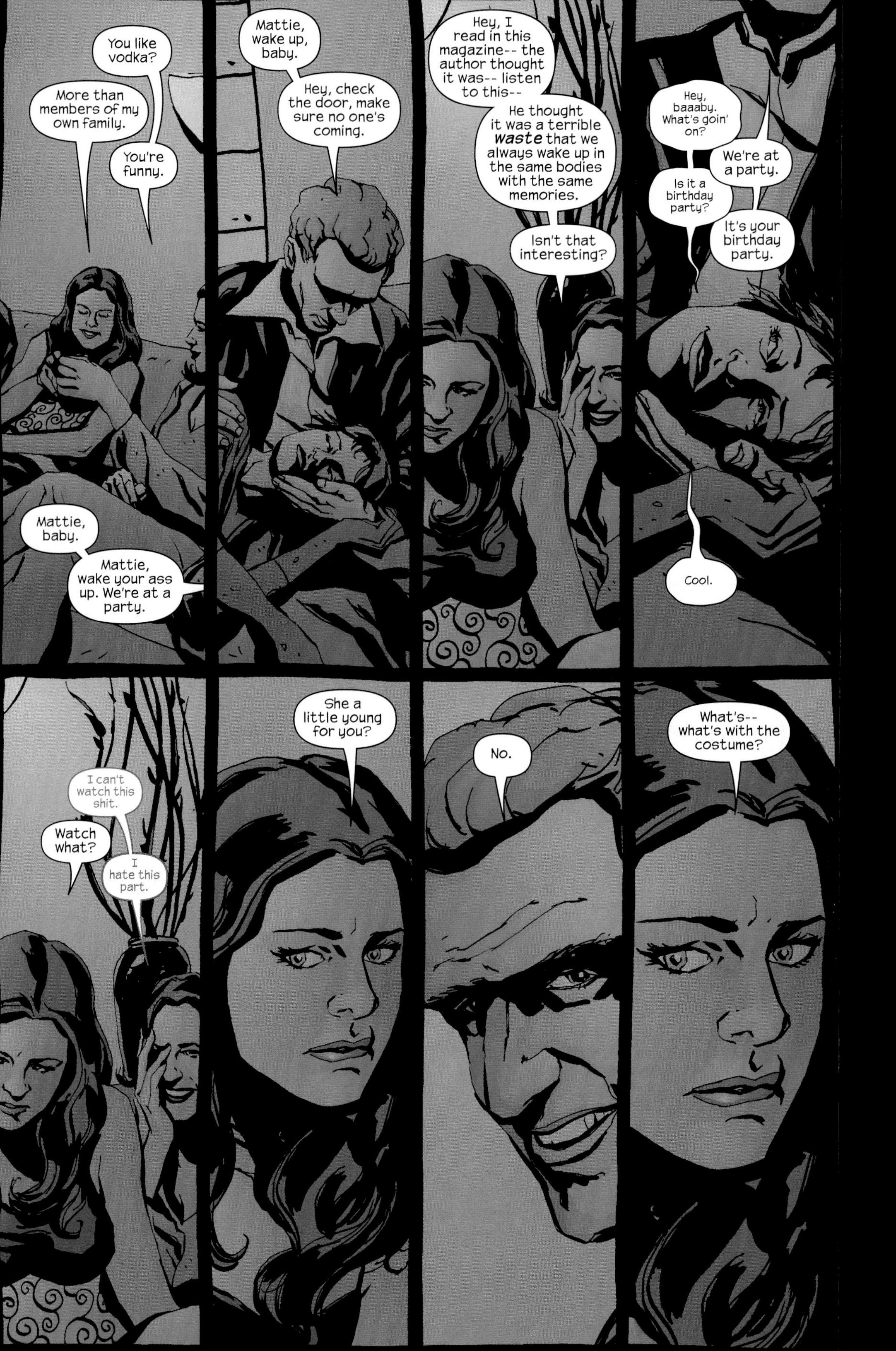
You like vodka?
More than members of my own family.
You're funny.
Mattie, baby.
Mattie, wake your ass up. We're at a party.
Mattie, wake up, baby.
Hey, check the door, make sure no one's coming.
Hey, I read in this magazine-- the author thought it was-- listen to this--
He thought it was a terrible *waste* that we always wake up in the same bodies with the same memories.
Isn't that interesting?
Hey, baaaby. What's goin' on?
We're at a party.
Is it a birthday party?
It's your birthday party.
Cool.
I can't watch this shit.
Watch what?
I hate this part.
She a little young for you?
No.
What's-- what's with the costume?

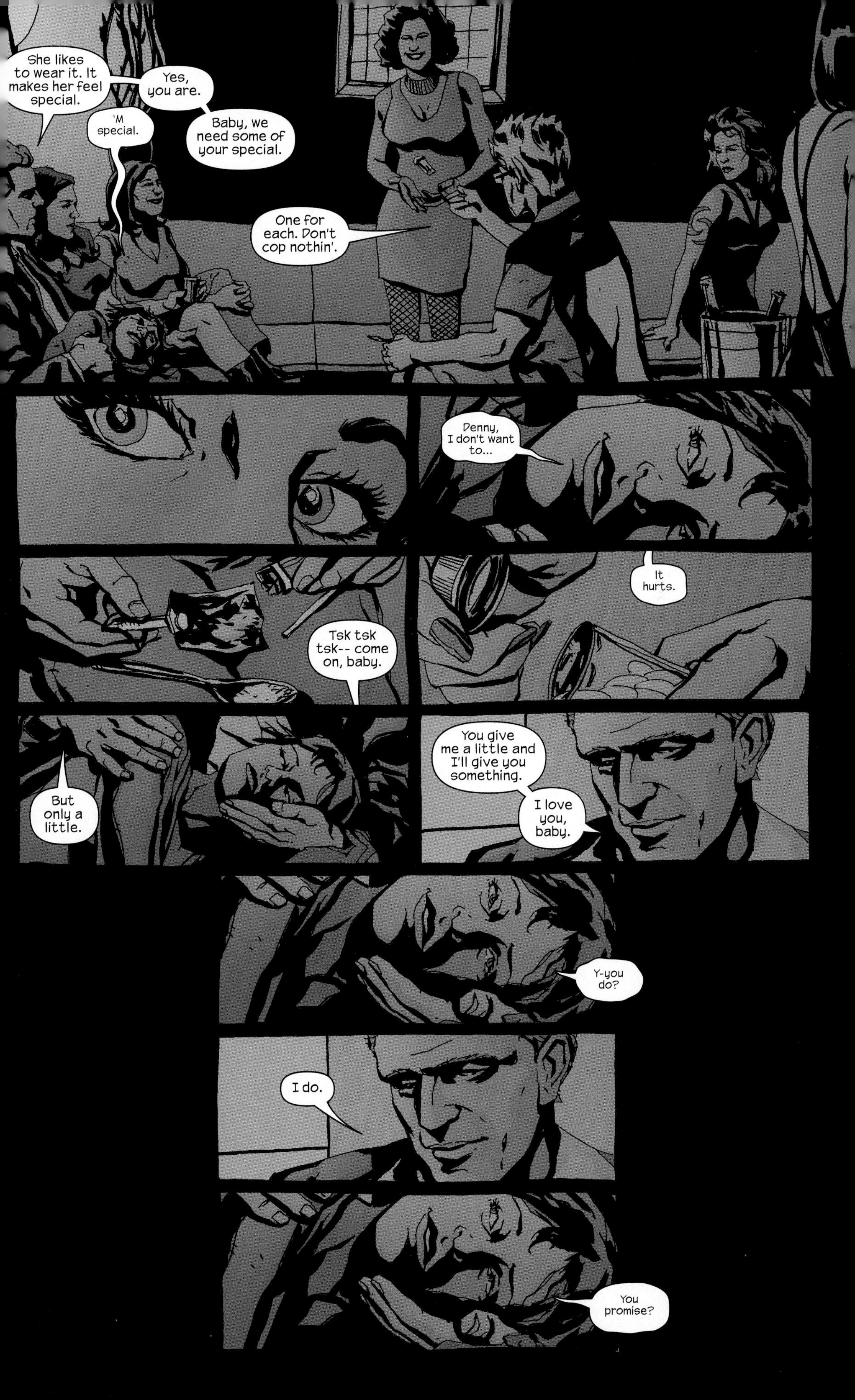
She likes to wear it. It makes her feel special.
Yes, you are.
'M special.
Baby, we need some of your special.
One for each. Don't cop nothin'.
Denny, I don't want to...
Tsk tsk tsk-- come on, baby.
It hurts.
But only a little.
You give me a little and I'll give you something.
I love you, baby.
Y-you do?
I do.
You promise?

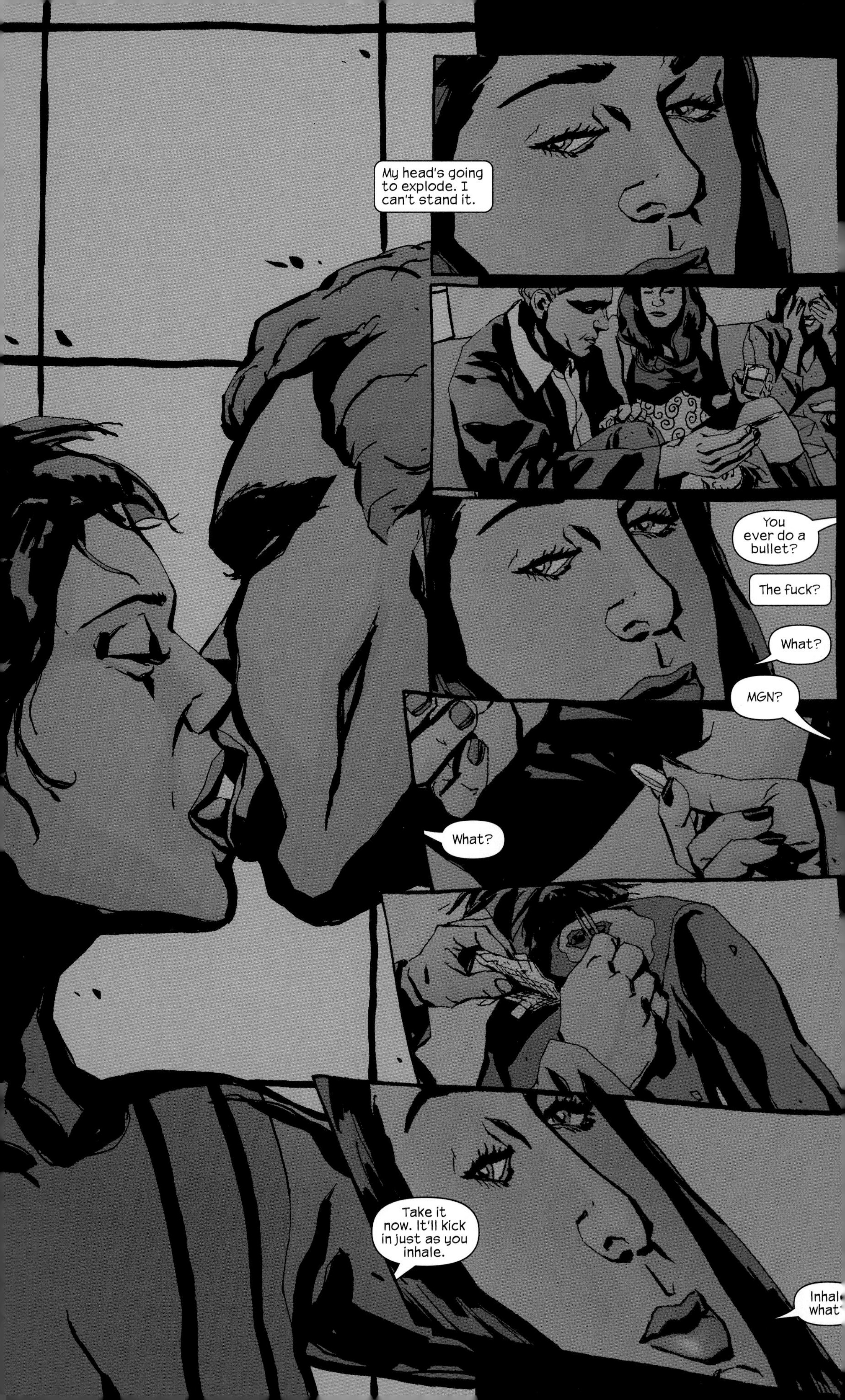
My head's going to explode. I can't stand it.
You ever do a bullet?
The fuck?
What?
MGN?
What?
Take it now. It'll kick in just as you inhale.

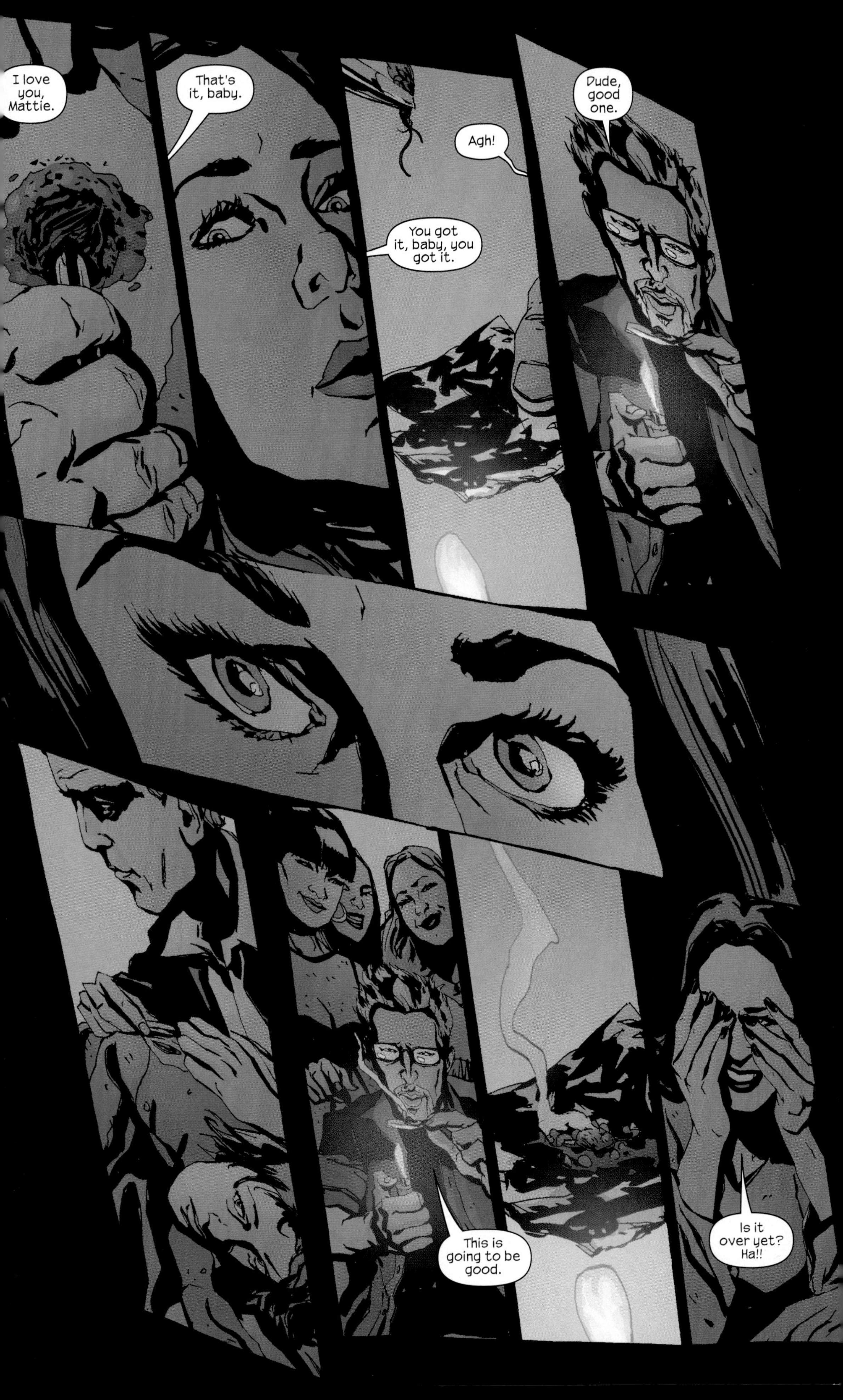
I love you, Mattie.
That's it, baby.
Agh!
You got it, baby, you got it.
Dude, good one.
This is going to be good.
Is it over yet? Ha!!

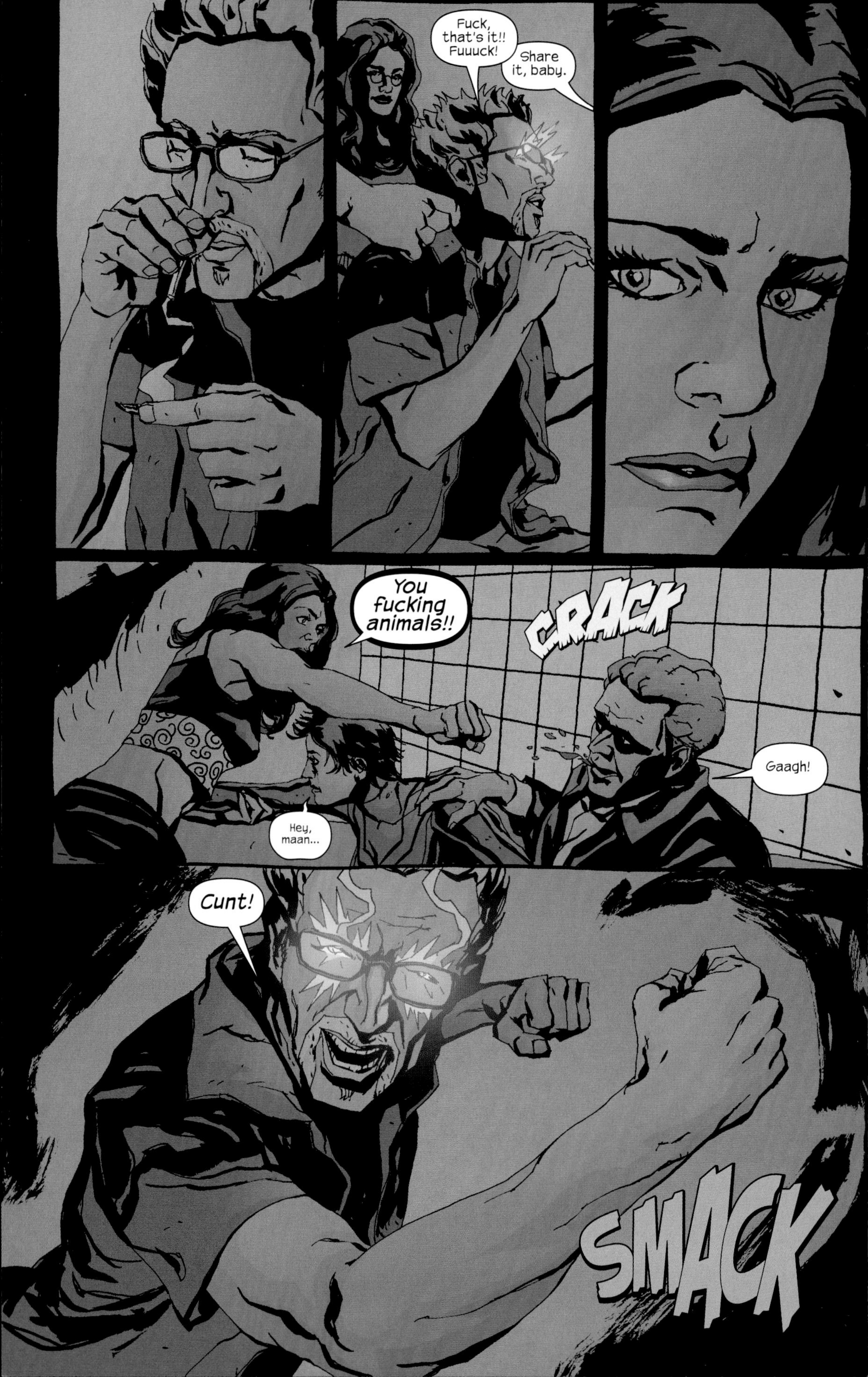
Fuck, that's it!! Fuuuck!
Share it, baby.
You fucking animals!!
CRACK
Gaagh!
Hey, maan...
Cunt!
SMACK

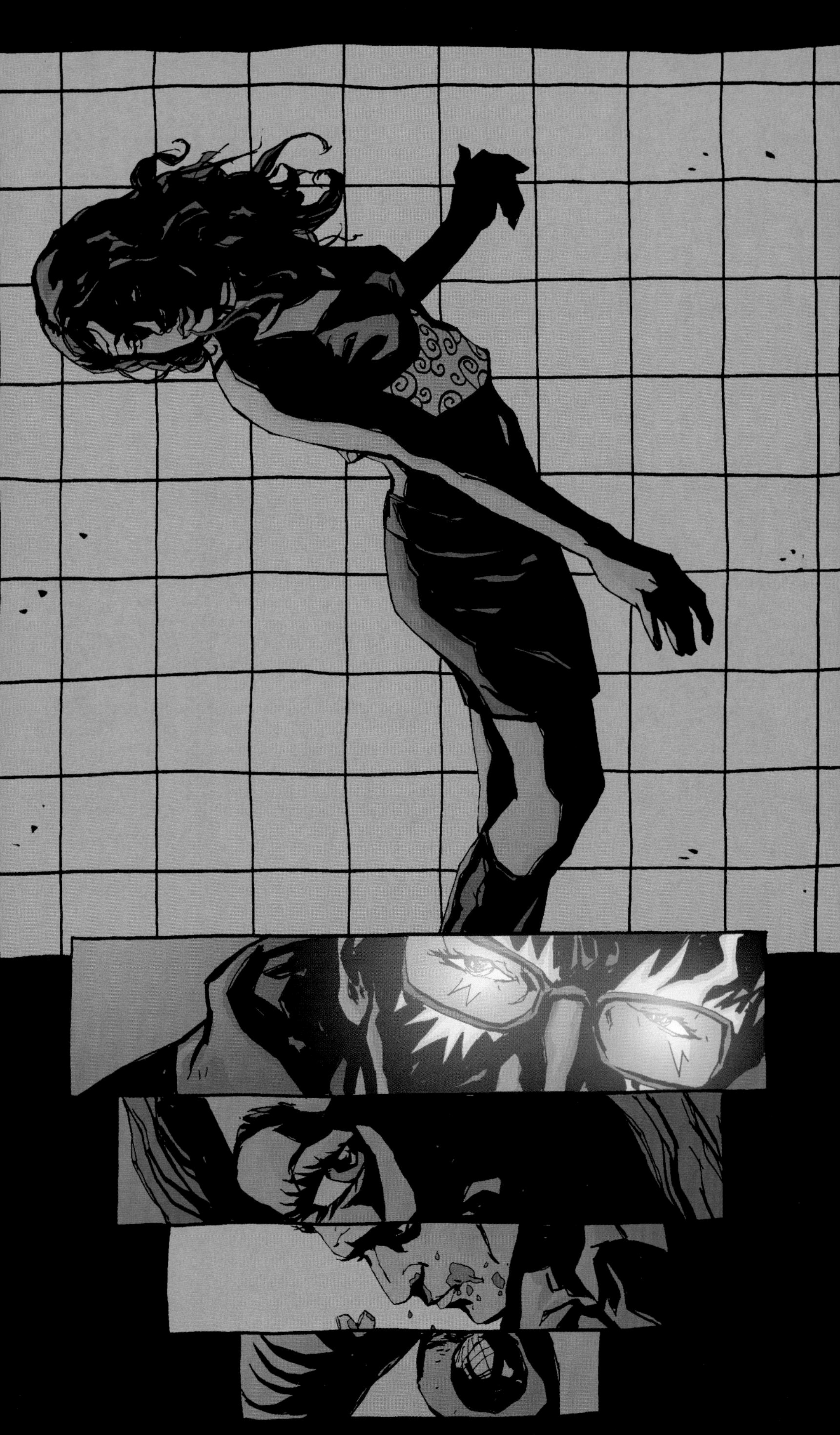

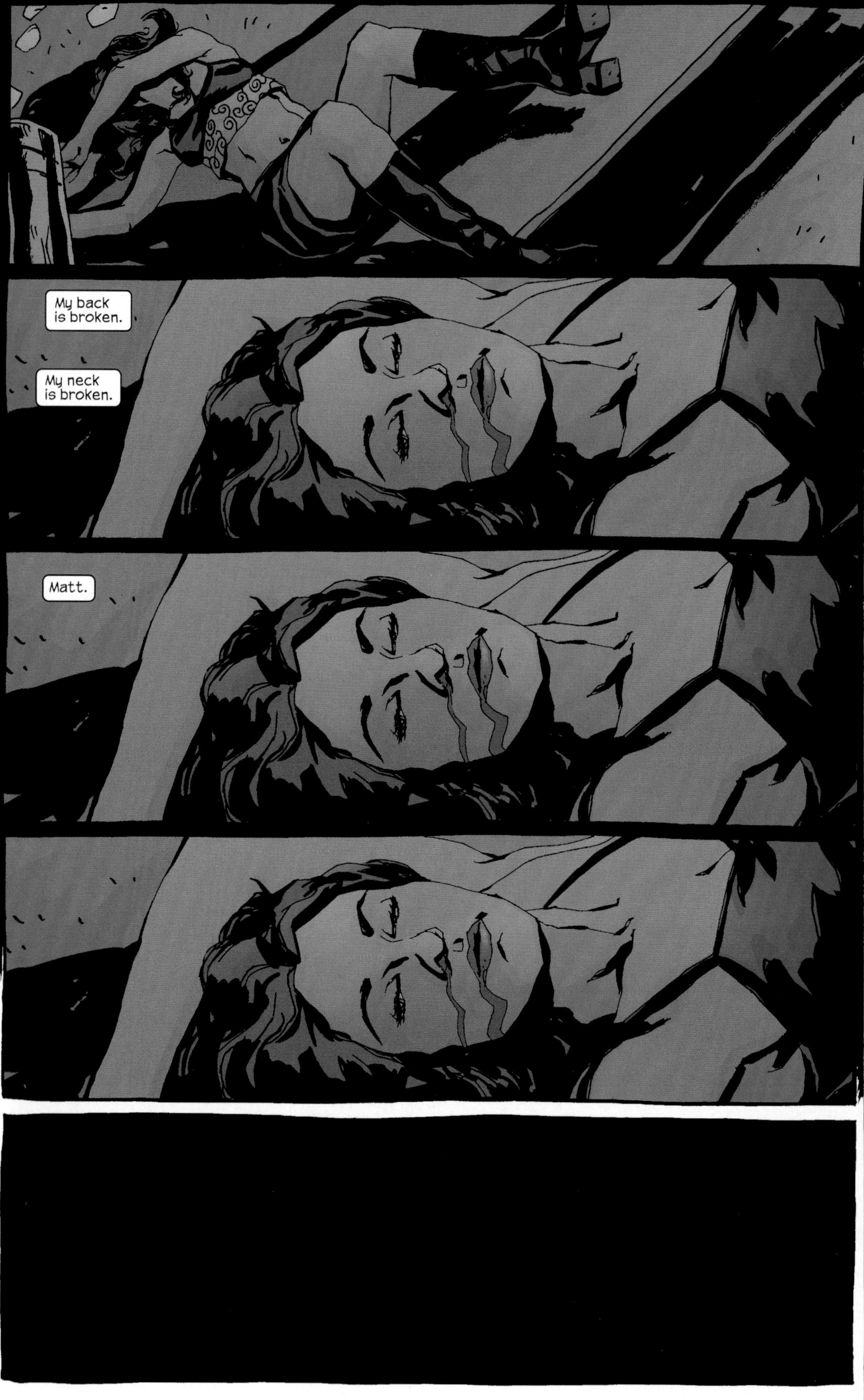
My back is broken.
My neck is broken.
Matt.

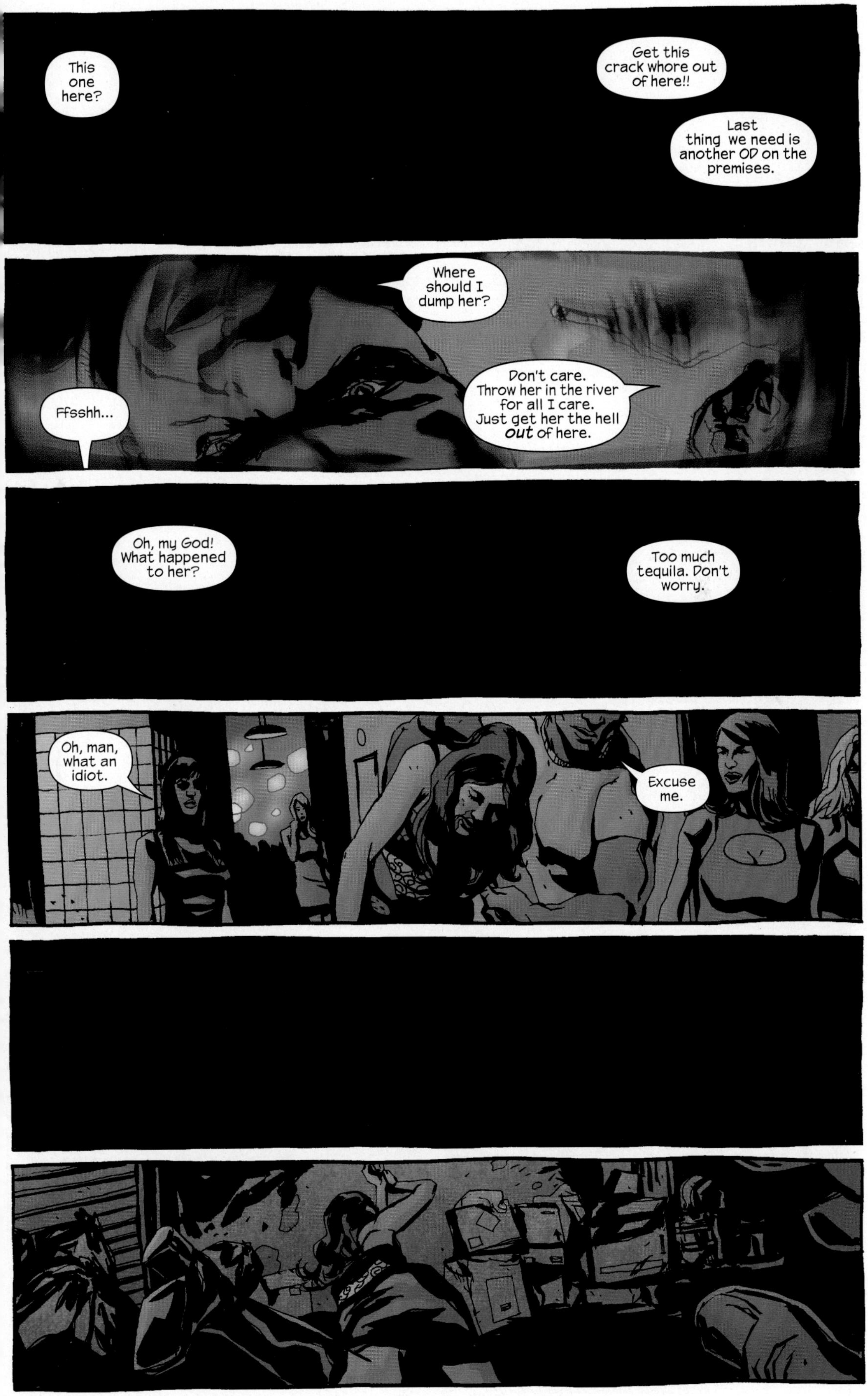
This one here?
Get this crack whore out of here!!
Last thing we need is another OD on the premises.
Where should I dump her?
Ffsshh...
Don't care. Throw her in the river for all I care. Just get her the hell out of here.
Oh, my God! What happened to her?
Too much tequila. Don't worry.
Oh, man, what an idiot.
Excuse me.

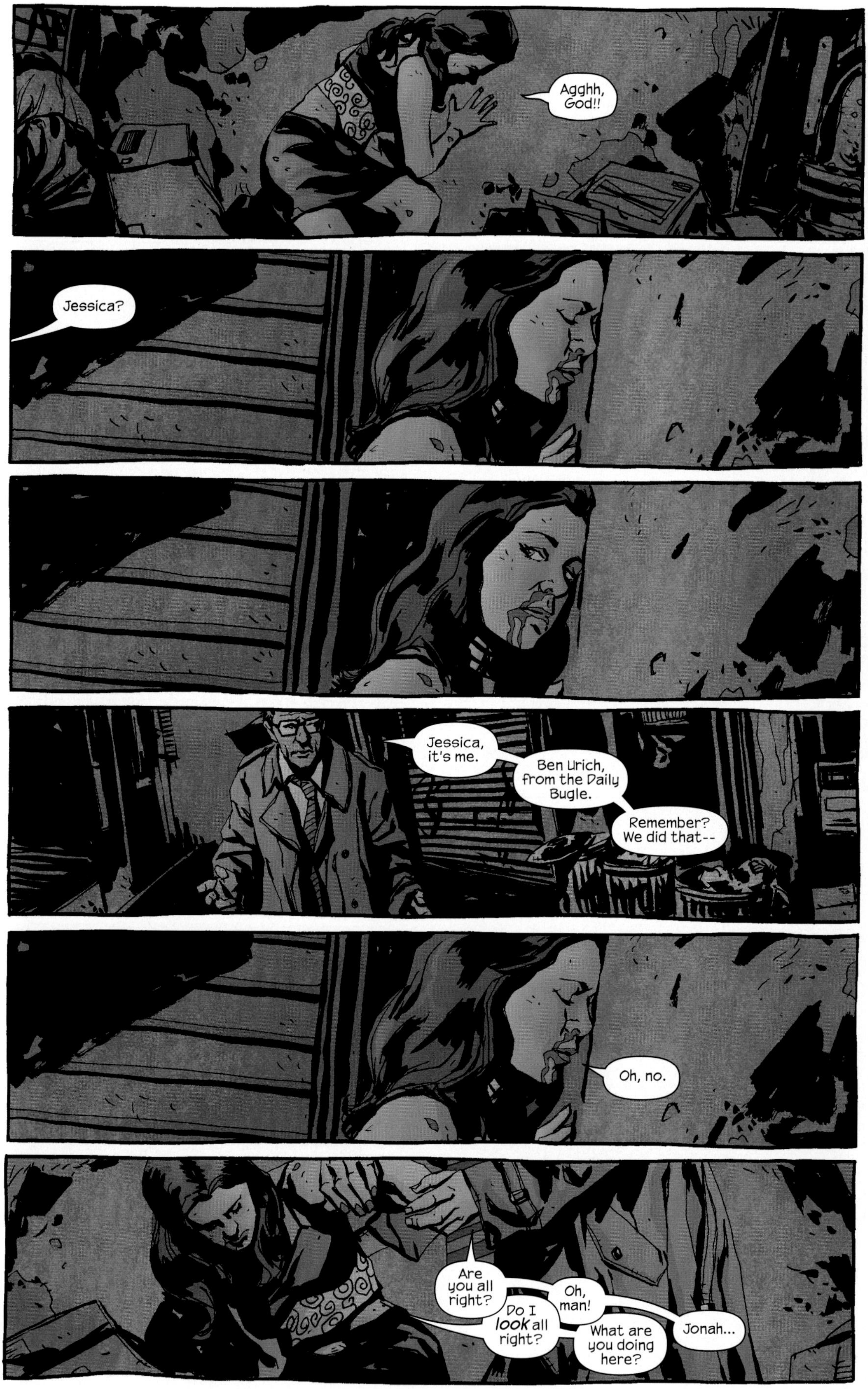

Agghh, God!!
Jessica?
Jessica, it's me.
Ben Urich, from the Daily Bugle.
Remember? We did that--
Oh, no.
Are you all right?
Do I *look* all right?
Oh, man!
What are you doing here?
Jonah...

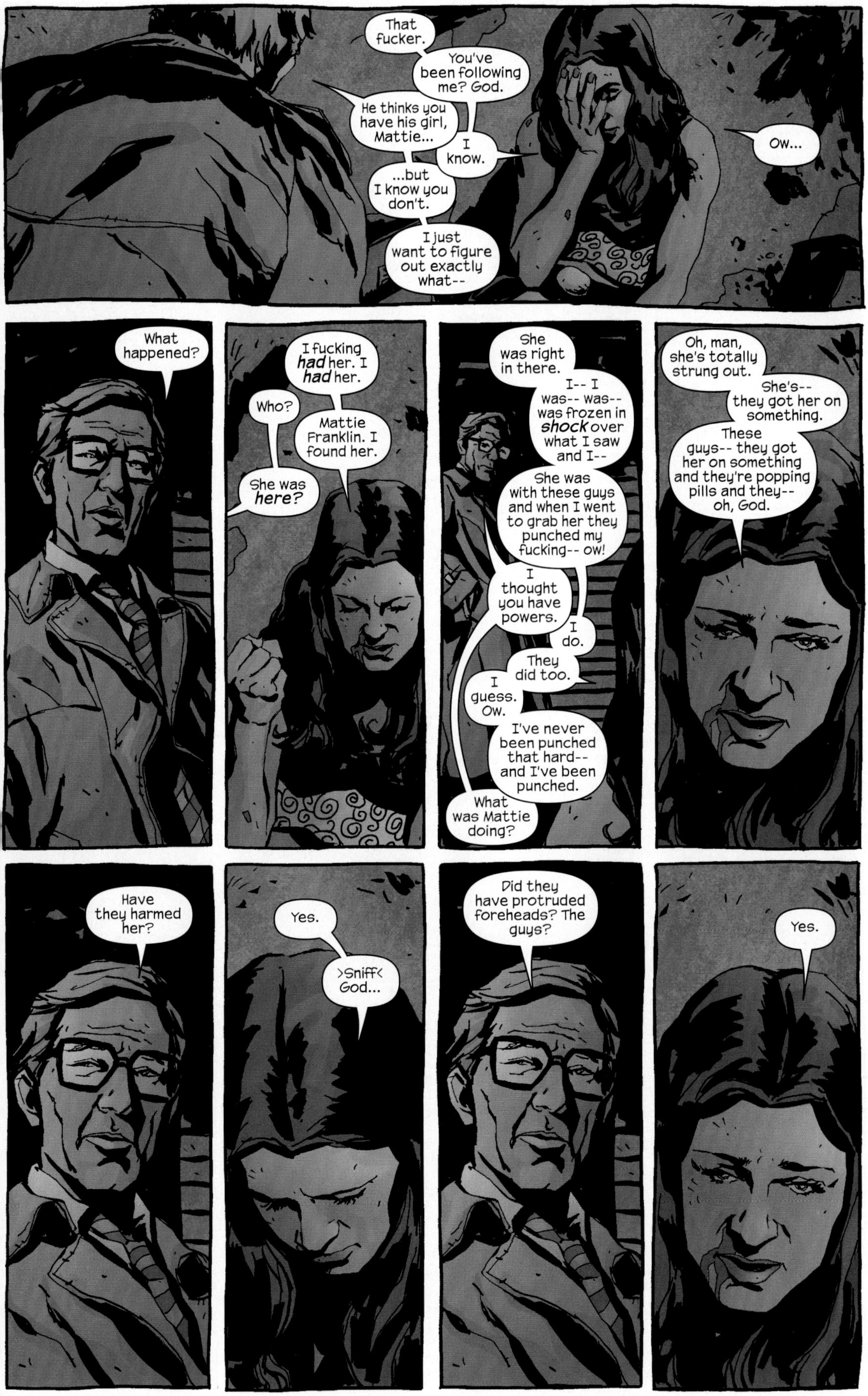
That fucker.
You've been following me? God.
He thinks you have his girl, Mattie...
I know.
...but I know you don't.
I just want to figure out exactly what--
Ow...
What happened?
I fucking **had** her. I **had** her.
Who?
Mattie Franklin. I found her.
She was **here?**
She was right in there.
I-- I was-- was-- was frozen in **shock** over what I saw and I--
She was with these guys and when I went to grab her they punched my fucking-- ow!
I thought you have powers.
I do.
They did too.
I guess. Ow.
I've never been punched that hard-- and I've been punched.
What was Mattie doing?
Oh, man, she's totally strung out.
She's-- they got her on something.
These guys-- they got her on something and they're popping pills and they-- oh, God.
Have they harmed her?
Yes.
>Sniff< God...
Did they have protruded foreheads? The guys?
Yes.

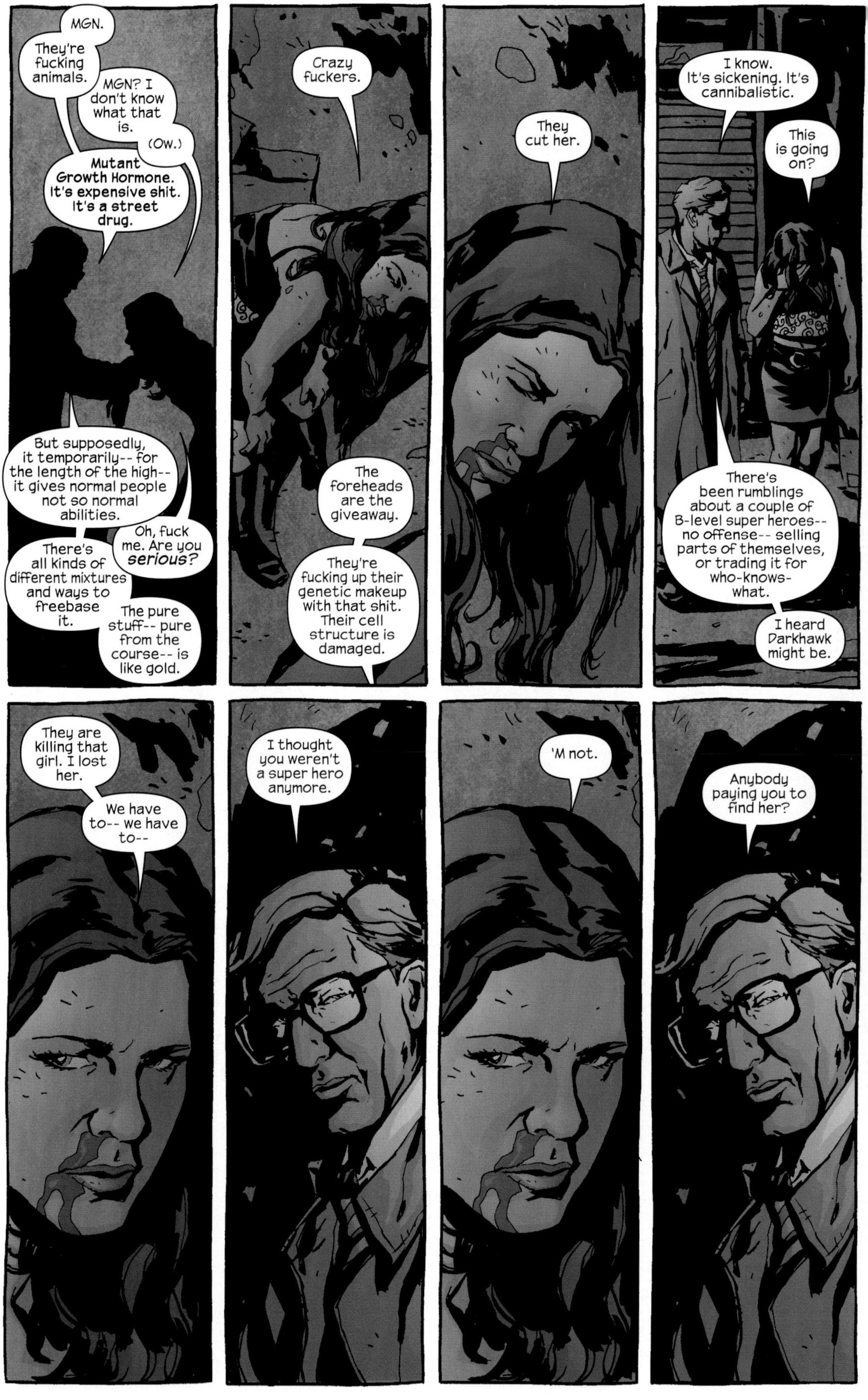
MGN.
They're fucking animals.
MGN? I don't know what that is.
(Ow.)
Mutant Growth Hormone. It's expensive shit. It's a street drug.
But supposedly, it temporarily-- for the length of the high-- it gives normal people not so normal abilities.
Oh, fuck me. Are you *serious?*
There's all kinds of different mixtures and ways to freebase it.
The pure stuff-- pure from the course-- is like gold.
Crazy fuckers.
The foreheads are the giveaway.
They're fucking up their genetic makeup with that shit. Their cell structure is damaged.
They cut her.
I know. It's sickening. It's cannibalistic.
This is going on?
There's been rumblings about a couple of B-level super heroes-- no offense-- selling parts of themselves, or trading it for who-knows-what.
I heard Darkhawk might be.
They are killing that girl. I lost her.
We have to-- we have to--
I thought you weren't a super hero anymore.
'M not.
Anybody paying you to find her?

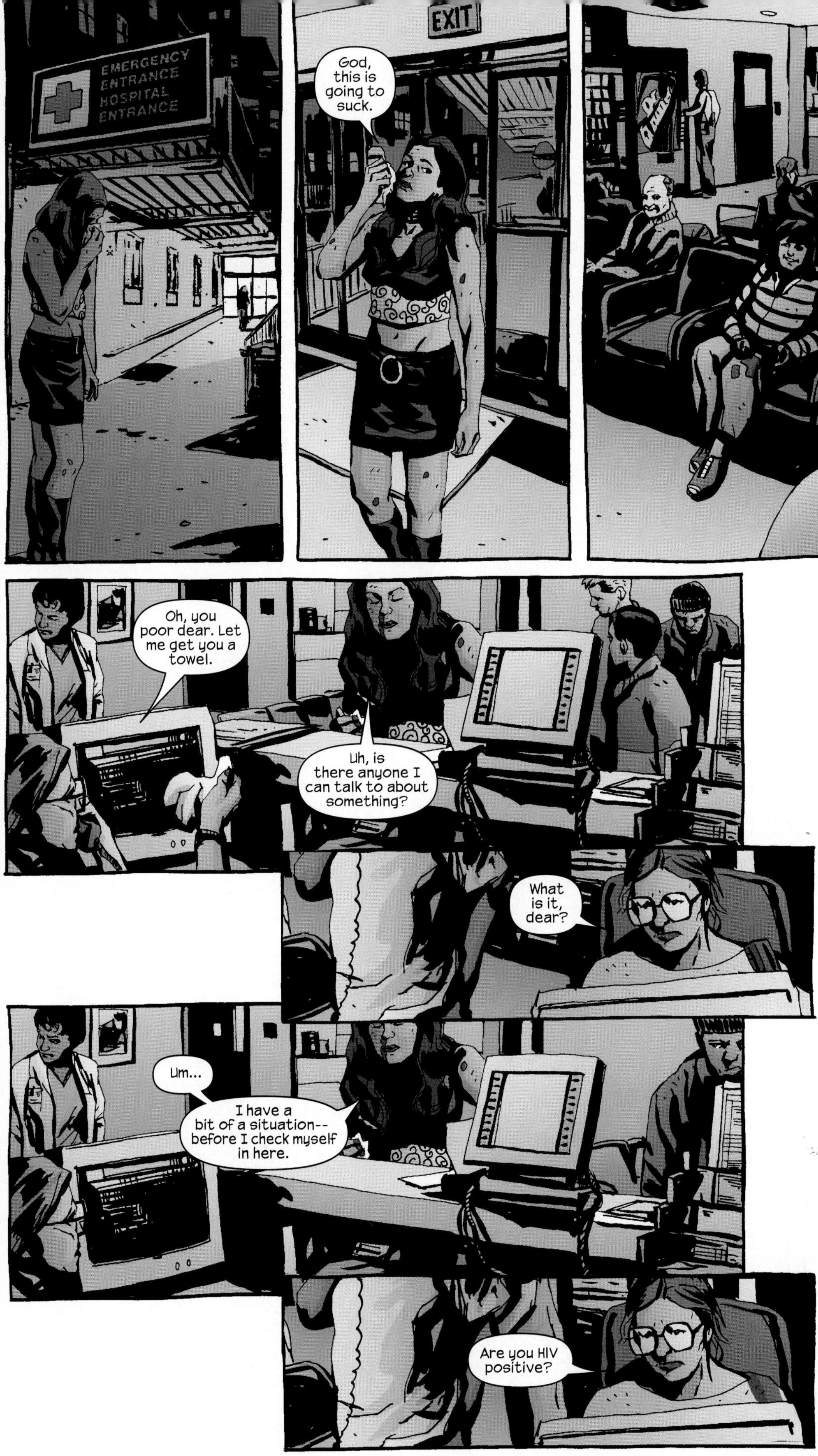
EMERGENCY
ENTRANCE
HOSPITAL
ENTRANCE
EXIT
God, this is going to suck.
Oh, you poor dear. Let me get you a towel.
Uh, is there anyone I can talk to about something?
What is it, dear?
Um...
I have a bit of a situation-- before I check myself in here.
Are you HIV positive?

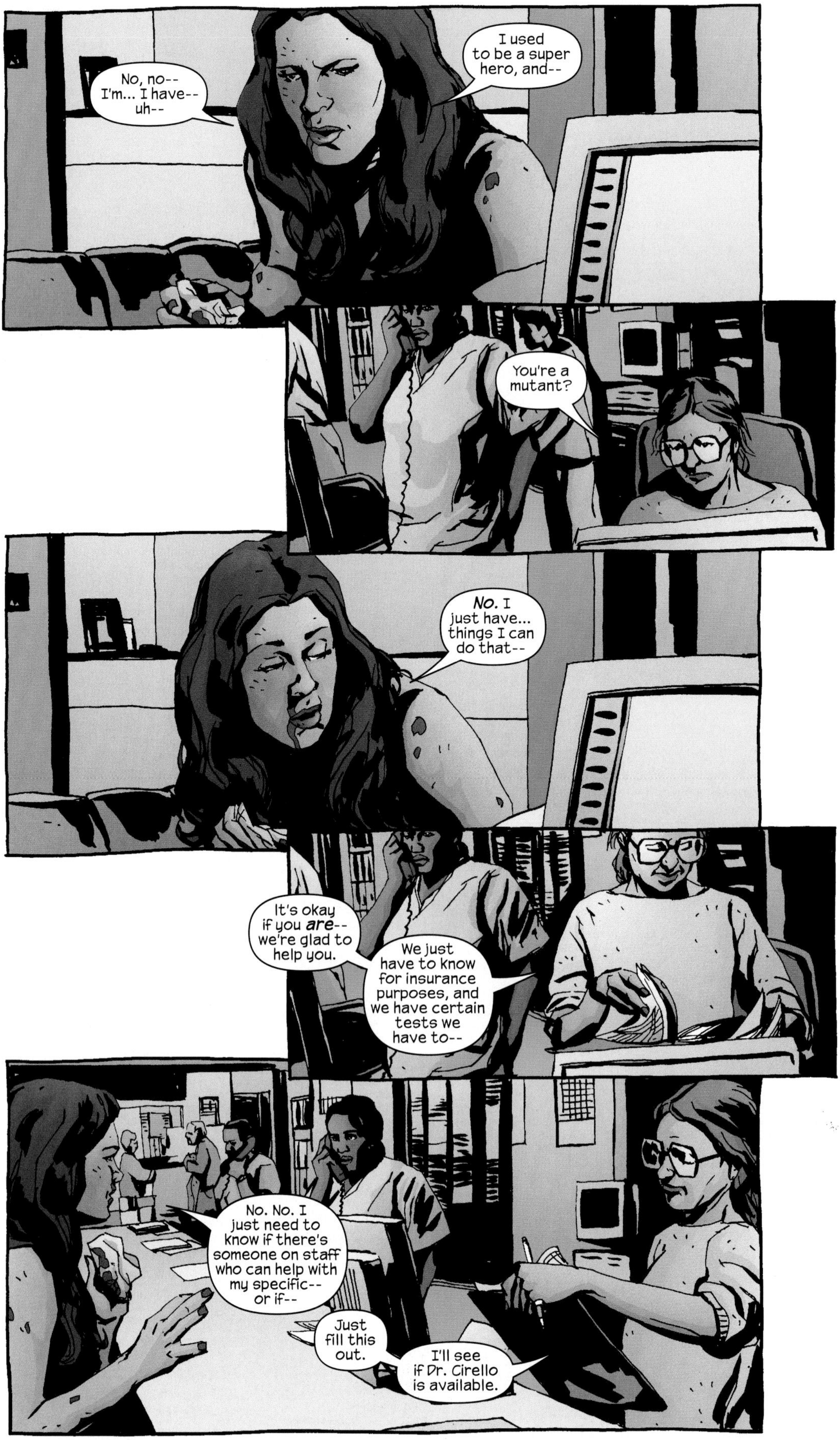
No, no--
I'm... I have--
uh--
I used
to be a super
hero, and--
You're a
mutant?
No. I
just have...
things I can
do that--
It's okay
if you *are*--
we're glad to
help you.
We just
have to know
for insurance
purposes, and
we have certain
tests we
have to--
No. No. I
just need to
know if there's
someone on staff
who can help with
my specific--
or if--
Just
fill this
out.
I'll see
if Dr. Cirello
is available.

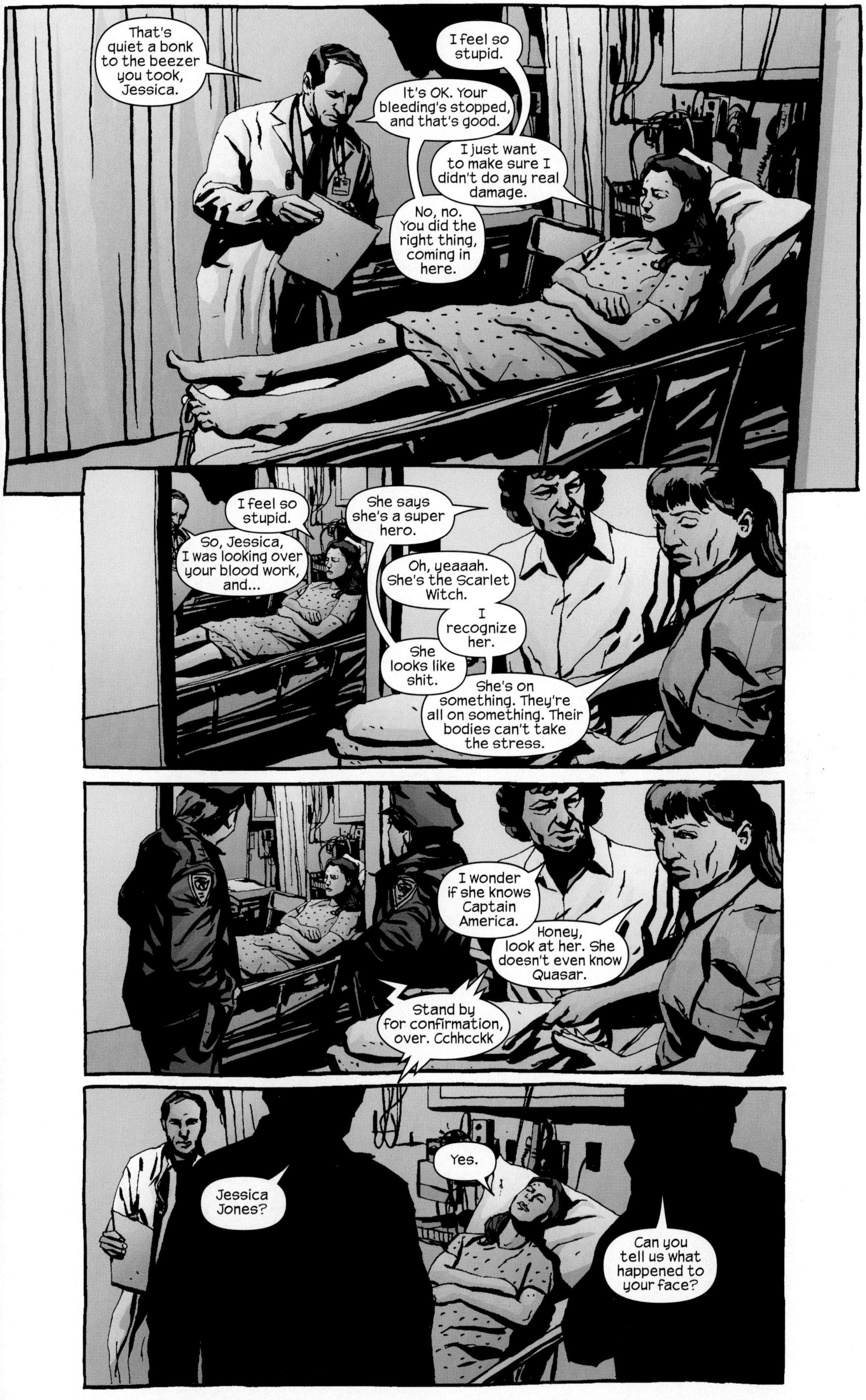
That's quiet a bonk to the beezer you took, Jessica.
I feel so stupid.
It's OK. Your bleeding's stopped, and that's good.
I just want to make sure I didn't do any real damage.
No, no. You did the right thing, coming in here.
I feel so stupid.
So, Jessica, I was looking over your blood work, and...
She says she's a super hero.
Oh, yeaaah. She's the Scarlet Witch.
I recognize her.
She looks like shit.
She's on something. They're all on something. Their bodies can't take the stress.
I wonder if she knows Captain America.
Honey, look at her. She doesn't even know Quasar.
Stand by for confirmation, over. Cchhcckk
Jessica Jones?
Yes.
Can you tell us what happened to your face?

Short of being chopped in half and waking up to find out that I have been turned into a half woman/ half robot cyborg...

...I can't imagine how that little adventure could have gone any worse.

The cops were so goddamn condescending. Bunch o' fucking power-tripping motherfuckers.

I enjoyed every bullshit lie I told them about how I was mugged.

Fuckers.

Fuck them!

Treat a woman like she's a child that shouldn't be out after dark.

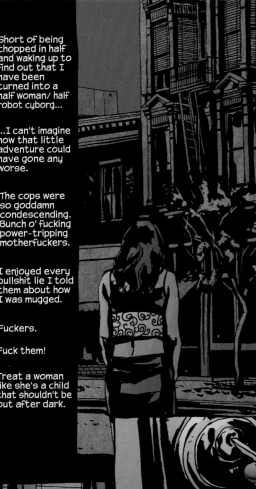

Eff you, little-dick, badge-wearing assholes.

Do your job!!

That whole thing was fucking awful.

I hope that Urich guy finds out something about where Mattie is, and I hope he tells Jonah to leave me alone.

I just want to get that girl home safe. Then I want to be left alone.

My body can't take this kind of abuse. I'm not that kind of person. I don't have the--

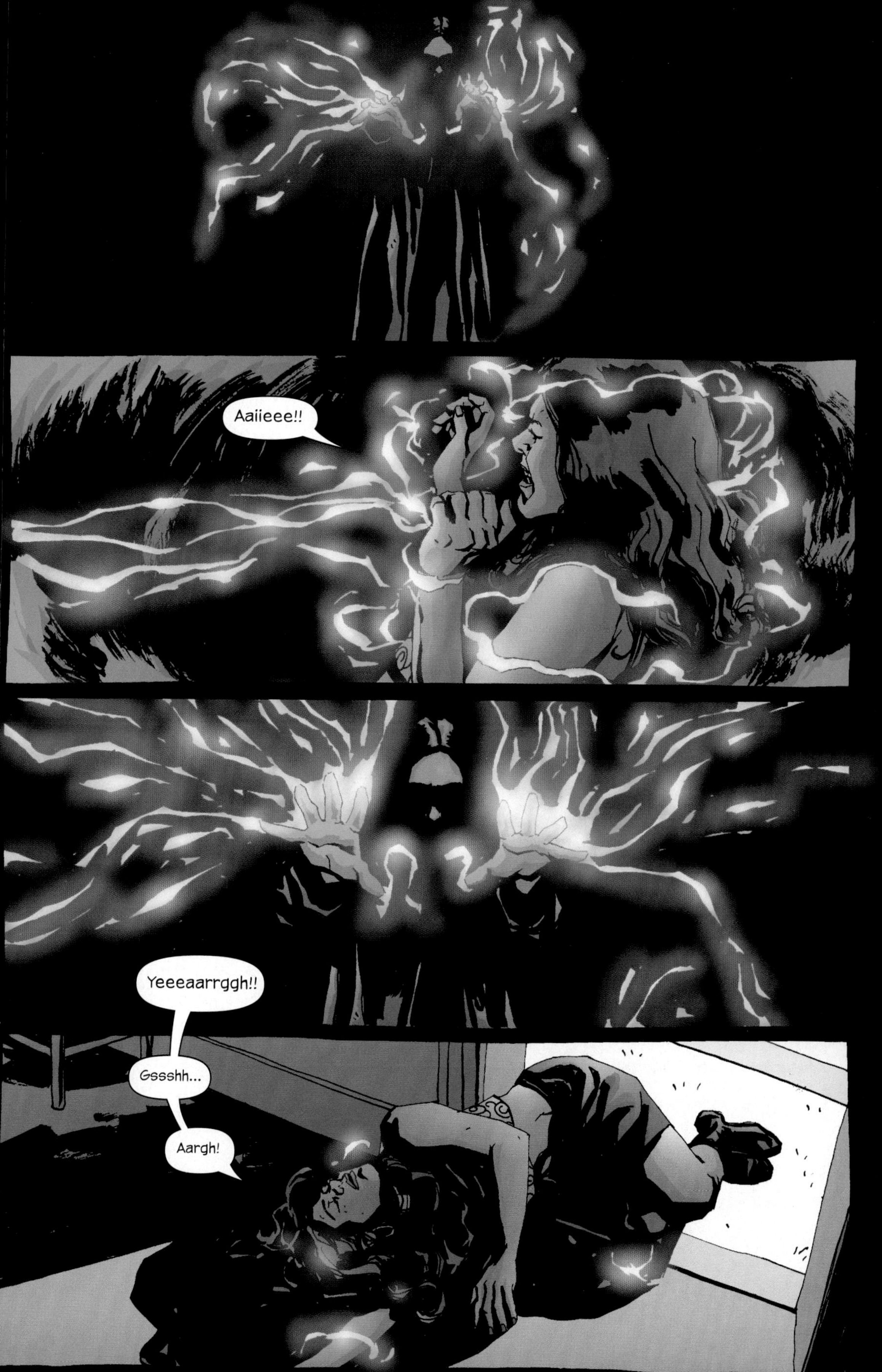
Aaiieee!!
Yeeeaarrggh!!
Gssshh...
Aargh!

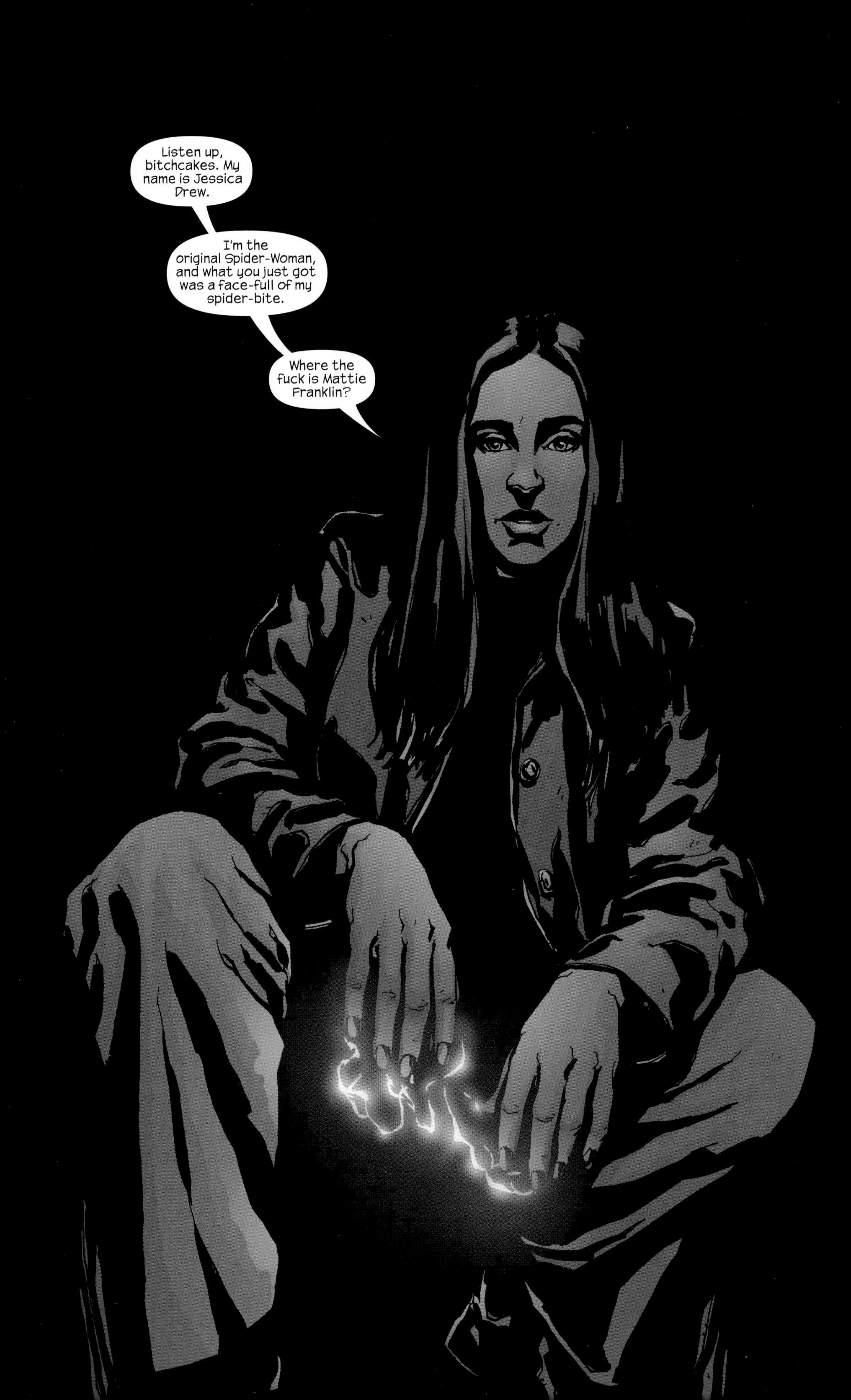
Listen up, bitchcakes. My name is Jessica Drew.
I'm the original Spider-Woman, and what you just got was a face-full of my spider-bite.
Where the fuck is Mattie Franklin?

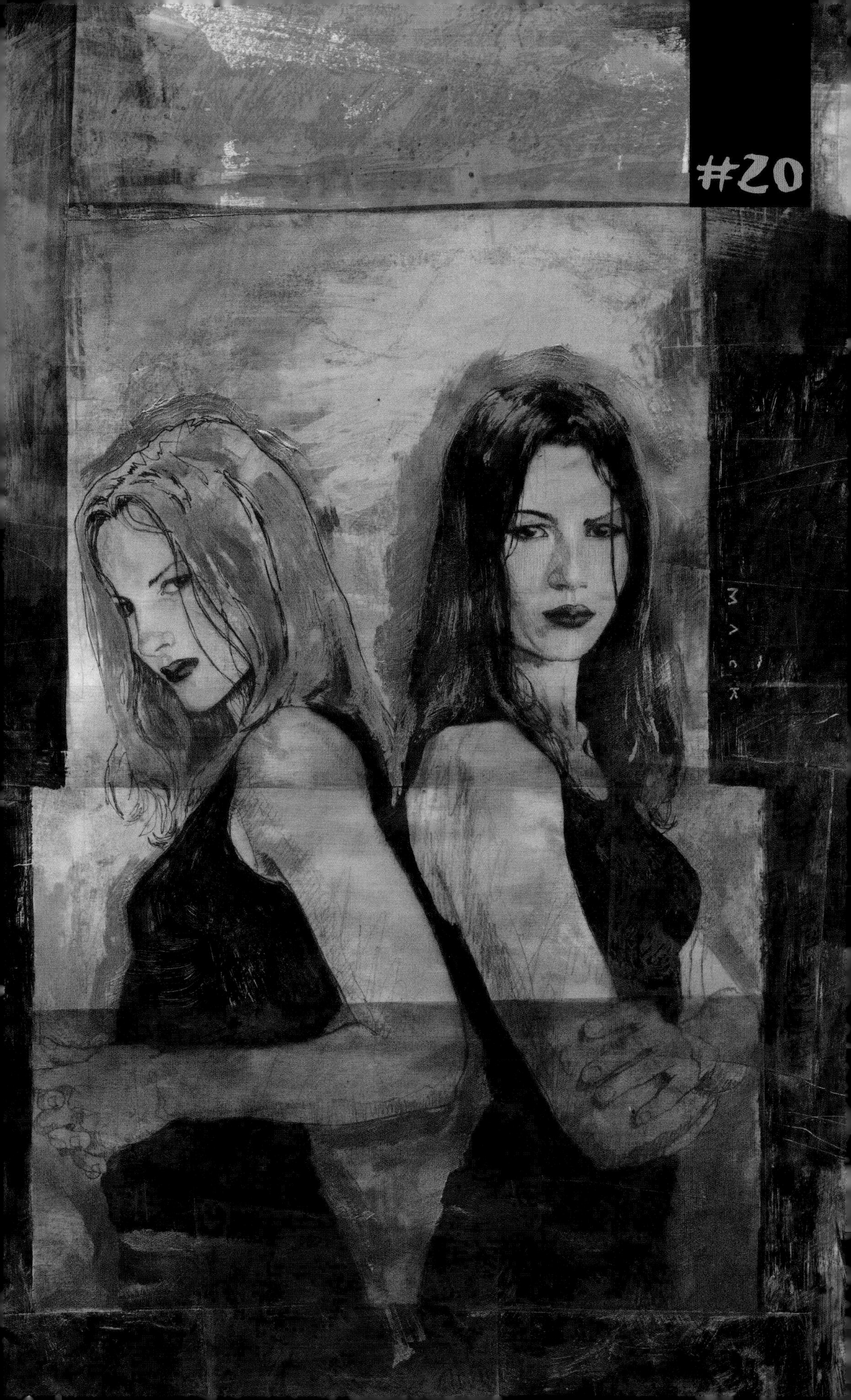
#20
MACK

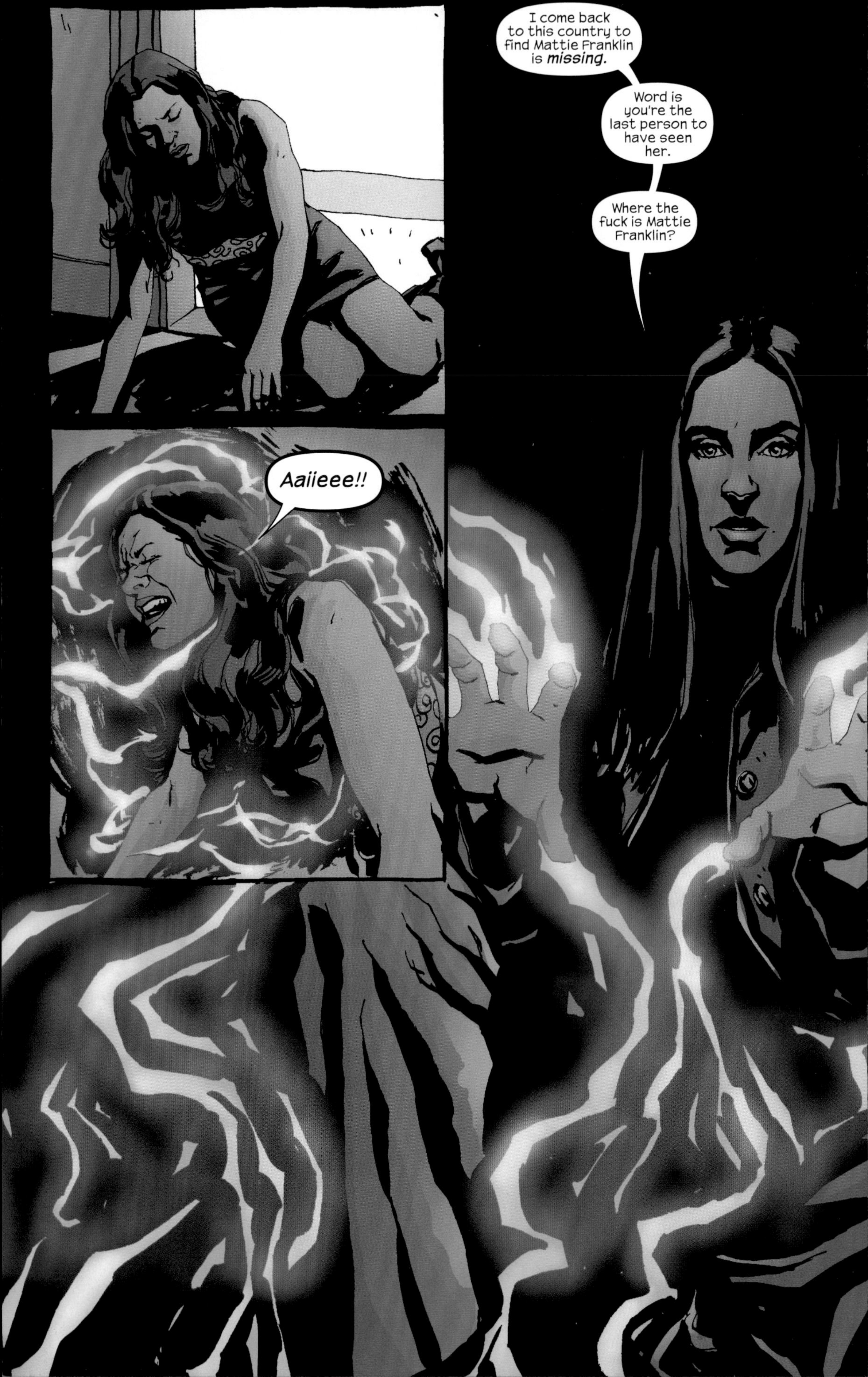
I come back to this country to find Mattie Franklin is *missing.*
Word is you're the last person to have seen her.
Where the fuck is Mattie Franklin?
Aaiieee!!

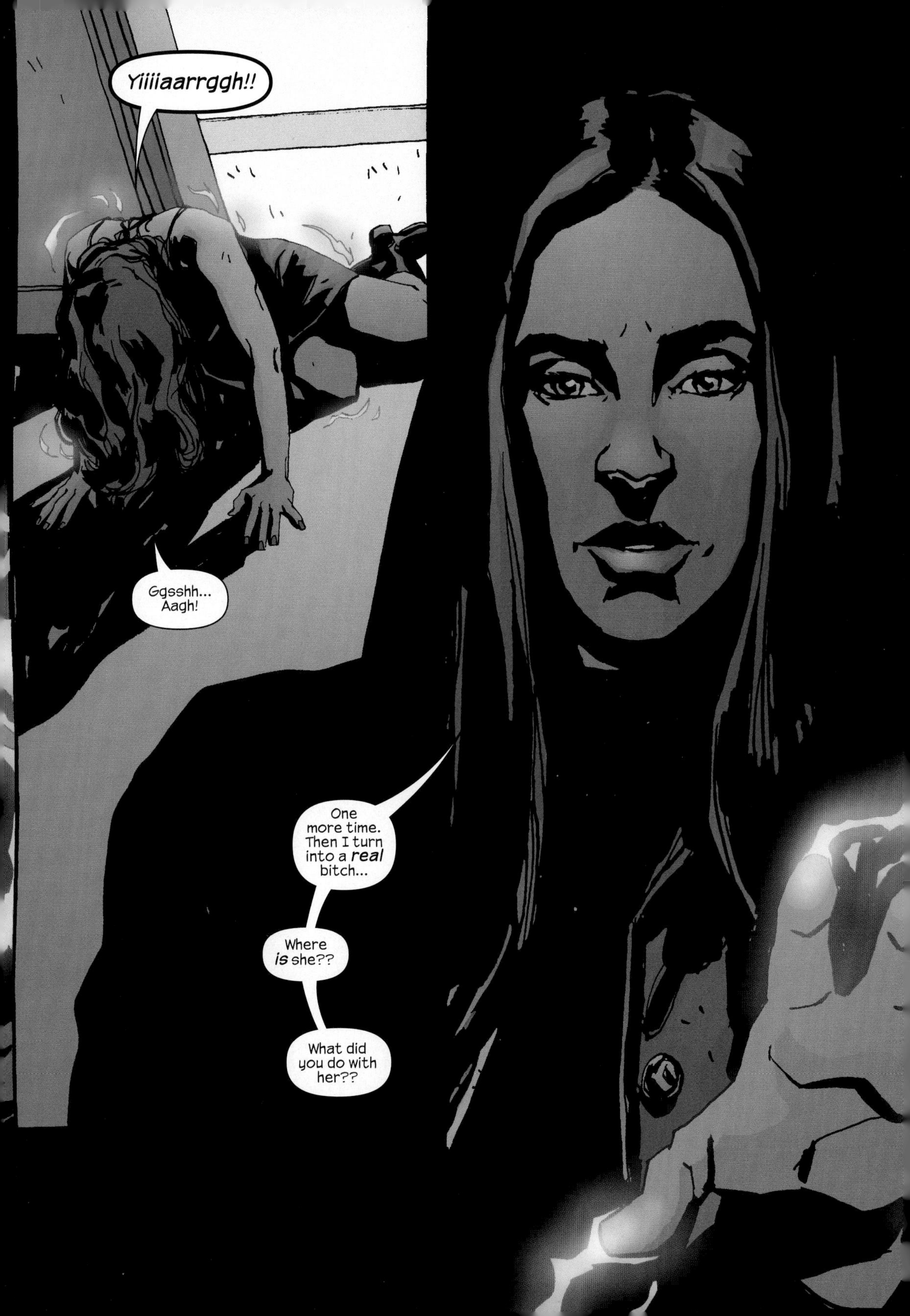
Yiiiiaarrggh!!
Ggsshh... Aagh!
One more time. Then I turn into a *real* bitch...
Where *is* she??
What did you do with her??

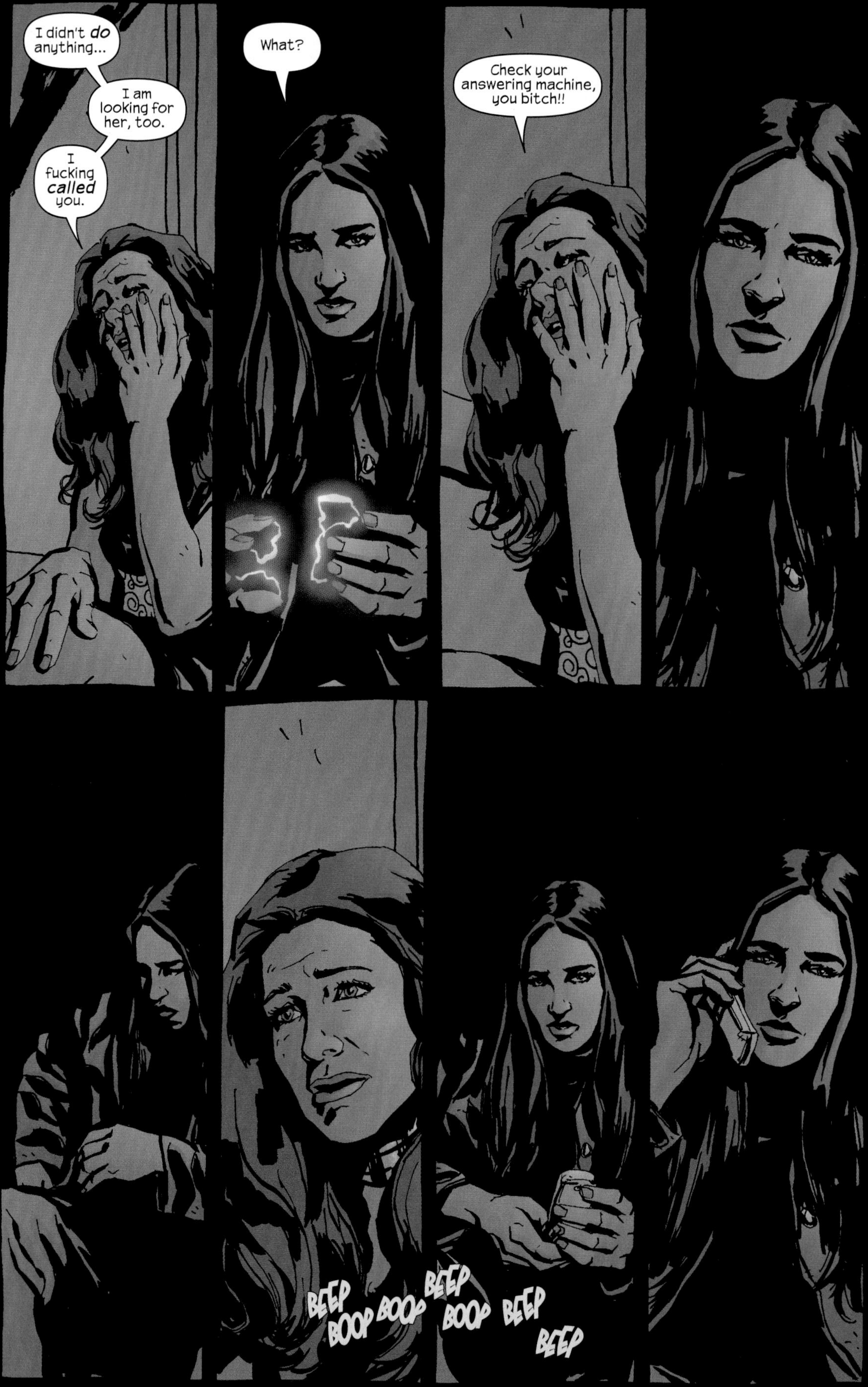
I didn't do anything...
I am looking for her, too.
I fucking called you.
What?
Check your answering machine, you bitch!!
BEEP
BOOP
BOOP
BEEP
BOOP
BEEP
BEEP

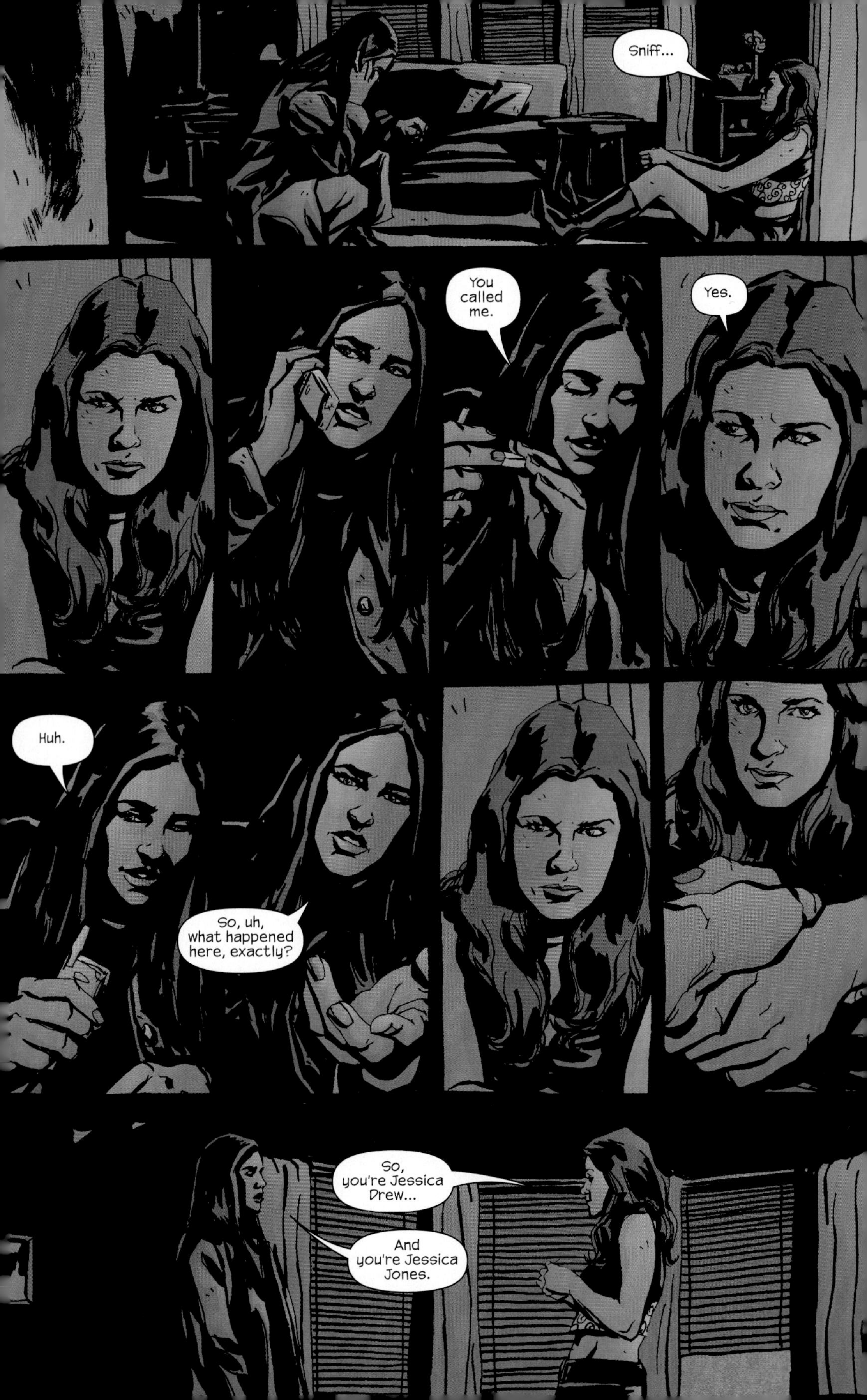
Sniff...
You called me.
Yes.
Huh.
So, uh, what happened here, exactly?
So, you're Jessica Drew...
And you're Jessica Jones.

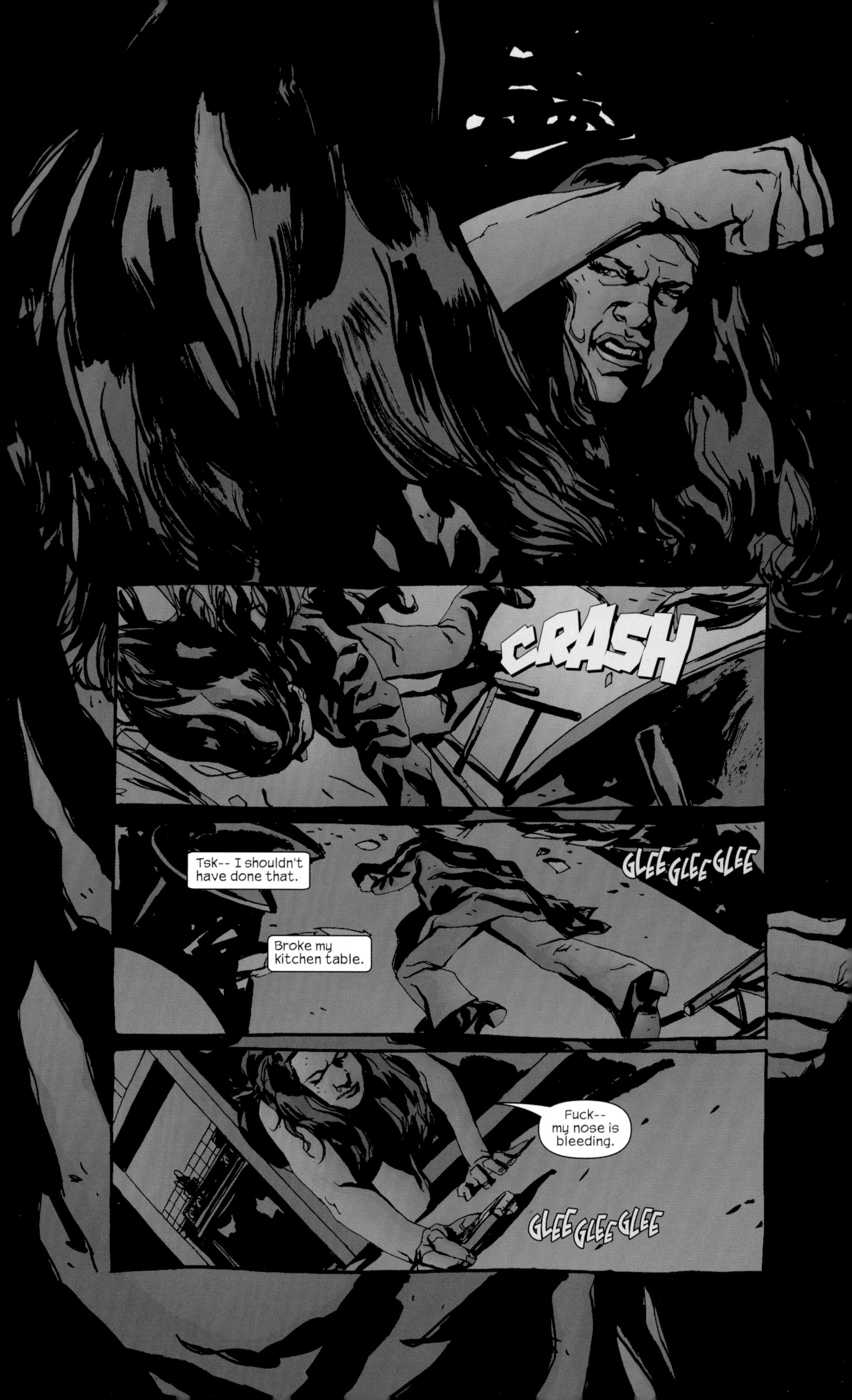
CRASH
Tsk-- I shouldn't have done that.
GLEE GLEE GLEE
Broke my kitchen table.
Fuck-- my nose is bleeding.
GLEE GLEE GLEE

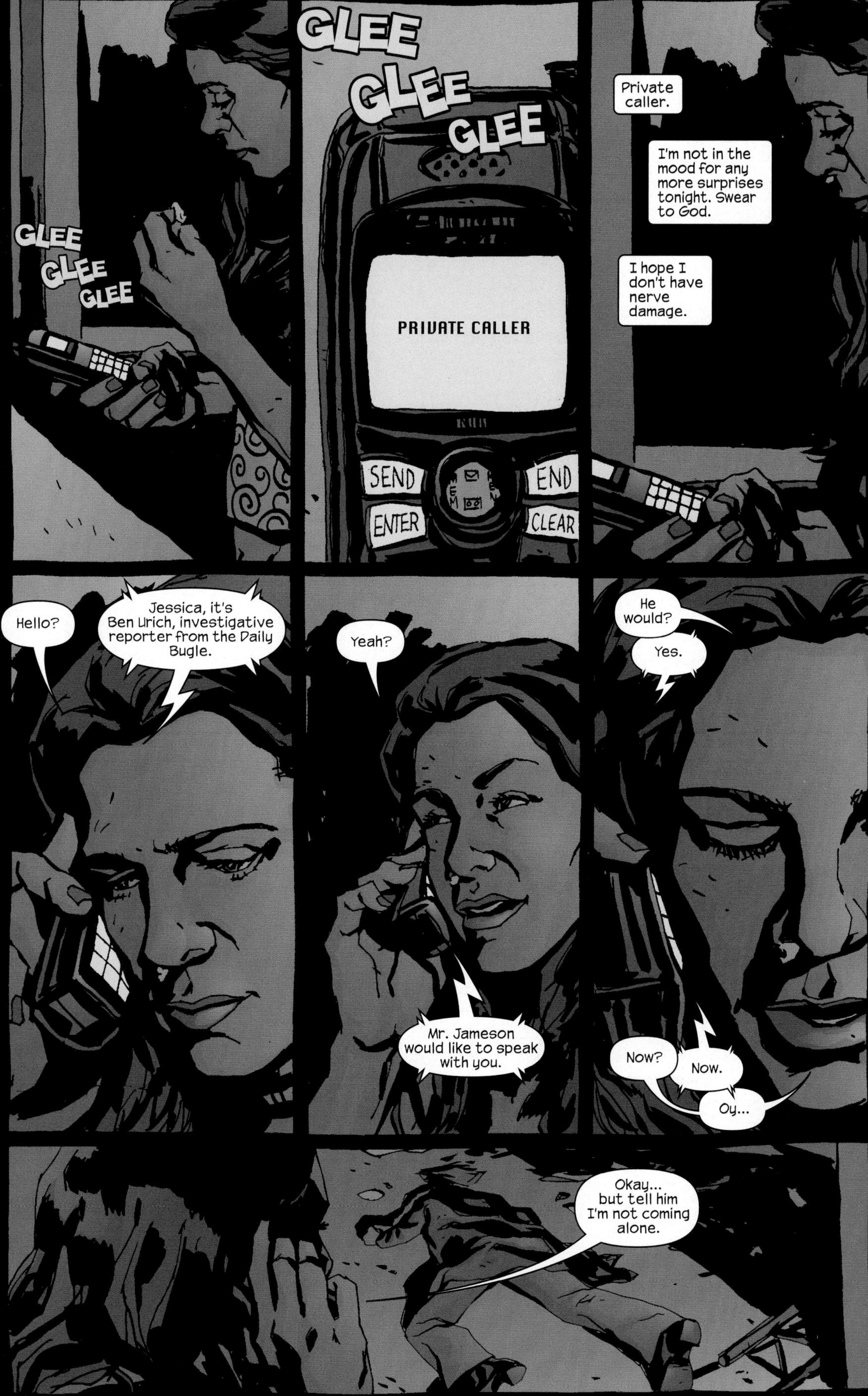
GLEE
GLEE
GLEE
GLEE
GLEE
GLEE
PRIVATE CALLER
SEND
END
ENTER
CLEAR
Private caller.
I'm not in the mood for any more surprises tonight. Swear to God.
I hope I don't have nerve damage.
Hello?
Jessica, it's Ben Urich, investigative reporter from the Daily Bugle.
Yeah?
Mr. Jameson would like to speak with you.
He would?
Yes.
Now?
Now.
Oy...
Okay... but tell him I'm not coming alone.

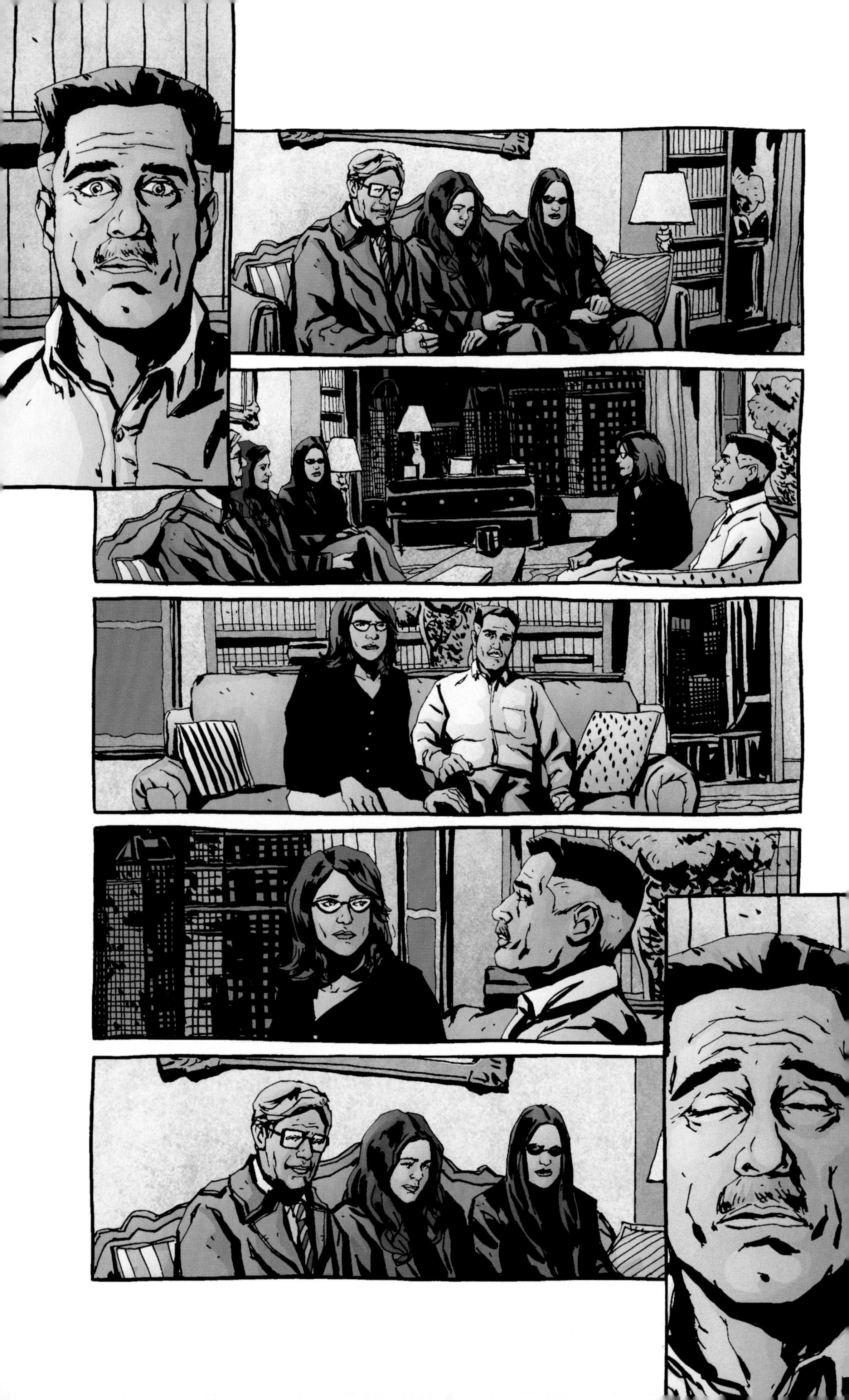

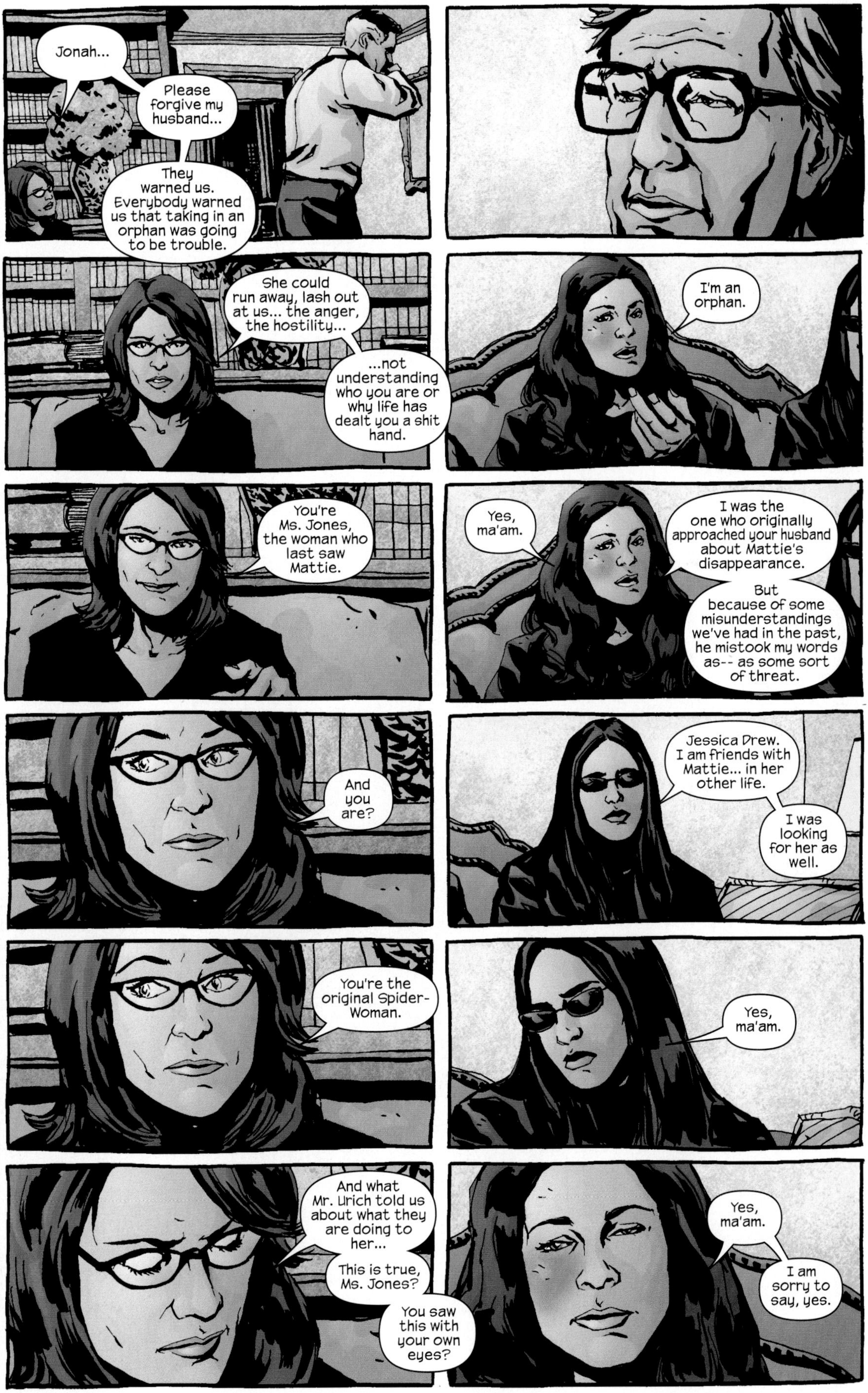
Jonah...
Please forgive my husband...
They warned us. Everybody warned us that taking in an orphan was going to be trouble.
She could run away, lash out at us... the anger, the hostility...
...not understanding who you are or why life has dealt you a shit hand.
I'm an orphan.
You're Ms. Jones, the woman who last saw Mattie.
Yes, ma'am.
I was the one who originally approached your husband about Mattie's disappearance.
But because of some misunderstandings we've had in the past, he mistook my words as-- as some sort of threat.
And you are?
Jessica Drew. I am friends with Mattie... in her other life.
I was looking for her as well.
You're the original Spider-Woman.
Yes, ma'am.
And what Mr. Urich told us about what they are doing to her...
This is true, Ms. Jones?
You saw this with your own eyes?
Yes, ma'am.
I am sorry to say, yes.

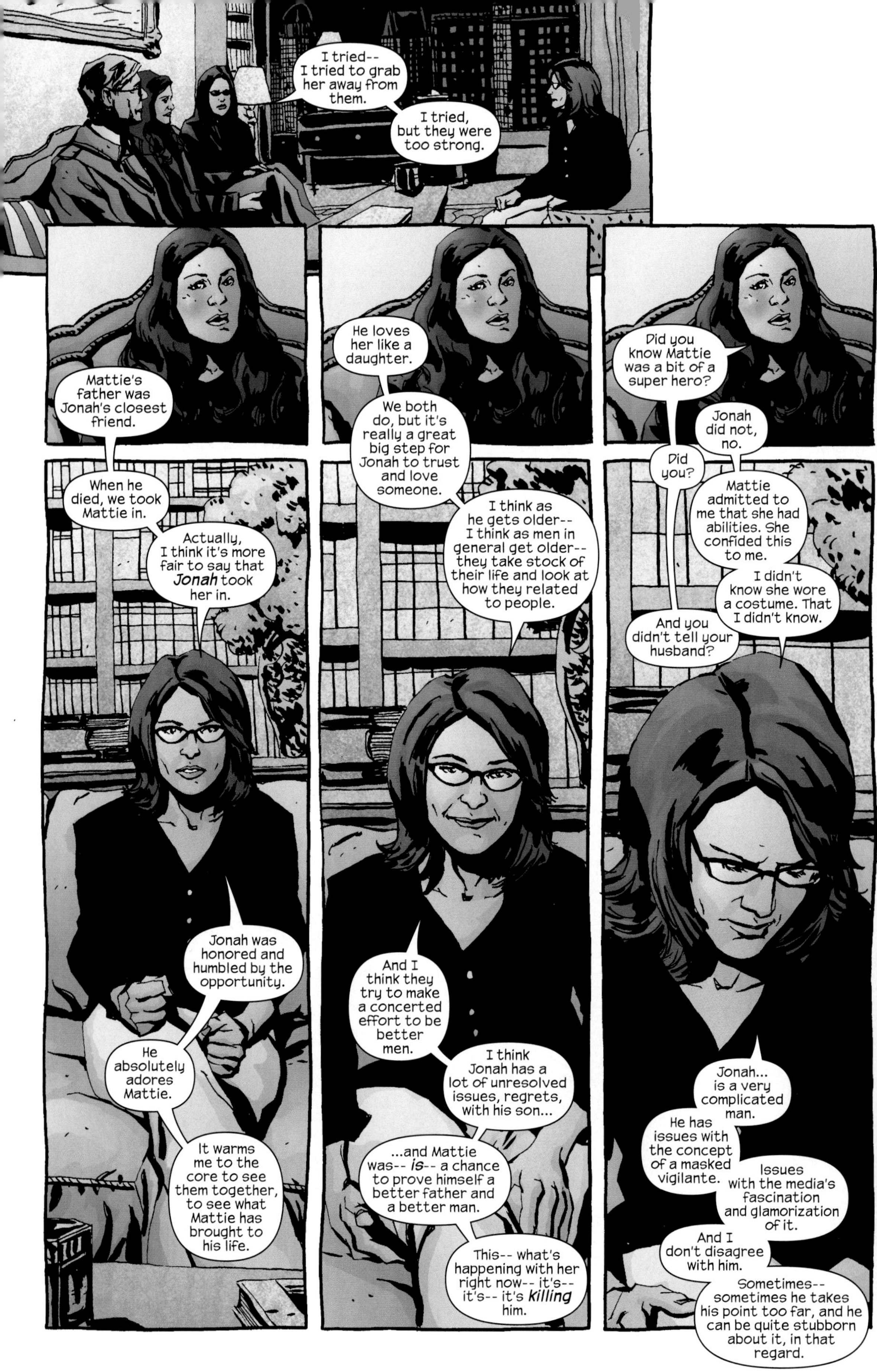
I tried-- I tried to grab her away from them.
I tried, but they were too strong.
Mattie's father was Jonah's closest friend.
When he died, we took Mattie in.
Actually, I think it's more fair to say that *Jonah* took her in.
Jonah was honored and humbled by the opportunity.
He absolutely adores Mattie.
It warms me to the core to see them together, to see what Mattie has brought to his life.
He loves her like a daughter.
We both do, but it's really a great big step for Jonah to trust and love someone.
I think as he gets older-- I think as men in general get older-- they take stock of their life and look at how they related to people.
And I think they try to make a concerted effort to be better men.
I think Jonah has a lot of unresolved issues, regrets, with his son...
...and Mattie was-- *is*-- a chance to prove himself a better father and a better man.
This-- what's happening with her right now-- it's-- it's-- it's *killing* him.
Did you know Mattie was a bit of a super hero?
Jonah did not, no.
Did you?
Mattie admitted to me that she had abilities. She confided this to me.
I didn't know she wore a costume. That I didn't know.
And you didn't tell your husband?
Jonah... is a very complicated man.
He has issues with the concept of a masked vigilante.
Issues with the media's fascination and glamorization of it.
And I don't disagree with him.
Sometimes-- sometimes he takes his point too far, and he can be quite stubborn about it, in that regard.

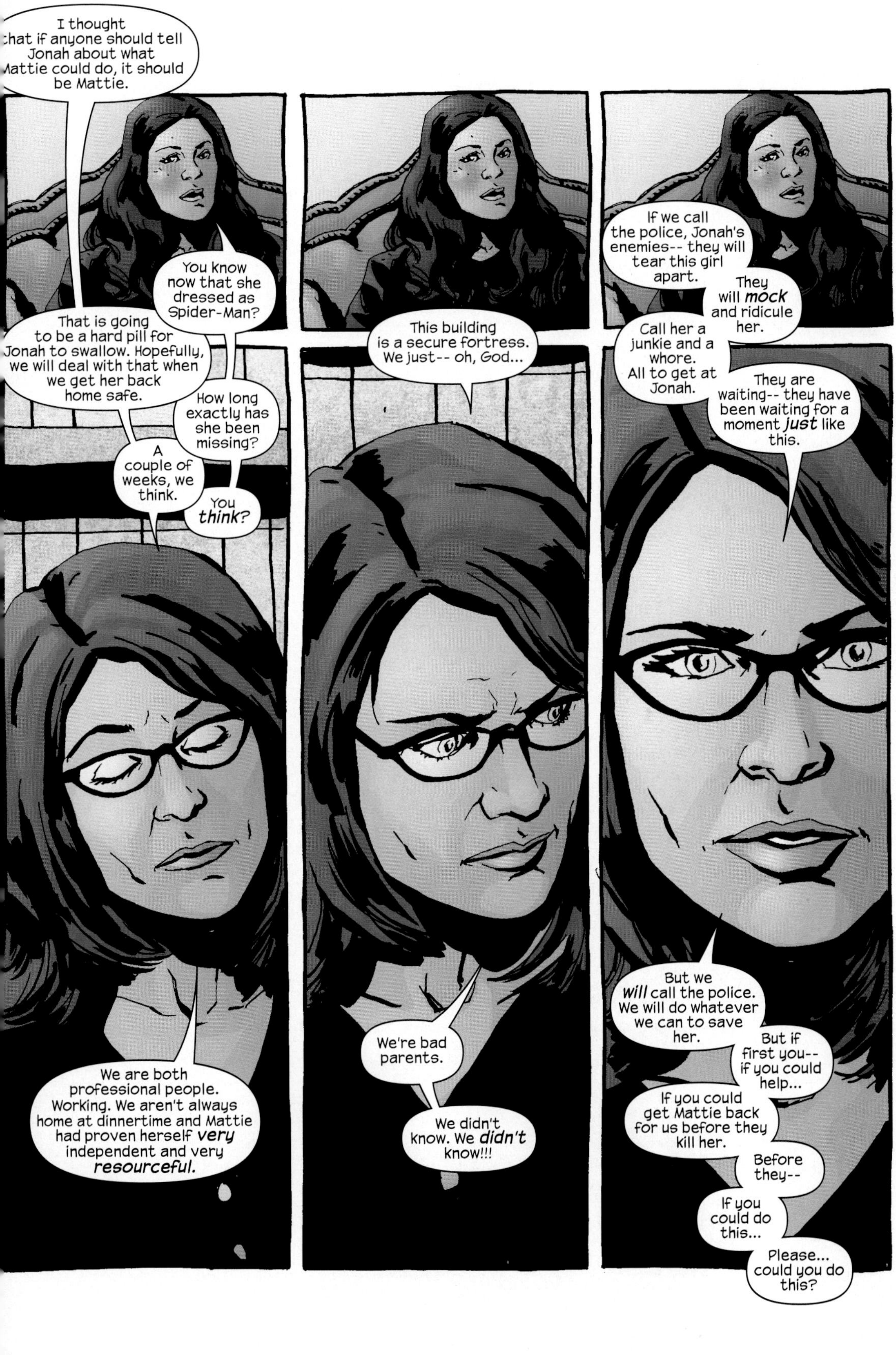
I thought that if anyone should tell Jonah about what Mattie could do, it should be Mattie.
You know now that she dressed as Spider-Man?
That is going to be a hard pill for Jonah to swallow. Hopefully, we will deal with that when we get her back home safe.
How long exactly has she been missing?
A couple of weeks, we think.
You *think*?
We are both professional people. Working. We aren't always home at dinnertime and Mattie had proven herself *very* independent and very *resourceful.*
This building is a secure fortress. We just-- oh, God...
We're bad parents.
We didn't know. We *didn't* know!!!
If we call the police, Jonah's enemies-- they will tear this girl apart.
They will *mock* and ridicule her.
Call her a junkie and a whore. All to get at Jonah.
They are waiting-- they have been waiting for a moment *just* like this.
But we *will* call the police. We will do whatever we can to save her.
But if first you-- if you could help...
If you could get Mattie back for us before they kill her.
Before they--
If you could do this...
Please... could you do this?

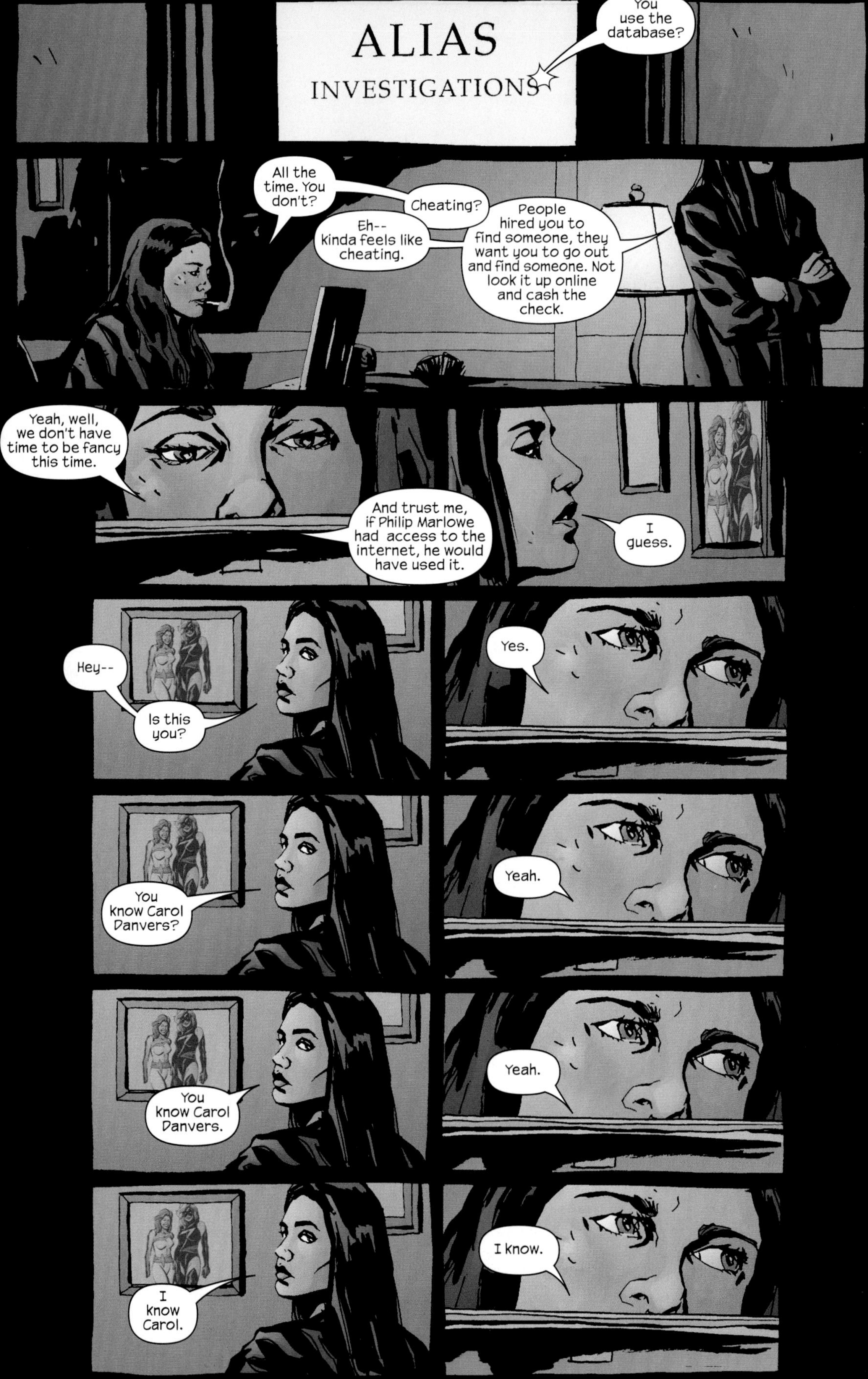
ALIAS INVESTIGATIONS
You use the database?
All the time. You don't?
Eh-- kinda feels like cheating.
Cheating?
People hired you to find someone, they want you to go out and find someone. Not look it up online and cash the check.
Yeah, well, we don't have time to be fancy this time.
And trust me, if Philip Marlowe had access to the internet, he would have used it.
I guess.
Hey--
Is this you?
Yes.
You know Carol Danvers?
Yeah.
You know Carol Danvers.
Yeah.
I know Carol.
I know.

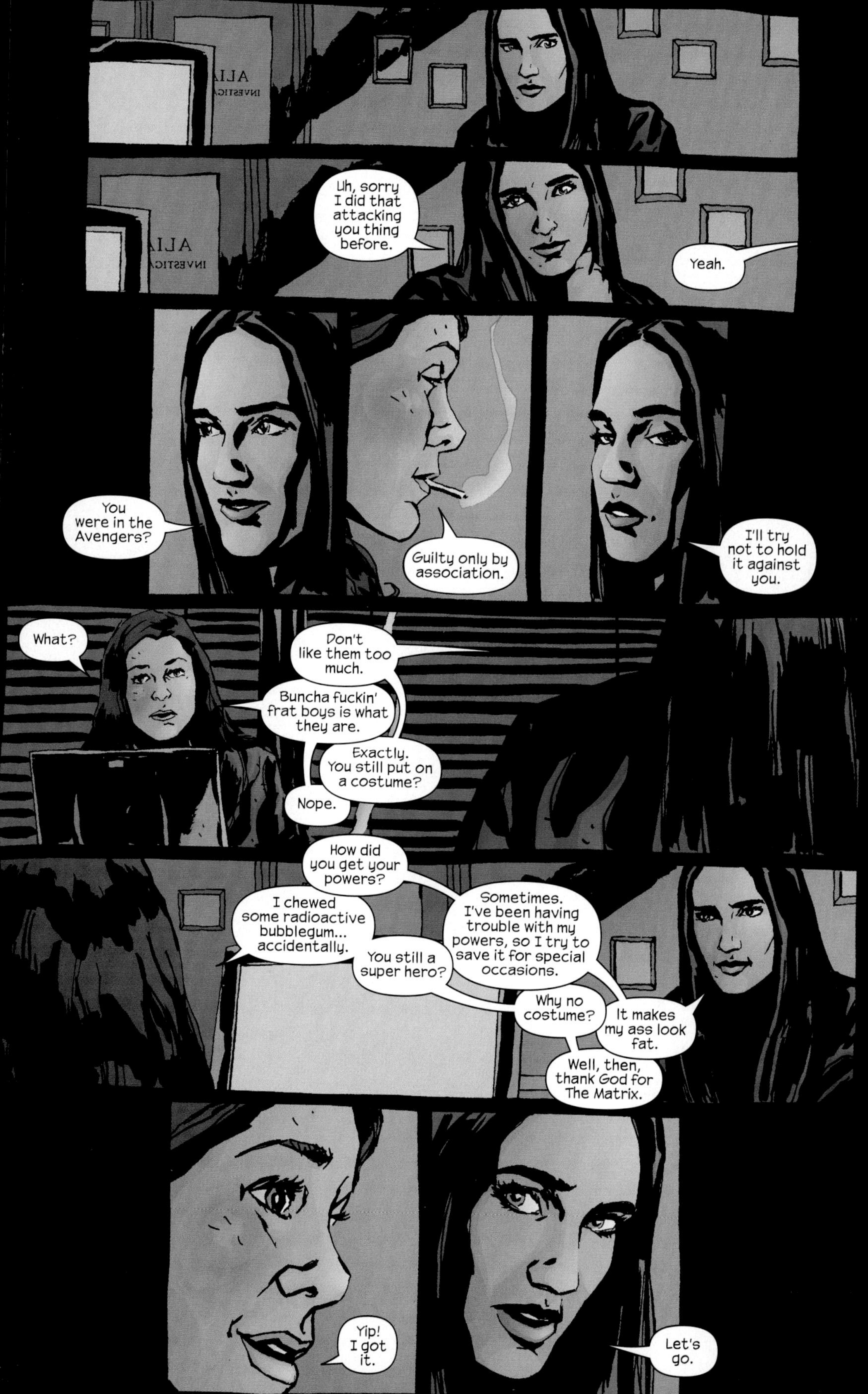

Uh, sorry I did that attacking you thing before.
Yeah.
You were in the Avengers?
Guilty only by association.
I'll try not to hold it against you.
What?
Don't like them too much.
Buncha fuckin' frat boys is what they are.
Exactly. You still put on a costume?
Nope.
How did you get your powers?
I chewed some radioactive bubblegum... accidentally.
You still a super hero?
Sometimes. I've been having trouble with my powers, so I try to save it for special occasions.
Why no costume?
It makes my ass look fat.
Well, then, thank God for The Matrix.
Yip! I got it.
Let's go.

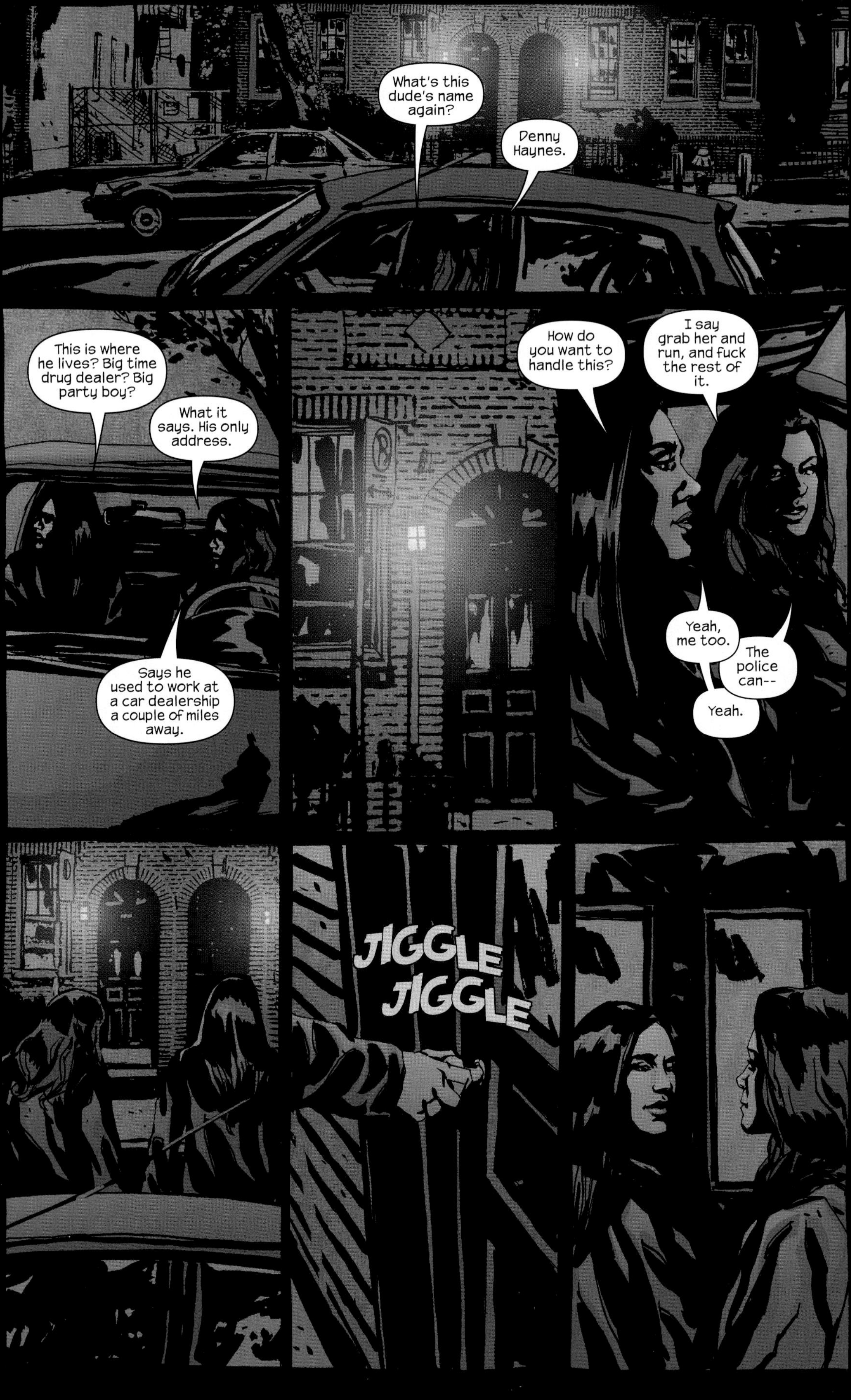
What's this dude's name again?
Denny Haynes.
This is where he lives? Big time drug dealer? Big party boy?
What it says. His only address.
Says he used to work at a car dealership a couple of miles away.
How do you want to handle this?
I say grab her and run, and fuck the rest of it.
Yeah, me too.
The police can--
Yeah.
JIGGLE JIGGLE

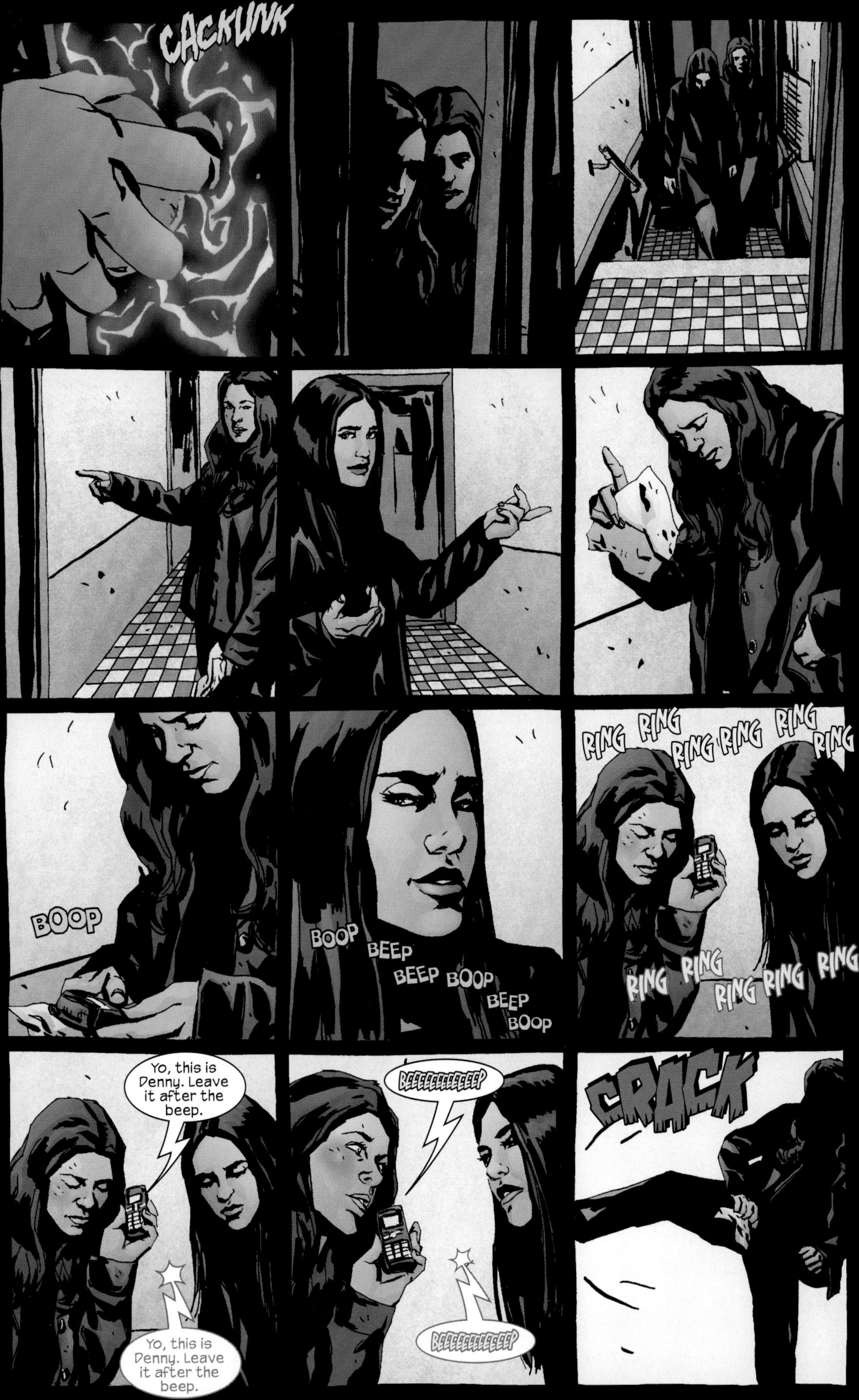
CACKUNK
BOOP
BOOP
BEEP
BEEP BOOP
BEEP
BOOP
RING RING RING RING RING RING RING
RING RING RING RING RING
Yo, this is Denny. Leave it after the beep.
Yo, this is Denny. Leave it after the beep.
BEEEEEEEEEEEEP
BEEEEEEEEEEEEP
CRACK

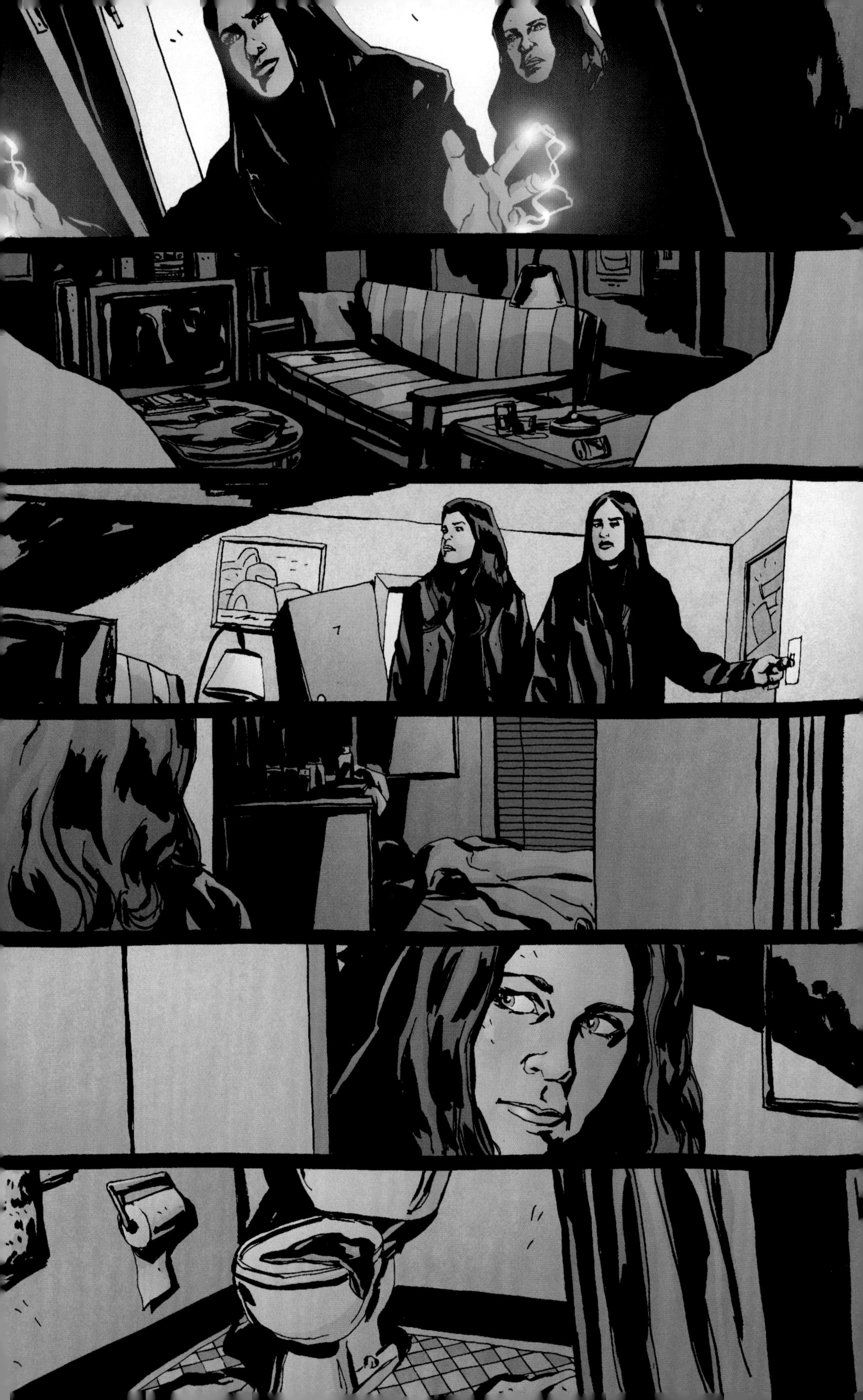

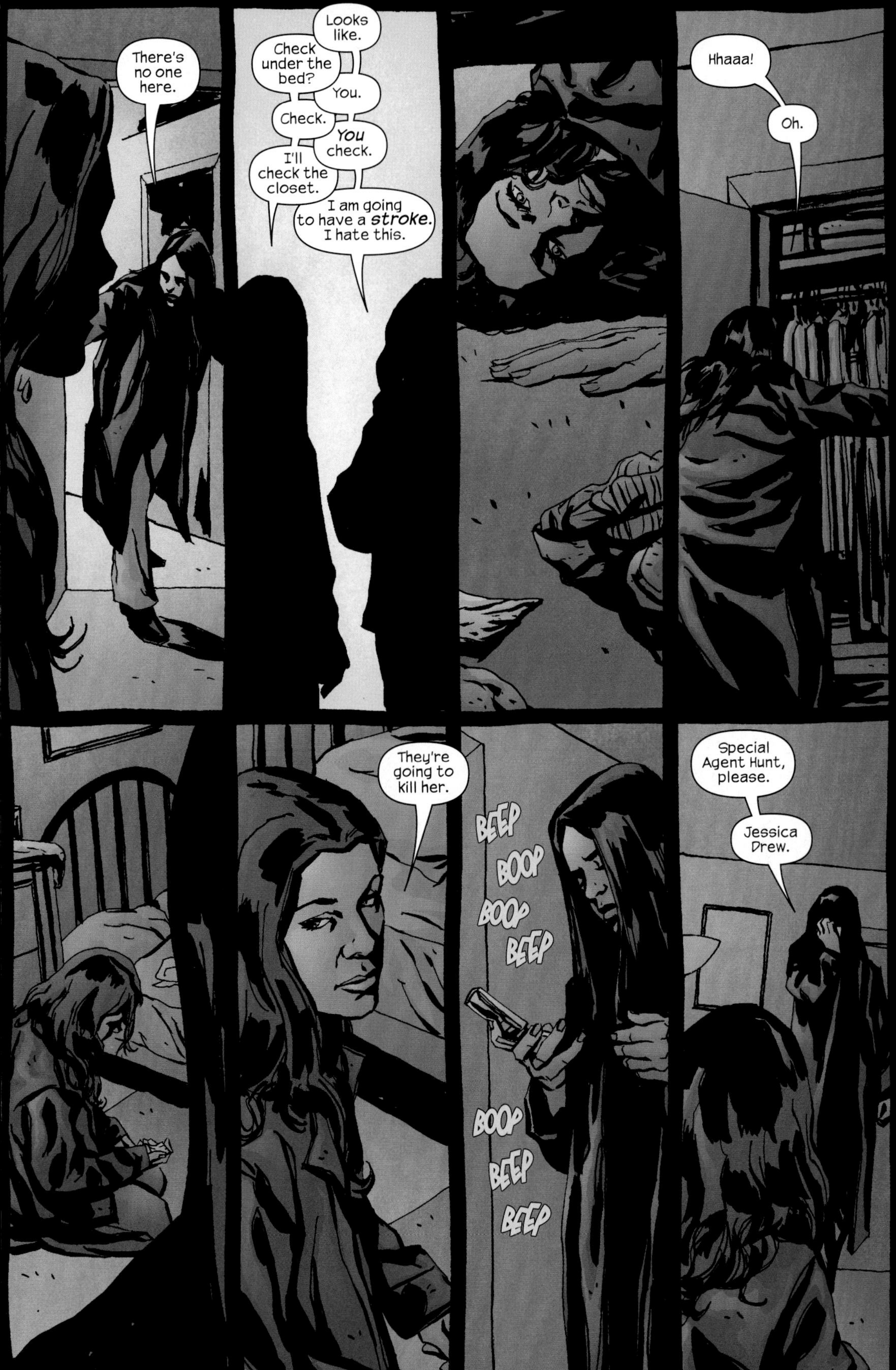

There's no one here.
Looks like.
Check under the bed?
You.
Check.
You check.
I'll check the closet.
I am going to have a **stroke.** I hate this.
Hhaaa!
Oh.
They're going to kill her.
BEEP
BOOP
BOOP
BEEP
BOOP
BEEP
BEEP
Special Agent Hunt, please.
Jessica Drew.

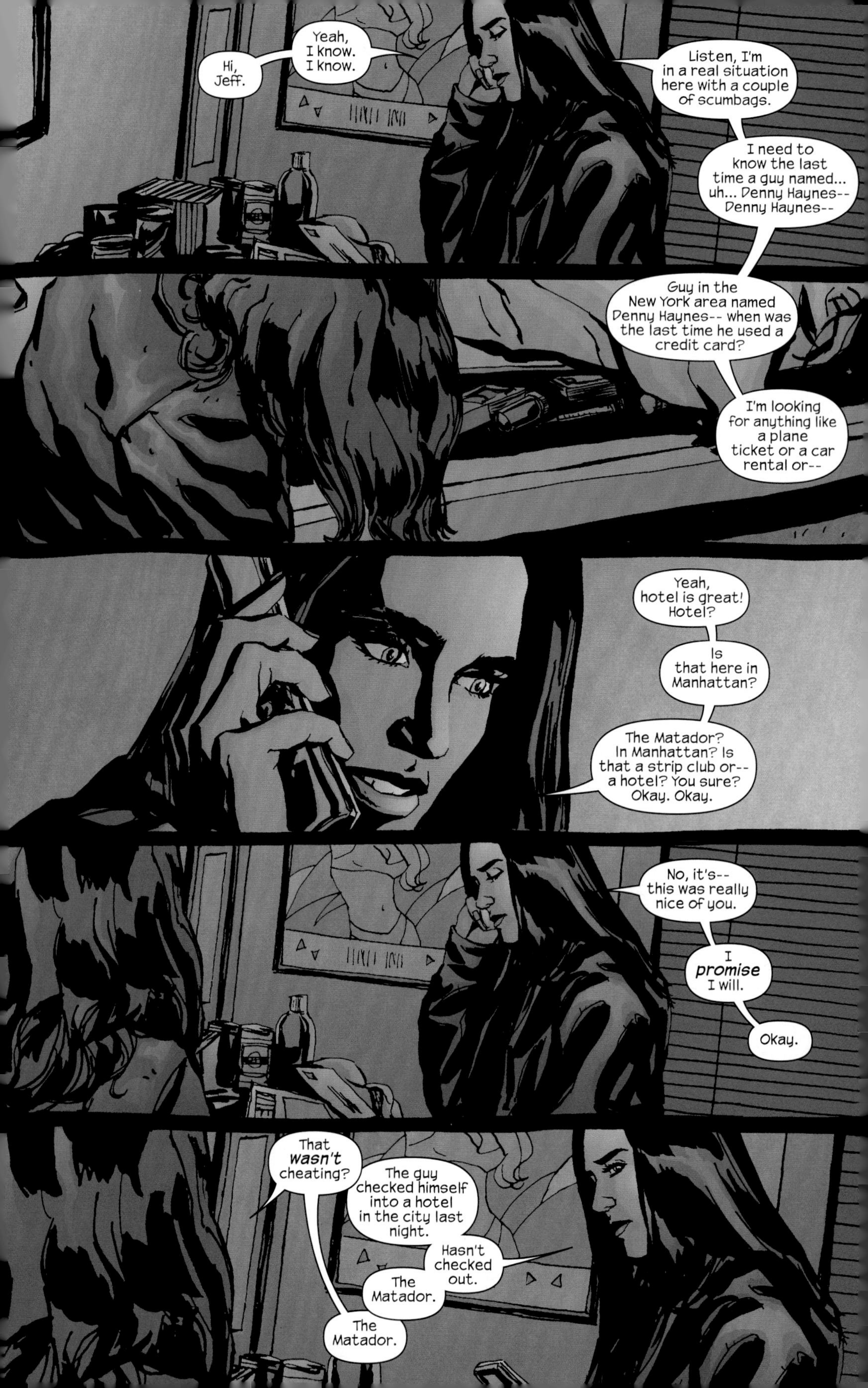
Hi, Jeff.
Yeah, I know. I know.
Listen, I'm in a real situation here with a couple of scumbags.
I need to know the last time a guy named... uh... Denny Haynes-- Denny Haynes--
Guy in the New York area named Denny Haynes-- when was the last time he used a credit card?
I'm looking for anything like a plane ticket or a car rental or--
Yeah, hotel is great! Hotel?
Is that here in Manhattan?
The Matador? In Manhattan? Is that a strip club or-- a hotel? You sure? Okay. Okay.
No, it's-- this was really nice of you.
I *promise* I will.
Okay.
That *wasn't* cheating?
The guy checked himself into a hotel in the city last night.
Hasn't checked out.
The Matador.
The Matador.

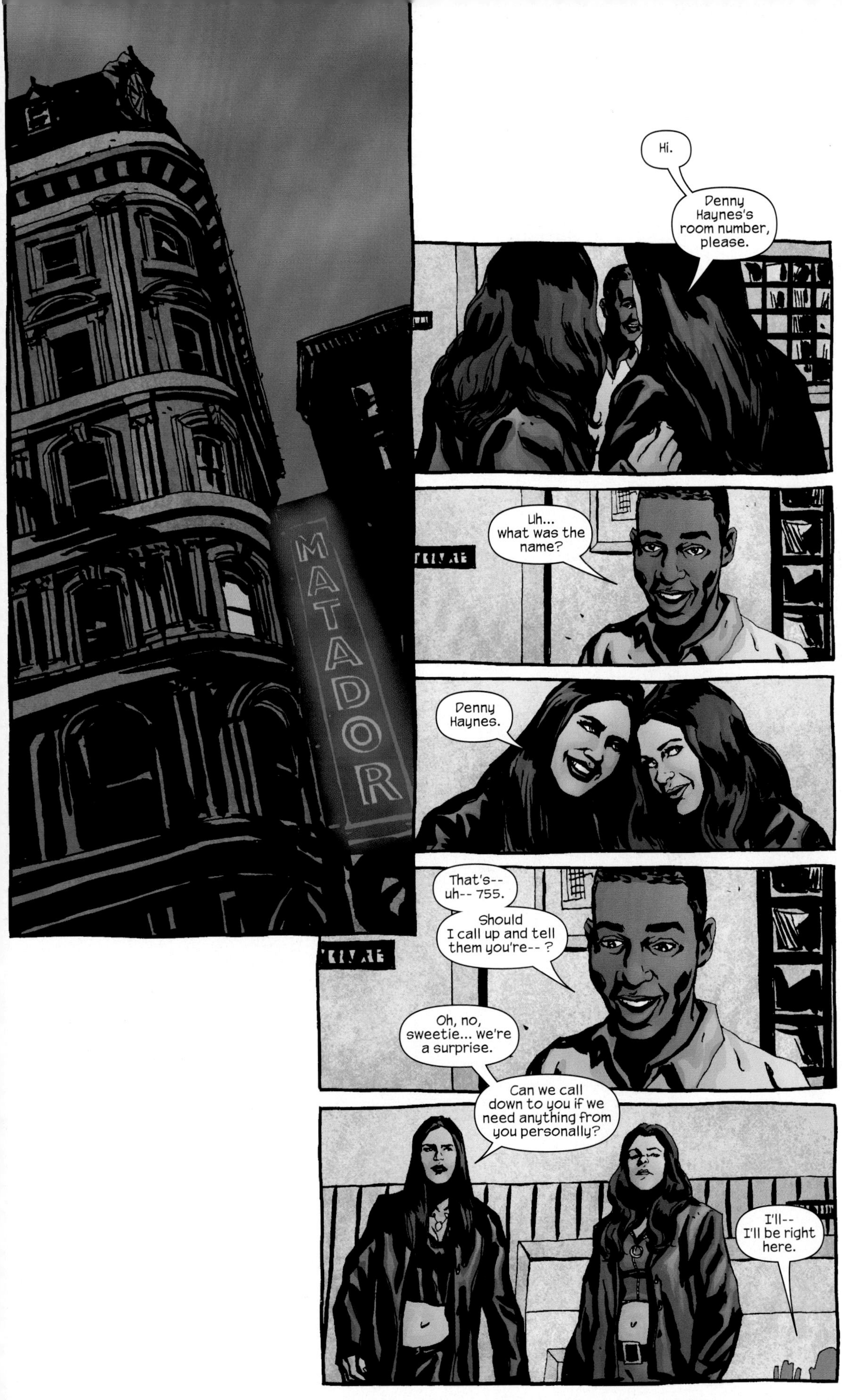
MATADOR
Hi.
Denny Haynes's room number, please.
Uh... what was the name?
Denny Haynes.
That's-- uh-- 755.
Should I call up and tell them you're-- ?
Oh, no, sweetie... we're a surprise.
Can we call down to you if we need anything from you personally?
I'll-- I'll be right here.

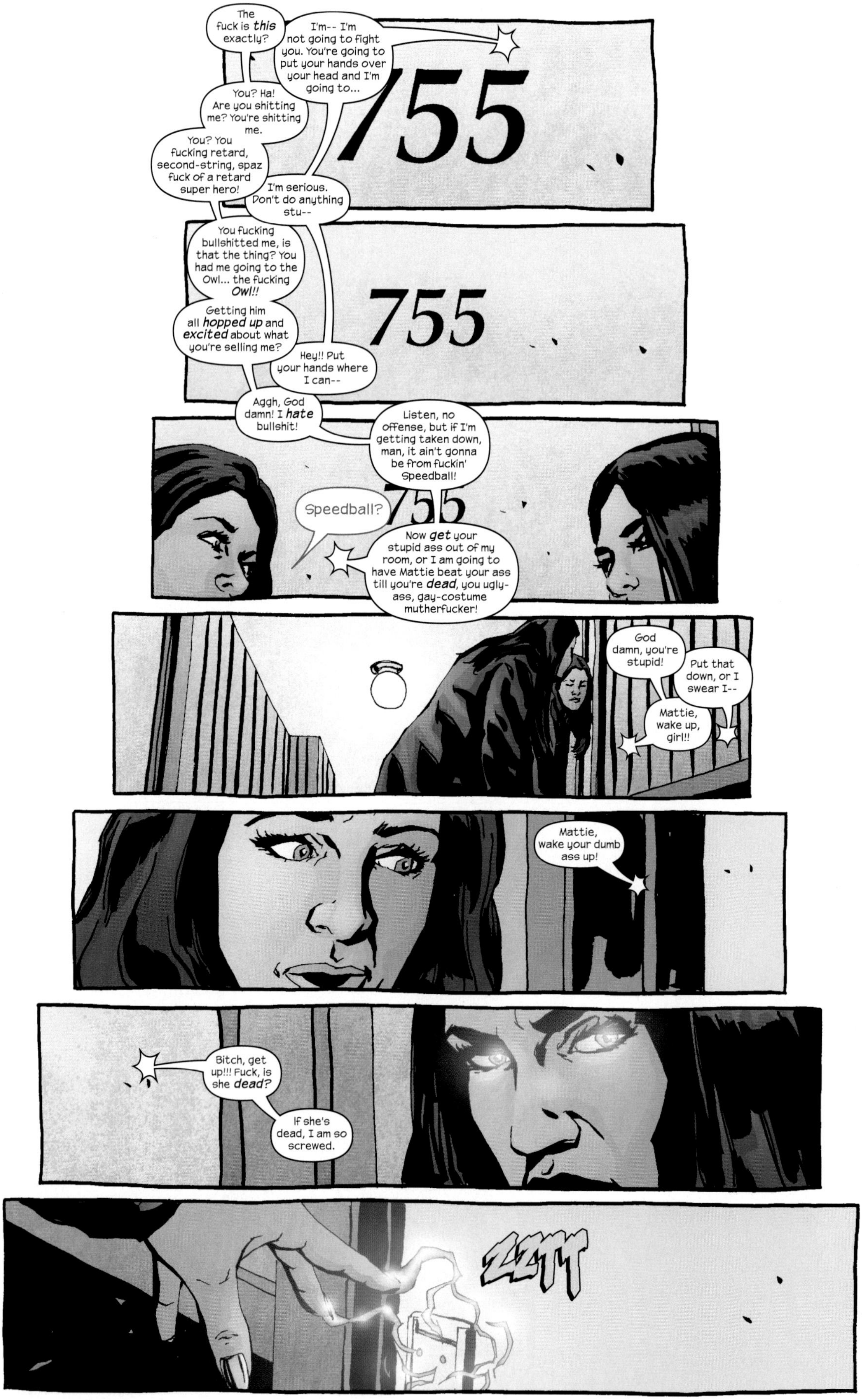
The fuck is *this* exactly?
I'm-- I'm not going to fight you. You're going to put your hands over your head and I'm going to...
755
You? Ha! Are you shitting me? You're shitting me.
You? You fucking retard, second-string, spaz fuck of a retard super hero!
I'm serious. Don't do anything stu--
You fucking bullshitted me, is that the thing? You had me going to the Owl... the fucking *Owl!!*
755
Getting him all *hopped up* and *excited* about what you're selling me?
Hey!! Put your hands where I can--
Aggh, God damn! I *hate* bullshit!
Listen, no offense, but if I'm getting taken down, man, it ain't gonna be from fuckin' Speedball!
755
Speedball?
Now *get* your stupid ass out of my room, or I am going to have Mattie beat your ass till you're *dead*, you ugly-ass, gay-costume mutherfucker!
God damn, you're stupid!
Put that down, or I swear I--
Mattie, wake up, girl!!
Mattie, wake your dumb ass up!
Bitch, get up!!! Fuck, is she *dead?*
If she's dead, I am so screwed.
ZZTT

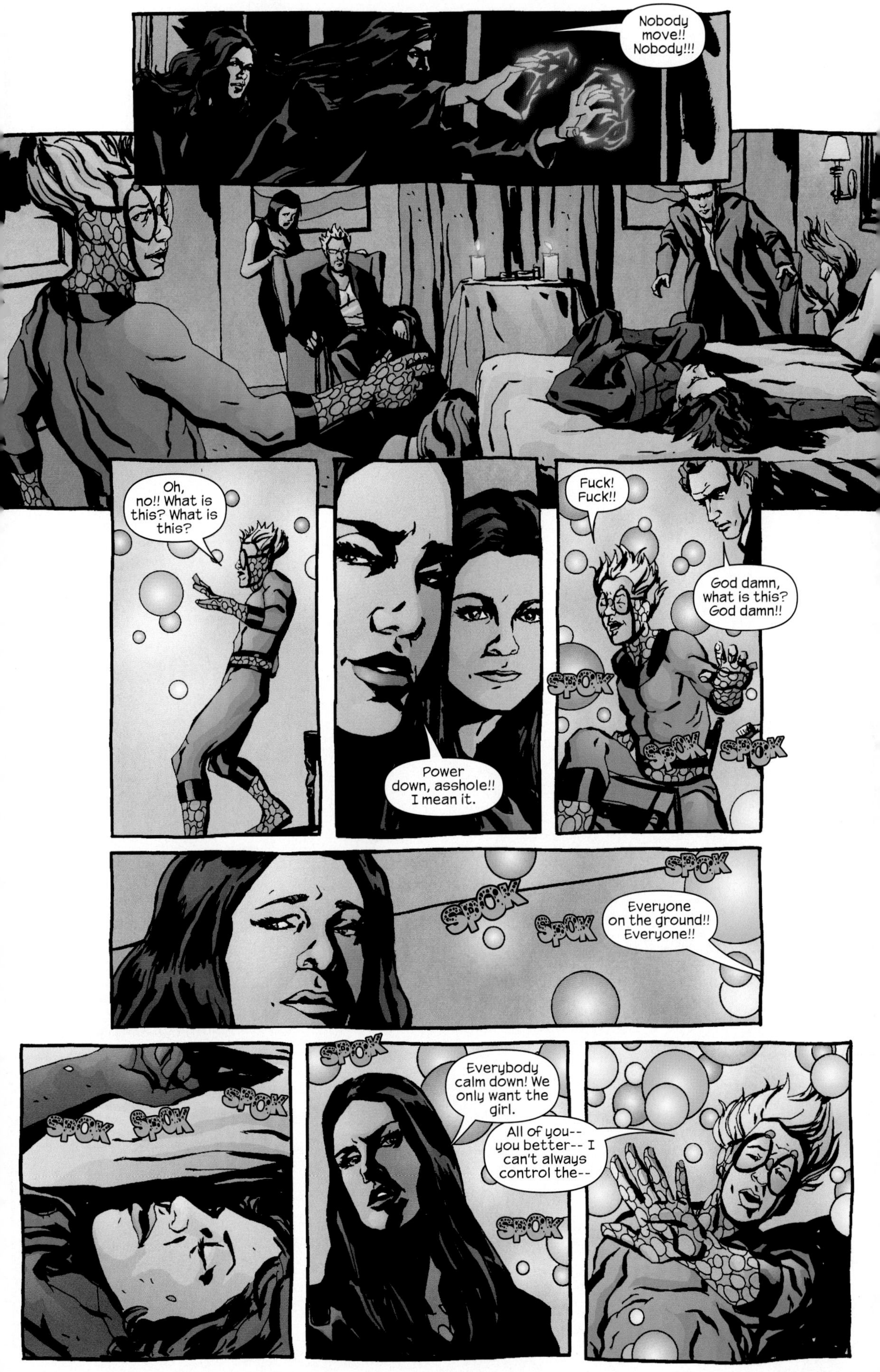
Nobody move!! Nobody!!!
Oh, no!! What is this? What is this?
Power down, asshole!! I mean it.
Fuck! Fuck!!
God damn, what is this? God damn!!
SPOK
SPOK
SPOK
SPOK
SPOK
Everyone on the ground!! Everyone!!
SPOK
SPOK
SPOK
SPOK
SPOK
SPOK
Everybody calm down! We only want the girl.
All of you-- you better-- I can't always control the--

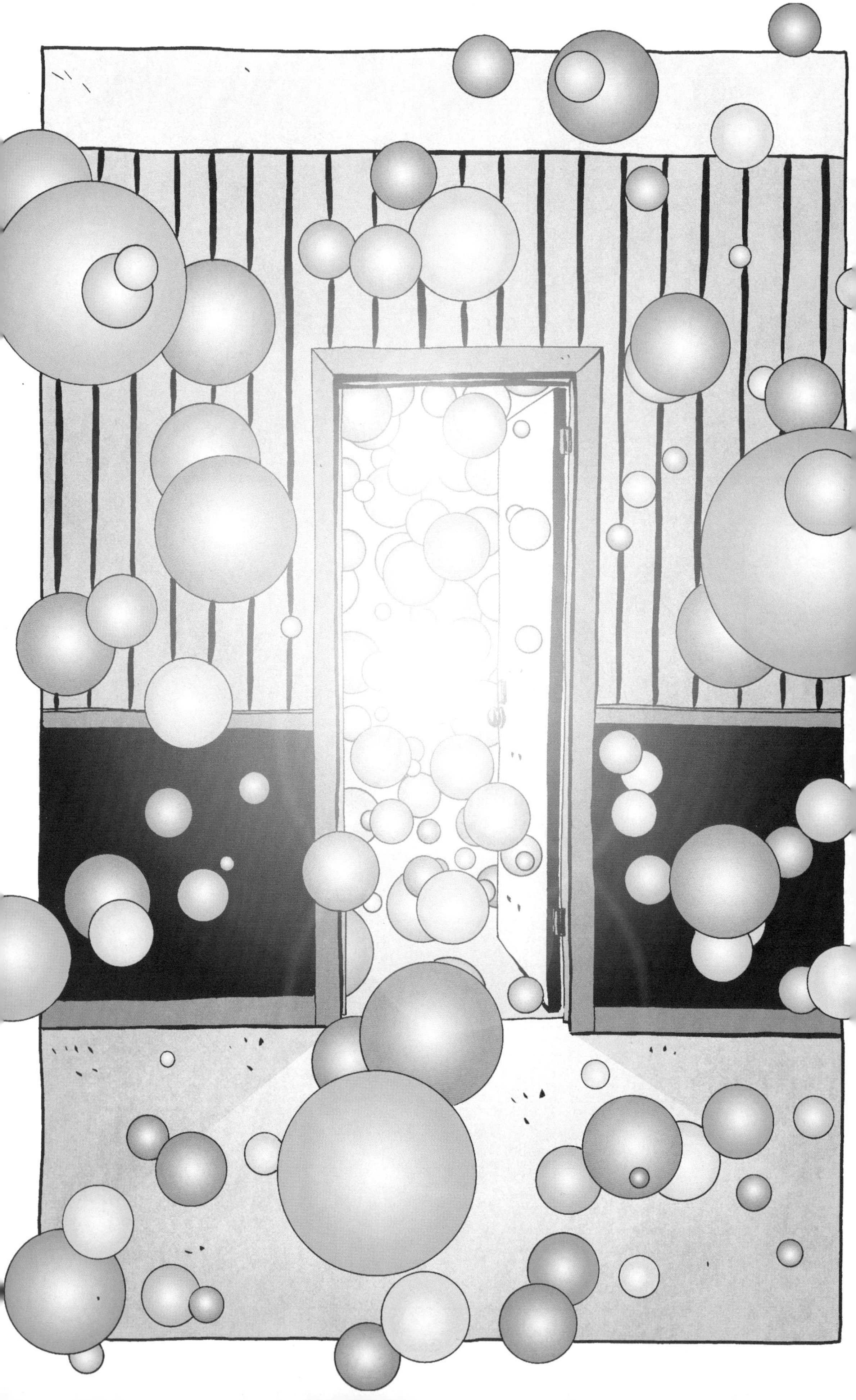

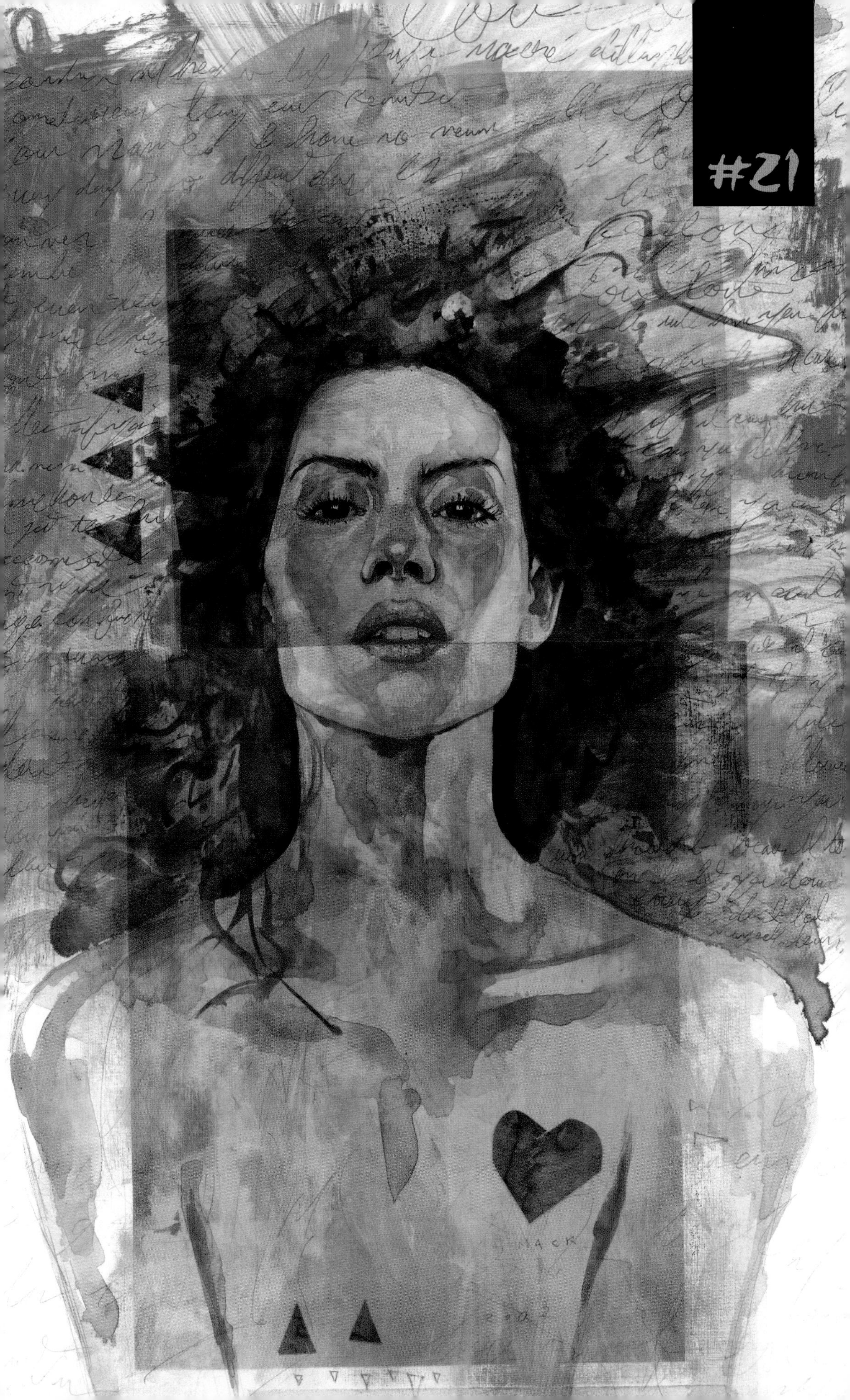
#21

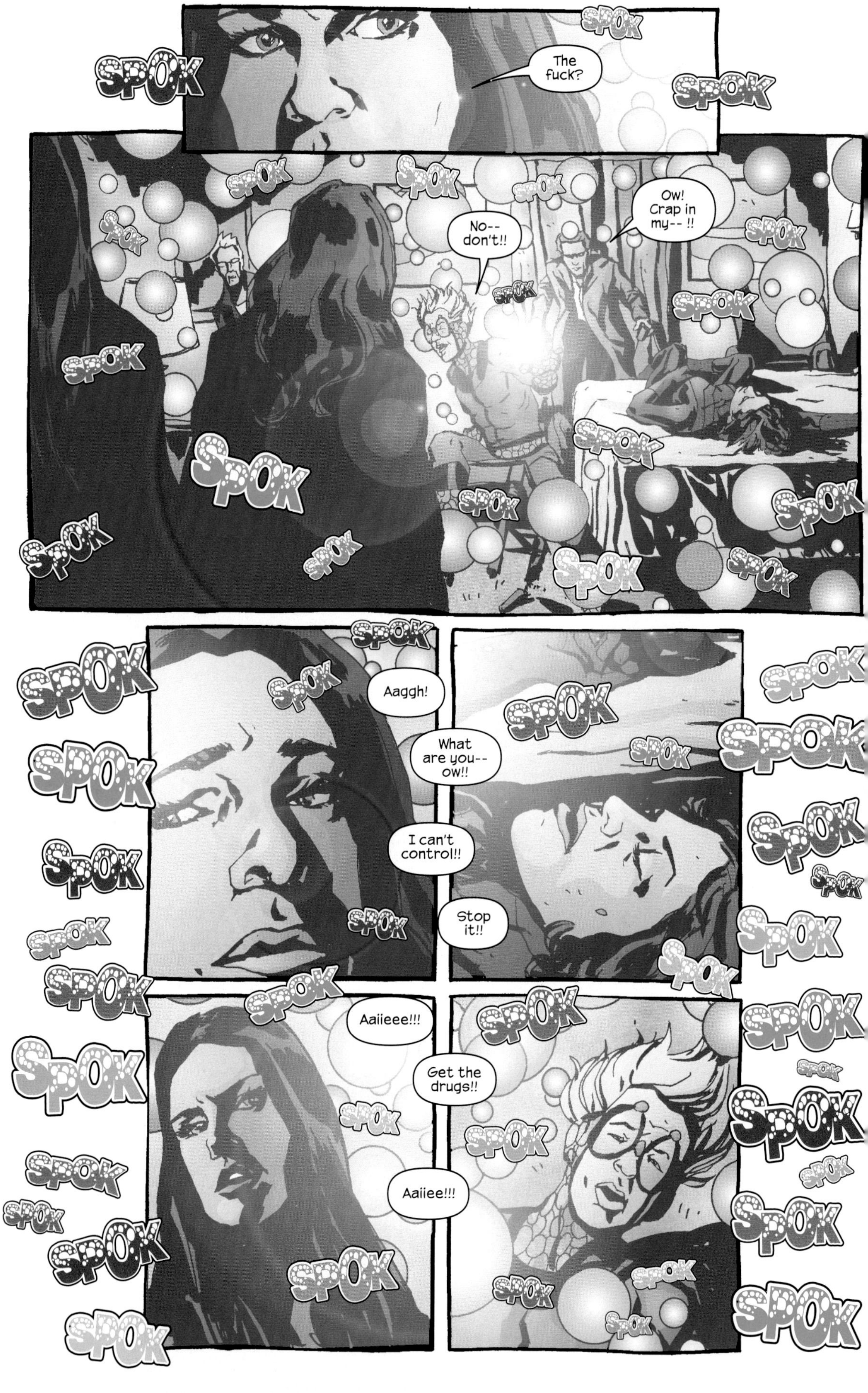

SPOK
The fuck?
SPOK
No-- don't!!
Ow! Crap in my-- !!
SPOK
Aaggh!
What are you-- ow!!
I can't control!!
Stop it!!
SPOK
Aaiieee!!!
Get the drugs!!
Aaiiee!!!
SPOK

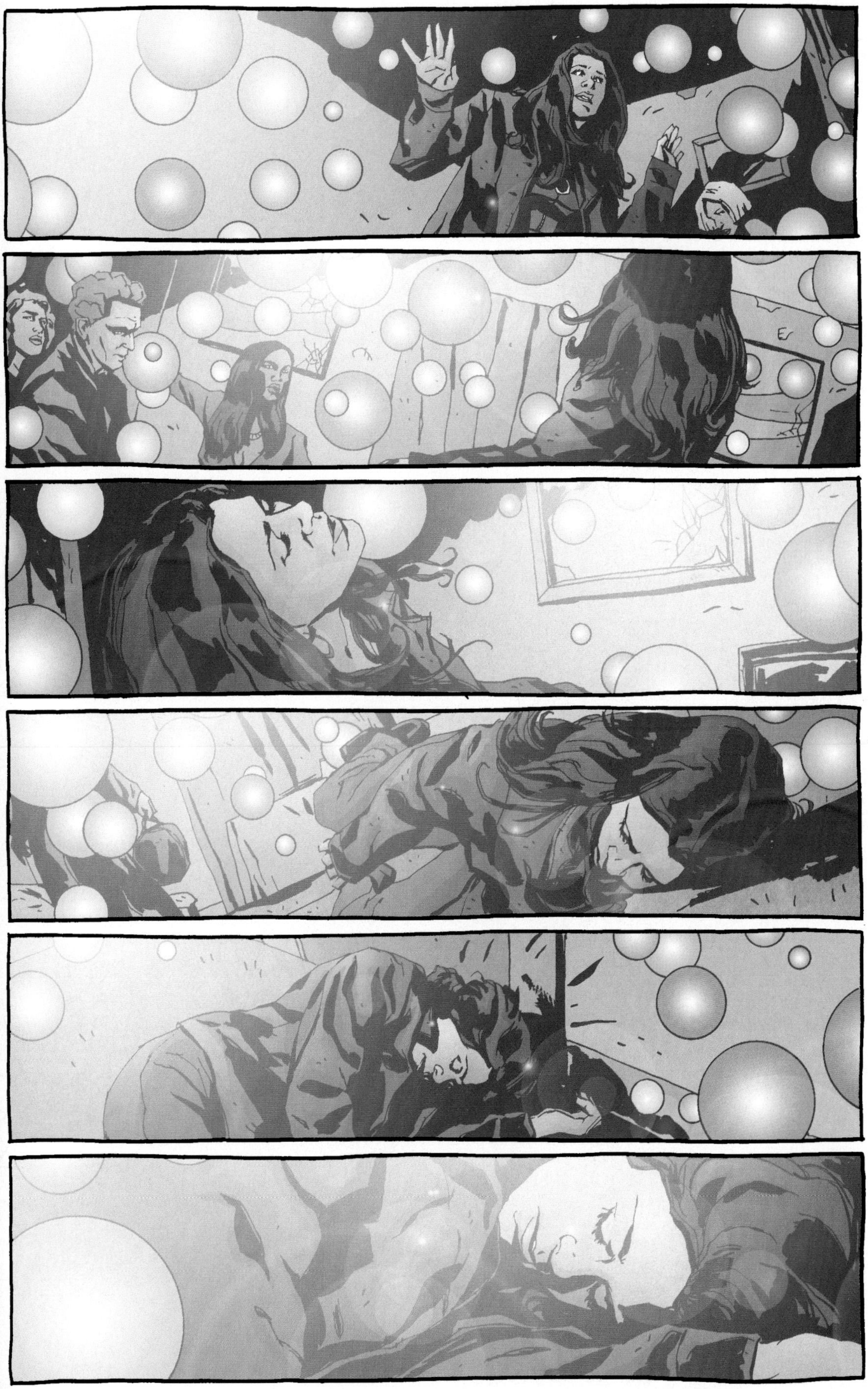

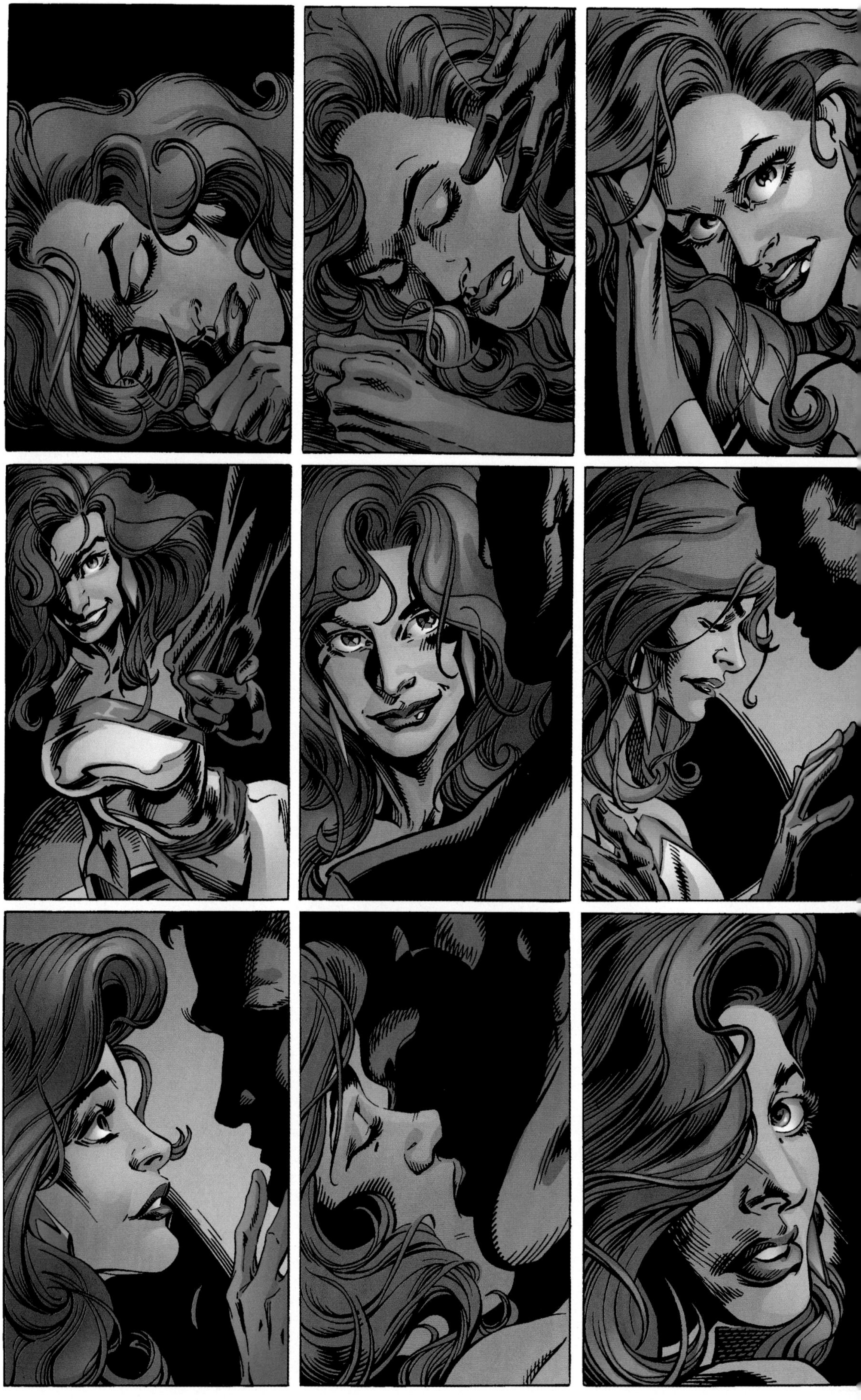

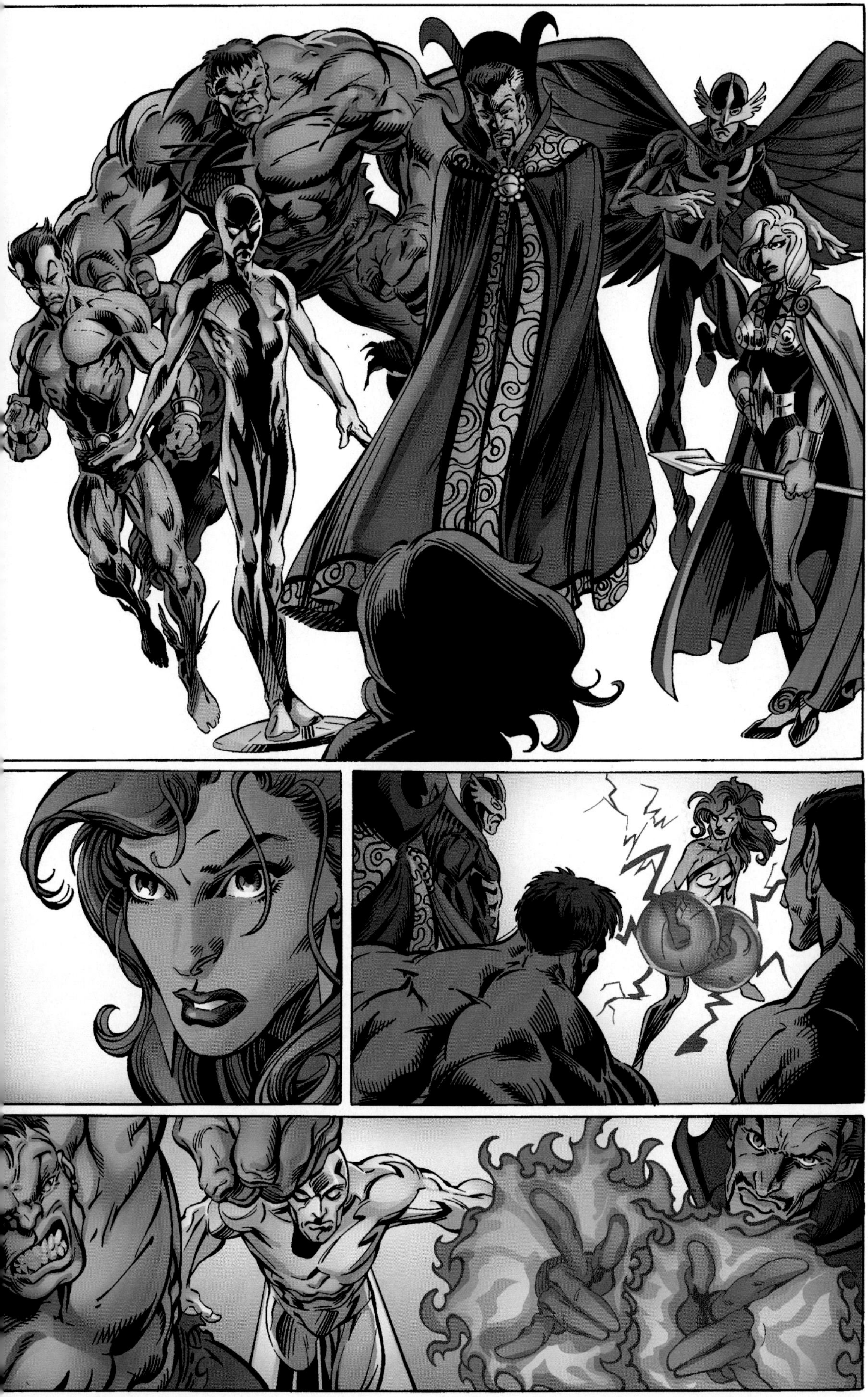

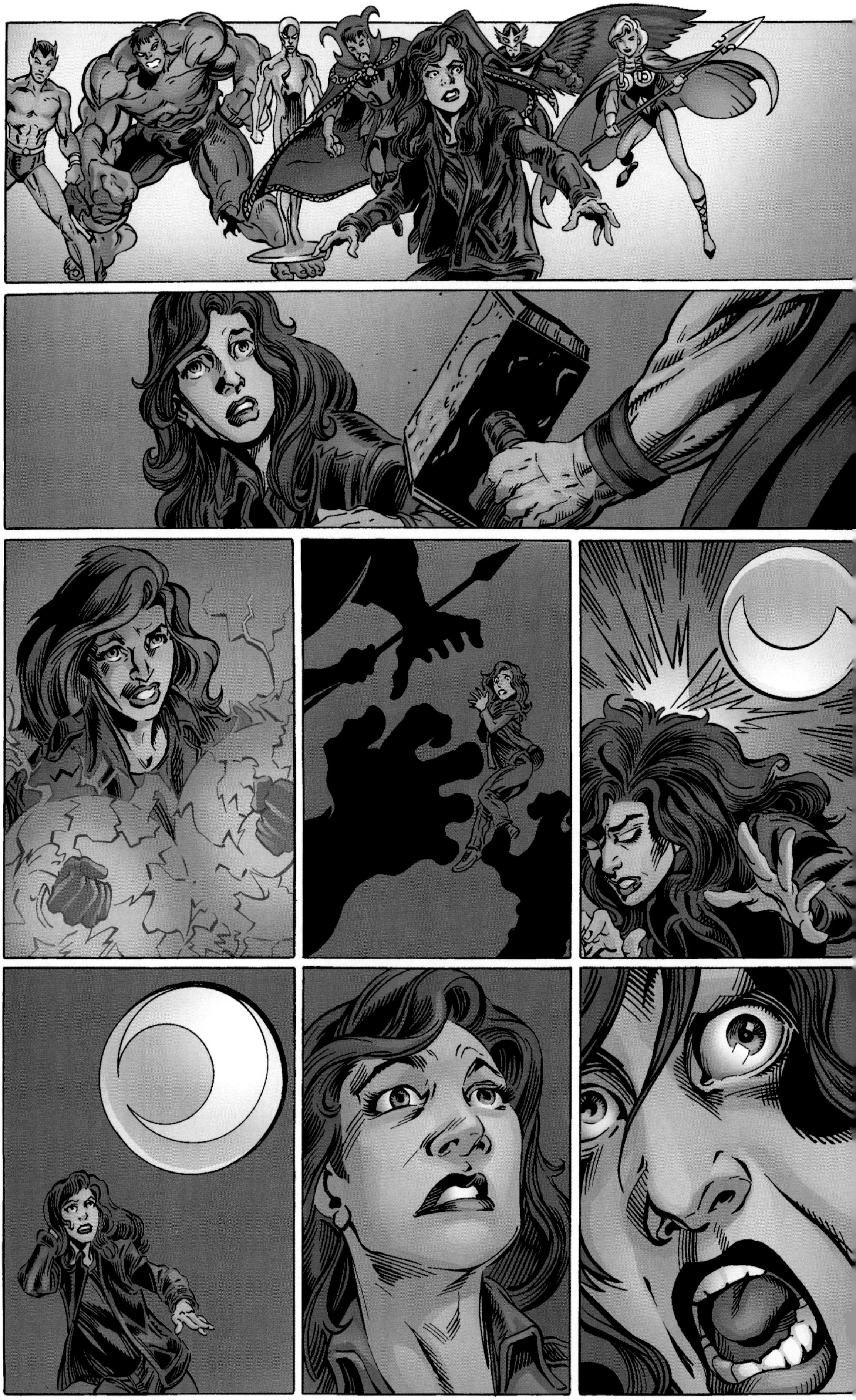

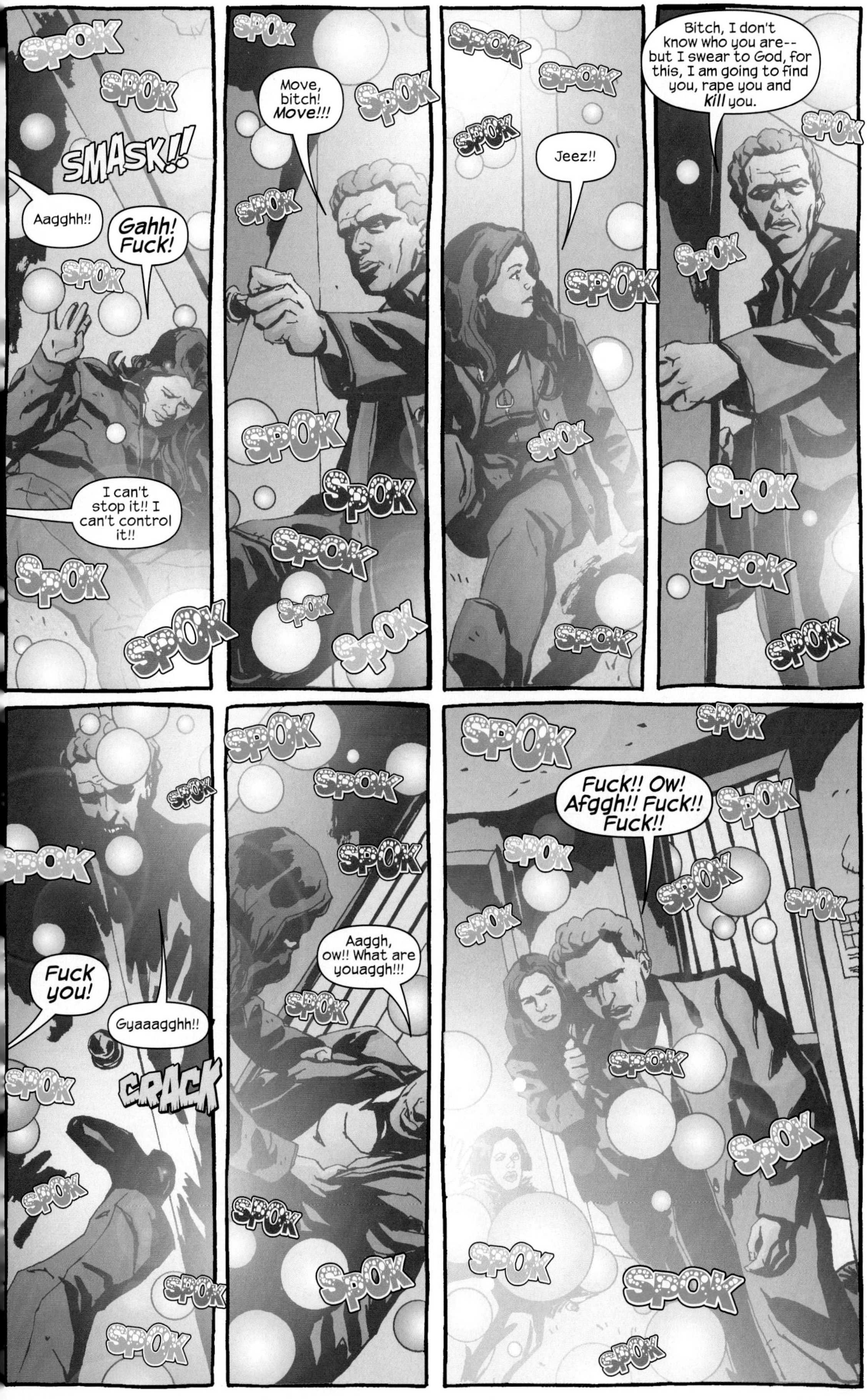
SPOK
SPOK
SMASK!!
Aagghh!!
Gahh! Fuck!
SPOK
I can't stop it!! I can't control it!!
SPOK
SPOK
SPOK
Move, bitch! Move!!!
SPOK
SPOK
SPOK
SPOK
SPOK
SPOK
SPOK
SPOK
SPOK
SPOK
Jeez!!
SPOK
SPOK
SPOK
Bitch, I don't know who you are-- but I swear to God, for this, I am going to find you, rape you and kill you.
SPOK
SPOK
SPOK
SPOK
SPOK
SPOK
SPOK
Fuck you!
Gyaaagghh!!
SPOK
CRACK
SPOK
SPOK
SPOK
SPOK
SPOK
SPOK
Aaggh, ow!! What are youaggh!!!
SPOK
SPOK
SPOK
SPOK
SPOK
Fuck!! Ow! Afggh!! Fuck!! Fuck!!
SPOK
SPOK
SPOK
SPOK
SPOK
SPOK
SPOK
SPOK
SPOK
SPOK

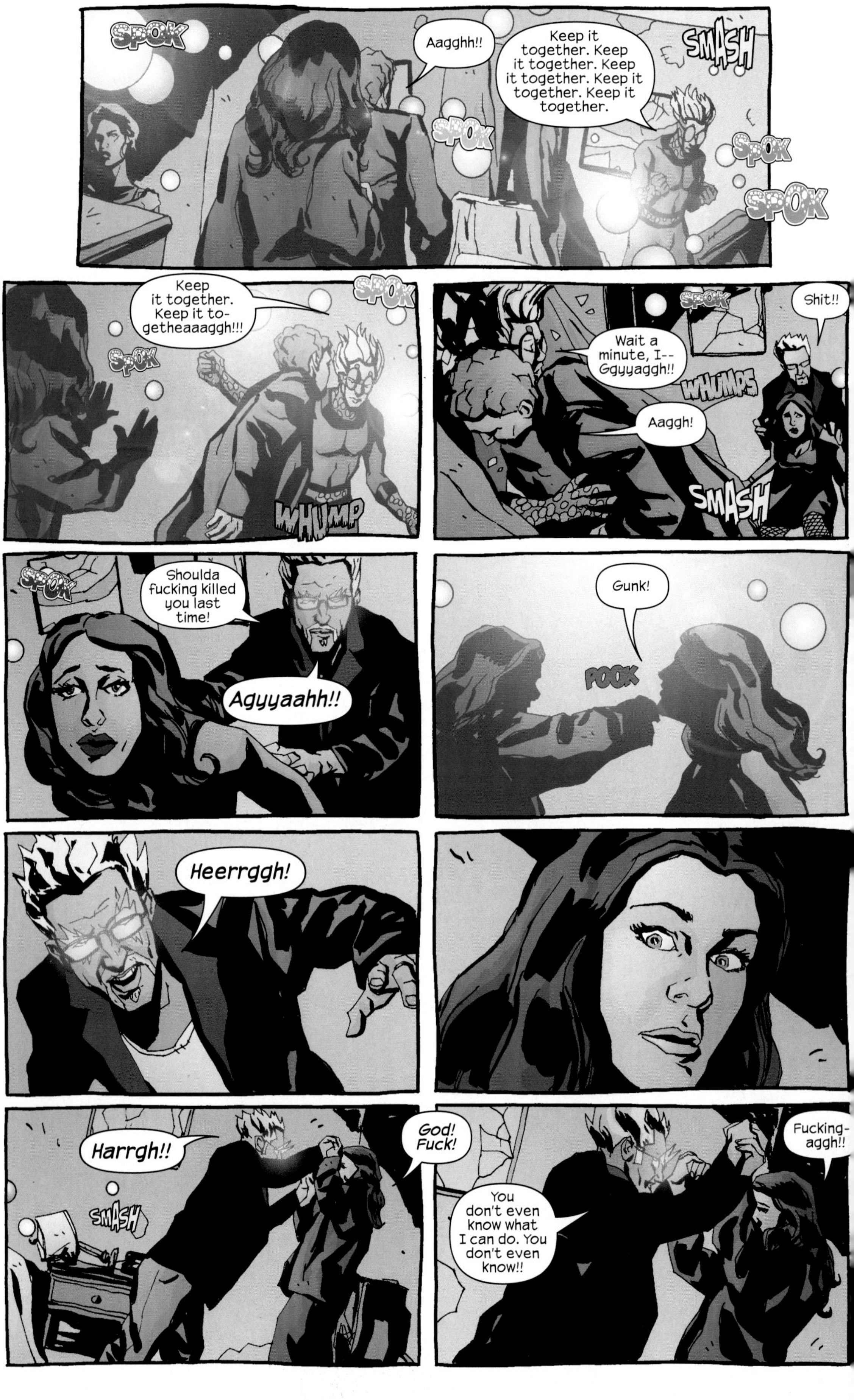
SPOK
Aagghh!!
Keep it together. Keep it together. Keep it together. Keep it together. Keep it together.
SMASH
SPOK
SPOK
SPOK
Keep it together. Keep it to-getheaaaggh!!!
SPOK
SPOK
WHUMP
SPOK
Wait a minute, I-- Ggyyagggh!!
Shit!!
WHUMPS
Aaggh!
SMASH
SPOK
Shoulda fucking killed you last time!
Agyyaahh!!
Gunk!
POOK
Heerrggh!
Harrgh!!
SMASH
God! Fuck!
You don't even know what I can do. You don't even know!!
Fucking-aggh!!

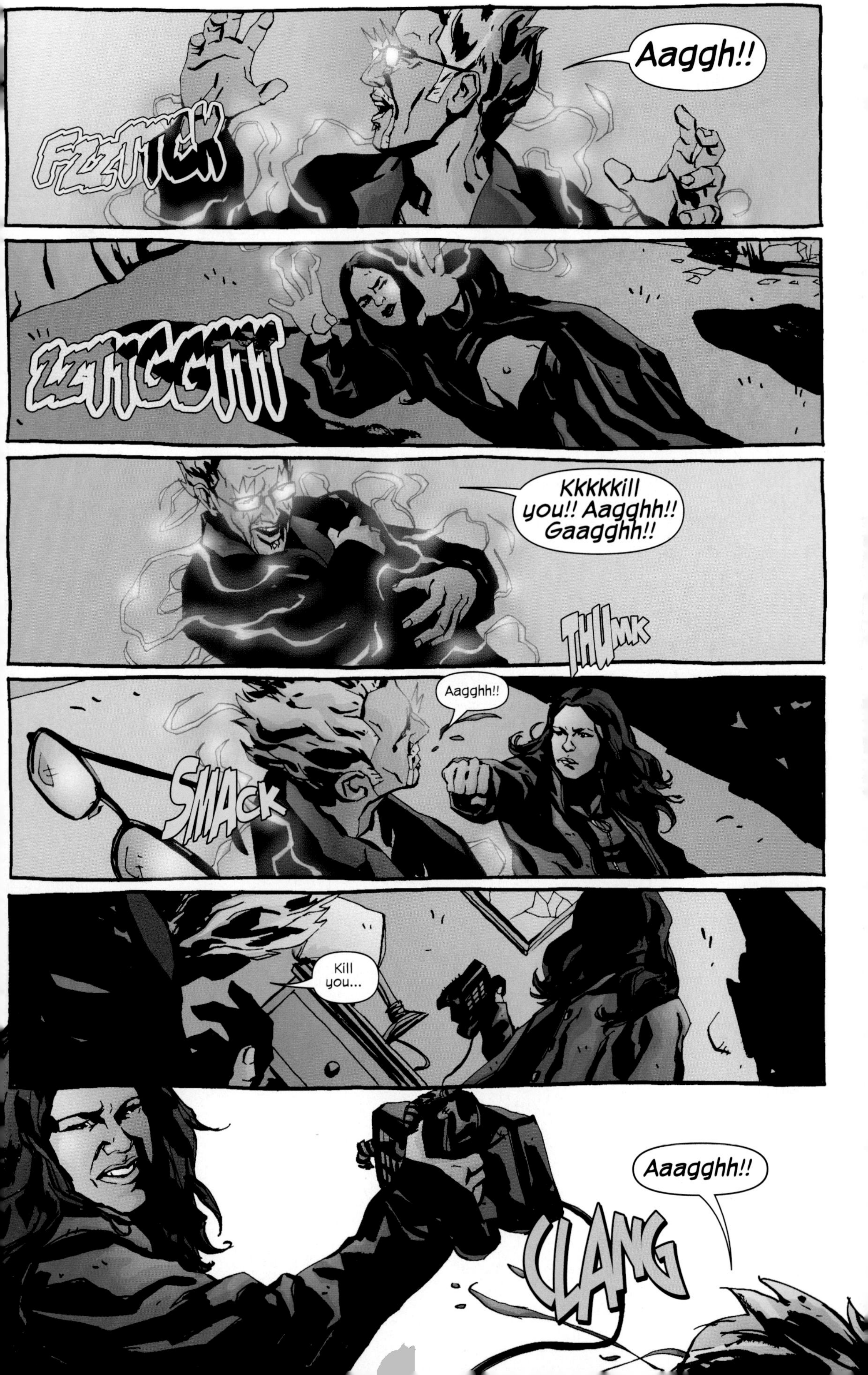
Aagggh!!
FZZTTCH
ZZTTGGHHH
Kkkkkill you!! Aagghh!! Gaagghh!!
THUMK
Aagghh!!
SMACK
Kill you...
Aaagghh!!
CLANG

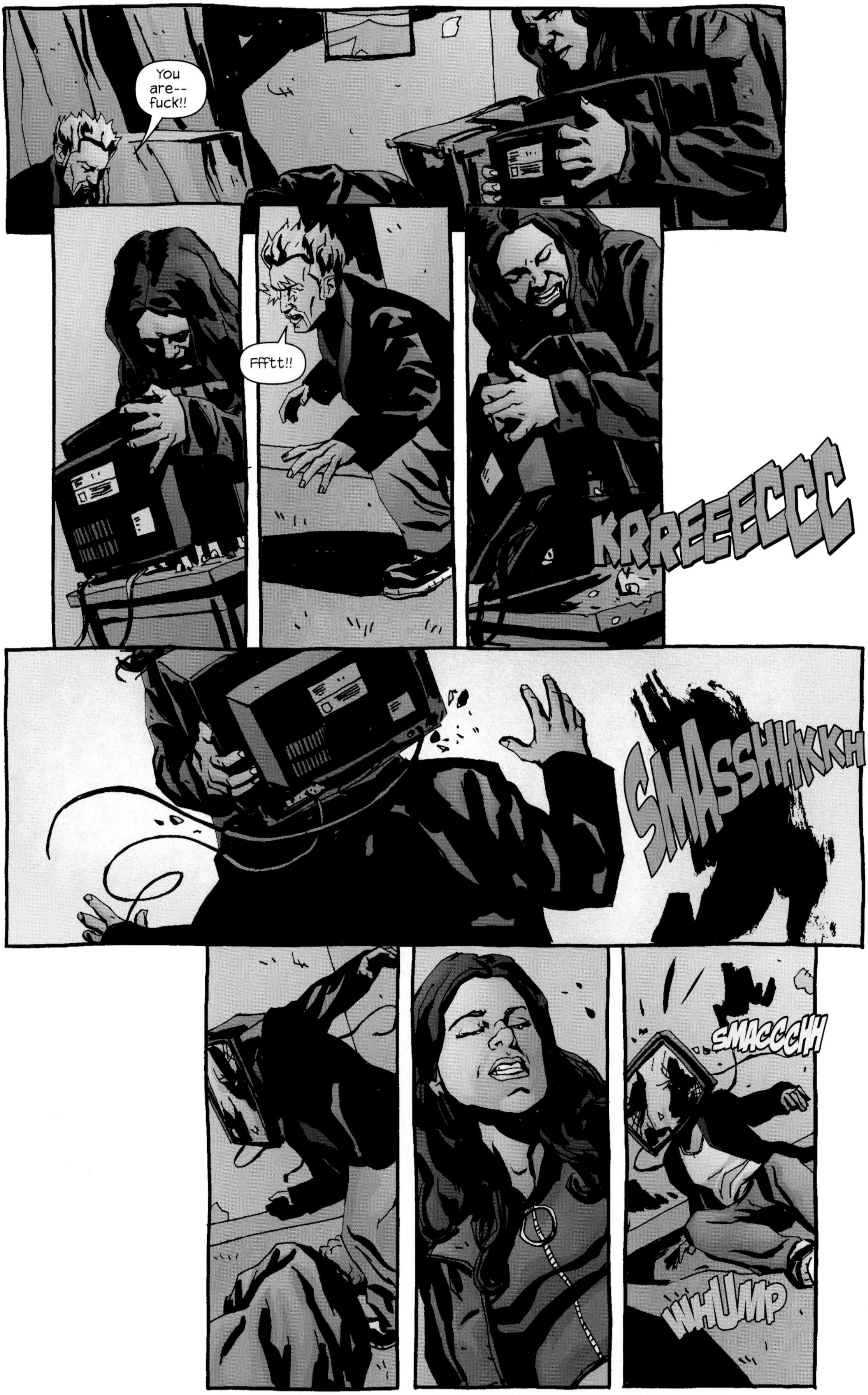
You are-- fuck!!
Ffftt!!
KRREEECCC
SMASSHHKKH
SMACCCHH
WHUMP

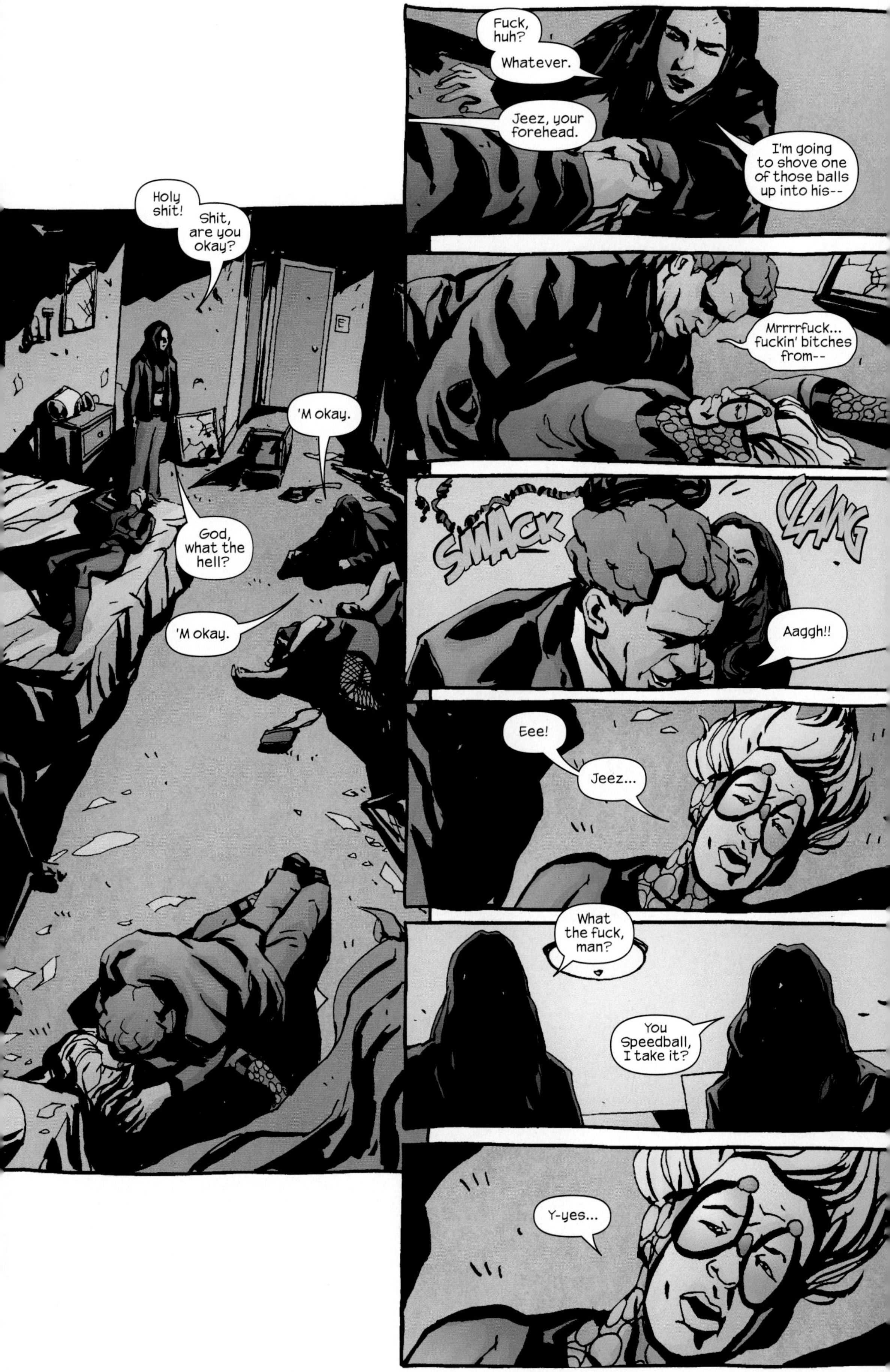
Fuck, huh?
Whatever.
Jeez, your forehead.
I'm going to shove one of those balls up into his--
Mrrrrfuck... fuckin' bitches from--
SMACK
CLANG
Aaggh!!
Eee!
Jeez...
What the fuck, man?
You Speedball, I take it?
Y-yes...
Holy shit!
Shit, are you okay?
'M okay.
God, what the hell?
'M okay.

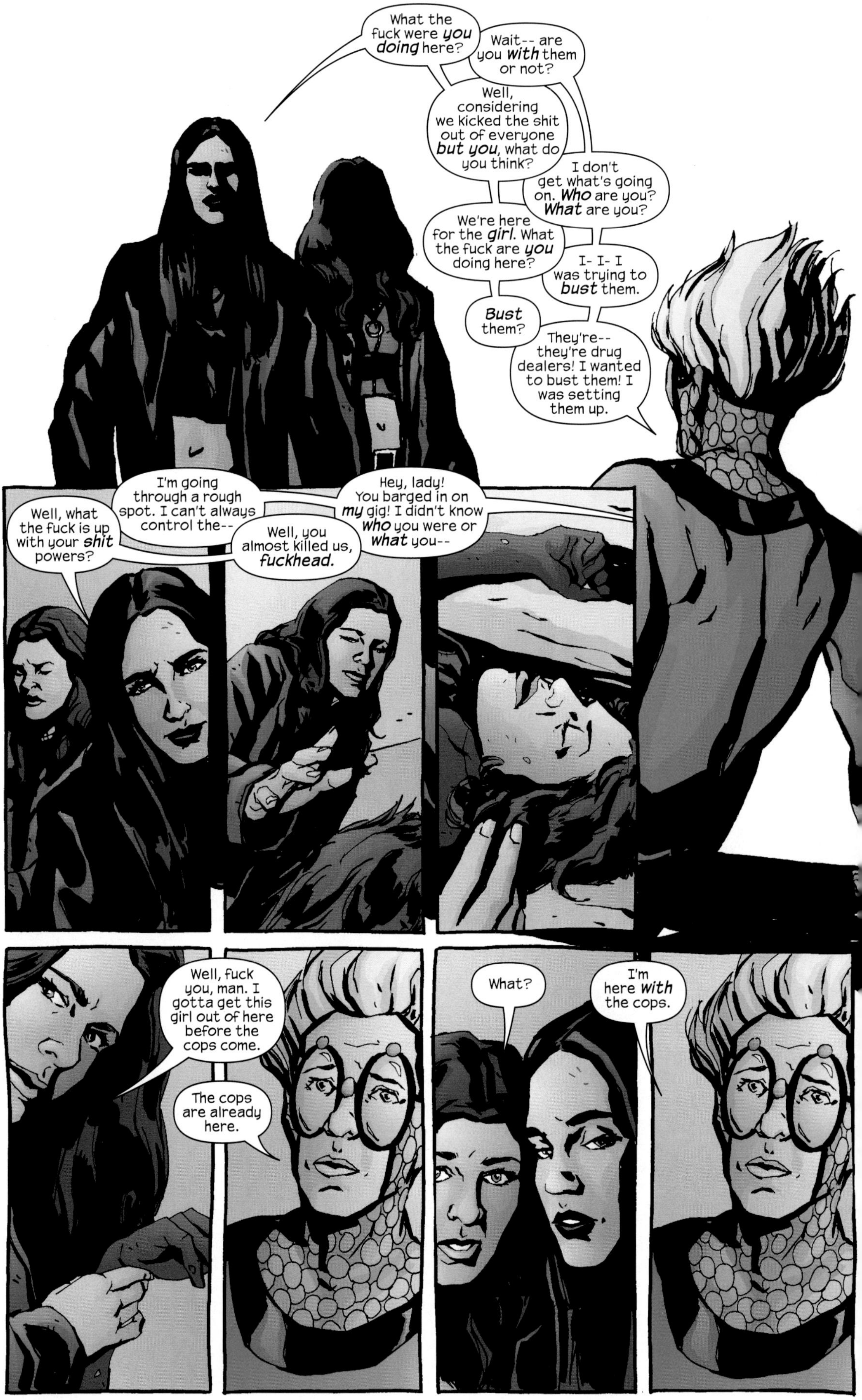
What the fuck were *you doing* here?
Wait-- are you *with* them or not?
Well, considering we kicked the shit out of everyone *but you*, what do you think?
I don't get what's going on. *Who* are you? *What* are you?
We're here for the *girl*. What the fuck are *you* doing here?
I- I- I was trying to *bust* them.
Bust them?
They're-- they're drug dealers! I wanted to bust them! I was setting them up.
Well, what the fuck is up with your *shit* powers?
I'm going through a rough spot. I can't always control the--
Well, you almost killed us, *fuckhead.*
Hey, lady! You barged in on *my* gig! I didn't know *who* you were or *what* you--
Well, fuck you, man. I gotta get this girl out of here before the cops come.
The cops are already here.
What?
I'm here *with* the cops.

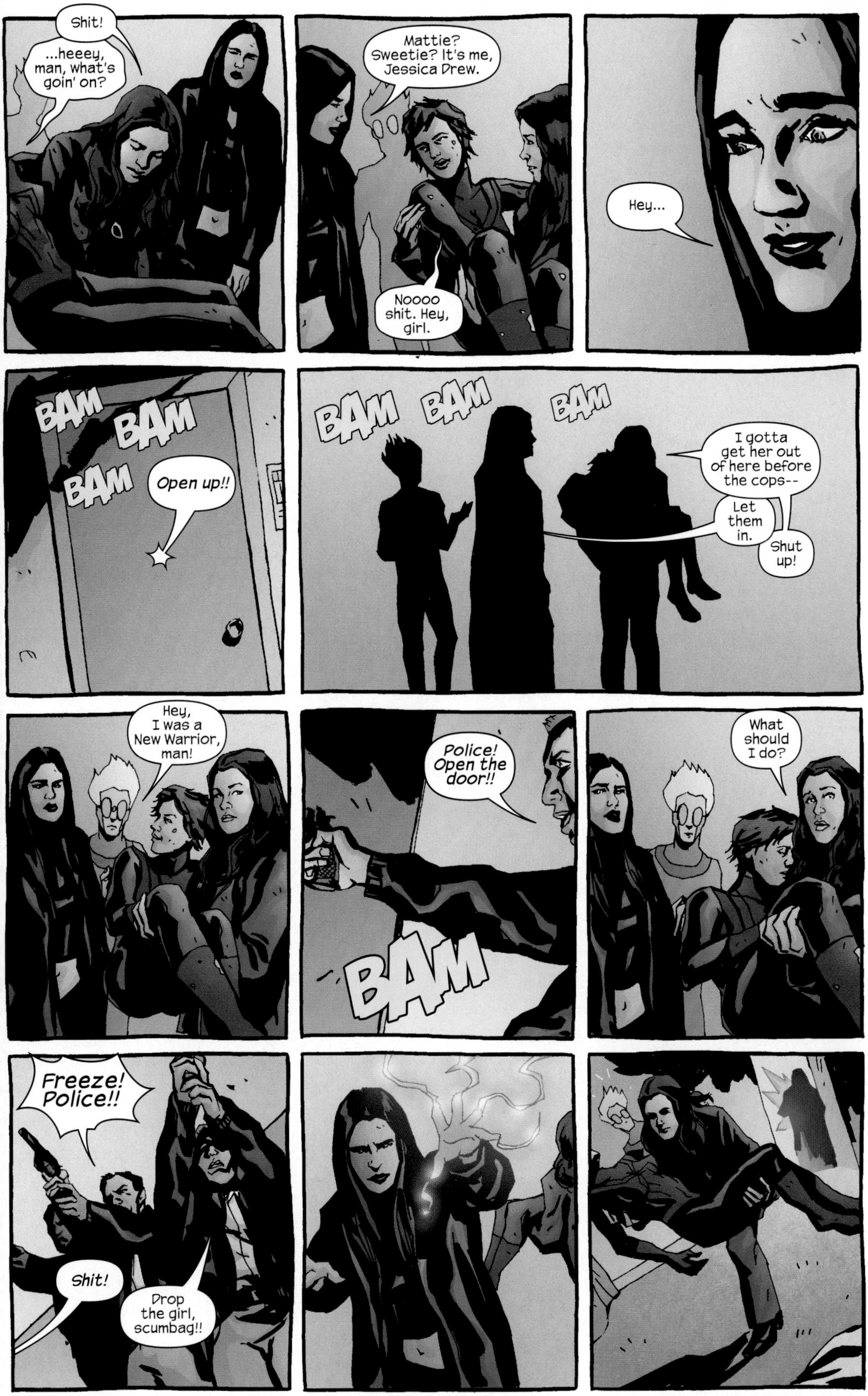
Shit!
...heeey, man, what's goin' on?
Mattie? Sweetie? It's me, Jessica Drew.
Noooo shit. Hey, girl.
Hey...
BAM
BAM
BAM
Open up!!
BAM
BAM
BAM
I gotta get her out of here before the cops--
Let them in.
Shut up!
Hey, I was a New Warrior, man!
Police! Open the door!!
BAM
What should I do?
Freeze! Police!!
Shit!
Drop the girl, scumbag!!

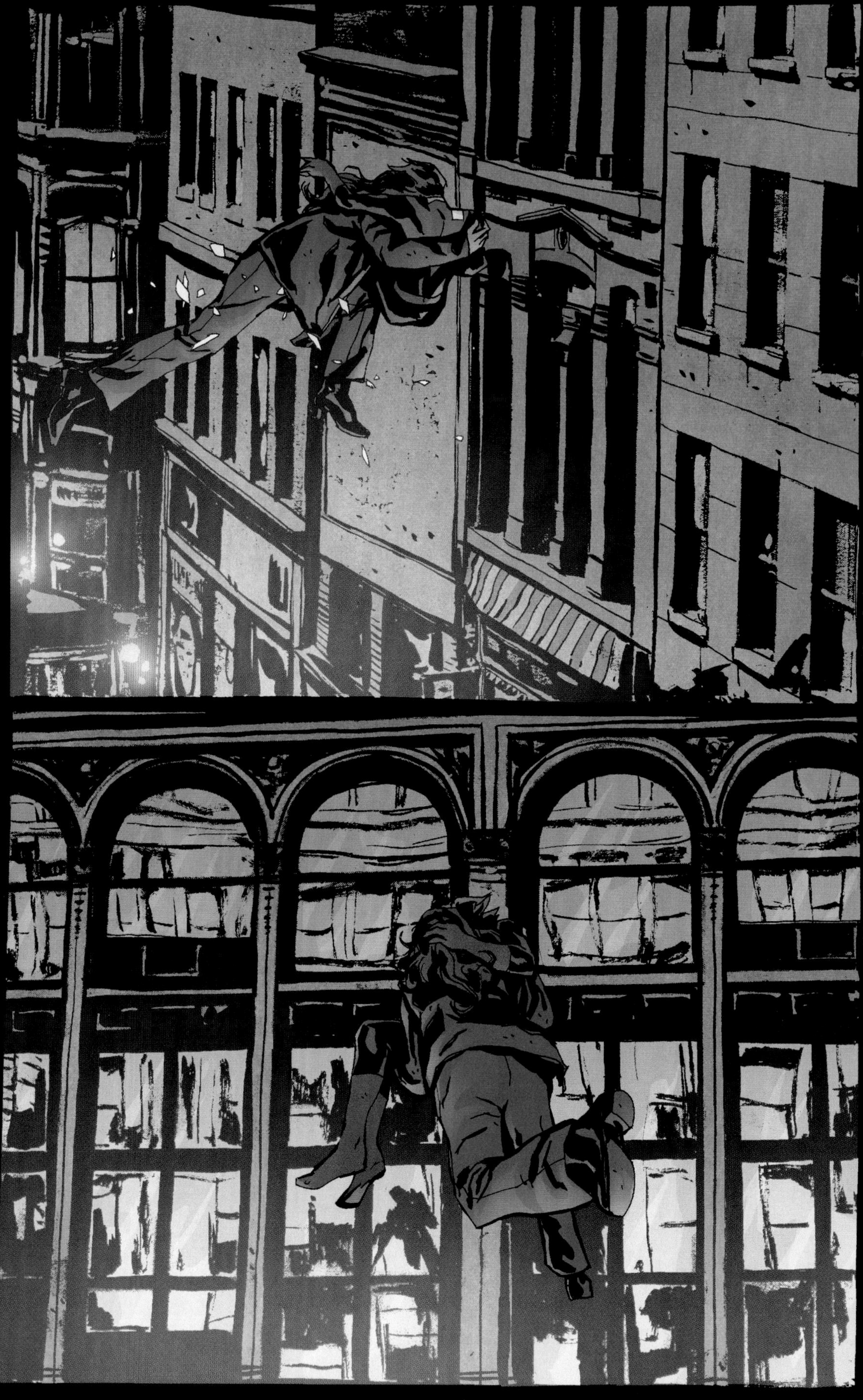

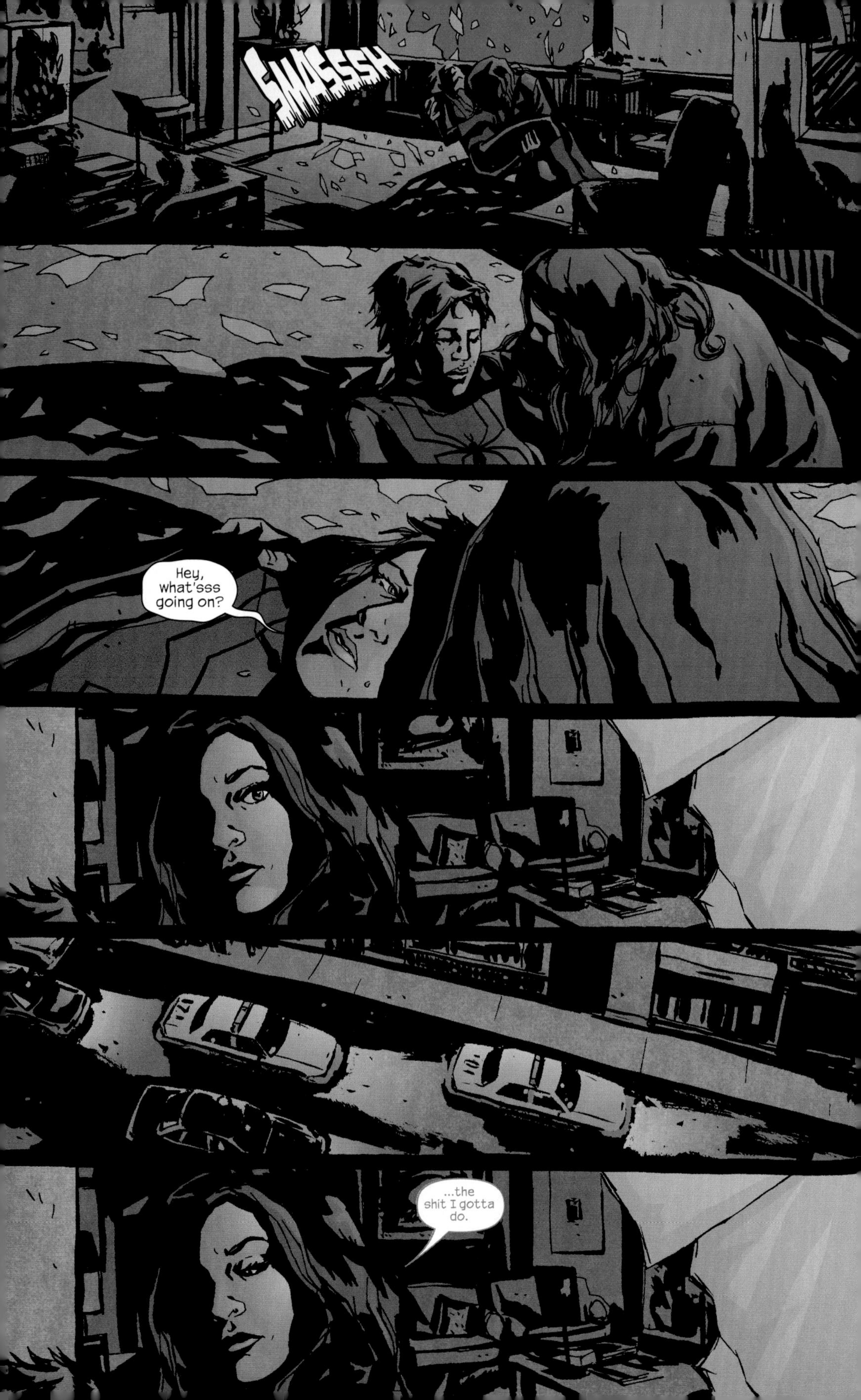
SMASSSH
Hey, what'sss going on?
...the shit I gotta do.

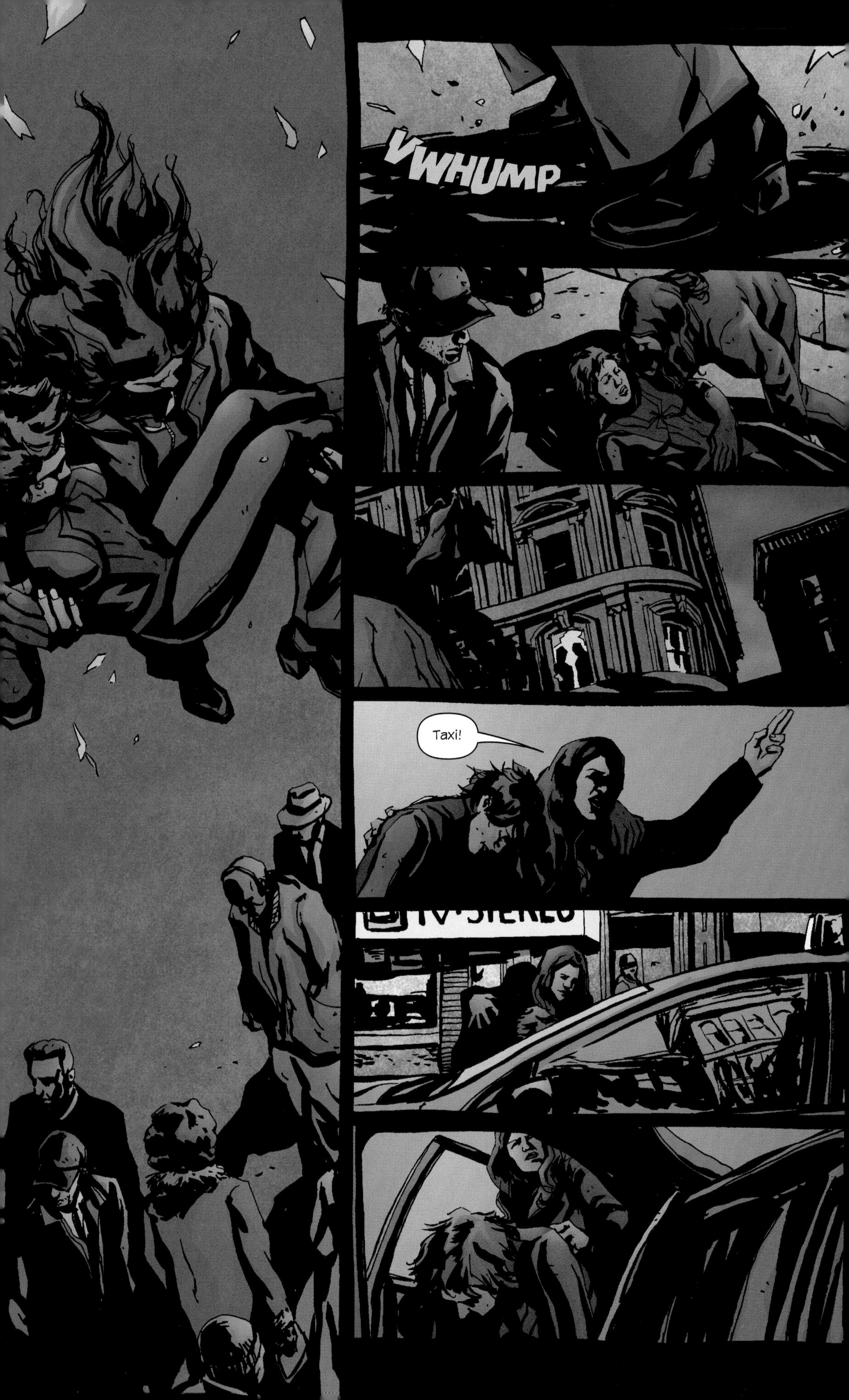
VWHUMP
Taxi!

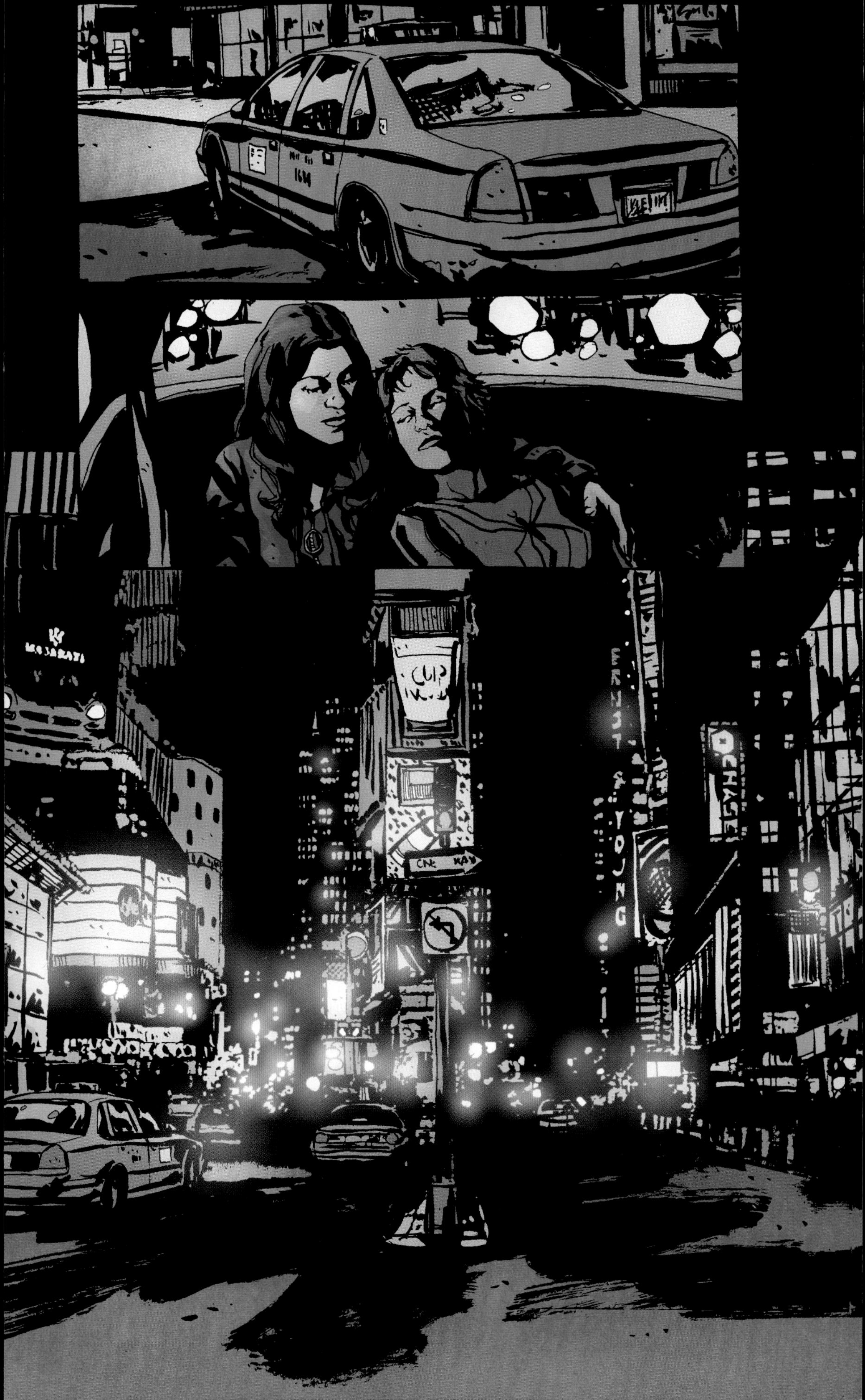
ERNST
YOUNG
CHASE

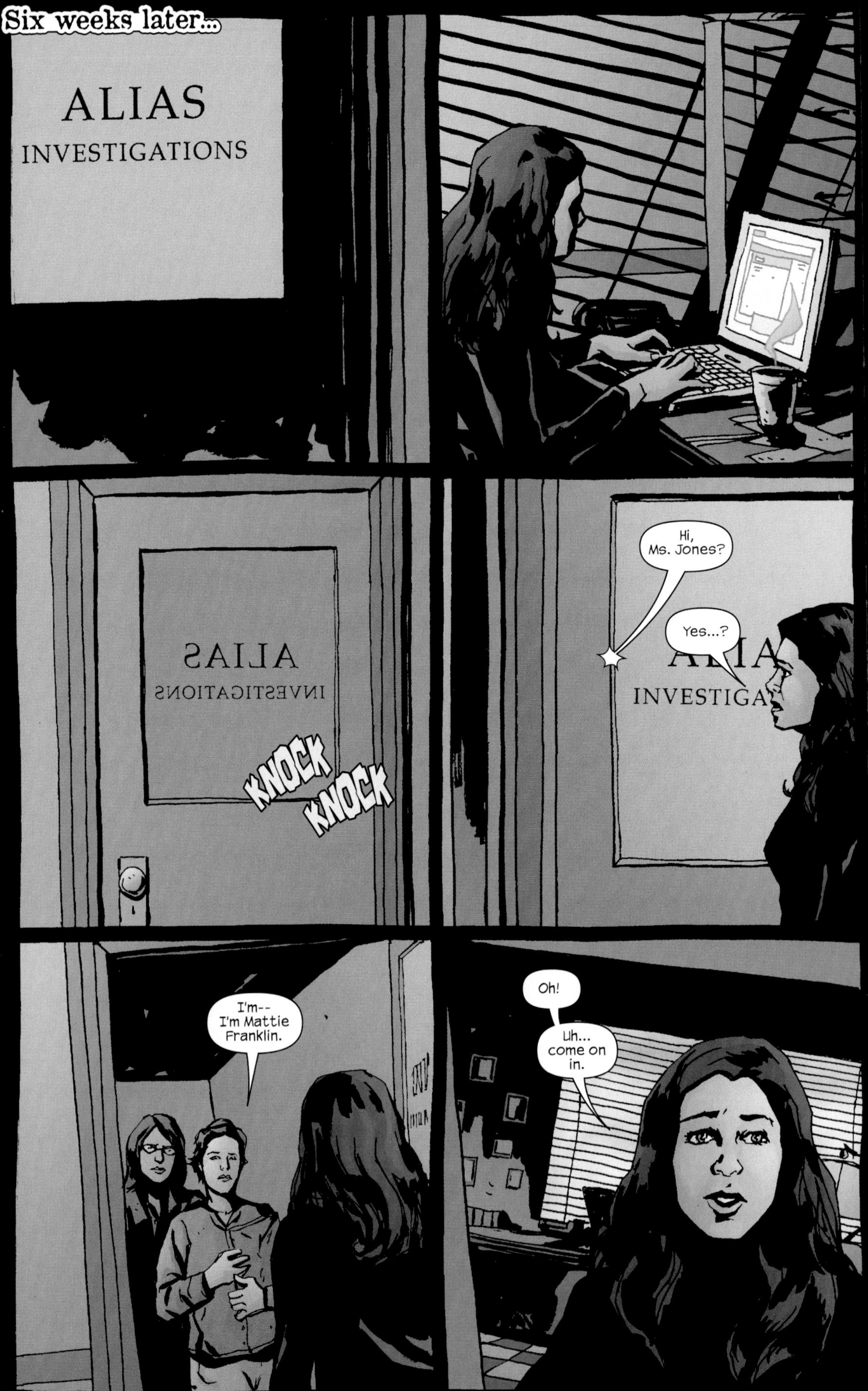

Six weeks later...
ALIAS
INVESTIGATIONS
ALIAS
INVESTIGATIONS
KNOCK
KNOCK
Hi,
Ms. Jones?
Yes...?
INVESTIGA
I'm--
I'm Mattie
Franklin.
Oh!
Uh...
come on
in.

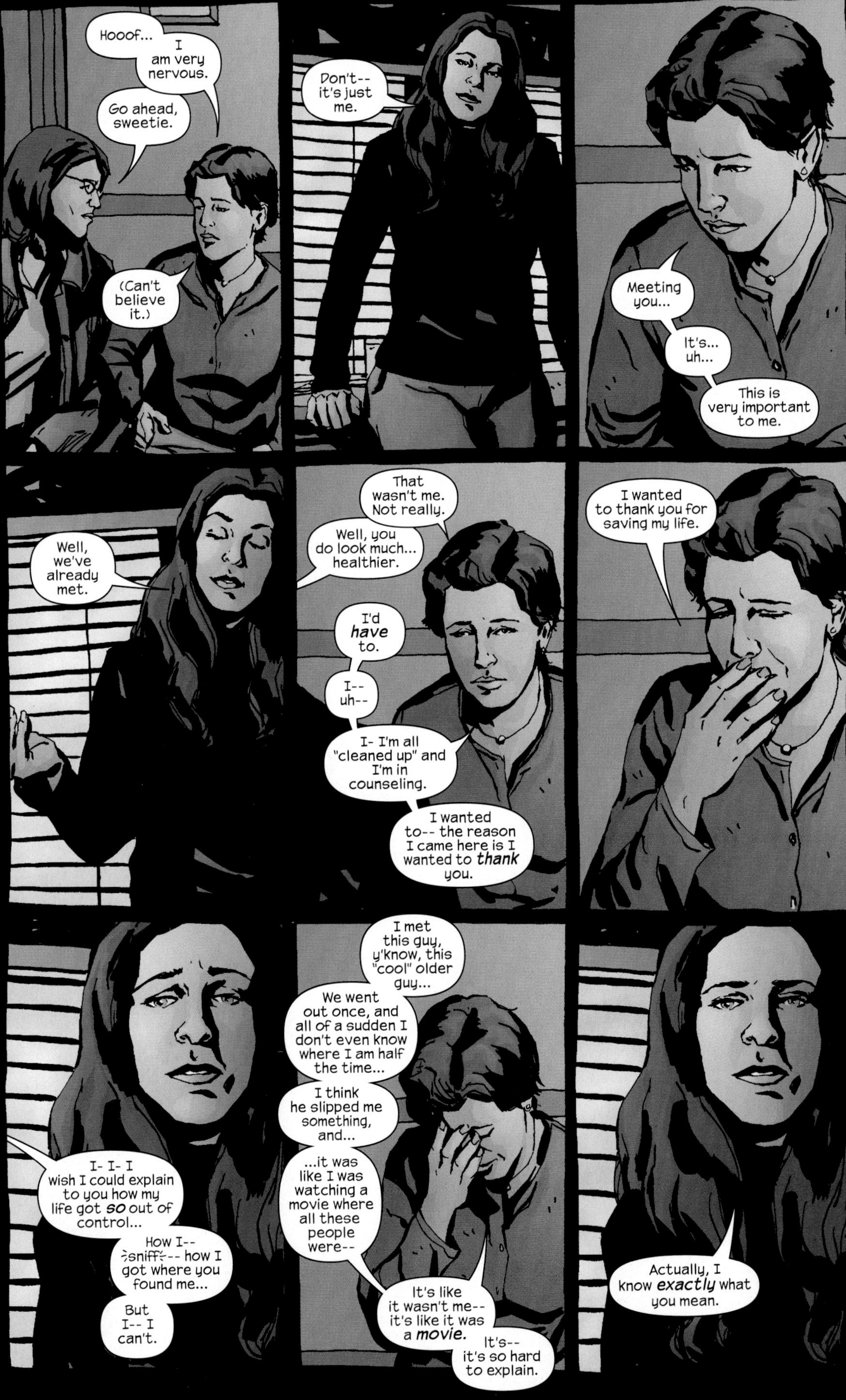
Hooof... I am very nervous.
Go ahead, sweetie.
(Can't believe it.)
Don't-- it's just me.
Meeting you...
It's... uh...
This is very important to me.
Well, we've already met.
That wasn't me. Not really.
Well, you do look much... healthier.
I'd *have* to.
I-- uh--
I- I'm all "cleaned up" and I'm in counseling.
I wanted to-- the reason I came here is I wanted to *thank* you.
I wanted to thank you for saving my life.
I- I- I wish I could explain to you how my life got *so* out of control...
How I-- sniff-- how I got where you found me...
But I-- I can't.
I met this guy, y'know, this "cool" older guy...
We went out once, and all of a sudden I don't even know where I am half the time...
I think he slipped me something, and...
...it was like I was watching a movie where all these people were--
It's like it wasn't me-- it's like it was a *movie.*
It's-- it's so hard to explain.
Actually, I know *exactly* what you mean.

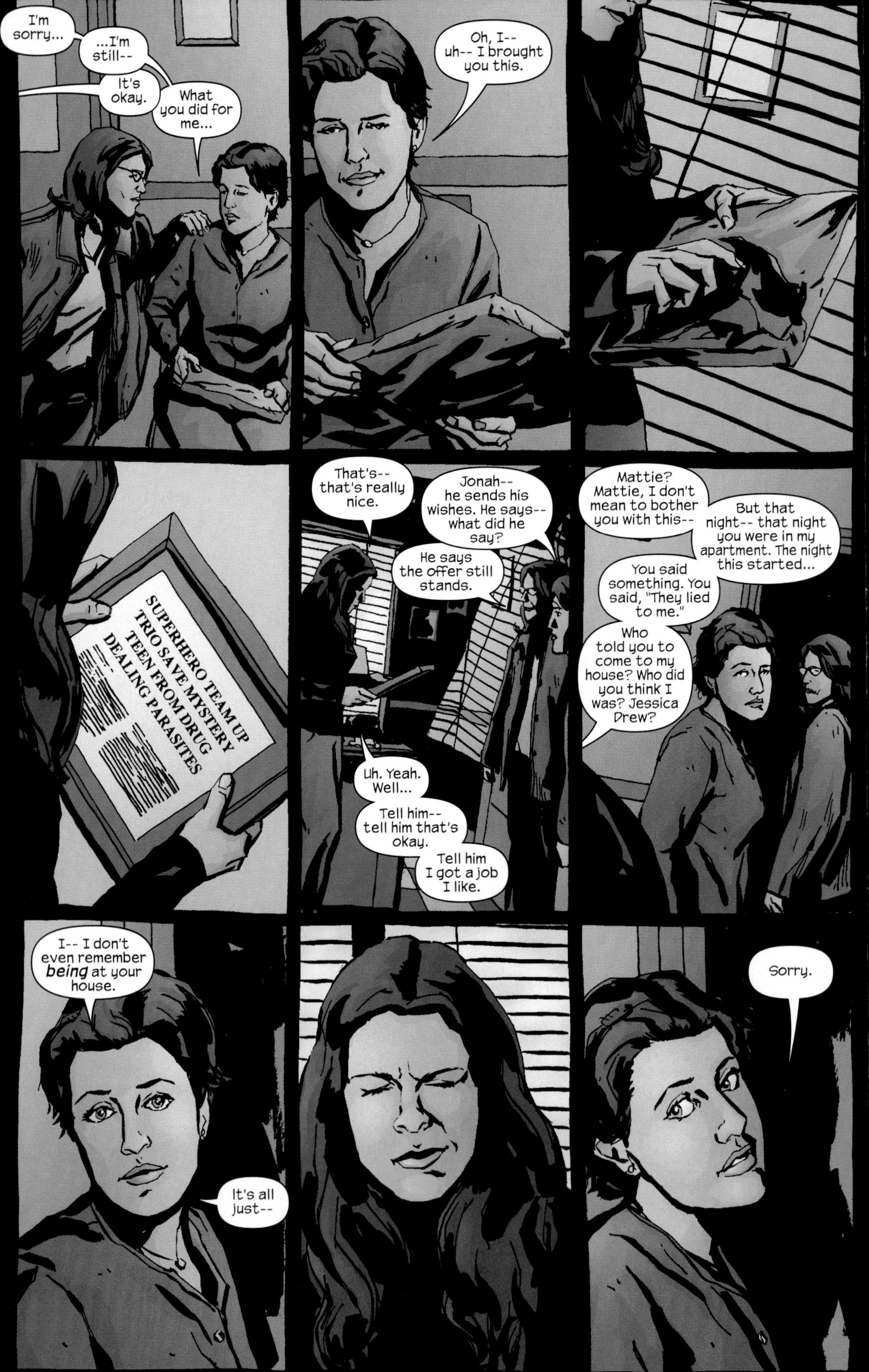
I'm sorry...
...I'm still--
It's okay.
What you did for me...
Oh, I-- uh-- I brought you this.
SUPERHERO TEAM UP TRIO SAVE MYSTERY TEEN FROM DRUG DEALING PARASITES
That's-- that's really nice.
Jonah-- he sends his wishes. He says-- what did he say?
He says the offer still stands.
Uh. Yeah. Well...
Tell him-- tell him that's okay.
Tell him I got a job I like.
Mattie? Mattie, I don't mean to bother you with this--
But that night-- that night you were in my apartment. The night this started...
You said something. You said, "They lied to me."
Who told you to come to my house? Who did you think I was? Jessica Drew?
I-- I don't even remember *being* at your house.
It's all just--
Sorry.

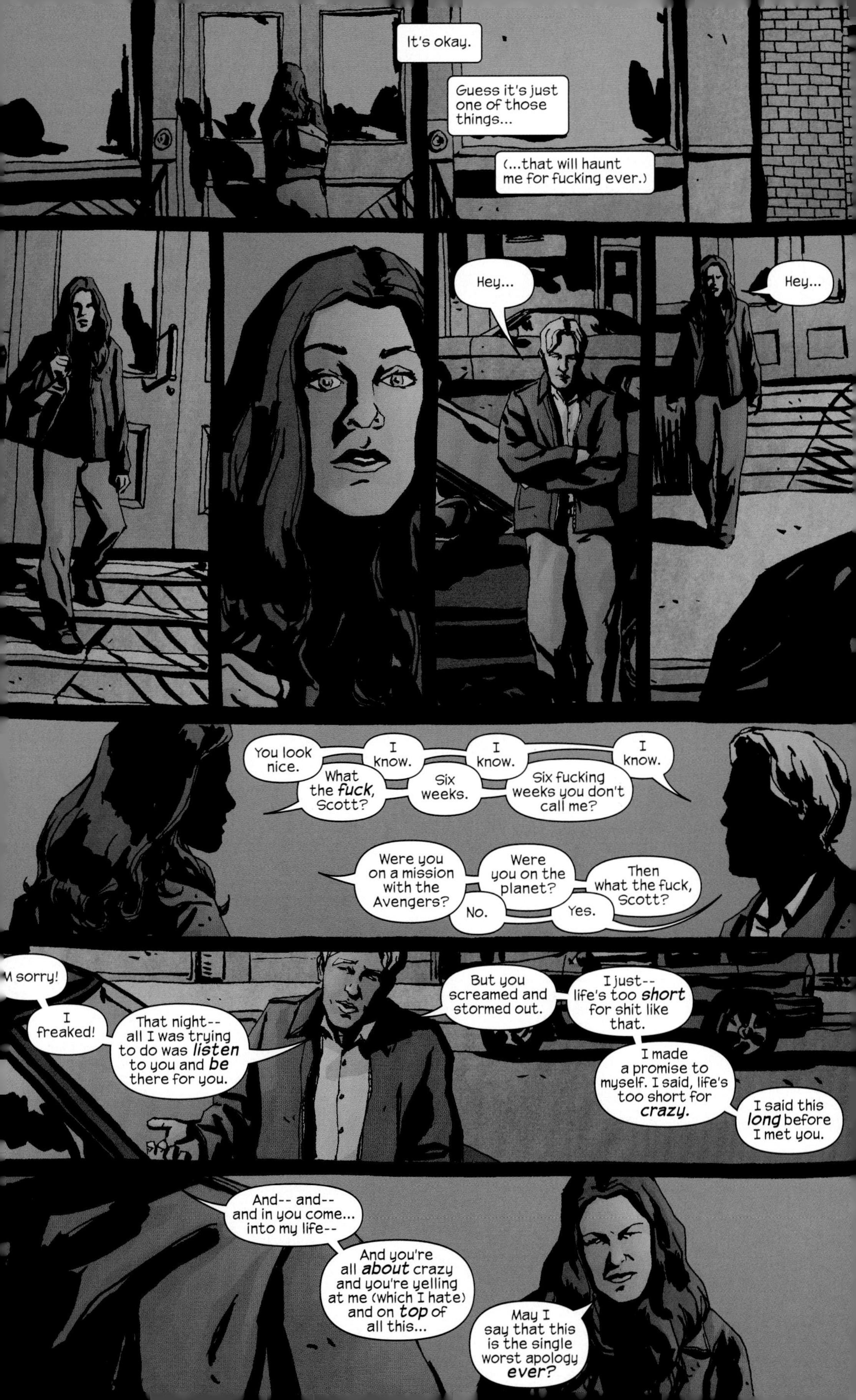
It's okay.
Guess it's just one of those things...
(...that will haunt me for fucking ever.)
Hey...
Hey...
You look nice.
I know.
What the *fuck*, Scott?
I know.
Six weeks.
I know.
Six fucking weeks you don't call me?
Were you on a mission with the Avengers?
No.
Were you on the planet?
Yes.
Then what the fuck, Scott?
M sorry!
I freaked!
That night-- all I was trying to do was *listen* to you and *be* there for you.
But you screamed and stormed out.
I just-- life's too *short* for shit like that.
I made a promise to myself. I said, life's too short for *crazy*.
I said this *long* before I met you.
And-- and-- and in you come... into my life--
And you're all *about* crazy and you're yelling at me (which I hate) and on *top* of all this...
May I say that this is the single worst apology *ever?*

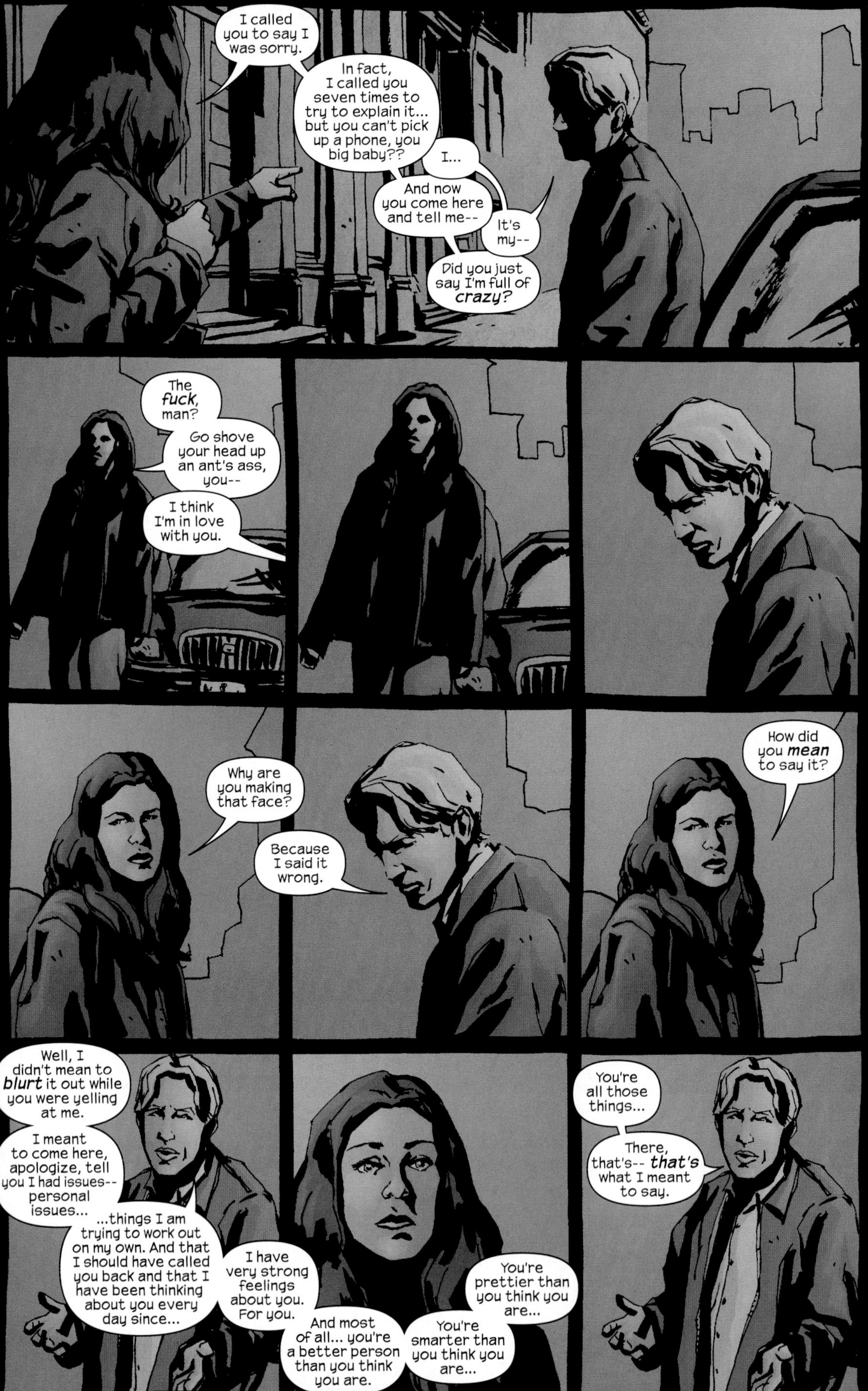
I called you to say I was sorry.
In fact, I called you seven times to try to explain it... but you can't pick up a phone, you big baby??
I...
And now you come here and tell me--
It's my--
Did you just say I'm full of *crazy?*
The *fuck*, man?
Go shove your head up an ant's ass, you--
I think I'm in love with you.
Why are you making that face?
Because I said it wrong.
How did you *mean* to say it?
Well, I didn't mean to *blurt* it out while you were yelling at me.
I meant to come here, apologize, tell you I had issues-- personal issues...
...things I am trying to work out on my own. And that I should have called you back and that I have been thinking about you every day since...
I have very strong feelings about you. For you.
You're prettier than you think you are...
You're smarter than you think you are...
And most of all... you're a better person than you think you are.
You're all those things...
There, that's-- *that's* what I meant to say.

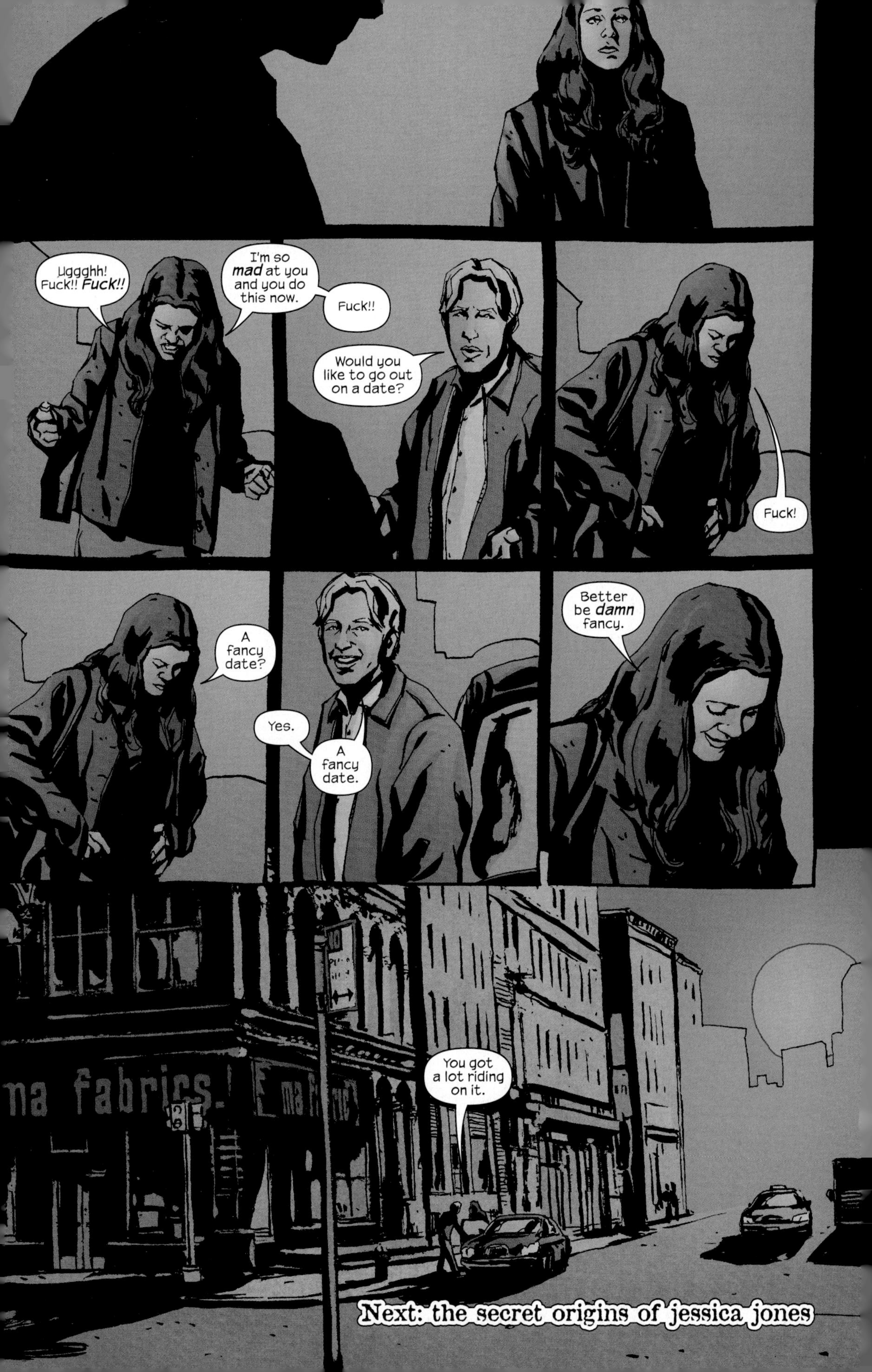
Uggghh! Fuck!! *Fuck!!*
I'm so *mad* at you and you do this now.
Fuck!!
Would you like to go out on a date?
Fuck!
A fancy date?
Yes.
A fancy date.
Better be *damn* fancy.
ma fabrics
You got a lot riding on it.
Next: the secret origins of jessica jones